THE DECORATING BOOK

THE DECORATING BOOK

MARY GILLIATT

Special photography by
Michael Dunne

Published by
The Reader's Digest Association, Inc.
Pleasantville, New York / Montreal
by permission of
Pantheon Books, a division of Random House, Inc.

Project Editor   **Art Editor**
Yvonne McFarlane   Ronald Pickless

Editor   **Designer**
Fiona MacIntyre   Derek Coombes

Managing Editor
Amy Carroll

Library of Congress Cataloging in Publication Data

Gilliatt, Mary.
   The decorating book.

   Originally published: New York: Pantheon Books, © 1981
   Accompanied by The design kit.
   Includes index.
   1. Interior decoration. I. Title.
NK2110.G48   1983   747   83-10975
ISBN 0-89577-173-X (set)

Printed in the United States of America

CONTENTS

THE PRINCIPLES OF DESIGN

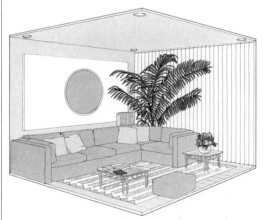

THE ROOM-BY-ROOM GUIDE

THE SAMPLE BOOK

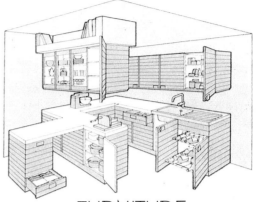

FURNITURE AND FURNISHINGS

APPENDIX

THE DESIGN KIT

INTRODUCTION

More than a decade ago, I started writing a book called *Doing Up A House* by saying, rather diffidently, that it was *not* a guide to the complicated subject of interior decorating. It simply offered, I said, elementary practical advice to all those who had limped over the preliminary hurdles of looking for, finding, buying or renting a home, and were now faced with a shell to organize into comfortable living space.

I have written several books since on various aspects of interiors from individual rooms through general precepts to lighting; but more important to me, I have had the practical experience of decorating houses, apartments and rooms of every sort and scale and not only had I to learn the hard way in the beginning, but I have inevitably gone on learning. So this book is different: it *is* as complete a guide to decoration as I have found possible to write. After all, having experienced more, seen more, traveled more and learned more, if only with the passing of time, I am equally aware both of the great increase in interest in domestic design and the attendant confusion and the frustration of so much choice.

Most people at one time or another in their lives are faced with renovating and/or decorating at least a room, if not an apartment or house. And this is where the difficulties start, for people who think nothing of choosing their own clothes suddenly find themselves at a loss when it comes to choosing ways of dressing a house or apartment.

Some people feel that they ought to be able to design their own home but simply cannot get it together; others would prefer to hire an interior decorator to take the responsibility off their shoulders, but feel that they cannot afford one or that it would be giving in to self-indulgence. Others still, with quite enough ideas have no time, or no money, or no entrée into showrooms to see the full choice available (a problem that is worse in America than anywhere else).

Yet decoration is in no way an absolute speciality. It is not like law or medicine. It is, or should be, highly personal; an expression of self; the sum of your interests as an individual or as a family; a personal and practical statement about living which anybody can make and feel comfortable about.

Successful decoration is a question of gaining confidence more than anything else; of feeling at ease with your choice of color and pattern, scale and texture, furniture and objects. And choices have to be made somewhere along the line, even when there is help from a professional at hand. In this book I have tried to cover as many aspects of the subject as possible, to answer as many queries as I can think of asking, to give as many alternatives to problems and variously shaped rooms, and to show as many examples of the ingredients available. I use the word ingredients advisedly, for to my mind, decoration is much like cooking, and fabrics and papers, floor and wallcoverings can be chosen and mixed together and spiced and seasoned with accessories in just the same way as one experiments with tastes and flavors. In both cases, familiarity with the ingredients is one half of the battle; interest and the will to experiment the other. If this book in any way helps to prove that interior decorating is not so very hard to master, I shall be very pleased.

HOW TO USE THIS BOOK

The Decorating Book will help you design your home so that it will look the way you've always wanted it to look. Its five main sections cover every aspect of decorating and put successful decors within the grasp of every reader.

Turn to **The Principles of Design** to find out about how to manipulate space, how to use the correct lighting, how to choose color schemes and mix texture and pattern.

Study the pages of the **Room-by-Room Guide** which covers every area of a house and gives hundreds of ideas for room schemes. Whatever the shape, or size of your room, whatever its problems, you will find out how to achieve a totally new look without resorting to expensive structural changes. Whether you are drawn to the photographic view of a room or to the illustrations, you will find listed the materials used in each scheme so that you can adapt and adopt the look to suit your own personal requirements.

Choosing your decorating materials is easy with the **Sample Book**. This comprehensive, visual catalog shows all types of materials from paint, paper and other wallcoverings through all kinds of carpets and floorcoverings, fabrics, shades, blinds, oriental carpets and ethnic rugs. (The Directory of Sources in the Appendix at the back of the book gives information on stockists for all of the materials in the Sample Book, so readers can order the same, or very similar, materials themselves.) There is also plenty of practical advice on how to go about putting up wallpaper and laying floor tiles, as well as information about the less usual decorative painting techniques and fabric treatments, including using material to line walls or make shades.

Should you want to know about **Furniture and Furnishings**, this chapter details the development of furniture and also gives information on lighting, fixtures and fittings and storage, plus plenty of ideas on how to go about displaying collections of paintings or prints, *objets d'art* and plants, as well as interesting treatments for beds and windows.

Finally, whether you plan to call in a professional or aim to do any redecorating work yourself, you need to know how to go about drawing up schedules of work, how to calculate quantities of materials like paint, wallpaper or tiles. **The Design Kit** contains all this practical information, plus unique, three-dimensional graph paper and furniture cutouts, which allow you to visualize how a new scheme will look, before you spend any money.

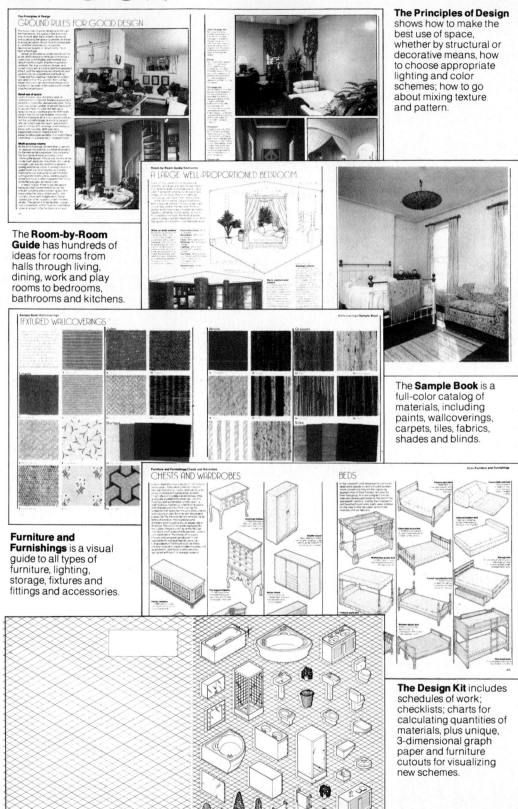

The Principles of Design shows how to make the best use of space, whether by structural or decorative means, how to choose appropriate lighting and color schemes; how to go about mixing texture and pattern.

The **Room-by-Room Guide** has hundreds of ideas for rooms from halls through living, dining, work and play rooms to bedrooms, bathrooms and kitchens.

The **Sample Book** is a full-color catalog of materials, including paints, wallcoverings, carpets, tiles, fabrics, shades and blinds.

Furniture and Furnishings is a visual guide to all types of furniture, lighting, storage, fixtures and fittings and accessories.

The Design Kit includes schedules of work; checklists; charts for calculating quantities of materials, plus unique, 3-dimensional graph paper and furniture cutouts for visualizing new schemes.

THE PRINCIPLES OF DESIGN

GROUND RULES FOR GOOD DESIGN

The basic rule of good design is first to get the framework of a space right and only then to look after the contents. It means first assessing the space available and then making decisions about how to manipulate it – whether cosmetically, by purely decorative means, or structurally – to its best advantage.

Design is also about understanding how scale and balance contribute to making a room look comfortable and inviting. It is about handling light, whether natural or artificial; the way a color is chosen and mixed, matched or contrasted to its greatest effect; and the way mixtures of texture and pattern can be assembled and built up. These are the essential ingredients which are dealt with in this section. All must be taken into consideration if the design of a home is to be given a firm basis and create a lasting impression.

Good use of space

Lack of space, lack of rooms, lack of wherewithal to expand, these are perennial problems shared by almost everyone. Yet a curiously large number of people seem just to accept them. To alter the feeling of spaciousness in a place you do not necessarily have to change its basic structure. And the *feeling* is what most space is about, not the actual footage. Ironically, people who actually have too much space find it just as awkward to arrange comfortably as those with too little. With personal experience of both, I have found it far easier to sit people sensibly in a small sitting room than in a very large, L-shaped room.

Multi-purpose rooms

At the simplest level, a home that is owned, as opposed to a rental, could be improved by the elementary expedient of changing the functions of various rooms, or by altering the layout. Almost any room can be made multi-purpose. A kitchen, if it is large enough, can also be used for a general eating and family room. A dining room or a guest room can also double as a study; bedrooms can always be made into bed/sitting/work rooms just by adding appropriate furniture. It often happens that in the reshuffle you gain an extra room.

In every house, there is usually space being wasted somewhere that can be utilized: landing and corridor space; the area under the stairs; blank walls; odd corners. Used with imagination, these spaces can often relieve congestion elsewhere. The secret is to be flexible, to question convention and to have no rigid ideas when it comes to the function of a room.

Opposite page, top:
By using a cleverly-placed island unit, this kitchen-family room manages to combine eating, lounging, study and television-viewing space in one end of a long kitchen. The basic white background also helps to enlarge the space.

Below:
Spiral staircases always seem to make more room, and this one, winding up from a well-planned, landing-dining area, is no exception. A panel of mirror reflects similarly sized book-shelves to further enlarge the space.

This page, top:
Almost every room in the house can be adapted for a number of uses, provided that there is adequate space. In this cleverly-planned bathroom-study, the heated towel rail effectively divides work and bathing areas. Elaborate pull-up drapes and serene blue coloring of the walls make the room seem suitably sybaritic.

Below left:
Dining space can often be fitted into seemingly impossible spaces. The end of what could have been an uninspired and awkward corridor makes a slick little eating corner for two. The spare lines of table and chairs are further exaggerated by the colorful geometric painting above.

Below right:
Given a modicum of ingenuity, even a wide corridor can be used to accommodate a bed. In this studio apartment, a series of hardboard arches were installed to break up the space. The softly tented sleeping alcove in the hallway cuts out the need for a bed in the living room.

ALTERING SPACE COSMETICALLY

Limited space can be expanded or too much space lessened by thoughtful decoration. Knowing how to juxtapose height and width, when to use large patterns and when small, when to offset an angle with a curve, or vice versa, all are important when it comes to achieving well-designed and proportioned rooms. The following guidelines should be useful for when it comes to redecorating problem areas.

Expanding space

Since pale colors recede, the lighter the wall and floor colors, the larger a room will seem. If a ceiling seems too low, you can raise it visually with a coat of light paint. Shiny, reflecting surfaces always seemingly make for a sense of space in a room, so use glossy paint to push back walls. The removal of a picture molding or chair rail will also help make a room seem less constricted and cramped.

There is no doubt that patterns with a strong geometric or directional feel can appear to push out and extend floors and walls. Patterned carpets or wallcoverings with a light background give a feeling of depth and patterns on a dark background do tend to enclose.

Lessening space

Strong, dark colors seem to move in, so if a ceiling seems too high in proportion to the rest of the room, an intense color will help bring it down visually. To make a room seem more compact, add a continuous band or stripe of color, or a contrasting picture molding round a room. Soft, matt surfaces diminish a sense of space, so use non-shiny paint for the walls of an over-large room.

Learning about scale

At first, it always helps to look at possessions in other people's homes. Remember what furniture is used to enlarge an area, and what dwarfs it. Notice which colors, textures and patterns complement or contrast with each other.

Aim to balance solidity with delicacy, softness with hardness, height with depth. Furniture kept at much the same level makes for a greater sense of space. But remember that the effect of a continuous low level is enhanced by one or two judiciously placed objects: a rangy plant, or an arrangement of paintings.

A good sense of scale is quite easy to acquire if you always remember to look at closely and learn from other people's rooms which particularly please you.

Opposite page:
A neatly tiled pattern clearly defines the different areas of this otherwise open apartment. The lowered stair wall follows the design of the dado opposite, and all other colors are kept neutral so that the tile edging stands out.

This page, right:
Squares of different proportions form much of the pattern in this kitchen. The smaller alternate squares of the floor are echoed in the larger outlines of cupboard moldings and re-echoed in the broken quarters and diamonds of tiles.

Far right:
To make the room seem much larger, a diagonal stripe has been painted on the wall to repeat the pattern of the vinyl floor tiles. Different prints in the same scale take up the green and white colors of floor and walls.

Below left:
Small children love bright colors and extravagant patterns. In this child's room, painted clouds and mountains are set against a striped floor painted to match. All the colors coordinate, so the drapes slung through rings at the window tie in with the green of the bed, and the kite tied to the painted sky repeats the coloring of the walls.

Below right:
Painted birds fly between wood-backed shelves carved like clouds, and paper bees and flowers are suspended from the ceiling in this living end of a bed-sitting room. When the dividing drape is pulled back, both ends of the room are linked by the strong design.

USING MIRRORS

It is always useful to know how to create a feeling of depth in a room, how to achieve the illusion of extra space.

Creating a three-dimensional effect

Think consciously, first of all, of creating a foreground, middle ground and background, a definite, three-dimensional effect. The eye can be drawn out and along by diagonal or geometric lines painted on doors or walls, or by similar geometric or directional patterns on the floor. Any rectangular room can be made to look wider if the floor- or ceiling boards or tiles are run at an angle.

A mirror on a table or mantelpiece with plants or some small objects in front of it will also give depth, as will a hinged screen in a corner behind a sofa or table.

Using mirror

Mirrored surfaces will always give added length, depth and width to a room. Mirror tiles (see the Sample Book page 233 for ideas) are less expensive than whole sheets of mirror, but although there are no distracting divisions with whole sheets, bear in mind the size of vast expanses of mirror when it comes to getting them through doorways and around corners. It is always wise to consider the possibility of expensive waste when a sheet of mirror is cracked during installation – unfortunately not such a rare occurance these days.

Where to use mirror

If the space could do with doubling, use mirror to cover an entire wall, if it can be afforded and fit it from floor to ceiling, extending it right into the corners. If plain mirror seems unsubtle, one compromise is to insert metal supports between lengths of mirror to hold glass or plexiglass shelves for books and small objects.

To help lose definition at the edges of a small room, and add extra sparkle, use thin strips of mirror to edge the top of the walls, just below the ceiling. Mirror alcoves; mirror between long windows; mirror backs of doors; mirror the side wall of a narrow staircase; mirror the ceiling of a small room. If your windows have wide embrasures, mirror them to both double the reflected light and maximize the view outside.

Even the bases of sofas, seating units or chairs can be mirrored so they appear to float; tall screens can be mirrored for an illusion of extra height. And remember that etched or patterned mirror has a decorative quality all of its own, quite apart from its reflective value.

This page, left:
Large mirror panels cladding the side of a stair wall and the balustrade greatly enlarge the width of this space as well as its dramatic impact.

Below:
Mirrored ceiling panels exactly the same size as the translucent wall panels give architectural unity to this low, narrow space as well as doubling its height and width. Polished steel cubes give sharpness to the soft brown upholstery.

Opposite page, top:
A completely mirrored wall enormously expands the space and light in what could have been a cramped studio apartment.

Below left:
Ornate mirror is placed on plain on this totally reflective fireplace wall, again doubling both space and light. Shiny paint and polished floorboards add to the general sense of gleam and sparkle.

Below right:
Mirrored wall and end panel make this small bathroom seem generously large; an illusion helped further by the shiny ceiling.

CREATING SPACE STRUCTURALLY

The simplest and least expensive structural alterations can be made to doors. They can be adjusted to swing in the opposite direction so extra furniture can be fitted into a space. Old doors can be blocked off or new, more conveniently placed ones can be cut into the walls. If the space is minimal, but a door is necessary, put in a folding door or narrow swing doors. If a new partition wall is being put up anyway, it might be possible to put in a door which slides into it.

Internal windows

Long, thin slits can be cut in walls to give extra light and depth to a room and small, narrow windows set either side of a fireplace will add new views, give slivers of extra light and take up very little wall space. Remember that internal windows can be opened up between rooms for extra light and depth. Non-structural partition walls can be cut halfway to the floor, or to seating level.

Modifying the ceiling always makes an enormous difference to the space, style and interest of a room. It can be lowered all round at the perimeter so that the central space seems to soar, or the central area of the ceiling can be lowered, perhaps over a dining table, for greater intimacy.

This page, left: Conservatories always make splendid additions to existing space, and they can be used for other activities as well as for growing plants or collecting solar heat, hence their current revival. This one was built into a roof garden and provides a sybaritic setting for a whirlpool. A hammock slung over the top adds to the general feeling of heightened luxury.

Below left: Some of the grandeur of a Gothic church has been caught in the design for this new house. The massive octagonal central column echoeing the general shape manages to visually divide the space into different intimate areas.

Below right: The removal of a wall makes a huge difference to the feeling of space, as proved in this formerly cramped apartment. Partition walls were ripped down to open up the hall into the living room, flooding the area with light it had never received before.

CHANGING LEVELS

For many people, a flexible change in levels is seen as the best way of making the best of a small space. Multi-levels are especially useful for one-room living, and can be used to divide off the various areas without the space seeming muddled and confused.

Even if a room is of ordinary height, it is usually possible to build in a variety of platforms – depending on where the room is situated in a building and on the latter's structure. The extra weight is seldom any more than the normal furnishings and seating which it replaces.

Conversation pits

Conversation pits can be installed in the center of a room by building up the surrounding space with plywood. This change of level can be exaggerated by creating an extra level for work or study on one side of the pit and perhaps a dining platform on the other. Alternatively, low seating with plenty of cushions can be accommodated on slim platforms running round the perimeter of a room. Or levels can be stepped and sculpted in free-flowing forms which swoop down again to a lower level. These constructions look extra neat when comfortably carpeted and often can be used to conceal storage space below.

Above:
Molded plastic is formed into cushioned and uncushioned seating areas, bedhead, bed-foot and sleeping space in this platformed end of an old room. Interestingly, the sculpted shapes of the 20th century addition have close affinity to the deep embrasures of the massive stone walls built, of course, centuries before.

Below:
A neatly carpeted series of steps, seating areas and wells apportions this room into different living functions without losing any sense of its sweeping space. A mixture of track and uplighting makes for subtle variations in the lighting levels.

FURNITURE ARRANGEMENTS

If lack of space is a problem the first basic thing to remember is that tables, desks and chairs made of glass or plexiglass, or pieces of furniture that are surfaced in mirror, look much lighter and less bulky than more solid pieces. Two small couches always look neater than four chairs, and likewise, two small seating units pushed together will take up less room than a couple of chairs. Large articles of furniture should be kept against a wall.

Corners can be used more: beds placed on the diagonal make a room look much more interesting; closets and desks also look particularly effective straddling corners. Storage all down one side of a room can look neater than separate desks, bookshelves, liquor cabinets or other closets.

One-room living

In a one-room apartment, a double bed can look too obvious and bulky. Use a pair of day-beds or chaises instead, and pile them high with pillows. By day these can be used for seating and by night they can be pushed together to make a bed. Pare down as much as possible to avoid clutter, but beware of discarding pieces of furniture to the extent that all character and individuality is lost.

This page, left:
Built-in semi-circular seating in a platformed room makes the most of the space. It is balanced as much by the circular desk top "floating" above a carpeted base as by the round coffee table. The height of the plants effectively varies the otherwise low-level room.

Below left:
Transparent furniture can make a great deal of difference to the feeling of space in a small area, as, indeed, can curves as opposed to sharp angles. Both these precepts are followed out to good effect here.

Below right:
Angled, carpeted plat-forming and seating are economical on space as well as neat in this small room. Shelves above the seating units are counter-balanced by a tall plant which echoes the greenery outside as well as the foliage on the top shelves, and the brown stripe is repeated in the leather of the lounge chair and stool.

Opposite page:
Background, task and accent lighting are needed together in most living areas. Here, the background light is provided by concealed uplights; the task lighting by adjustable floor lamps set at the right position for reading, and the accents by small candles on the table top.

USING LIGHT

Artificial lighting has made more dramatic progress in this country than any other element in interior – and to a great extent exterior – design. It can be made to alter shape and color, to distort or enhance, dramatize or minimize, to increase working efficiency, and to form its own subtly changing decoration.

It is much easier to understand light and the various ways to manipulate it, if you realize that it is basically divided into three main types: general or background lighting; local or task lighting, and accent or decorative lighting. Most rooms, depending on their function, should include a combination of at least two of these types, and general living areas, all three. The level of each can be controlled at will by using dimmer switches.

Background lighting

Good general lighting means achieving a *low* level of light throughout the living area. This includes ceiling fixtures of one sort or another, from the ubiquitous central light to a whole illuminated ceiling; lighted valances; cornice or wall lighting; recessed fixtures inset into ceilings or floors, or judiciously placed, portable lights (such as table lamps or uplights), which bounce light off ceilings and walls.

Local or task lighting

At the very least, task lighting should provide adequate illumination for all normal household activities, as well as creating interesting pools of light. In living areas, the source is usually from table, floor or desk lamps; in kitchens, laundry and utility rooms by fixtures like fluorescent or incandescent tubes, or spots, over working surfaces. In bathrooms, bulbs could be installed all around a mirror (the ideal light for shaving or make-up, as theater stars discovered long ago), as well as downlights over bathtubs and basins.

Accent or decorative lighting

This type of light can be used to draw attention to any possessions or areas that you want to emphasize and also provides dramatic and interesting highlights. Fixtures for use here include the various types of spots, wallwashers, pinhole or framing projectors, as well as uplights and candles.

Artificial light used with this sort of understanding can be made to achieve as many moods and diverse effects as shifting, glancing, natural daylight, and will certainly make an immeasurable difference to night-time rooms.

A GUIDE TO LIGHTING TERMS

It is easy to be bewildered by the complexity of terms used by both lighting designers and manufacturers alike. To help sort out some of the confusion, there follows a brief guide to the sort of questions most commonly asked which should give an elementary working knowledge about the different lighting terms and their proper use. Further information is also given on pages 310 to 312.

Incandescent versus fluorescent lights

Also known as tungsten lights, incandescent bulbs give a pleasant, golden light and are a more popular choice for domestic use than the cheaper, colder looking fluorescents. The average incandescent bulb life ranges from 750 to 1,000 hours. Fluorescent bulbs are tubular in shape, and with normal domestic use and cleaning care, they will last four to five years. The tubes are best masked by a baffle.

Low-voltage bulbs

These have a precise beam and are particularly useful for pinpoint lighting. When connected to a normal voltage line, these bulbs must be operated on a transformer. Low-voltage bulbs come in spot and flood form and those designed to cast a rectangular beam are particularly useful for highlighting objects.

Reflector bulbs

These are incandescent bulbs with a silver or aluminum reflector coating. The projected beam can be wide or narrow, as in a flood or spot bulb and will direct light where needed. To make every watt count, you could replace all regular 100-watt bulbs in directional fixtures or task lamps with 50-watt R20 reflector bulbs. This way you will get the same amount of light for less running cost.

Wallwashers

These literally bathe a wall with light, expanding the feeling of space in a room. They are usually fixed about three feet (9 meters) away from the wall. Angled closer to a group of paintings or a collection of objects, the wallwashers splash light over the different surfaces, leaving contrasting shadows in between.

Downlights

These may be round or square metal cannisters that can be recessed into a ceiling, semi-recessed, or ceiling-mounted to cast pools of light on any surface below them. The type of light depends on whether the bulb is a spot, a flood or just an ordinary bulb. Most downlights are fitted with an anti-glare device, and some are baffled to give a directional light.

Uplights

Placed on the floor behind sofas or plants, under glass shelves and in corners, uplights give a beautiful, dramatic accent light.

Framing projectors

The beam of these fixtures can be shaped accurately so that a given surface such as a painting or a tabletop can be lit exactly.

Track lighting

A track makes it possible for one electric outlet to supply a number of separate fittings positioned at any point along its length. Its versatility is such that the track can be surface-mounted or recessed, used in or on ceilings, on walls, above baseboards or skirtings, and can be fixed vertically or horizontally, singly or in pairs, in squares, rectangles or large circles.

Dimmer switches

These give a variety of different light levels at the turn of a knob. They save energy, bulb life and running costs by reducing current consumption, and are an essential ingredient to any sort of flexible or subtle lighting scheme. Inexpensive dimmers are available that fit in place of the usual light switch, as well as multiple-control units that control several circuits from the same point. Most types can be installed quite easily.

Opposite page, far left:
An unelectrified chandelier with candles and matching wall sconces backed by crystal table lamps and uplights give romantic light and shade in this pretty, traditional room.

Left:
Three spots fixed between beams and angled down over the worktop give good general light as well as catching the prisms reflected from the glasses slotted into the ceiling.

This page, right:
An angled seating platform and the seats themselves are lit from below with strip lights for a light, floating effect. Further interesting light is provided by an uplight behind the wall flat and by the lamp suspended over the candlelit table.

Below, left:
Downlights and wall-washers are set into the ceiling to give both general and accent light in this simply furnished space. Note the extra dimension it adds to a space that would just look bland with overall light.

Below, right:
An uplight concealed behind large palms casts dramatic shadows on the ceiling and walls, doubling the plants' impact.

Halls should seem both warm and welcoming. In largish areas, uplights in corners or a series of downlights and wallwashers are ideal. Or if there are enough outlets, provide floor or table lamps. Stairs should be well lit from above.

For living rooms, the best light is undoubtedly a mixture of background, task and accent light. And remember the gentle but dramatic effect that uplights can give when concealed behind plants and pieces of furniture or other objects.

Lighting dining rooms and kitchens

The focal point of any dining room or area is the tabletop, and one of the best ways to light it is by downlights. Whichever type of fixture you choose, make sure the actual bulb is hidden from all usual seating angles. Candles combined with dimmed background lighting are a romantic alternative. Kitchens need good general light plus localized light over work surfaces.

If a bathroom is very small, the best solution is a central ceiling fixture. For larger rooms, use downlights above the tub and basin and boost these with shaving and make-up lights all around a mirror.

Bedroom lighting should be as flexible as that in the living area, with the same mixture of general, task and accent light.

Left:
Strips of small bulbs all around a bathroom mirror give the best light for make-up and shaving. Have them controlled by a dimmer switch if possible.

Below left:
Decorative or sculptural light can act as an art form as well as fulfilling its primary function. Here, a panel of painted glass stands in front of a tall tinted light.

Below right:
Neon tubing, though expensive, can also provide effective decoration. This series of circles above a dining table can be turned to red, blue or white, depending on the mood that is required.

LIGHTING ART AND POSSESSIONS

When it comes to lighting art there is a wide variety of fixtures on the market, ranging from the ubiquitous picture light itself through adjustable spotlights and framing projectors (see also pages 310 to 312 for additional information).

Lighting single pictures

If you are lighting a single painting the ideal is to place a fixture so that there is no distracting reflection, whether from the frame, glass or varnish. To get the best angle, it is worth experimenting with a clip-on work lamp attached to a long cord.

Conventional picture lights are easily installed and maintained, but they are inclined to throw light on the top of the painting to the detriment of the bottom. Downlights are the next simplest form to install. They can be mounted on or recessed into the ceiling, or they can be fixed to a track. The light is controlled either by a dimmer switch or according to the wattage of the bulbs used. The main disadvantage is that the beam from an ordinary downlight also forms an eliptical shape on the wall beside the painting. Conversely, pictures can be lit from below by uplights on the floor, or small spotlights concealed in vases positioned on mantels or other broad surfaces. The ideal, but expensive solution is to use a framing projector (see page 20).

Above:
Spherical lamps positioned on the floor throw up diffuse light which catches the edge of the plexiglass shelves so the oriental objects appear to be suspended on rims of light. They look all the more dramatic against the dark walls.

Far left:
A spotlight (not seen) angled from the ceiling, throws an aura of light around the early Italian carved wood statue mounted on a burlap-covered wall.

Left:
A handsome 19th century woodburning stove is shown up in interesting relief by the uplight placed behind. Another uplight placed under the spraying *ficus* casts effective shadows on the ceiling.

Lighting groups of pictures

When there is a number of pictures on a wall, wallwashers are the best solution because they light the whole area. They should be fixed in much the same way as downlights, or concealed behind cornices or valances. The pictures and prints can then be moved around at will without disturbing the balance of light. The main disadvantage with this method is that there is a lack of contrast between art and wall and a diminishing of textural qualities that a painting may possess. Of course, spot-lights mounted in the same way can be trained onto individual pictures. If there are several pictures on a wall, track lighting is very useful since it will hold a number of fixtures which are adjustable at will.

Again, as with single pictures and objects, light can be thrown up from beneath by adjustable uplights, or by wall-washers set on sections of track fixed along the top of the baseboards. These will give an interesting contrast of shadow and light and are utterly inconspicuous in a room.

Lighting wallhangings

Try first of all to experiment with a clip-on work lamp to see the kind of angle which will show up the intricate textural effects and weaves of tapestries, rugs or macramé. Remember that any light projected full on will almost certainly flatten a highly worked surface.

Lighting sculpture and other objects

The impact of any piece of sculpture depends very much on the interplay of light and shadows, so it is important that you experiment with what kind of light to use.

Almost any attractive object can be treated as a piece of sculpture, and it is useful to keep an adjustable fixture, or several, ready to light a plant, an arrange-ment of flowers, a piece of interesting porcelain or any found object.

Striplights concealed by a baffle are useful for lighting collections arranged on shelves, or you can use miniature eyeball spotlights or tiny spots concealed among the objects themselves. Items on the lower shelves should be as near the front as possible so that they will get the full benefit of the light.

Objects inside cabinets can be lit with slightly less emphasis. Rows of tiny bulbs or miniature tracks can be installed whether along the front edge of each shelf or vertically down the sides. Whatever method you choose, make sure that the equipment is hidden and does not distract from the objects themselves.

Left:
Track lighting with cannister spots can be trained on whatever needs light. Tracks are probably the most versatile lighting system, and can be added to and adjusted at will, however much pictures and objects are changed around.

Below:
A plexiglass lamp of just the right height illuminates the collection of glass and ceramics on the cube table. The large painting is lit by a recessed spotlight.

THE EFFECTS OF COLOR

Color can transform a home more quickly and cheaply than any other decorational device, disguising faults and altering the whole feeling of a space in as short a time as it takes to paint or cover the walls. Even one extra color, judiciously chosen and well-placed, can add instant extra pep to a room, even if it is only a pillow, a poster, or a flowering plant. Wrongly chosen or uninspired colors can make the most beautiful furniture seem dull, and hide the purity of good proportions.

The importance of color is proved again and again in the Room-by-Room Guide (see pages 33 to 192) in which I show how all types and sizes of rooms can be redecorated to achieve quite different visual effects.

New juxtapositions and injections of color can transform even the dullest space. A darkish room, for instance, can be painted white and spiced with plants and pillows in primary colors to make a totally fresh looking, unrecognizable space; a white room, painted, say, nutmeg brown, will take on an unprecedented warmth; an acquamarine blue room will look warm and inviting in the winter with the aid of red flowers and brown and rust accessories, while the same space will seem cool and restful in summer with greens, more blues and whites.

By absorbing certain key principles about using color and by learning to observe and remember combinations and harmonies that seem particularly pleasing (from diverse sources, whether in nature, or paintings, oriental rugs, or in other people's homes) a sure color sense can be built up to lasting effect. Color sense, unlike, for example, perfect pitch, is not an absolute, it can be absorbed and improved steadily over the years.

One important point to remember is that color will change radically according to the circumstances under which it is viewed. If red is put near blue, for example, the red appears yellower. Near yellow, the same red appears bluer; next to green, it appears purer and brighter; next to black, it seems duller; next to white, it becomes lighter and brighter; and next to gray, too, red seems brighter. If a dark color is placed beside a different, but lighter color, it appears deeper and the light color appears lighter. This is the result of contrast of tone.

A color is also greatly intensified by gloss: look at butterflies' wings, the feathers of some birds, the textures of some flower petals, and you will see that lacquered and shiny surfaces look so much more brilliant than matt ones.

Left:
A new wood-block floor was so unacceptable to its artist owner, that in a fit of indignation he painted it overnight. The blues and greens of the geometric design make a striking background for the ancient hutch and the foliage.

Below:
Making a virtue out of necessity, unsightly ducting is turned into a feature in the bedroom. The chrome yellow paint is repeated in the pillows and striped sheets, and the ceiling is gloss-painted to match the carpet.

USING COLOR

Working out the best combination of colors or the best scheme for a room is of prime importance in decorating, but there is no doubt that, when working from scratch, the task can be daunting.

It is all very simple, once you know how, but few of us are born with a sure enough sense of color to use it with ease and confidence – at least from the beginning. And, surprisingly, perhaps, many people who find no trouble at all in putting together clothes and accessories in interesting, bold or subtle combinations, seem to feel inhibited about combining the various components of a room with the same sort of verve and dash.

Apart from all the situations which affect the way color changes (dealt with on the previous page), it should also be remembered that colors can be considerably modified by the shape and form of an object, and according to the amount of light, or shade, that is in the room.

Accent colors

One approach to using color is to keep most of a room in one color, or shades and variations of it, using accent colors for accessories. Another solution is to keep most upholstered furniture, drapes and walls in one color and use a different one for the floor; accessories would be in another, third color, and in variations of the first two. Or a major color could be used for walls and the smaller items of furniture, with accent colors supplied by the larger pieces and the accessories.

Color sense in others

If inspiration is lacking when it comes to thinking up a new color scheme, one way is to cut out photographs from magazines that seem to look good. If such clippings are systematically put into a file over a period of time and then looked at all together, the same balance of colors will almost certainly tend to be repeated over and over again. This little experiment should prove, as nothing else will, the sort of colors that, even unconsciously, are most comfortable for the collector.

Collecting ideas

Another way is to always keep a notebook at hand and to jot down any color combination that seems particularly pleasing, whether it be in restaurants and art galleries, hotels and museums, shops, model rooms and hairdressers, quite apart from other people's homes. Study paintings in detail and see how color is laid against color, and tone upon tone.

Opposite page:
Any color used with white assumes a special clarity. Against these pale walls, the pastels of the painting, echoed in the throw pillows and repeated in the flowers, assume an interesting luminosity.

Below:
In this all-white bathroom, accents of color, the green of leaves, the reds and yellows of flowers, even the paler apricots of towels, stand out in sharp focus.

This page, right:
Brilliant red units are set against yellow walls and a green floor with matching blinds in this forceful statement of a kitchen area. Meshed wire guarding the staircase and the child's high chair are painted to match, so that nothing is out of key.

Below left:
To brighten up a brownstone townhouse, red walls and woodwork and a red-painted chair frame are contrasted with chrome yellow shutters, red and yellow patchwork, and green, yellow and red upholstery. The overall effect is smart and lively without being garish.

Right:
Shiny black walls sharpen colors and give them an even greater intensity than white ones. Here, the red light, the white china and a yellow box are also reflected on the aluminum worktop, so the effect is doubled. Dramatic low-level lighting adds extra depth.

CHOOSING COLOR SCHEMES

Planning a color scheme often seems an insurmountable task to the inexperienced. One way to begin is to take a color, any favorite color, and think of it in depth. Take green, for example, and think of trees through the seasons; the different greens of herbs, from the sharp, freshness of parsley or chives to the gray-green of sage and blue-green rosemary. Or try thinking of precious stones: jades and malachite and emeralds; or the striated, cool, greens of marble and the deep, dark green of some slates. Think of moss and lichen, algae and seaweed, variegated ivy and honeysuckle, the browny-greens of ponds and the clear, blue-green of sea struck by sun. Natural combinations like these can be used to build up interesting, monochromatic schemes, especially when contrasted or accented with other colors that set them off quite naturally.

Ideas for color schemes
In a white scheme, for example, the walls and drapes might be a pale string color, the carpet would be white, with sofa in honey and chairs a silver gray; cushions and plants or flowers would also be white. For a brown scheme, the walls would be a coca-cola color, the drapes would be chestnut brown and the carpet black and brown; the sofa would be white and the chairs natural-colored, with scarlet cushions and shocking pink flowers as accents. In rooms with pale beige walls, the drapes would match, the carpet would be dark brown and the sofa would be the color of milk chocolate; any chairs would be Chinese yellow, the cushions would be white and flowers, orange or yellow. In a gray scheme, the walls might be a pale gray, the drapes white and the carpet yellow; there would be a dark gray sofa and black chairs with lemon cushions; any flowers would be yellow. Where the walls are very pale pink, the drapes could be white and the carpet a sand color; the sofa would be moss green, with shocking pink cushions and scarlet flowers to spike the pastels. These are just some ideas; remember that texture is an important ingredient and will affect the impact of any color. And remember, too, that pale colors tend to look good in sunny rooms, while north facing ones always look more cheerful if warm, luminous colors are used rather than cold or dark ones.

A space will always seem more cohesive if more or less the same colors are used throughout. Ideas about continuing a feeling throughout a house or apartment are dealt with in the Room-by-Room Guide. See pages 184 to 192 for ideas.

Opposite page, top:
Brilliant yellow is combined with blue in different proportions in this canary-colored kitchen. Because of their shared coloring, drapery fabric harmonizes well with the ceramic floor tiles.

Below:
Satin throw cushions luminously pick up the colors in the Jim Dine painting which are reflected again by the roses in their specimen vases.

Right:
Grass green makes a bold, unifying theme here, used over walls and Art Nouveau table, repeated in wallpaper and fabric, and added to with plants and the green in the Tiffany lamp shade.

Far right:
Red, white and blue harmonize surprisingly calmly in this eclectically-furnished bedroom with its massive carved bed and striking geometric rug.

Below:
The predominant pink of the rosewood paneling in this bathroom is brought out with rose-colored accents and the paler tones of drapes, carpet and ceiling. The blue-gray miniprint of walls and shade act as a quiet foil.

USING TEXTURE AND PATTERN

If sure use of color is absolutely basic to good decorating, a feeling for texture and pattern is the refinement or gloss and should be considered just as seriously as the whole process of building up colors in a room. Colors can be so radically changed or modified by cleverly used texture and pattern, that through its subtlety of finish, even a one-color room can be made to look just as lively and interesting as a more vividly colored counterpart. And just as good juxtapositions of color add immediate interest in a room, so thoughtful contrasts of texture and pattern, or both, can add to the overall visual effect, but in a gentler, less obvious way.

Textural build-up

Interestingly, textures are often as evocative as colors. Take, for example, these well-known finishes: boarding, brick, burlap, brass, cane, ceramic, coir matting, corduroy, cotton, cork, denim, felt, glass, lace, lacquer, leather, linen, marble, mirror, plaster, plexiglass, rush, sailcloth, satin, silk, sisal, sheepskin, slub, slate, steel, stone, suede, terracotta, travertine, trellis, velvet, wicker, wood (natural and polished), wood slats, wool, woolcord. If you isolate each one in your mind, you can practically feel as well as see its surface. Imagine how each one would look appropriately applied to floors or ceilings, walls, furniture, windows and accessories. Contrast the varying qualities of the materials, and you begin to appreciate the possibilities inherent in intelligent mixing of textures, the ability to build up comfort, or crispness, or both; the combinations of hard with soft, smooth with rough, matt with shine.

Clearly, some textures seem to go better together than others, but this is mainly a matter of taste and practicality. Look at the Sample Book, pages 193 to 288 for ideas, and look around for samples of carpet, matting, fabrics, vinyls, wallpapers, wallcoverings and various tiles so you can see the possibilities for yourself. But rather than just color-matching or contrasting, find out which ones make the most interesting combinations, and which textures seem actually to enhance something else.

Most people know that rough textures probably mix well with smooth ones, that matt goes well with gloss, but *which* rough surfaces should be mixed with which smooth ones, what matt juxtaposed with what gloss? As a general rule, coarse fabrics like burlap or tweed will usually look

This page, left:
Although the various patterns and their scales are very different in this room, they work well together because of their similarity of color. The very difference in pattern sizes adds a touch of liveliness to this predominantly peach and green-toned space.

Below:
Based on various shades of apricot, this monotone scheme is given liveliness by the differences of scale: floor tiles and seat covers, the contrast of tile and wood, the brightly painted walls and pale shutters, the smooth plastic pedestals and the luxuriant foliage. Even the smallest details link up, so that the blue and white ceramics are repeated in the throw cushions and underscored by the more violent blue of the painting between the windows.

Opposite page, top:
The same pattern can be used extensively in a room for different surfaces. Here, one pattern is used lavishly for walls, drapes and bedspreads, and is complimented by a toning chair and painting. An extra layer of pattern is provided by the small embroidered pillows in repeating colors, but on a different scale. The tactile nubbliness of the quilted bedspreads is underscored by the thick pile of the shag carpet, and offset by the smoothness of painted wood bedheads, dado and bedside table.

Below:
Bright colors and exotic patterns can look good against plain, dark walls. Here, painted "drapery" exactly matches the color of the carpet, whose rich patterns are repeated again in the exotically painted ceiling, and in the gleaming, luxurious satin of the sofa and throw pillows. Frivolously ruched shades match the plain walls, while foliage and gleaming mahogany provide deeper but gently toning shades.

far better in rooms with rough, brick walls than more refined materials like silk or satin; lacquered furniture will look far more effective against velvet-covered walls than the same pieces made from plexiglass. Which of your furnishing accessories, for example, has a particular softness, or depth, or gleam to it, and what can you put beside it to make those qualities stand out?

Will the introduction of a plant or a vase of flowers help soften the shiny, hard-edged effect of a collection of silver or ceramics; or can a large, solid piece of sculpture be offset by a tall, yet insubstantial plant? Further information about building up pleasing arrangements of objects and mixing and matching textures and patterns is also given on pages 321 to 352.

Unusual paint techniques

Remember, too, the various methods for painting walls. Each type of finish, whether lacquered or glazed, rag-rubbed or dragged, combed or flat will, to a greater or lesser degree, alter the feel of a textural build-up. For more information about the more unusual painting techniques, see the Sample Book, pages 195 and 243.

Even when a room seems finished, the introduction of one more texture could make the same difference to its interest and vitality as a sudden and unexpected injection of color. A chance incident might point something out: a basket left on a floor; a heavy woollen cardigan thrown over a chair; a brass container lying on a table. Suddenly, a quite unexpected surface seems so right, so delineating of the other surfaces and colors in a room, that one cannot imagine why it was not thought of in the beginning. This gradual, relaxed accretion of experience, ideas and possessions is what decoration is about, after all.

Mixing patterns

Mixing patterns can be a daunting exercise to the uninitiated, who may fear the distracting effect pattern piled on pattern can have. Historically, of course, people have always mixed pattern and ornament, if not with abandon, at least with a fine air of certainty. Think of the fabulous linenfold paneling and plaster-work of the sixteenth century; the magnificent complication of paneling, cornices, fabrics and rugs of Europe in the seventeenth century; the elaborate ceilings, damask wallcoverings, moldings, chair coverings and carpets of the eighteenth century; the stripes and

GOOD USE OF PATTERN

silks, Turkey rugs, mahogany, figured velvets and lace antimacassars of the 1900s, the jazzy mixtures of the Twenties.

Grouping similar tones

Mixing patterns is really a question of achieving the right scale, color and balance. If you put together a number of prints which share much the same coloring or tones, some will appear to work together much better than others, and, as with textures, these might actually enhance one another (especially if linked by areas of a plain color predominant in the pattern). It is all too easy to under-estimate the intricate patterning of accessories such as plants and books, pictures, objects, and ceramics, and the shapes of furniture, even before you think of the choice of fabrics and wallpapers, rugs, carpets, wallcoverings and tiles.

Massed ethnic prints

Or think of the way a mass of Indian printed cottons can look effortlessly harmonious, their patterns all very much the same size and in good proportion with each other. Look at how their colors intermingle and repeat each other, and you begin to understand the principle of mixing and matching and will begin to feel more confident of putting it into practice.

Even the flimsiest of sheers can be used in the build-up of patterns in a room if they are chosen with a similar or matching design to the drapes. The pattern could be simply white on white, or in a toned-down version of the main colors, or it could be a simplified version of the drape motif, in one color on white. The effect will be no less interesting than less subtle combinations.

Playing with pattern

A play of pattern, properly manipulated, can be very beneficial to a room, influencing as it does the whole balance of color. And sensitively worked, pattern can often give the illusion of added depth and therefore space to a room, as well as giving it a recognisable personality. Many of the hazards of experimentation are taken out of one's hands these days now that manufacturers are producing coordinated ranges of fabrics, wallpapers, wallcoverings, tiles and sometimes carpets, all designed to be mixed and matched according to taste, space and circumstances.

As ever, the only way to learn is to observe and experiment, to find patterns and combinations that appeal and then try them out for yourself.

Left:
In this highly patterned and textured vignette, a large oriental rug on the wall, bamboo furniture, colorful glass lamps, coarse textured matting are teamed with zebra skins and a spiky plant. The interplay of very different textures and patterns makes for a richly warm, luxurious feel.

Below:
In this carefully-planned entrance hall, the interesting contrasts of texture all link up. The closely woven coir matting blends in with the terracotta painted walls, the silky, skin-covered upholstered stools tone with the dark, chunky, wooden bannisters, and the thick weave of the sofa looks good against the smooth cotton of the Roman shade.

THE ROOM-BY-ROOM GUIDE

CORRIDORS AND ENTRANCE HALLS

Since first impressions are as relevant to buildings as to people, it is logical to spend time and thought designing a warm and interesting entrance hall for a home. But all too often, mostly for budgetary reasons, these spaces are relegated to the bottom of the list of priorities and end up a rather formless miscellany of all the odds and ends left over from other rooms, other ideas.

Planning a hallway

In theory, they should be comparatively easy to design since most areas are not big enough to hold much in the way of furniture and accessories. Entrance halls in the majority of city houses and apartments are seldom much bigger than a corridor, and you rarely find anywhere else the kind of wide and generous space that seemed so commonplace in early Hollywood movies.

If at all possible, there should be at least one chair and a capacious enough table to take parcels, letters, magazines, a telephone, message pads, lists, and all the other paraphernalia that inevitably collects, however fleetingly, in this clearing house of the home. But if the space is too narrow for these, try to get a long bench, or at the very least a stool and shelf. And try to provide some place for coats and a stand for umbrellas.

Ideally, walls in halls, corridors and on staircases should be decorated with the same color throughout if they lead off from one another without any sort of real division. Sometimes a dominant feature, like the stained glass windows often to be found in turn-of-the-century houses in city suburbs, will suggest a color. Or the colors of any room seen opening off the space provide the key to the scheme. But avoid the temptation of using pale tones or delicate fabrics – especially in a family home – since all the constant traffic through the area, the occasional removal of furniture, appliances, suitcases, parcels, the deliveries of one sort and another, quite apart from the daily comings and goings, must clearly take their toll. Aim instead, to use a warm, rich color which will withstand the wear and tear better, unless you really prefer to keep the space as light as possible and are quite prepared to repaint or resurface the area whenever necessary.

Flooring should be tough, practical, and above all, easily cleaned. If you are going to have carpet in the hallway and up any stairs to landings, make sure that it is the heaviest weight Wilton or Axminster that can be afforded, though stairs do not necessarily need to be carpeted unless you have elderly people in the house, or young children, both liable to slip, or unless noise is a problem. And it is a good idea to avoid matting of any sort, however neat and crisp it might seem in theory, for it can be slippery on treads, and looser weaves can be a trap for heels.

Lighting hallways and stairwells

The safety aspect is particularly important for hall and staircase lighting. The treads of stairs should be well lit at all times, and light should never be placed in such a way that it could shine in people's eyes. Similarly, any irregularities like small steps or changes in level in corridors should be well-lit, and there should be enough light on walls to show up switches and door handles. If you are starting a lighting plan from scratch in these areas, the ideal would be either to have a night circuit of low-level lights, controlled by a dimmer switch that can turn them down to the right level at bedtime. Or you could have a separate circuit of miniature lights; these could be left on the full twenty-four hours, if necessary, because they consume a minimum of electricity and although more expensive to install, they are undoubedly convenient. A cheaper solution would be to use single, low-wattage bulbs in appropriate positions. Any of these systems would also provide a useful deterrant to burglars and prowlers. (More information about lighting can be found on pages 19 to 24.)

The final touches

One of the best things about these areas is that they will take any number of paintings, prints, objects, curiosities and of course, mirrors or mirror panels as long as you hang, place and light them with care. You can always fill alcoves, wider than usual corridors and awkward angles with closets or bookshelves, and quite often the most unpromising-looking space can be made to take a small dining table, or a desk which will double its usefulness.

If there is a window on a wide landing on the turn of the stairs, the space can be turned into a miniature conservatory or greenhouse area with trellis on the walls, or shelves of plants. Or the same window can be made into a lively focal point with an interesting window treatment.

Ideas for many of the more usual shapes and also problem areas are shown over the next few pages, and at the very least, they should start a new train of thought on the subject of decorating corridors and entrance halls.

Opposite page:
The dramatic cluster of pendant lights and an unusually low-hung drawing add further interest to this entrance hall with its textured floor and walls. A large mirror reflects the boarded table and branches as well as doubling the space in what could easily have been an undistinguished, awkward area.

This page, right:
Warm color is especially appealing in large halls like this one. Extra interest is added here by the arched niches which are ideal for showing off a collection of sculpture.

Below left:
A herringboned brick floor, waxed wood and rough stone walls make a sympathetic background for the solid wood chest and early candle holders in this country entrance hall.

Below right:
Hallways are often just the place for a touch of fantasy. The painted mural and false marbled dado in this actually narrow and corridor-like hall makes the "crowded" space seem like part of a modern cloister.

AN UNUSUALLY LARGE ENTRANCE HALL

With conscientious attention to detail and a good eye for arrangement, an unusually large entrance hall can be used to show off an eclectic collection of furniture and objects. The scheme opposite has a warm, natural background which does not detract from the collection; the second has a more sophisticated feel, concentrating on low key colors, and another has a spare, Spanish influence.

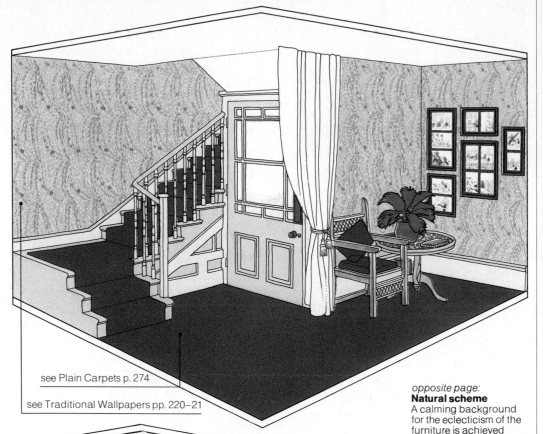

see Plain Carpets p. 274

see Traditional Wallpapers pp. 220–21

Sophisticated scheme

Lines are kept crisp and uncluttered and are emphasized by the use of dark, all-over carpet with matching colored cushions and the mass of small prints on similar colored matts. The marbled paper merges into the painted door. While the muted shades of walls and woodwork are very pleasing, the bright color of the table top is used here to add a splash of warmth.

Walls: Marbled paper in cream, beige and terracotta
Ceiling: Cream latex paint
Floor: Plain brown twist carpet
Woodwork: Coffee and cream semi-gloss paint
Furniture: Gilded turn-of-the-century chair with brown cushions; cloisonné-topped table
Lighting: Uplights; spotlights (not seen)
Accessories: Collection of small prints on dark brown matts; fern in copper container; drapes; basket for letters and cards

Spare Spanish scheme

A basic, uncluttered look is achieved by stripping the stairs to their original pine and leaving them uncarpeted. The floor is covered with Mexican tiles in faded terracotta and the walls are left plain. A simple oak refectory table and a seventeenth-century oak chair are the only furniture, and terracotta pots on the wall the only decoration.

Walls: White latex paint
Ceiling: Pale terracotta latex paint
Floor: Stripped pine stairs; large Mexican terracotta tiles
Woodwork: All stripped pine
Furniture: Early refectory table; seventeenth-century oak chair
Lighting: Uplights; wall spotlight
Accessories: Terracotta pots on wall; large majolica dish; portrait; clock; candles; plant

see Natural Tiles p. 265

opposite page:
Natural scheme

A calming background for the eclecticism of the furniture is achieved here by the use of natural colors and textures – the door is stripped pine with simple brass fittings, herring-bone coir matting covers the floor, and a dark carpet the stairs. Natural raw silk curtains are tied back with cord and walls are painted terracotta to add to the warm effect. The same atmosphere could be achieved with cork-colored or ocher walls.

Walls: Terracotta latex paint
Ceiling: White latex paint
Floor: Coir matting; brown wool stair carpet
Woodwork: Stripped pine or white semi-gloss paint
Furniture: Gilded turn-of-the-century chair; blue, green and terracotta cloisonné-topped table
Lighting: Uplights concealed behind table; wall spotlight
Accessories: Plants; naïve paintings; small bust; books; drapes

A LONG DARK CORRIDOR

Town apartments often have rather dark, meandering internal halls which present something of a challenge because they should be made both welcoming and utilitarian, in spite of the natural gloom. They are, of course, obvious places for fitting in extra storage and walls can be lined with units to take any excess household paraphernalia, china and glass, especially when they lead between dining room and kitchen like this one. For such a functional area the scheme opposite is unexpectedly rich and dramatic; the second is deliberately cool and clean-lined, while the third is crisp and cheerful.

see Paints pp. 210–11

Clean-lined scheme
To make the area seem less confining the corridor and units are painted the same cream as the kitchen beyond. The space is further enlarged by using glass for the unit doors. Downlights are inset into the ceiling, with strip lights inside the units to illuminate the china and glassware.

Walls and ceiling: Cream latex paint
Woodwork: Cream semi-gloss paint
Floor: Terracotta tiles
Lighting: Downlights and strip lights
Fittings: Built-in units with tiled tops and cream semi-gloss painted frames with glass-fronted doors
Accessories: Baskets on wall; units filled with china and glass

see Ethnic Tiles p. 238

see Natural Tiles p. 265

Chrome yellow scheme
Brilliant chrome yellow makes a dazzling approach to the kitchen. Counter tops are covered with melamine and the shade on the window picks up the scheme's bright colors.

Walls: Chrome yellow high-gloss paint
Ceiling: White latex paint
Woodwork: Cream semi-gloss paint
Floor: Terracotta tiles
Window: Striped cotton shade
Lighting: Strip lights inside units, over counter tops; inset downlights in ceiling
Fittings: Units with full-gloss louvered doors; counter tops in white melamine
Accessories: Plants; china mugs

opposite page:
Rich and dramatic scheme
To give the space an air of lacquered elegance, high-gloss paint is used on the walls, ceiling and units. The effect is heightened by using shiny terracotta tiles on the floor and by flooding the area with dramatic lighting. Cool-colored plates on the wall counter-balance the richness as do the walls of the kitchen beyond. The same feeling could be achieved with shiny blue-green walls.

Walls and ceiling: Indian red high-gloss paint
Woodwork: Indian red high-gloss paint; butcher block work tops
Floor: Provençal terracotta tiles
Window: Striped Roman shade and café curtain
Lighting: Track with adjustable downlights fitted with flood bulbs
Accessories: Blue and white plates; baskets and brown pottery

AN OLD-FASHIONED STAIRWELL

The sweeping staircases and high ceilings sometimes found in old town and country houses certainly create a great feeling of space, although they are often difficult to decorate – as well as expensive. The best solution is to look for some natural asset which can dictate the scheme: the balustrade, a molding, the color of the wood, or, as in this case, a window, which is usefully endowed with brilliantly colored stained glass. In each scheme, the window is allowed to dominate but in quite different ways. The scheme opposite is calm and dignified, the second is like a jeweled box, and the scheme on the right is fresh and clear-cut.

see Paints pp. 210–11

Clear-cut scheme
Contrasting bright colors can be used to great effect to produce a razor-sharp, crisp look. To give definition to the dazzling background of white lacquered walls, colors in the stained glass window are again picked out in the carpet, the small cornice and the top rail of the dado.

Walls: White super-gloss paint
Ceiling: White latex paint
Woodwork: White semi-gloss paint; cornice and rail of dado in blue semi-gloss paint to match the glass
Floor: Red wool carpet to match window
Window: Stained glass
Lighting: Four inset downlights in ceiling; light behind window

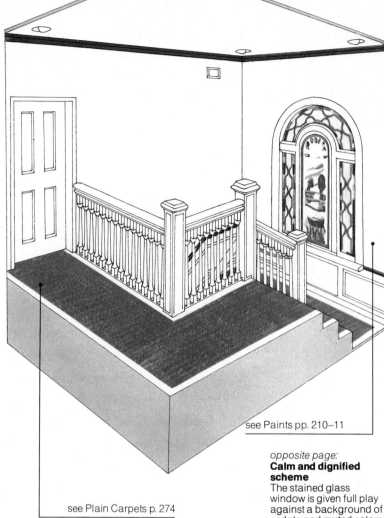

see Paints pp. 210–11

see Plain Carpets p. 274

see Plain Carpets p. 274

Jeweled box scheme
The background colors in this scheme echo those in the stained glass window, so both walls and woodwork pick out the predominant color of the glass and have its sheen. The carpet, too, is the same color and its border repeats the border of the window to achieve a jeweled-box effect. Another way of achieving the same effect would be to take the green of the central panel as the *leitmotif*, and vary the colors of the carpet to green and red.

Walls, ceiling and woodwork: Bristol blue semi-gloss paint; cornice in red semi-gloss paint; mahogany balustrade and moldings
Floor: Bristol blue Brussels weave carpet with red, pinky-beige and blue border
Window: Stained glass
Lighting: Wallwashers in four corners of ceiling; light behind window

opposite page:
Calm and dignified scheme
The stained glass window is given full play against a background of sedate and muted colors. The carpet has a small Greek key motif bordered with Greek key in a larger, sharper scale. The use of subtle-colored silk for the walls continues the calming effect. The same feeling would be given by using gray silk or *moiré* paper, or pale gray felt or flannel with a string-colored cornice.

Walls: String-colored silk paper
Floor: Carpet in black and white Greek key pattern
Woodwork: White semi-gloss paint; cornice in gray latex paint
Window: Stained glass
Lighting: Downlight above stairs and light behind stained glass

A SMALL ENTRANCE HALL

This entrance hall is typical of many small houses, with its staircase at one end and a living room off to one side. The exercise is to make it as warm and welcoming and, of course, as interesting, as possible. The scheme opposite relies on the tawny colors and different textures of matting, furniture and rug to provide warmth against the brilliant white background. The next scheme takes the Afghan rug as a starting point, and this is echoed in a series of mellow browns and golds. The third scheme visually doubles the space with dramatically colored carpet and a wall of mirror.

Warm, mellow scheme
Light and warmth is injected into the space here with a scheme in which the colors of the flooring, walls and woodwork are based on the Afghan rug. The overall effect is certainly warm and welcoming.

Walls and ceiling:
Golden brown latex paint
Cornice, door frame and bannisters: Dark polished wood
Other woodwork:
Stripped and waxed
Floor: Coir matting; Afghan rug
Lighting: Recessed wall-washers
Furniture: 19th-century pine table; pine-framed mirror
Accessories: Prints; plants

see Patterned carpets p. 277

see Paints pp. 210–11

see Matting pp. 278–9

see Paints pp. 210–11

opposite page:
Light, natural scheme
To boost the meager ration of natural light that actually reaches this area (most is "borrowed" from the stairwell and adjoining room), the walls and ceiling are painted the color of pure snow. Visual interest is provided by the crisp texture of the matting, which complements the glowing color of the stripped wood stairs, the mirror and side table.

Walls and ceiling:
White latex paint
Woodwork: White semi-gloss paint
Floor: Coir matting and stripped wood; Afghan rug
Lighting: Paper shade (not seen)
Furniture: 19th-century pine table; pine-framed mirror
Accessories: Prints; plants; china bowl full of *pot pourri*

Brilliantly colored scheme
The strong colors and bold pattern of the carpet used here seemingly push out the walls and change the feel of the space. The area is visually expanded further by the use of a mirror on the wall opposite the living room entrance – there now appear to be *two* large rooms opening off the central space. The colors of the carpet are picked out and used in separate blocks for further dramatic impact.

Walls of hall: Green latex paint; mirror

Walls of stairwell (and living room): Chrome yellow latex paint
Ceiling: White latex paint
Cornice, baseboards and door frames: White semi-gloss paint
Bannisters: Polished wood
Floor: Yellow, green and apricot wool and nylon carpet
Lighting: Ceiling-recessed wallwashers and downlights
Furniture: 19th-century chair; prints; plants

A DARK HALLWAY

Dark, meandering, windowless halls are, unfortunately, typical of thousands of city studio apartments, and unless they are to appear somber and featureless, these spaces need imaginative decoration. The scheme opposite produces a discreet but well delineated effect, the second is airy, light and space-stretching, and the third depends on walls of books to add interest.

Space-stretching scheme
To exaggerate the space, seemingly pushing out the walls, oriental, trellis-patterned paper is used for the walls, in conjunction with a plain color for the slight alcoves. Ceiling, woodwork and floor are kept plain. The tiered rosewood and lacquer chest builds up the *Chinoiserie* effect. Green or apricot could be used as alternative colorways.

Walls: Red and white oriental trellis wallpaper
Ceiling: White latex paint
Woodwork: White semi-gloss paint
Floor: White vinyl tiles
Furniture: Tiered rosewood and lacquer chest; chairs
Lighting: Track with wallwashers; downlight
Accessories: Mirror; plant

see Tiles p. 270

see Wallpapers p. 215

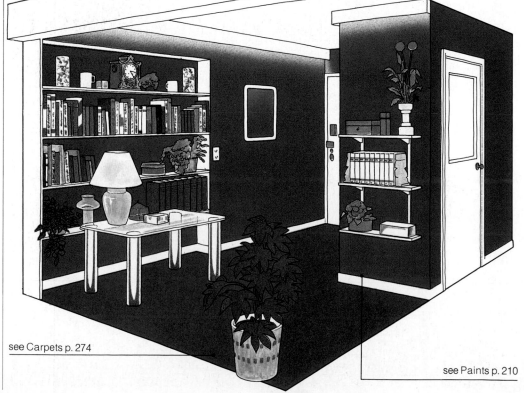

see Carpets p. 274

see Paints p. 210

Book-lined scheme
To add interest and color to the hall, the large alcove and both facing walls are lined with bookshelves; these are lit from above by tube lights hidden behind a continuous valance. The muted color of the carpet is taken up in the walls. Bibliophiles can read the books at the functional, steel and glass table standing near the door.

Walls: Chestnut brown semi-gloss paint
Ceiling and other woodwork: White latex and semi-gloss paint
Floor: Dark brown nylon carpet
Furniture: Bookshelves; steel and glass side table
Lighting: Concealed tubes
Accessories: Lamp; books, occasional objects on shelves

opposite page:
Dark, discreet scheme
To create a subdued, yet interesting effect, the dark walls have been lit by a mixture of wallwashers and downlight. Coir matting the same color as the ceiling has been used both to coordinate the colors and provide textural contrast. The prints and elaborate mirror are shown off to good effect against the dark walls. Plum or eggplant could be used as alternative color schemes.

Walls: Spruce green latex paint
Ceiling: Pale coffee latex paint
Woodwork: Spruce green semi-gloss paint
Floor: Coir matting
Furniture: Mahogany chest
Lighting: Track with wallwashers and downlight
Accessories: Wooden box; carved ivory figure; elaborate mirror; flowers

LIVING ROOMS

Exactly what style of living room suits you best will depend on a number of factors, not least of which is whether it is to be for single, a couple's or family use. Will you, or other members of the household, ever need to work there, or will the living room only ever be used for relaxing in, for reading, talking, listening to music perhaps, or watching television?

Pay particular attention, first of all, to making an interesting framework for the living room. Decorate the walls and windows with care, for even the best furniture and accessories will look poor against a shabby background. Generally speaking, colors should be restful without being insipid, interesting but never frenetic.

When it comes to the style of a room, remember that while a room furnished all of a period rarely looks anything but dull, mixing a great many styles demands experience and a great sureness of taste. On a general level, a collection of contemporary art will look good in an otherwise antique room, and just one or two old things will make a vast difference to a roomful of modern furniture and contemporary fabrics.

The first rule here is to put practicality before esthetics. Even if you have no children or animals at the present time, it is always as well to plan a room bearing in mind future visits by one or other, or both together. And if you do have children, there is no reason why a stylish room cannot be evolved which will comfortably accommodate them as well as the adults. Just avoid using fragile furniture and accessories, and choose fabrics and carpeting that are easily cleaned.

The second rule is to be realistic, to plan a room that reflects, first of all, your needs, your tastes and your interests, but which, at the same time must be as comfortable and relaxing for guests as it is for you and your family.

Living room furniture

The choice and arrangement of furniture for a living room is, to a great extent, predetermined by the fact that the space will probably be used for a variety of activities. As well as general seating, therefore, you may also have to find room for a work-table or desk, and perhaps, a dining table.

For the young and impecunious, modular seating, which can be added to and moved around as necessary, makes a good start. Open armchairs, or occasional chairs with upholstered backs and seats, whether traditional or modern in style, don't look bulky and are particularly useful for adding accents of color in a monochromatic scheme. Fully upholstered sofas, love seats, chesterfields and so on are certainly more expensive and altogether more bulky.

A good general rule is to balance a sofa with two occasional chairs, or another sofa, set at right angles to it; aim to provide table surfaces within easy reach of each seating place. A sturdy coffee table will not only accommodate all the usual family impedimenta, but can also be used for serving an occasional meal.

Whatever arrangement you choose, keep a sense of balance and proportion. Small-scale furniture in a small space, for instance, will make the area seem larger, whereas a good-sized room can absorb bulkier items.

Living room flooring

If you have children, lead a fairly gregarious life, or cannot afford close carpeting, you might just as well have a plain wood or tiled floor, softened by area rugs. If, however, you prefer carpeting, and even if you can afford the best quality wool or wool and nylon mixture, remember that interestingly textured matting, sisal or woolcord is sometimes more effective. Where different textures or colors meet at doorways, the effect is neater if a threshold strip is inserted between the two. This will both protect the edges of the materials and delineate the areas.

Living room lighting

Plenty of general background light is obviously necessary and this should be boosted by task lighting and well-controlled highlighting for interesting arrangements of plants, paintings and objects. Detailed information about lighting is given on pages 19 to 24.

Ultimately, the colors and textures you use, the pieces of furniture you finally decide on, and what kind of accessories you amass, are very much a question of taste, and pocket. The varied rooms shown in this section cover a cross-section of ideas and styles and can be adopted and adapted to suit whatever type and size of space you have.

Opposite page:
A build-up of different textures – stripped wood-work, matting, cane and glass – can make a gently-colored room look as varied as a much more vibrant space. Here, too, the diagonal arrangement of furniture makes a square area seem much more interesting.

This page, above left:
The point of departure in this subtly colored room was the bleached Indian rug, whose colors are repeated in throw pillows on the white satin-covered seating.

Above right:
Dramatic lighting in this loft accentuates the subtle use of natural textures. Bare brick walls, polished wood floor, sailcloth floor pillows and upholstery still manage to look neatly sophisticated.

Right:
Polyurethaned white deck paint on the floor, white walls, a huge white sofa and an eclectic collection of furnishings make this generous space look un-expectedly intimate.

A SPACIOUS LIVING ROOM

City living rooms can look dark and drab by day, especially in a built-up area, but any room with long windows and good natural light can be made to look bright. This particular room overlooking a garden square is so light and spacious it could be in the country. The first scheme, based on honeysuckle motifs, creates a warm, restful effect, the second is based on clear, fondant colors, making the room bright and airy, and the third takes advantage of the space and nineteenth century detailing.

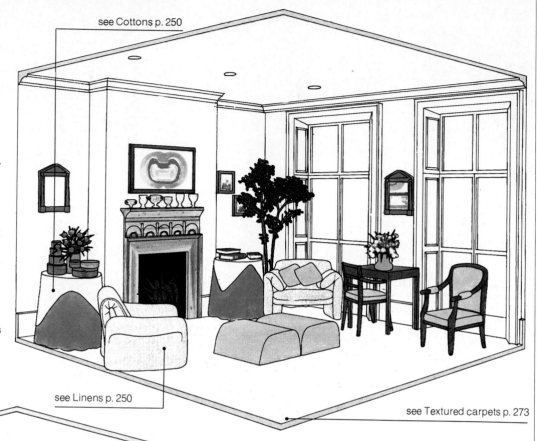

see Cottons p. 250

see Linens p. 250

see Textured carpets p. 273

Candy-colored scheme
Pale backgrounds make clear colors stand out with a luminous intensity, and here, walls, ceiling and shutters are vanilla colored, with a thickly woven carpet to match. The upholstered chairs, stools and tables are covered in a mixture of bright, candy colors to add a splash of color.

Walls, ceiling and woodwork: Brilliant white latex and semi-gloss paint

Floor: Thick-textured vanilla carpet
Furniture: Armchairs in natural linen; occasional tables with scarf-shaped tablecloths; desk chair; occasional chairs; upholstered stools
Lighting: Uplights; recessed wallwashers
Accessories: Plants; mirrors; paintings; books; collection of glass on glass shelves; pillows

see Textured wallcoverings p. 228

see Fabrics p. 244

see Fabrics p. 250

Neo-Victorian scheme
Natural details should be emphasized wherever possible. Here the stripped woodwork is set off by the dark burlap wallcovering, the pale ceiling and the dark oriental rug.

Walls: Pine green burlap
Ceiling: White latex paint
Woodwork: Stripped pine
Floor: Polished boards with oriental rug
Windows: Stripped pine shutters
Furniture: Tables covered in cloths with scarf tops; stools covered in Turkey carpet; armchairs; tables
Lighting: Uplights; recessed wallwashers
Accessories: Plants; collection of framed photographs; books; bird sculpture

opposite page:
Honeysuckle scheme
Honeysuckle, the central color in this scheme, is used for a build-up of tones to create an overall effect of warmth and calm. The walls are rag-rubbed, continuing the softness of the feeling.

Walls: Rag-rubbed paint in pale creamy-yellow
Ceiling: Off-white latex paint
Moldings: White latex paint
Woodwork: Stripped pine, or dragged a slightly darker yellow
Floor: Yellow and apricot Brussels weave carpet
Windows: Roller shades
Furniture: Antique and modern chairs and tables; upholstered stools
Lighting: Uplights; recessed wallwashers
Accessories: Flowers; plants; paintings; mirrors; books

A HIGH-CEILING'D ROOM

Although huge soaring living spaces might seem an ideal situation to cramped apartment dwellers, the fact remains that too much space is as difficult to manipulate as too little. The answer generally lies in thoughtful arrangement and a clever use of color. The scheme opposite has a cool, sophisticated look achieved with a distinguished use of monotones. The second tames the space with color and pattern, while in the third, an indoor-outdoor effect is created using natural textures, plants and generously comfortable seating.

Patterned scheme
A cheerful, large-scale flower-patterned fabric blooms over all these windows making the space seem both comfortable and more intimate. The sloping window wall of the scheme opposite has been filled in to give a more enclosed feel, which is further enhanced by the all-over pattern of the dhurrie rug.

Walls and ceiling: Ivory latex paint

Woodwork: Buff satin finish paint
Floor: All-over dhurrie rug
Windows: Drapes and shades in hydrangea and rose-patterned glazed chintz
Lighting: Uplights; floor and wall lamps
Furniture: Refectory table; sofa; occasional chairs and table; upholstered stools
Accessories: China; plates; flowers; plants

see Fabrics pp. 258–9

see Ethnic rugs p. 280

Indoor-outdoor scheme
Natural textures are combined with greenery, pale colors, a stenciled floor and a woodburning stove to create a pleasantly conjoined atmosphere with the outside. The shades are painted to match the floor and co-ordinate with the canvas-covered seating and the throw pillows.

Walls and ceiling: White satin finish paint
Woodwork: White satin finish paint
Floor: White deck-painted boards stenciled with ferns
Windows: Canvas shades self-painted with ferns
Lighting: Floor and table lamps
Furniture: White canvas-covered chairs and sofa; side and coffee tables; bookshelves
Accessories: Wood-burning stove; plants; books

opposite page:
Cool, sophisticated look
Effectively minimizing the lofty space, the deliberate monotones used here make for a calm and leisured feel, which is enhanced by the filtering effect of the blinds, and the clean lines of the furnishings. The horizontal lines of the blinds also serve to counteract the high ceiling

Walls and ceiling: Pale gray latex paint
Woodwork: Darker gray satin finish paint
Floor: Polished wood boards with tawny brown rug
Windows: Venetian blinds
Lighting: Floor lamps and uplights
Furniture: Upholstered armchairs; sofa; chaise longue; coffee and side tables
Accessories: Framed posters; ceramics; dried flowers; throw pillows; magazines

see Stencils p. 242

see Shades p. 263

51

A LIVING ROOM WITH PERIOD DETAIL

Small, square living rooms lend themselves to a variety of different color schemes, arrangements and treatments which depend on taste and pocket. They have the advantage of not swallowing up too much furniture, although it is often difficult to decide how best to arrange possessions and seating in these confined spaces. The scheme opposite is simple and undemanding and takes the room's natural assets as focal points. The scheme, right, uses mirror to prevent the space closing in, while the vivid colors of the upholstery in the third one make for a permanently summery effect.

see Shades p. 263

see Fabrics p. 244

see Carpets p. 273

see Blinds p. 262

Dark, glossy scheme
The whole mantelpiece wall is mirrored here to give the room extra depth and sparkle. The dark glazed walls contrast well with the crisp cornice and baseboards and the pale, self-patterned carpet. The colors of the upholstery and ceiling are the palest possible version of the surrounding walls.

Walls: Dark emerald green glazed walls
Ceiling: Pale green semi-gloss paint
Woodwork: White gloss paint

Floor: White zig-zag-patterned wool and nylon carpet
Window: White gloss-painted shutters; white Roman shade
Lighting: Uplight concealed behind plant; floor reading lamp; chandelier
Furniture: White cotton covered chaise and pale green ottoman and slipper chairs; clear plexiglass coffee table; side table
Accessories: Large plant; mirror; pillows; books; paintings; checked pillow and blanket

Candy-colored scheme
The pale background makes this space seem larger and acts as a foil for the brightly colored accessories. The walls either side of the fireplace are mirrored to help visually double the space.

Walls and ceiling: White semi-gloss paint
Woodwork: White semi-gloss paint
Floor: White sisal carpeting
Windows: White-painted shutters; white matchstick blinds
Lighting: Concealed uplights; recessed spotlights in ceiling
Furniture: Sofa covered in striped cotton; cane chairs covered in soft pink or white cotton; cane and glass coffee table; pine tables
Accessories: Plants; painting; striped pillows; books; magazines

see Matting p. 278

see Fabrics p. 252

opposite page:
Stripped wood scheme
The stripped wooden shutters, mantelpiece, mirror frame, and floorboards are shown off here against the pale walls and ceiling. The cane furniture fits in well with the basic colors.

Walls and ceiling: White latex paint
Woodwork: Stripped pine; white semi-gloss cornice and baseboards
Floor: Stripped pine boards; rugs
Window: Stripped pine shutters
Lighting: Table lamps
Furniture: White cotton-covered sofa; cane chairs; cane and glass coffee table; side tables
Accessories: Mirror; prints; flowers; china; cushions

A FEATURELESS LIVING ROOM

So many modern apartment rooms are like featureless boxes, with, perhaps, a large expanse of window as their main asset. To give them some individuality, therefore, they have to be injected with a style of their own – sometimes by a striking use of color, pattern or texture, sometimes with accessories, more often than not with a mixture of both. In the scheme opposite, a western interior has been given an oriental feel with low, modular seating and translucent sliding shades. The second scheme, while less extravagant in its use of color, still maintains interest and has textures and pattern as the focus. The third scheme gives the room a summery look with sky blue, pinks and greens.

Textured and patterned scheme
Background anonymity is completely forgotten in this scheme with its build-up of textures and patterns. Wool-covered walls and a shaggy carpet of similar color are teamed with bamboo blinds and a forceful check cotton.

Walls: Caramel wool finished with a strip of natural wood

Ceiling: White latex paint
Floor: Caramel shag acrilan and wool carpet
Window: Bamboo blinds
Lighting: Paper shades; white ceramic table lamp
Furniture: Brown and white checked cotton-covered modular unit seating; cream lacquered tables
Accessories: Plants; pottery; books

see Smooth Wallcoverings p. 230

see Blinds p. 262

see Textured Carpets p. 232

see Shades p. 263

see Fabrics p. 244

See Paints pp. 210–11

Summery scheme
Against the background of pale, shiny floor and walls, the pastel-colored seating and brightly striped cotton rug make this dull space look like perpetual June. The sun abstract completes the illusion. Vertical louvers at the windows can shield or reveal the day as required.

Walls and ceiling: Ivory gloss paint
Floor: Ivory deck paint; cotton rug
Window: White vertical louver shades
Lighting: Recessed downlights; spotlights
Furniture: Lilac cotton-covered seating; ivory lacquered tables; upholstered stool
Accessories: Painting; plants; flowers; books; cushions

opposite page:
Oriental-style scheme
The brilliant color and simple forms of the seating give a strong and immediate character to the space. This is further enhanced by the translucent sliding window shades. The low, modular, upholstered squares are interspersed with similarly shaped lacquered tables to form a variety of choices for sitting and lounging.

Walls and ceiling: Pinky-beige latex paint with a double white line
Floor: Chestnut brown carpet
Window: Sliding white shades
Lighting: White paper shades; reading lamp
Furniture: Red wool-covered upholstered modular unit seating; white lacquered tables
Accessories: Oriental sculpture and objects; ethnic pots; plants

A SMALL SQUARE LIVING ROOM

Old fashioned apartments can be given gleam and gloss as much by clever use of color and texture as by furnishings. In this room, whose main assets are its large expanse of leaded glass window and ornate fireplace, the scheme opposite is all lavender and gray, spiked by the shiny chrome furniture and flowers. The second uses sunset colors for a year-round glow, and the third, with its updated wood paneling, uncarpeted floor and firm fabrics, achieves a cool, textured look.

see Shades p. 263

see Carpets p. 273

Cheerful scheme
Sunset colors distributed throughout a room ensure a warm glow, whatever the external circumstances. Painted walls merge into a woolcord carpet and both are repeated and exaggerated in the striped covering on the soft furnishings. The simple shades at the window and the outsize coffee table covered in coir matting fit in with the general color scheme.

Walls and ceiling:
Pinky-apricot semi-gloss paint.

see Blinds p. 262

Woodwork: As walls; mantelpiece left natural
Window: Warm cream Roman shades
Floor: Pink woolcord carpet
Lighting: Plugmold lighting behind valance all round room; uplights
Furniture: Unit seating covered in striped rough moiré; coffee table covered in coir matting; side table
Accessories: Painting; plants; flowers; ceramics

see Flooring p. 264

see Wallcoverings p. 234

Cool, textured scheme
With its leaded windows and ornate fireplace, this room is a natural for wood paneling. Here parana pine is used for a thoroughly updated look. It provides good heat and sound insulation as well as interesting textural finish. The stripped wood floor and natural canvas upholstery make for a cool, pared-down feeling.

Walls: Parana pine tongue-and-groove paneling
Ceiling: White latex paint
Woodwork: White semi-gloss paint
Floor: Stripped and bleached boards
Window: Vertical louvered blinds
Lighting: Spotlights; uplights; reading light
Furniture: Unit seating in natural canvas; coffee table; side table
Accessories: Painting; plants; ceramics; flowers; books; cushions

opposite page:
Lavender and gray scheme
Color plays a vital role in this room, since walls, ceiling, woodwork and floor are painted or covered the same. They make a cool framework for the warmer colors of the seating and mantelpiece, the glossy plant leaves and gleaming modern furniture.

Walls and ceiling: Dove gray latex paint
Woodwork: Dove gray semi-gloss paint; mantelpiece in carved mahogany
Floor: Dove gray wool carpet
Window: Left bare
Lighting: Track with spotlights (not seen)
Furniture: Lavender wool-covered unit seating; chrome and glass coffee table; cantilevered wooden side table
Accessories: Painting; plants; flowers; ceramics; books; vases

A LONG BEAMED ROOM

Beams are such a dominant feature in any room, tending to make the space seem long and low, that they need special treatment if they are not to overwhelm a space. In two of the three schemes, the beams are kept as an intrinsic decorative feature; in one they tone in with the background, while in the other, they form their own graphic design. In the third scheme, right, they have been paneled over, and the ceiling is kept pale to make the room seem light and airy. The lowered ceiling also allows lights to be recessed into the wood, which obviates too much interruption of the surface. And the geometric pattern of the carpet tends to make the space seem a good deal wider than it actually is.

Pastel scheme
The beams are paneled in here and ceiling and woodwork are kept pale both to make a pristine framework for the other colors in the room, and to expand the space. Interest is provided by the patterned fabric of the sofa and the geometric carpet.

Walls: Pink latex paint
Ceiling and woodwork: Brilliant white semi-gloss paint
Floor: Gray, pink and white geometric carpet
Window: White bamboo roll-up blinds
Lighting: Recessed downlights
Furniture: Heavy cotton covered sofa; chairs; coffee tables; chest; bookcases
Accessories: Wood-burning stove; pottery; books; plants; prints

see Lighting p. 312

see Fabrics p. 248

see Carpets p. 276

see Fabrics p. 258

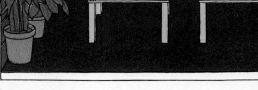

Yellow ocher scheme
In a neat, graphic link-up, the interesting pattern of pale beams against the brightly colored background is echoed in the vertical design of the louvers at the window. To make the space seem larger, the sofa and upholstered chair are covered to tone with the walls. The dark carpet is strong enough to balance the beams.

Walls and ceiling: Yellow ocher latex paint
Woodwork: White semi-gloss paint
Floor: Nutmeg brown wool and nylon carpet
Window: White vertical louver blinds
Lighting: Downlights
Furniture: Sofa in Liberty print linen union; chairs; bookshelves; tables; chest
Accessories: Books; pottery; plants; print

opposite page:
Monotone scheme
The weathered color of the beams is repeated in various degrees throughout this room, so instead of being over-powering they fit neatly into it.

Walls: Gray bricks and wood paneling
Ceiling: Weathered gray beams; pale gray latex paint
Woodwork: Left natural
Floor: Dark gray bricks
Window: Linen drapes
Lighting: Downlights
Furniture: Sofa in gray flannel; chairs; book-shelves; tables; chest
Accessories: Wood-burning stove; books; pottery; old bath; dried flowers.

A LARGE, SQUARE LIVING ROOM

Large rooms can be much more difficult to furnish and arrange satisfactorily than smaller areas. Informal, yet uncluttered, an easy grouping of modular seating against a pale background solves the problem in the scheme opposite; in the scheme, right, the spacious feeling is maintained with pale upholstery and a geometric carpet. In the scheme below, the fireplace and moldings are accentuated against a more traditional background coloring.

Light, airy scheme
Shiny, dark walls make a space warm and distinguished, and here the furniture and floor are kept pale so that even with a dark background, the room seems spacious and filled with light. The color contrast between furniture and walls is diffused by the geometric carpet and the patterned throw pillows.

Walls: Mustard gloss paint with an extra coat of varnish
Ceiling: Cream latex paint

Woodwork and molding: White gloss paint
Floor: Brown and white geometric carpet
Window: White-painted shutters
Lighting: Uplights (not seen); wall lamps
Furniture: Unit seating covered in white, figured cotton; floor cushions; plexiglass table
Accessories: Paintings; plants; throw cushions; books; magazines; ceramics

see Carpets p. 276

see Shades p. 263

see Fabrics p. 247

see Fabrics pp. 258–9

see Carpets p. 277

Warm-colored scheme
To accentuate the traditional ingredients of this room (the molding, the marble fireplace and handsome window) the walls are painted a warm, cheerful color against which these details stand out with great clarity.

Walls and ceiling: Deep apricot latex paint
Molding and woodwork: White semi-gloss paint
Floor: Brussels weave patterned carpet
Window: White canvas Roman shade
Lighting: Uplights (not seen); floor lamps
Furniture: Bookshelves: sofa covered in green heavy cotton; chair; cane and glass coffee table
Accessories: Books; painting; silhouettes; mirror; throw cushions; plant; jars; coal box

opposite page:
Light, bright scheme
Low-level seating and tables, casual floor cushions and brightly-colored throw pillows give an air of easy informality to this room. The floor and walls are kept pale to exaggerate the generous space.

Walls and ceiling: Off-white latex paint
Woodwork and moldings: Brilliant white semi-gloss paint
Mantelpiece: White marble
Floor: White wool carpet; rug
Window White vertical louvers
Lighting: Uplights (not seen); table lamp
Furniture: Soft brown unit seating; large floor cushions; white modular tables
Accessories: Throw cushions; plants; magazines

A ROOM WITH A VIEW

Town houses and apartments often have rectangular living rooms which, failing interesting treatment, can look plain and uninspired. Here, all three rooms take the unusual window as their focal point, but there the similarity ends. The scheme opposite is bleached and polished, allowing the foliage to dominate; the second has been turned into one large garden room, and the third has a definite Moorish theme.

see Blinds p. 262

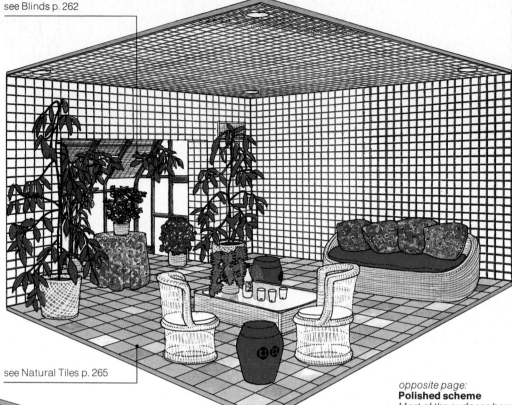

see Natural Tiles p. 265

Garden room scheme
The use of green trellis completely covering the walls and ceiling seems to add extra width to the room as well as extending the greenhouse-conservatory feel. Quarry tiles for the floor and wicker and glass for the furniture continue the rustic effect and print-covered pillows and a round, cloth-covered table complete the scheme. A similarly fresh effect would be gained by using sky blue latex paint with white trellis, or vice versa.

Walls and ceiling:
White latex paint with green squared trellis
Floor: Pale terracotta quarry tiles
Window: Green matchstick blinds
Furniture: Wicker sofas and chairs; cane and glass table; cloth-covered table
Lighting: Recessed downlights and uplights in corners
Accessories: Green ceramic stools; wide rush planters; massed plants in baskets

see Paints p. 210

see Tiles pp. 270–71

Moorish scheme
To create a cool, yet exotically North African look, the seating units are covered in Moroccan cotton fabric, with matching bolsters and pillows picked out in embroidery; terracotta urns stand at either end. To continue the oriental feel of the room, the low, rug-covered table in the center is surrounded by large floor cushions. A built-in arch of small trellis divides the window area from the rest of the room.

Walls: Pale blue latex paint
Ceiling: White latex paint
Floor: Moorish patterned tiles
Window: Tightly trellised dark blue arch
Furniture: Two seating units made to look like couches; long bolsters and pillows; low round table; floor cushions
Lighting: Recessed downlights; uplights in corners

opposite page:
Polished scheme
Most of the surfaces here gleam as if to reflect the expanse of glass at the far end. The walls and floor seem bleached out in deference to the foliage, and the tight-rolled matchstick blind at the top of the window embrasure creates its own demarcation line. Polished chrome furniture frames and planter contrast with the softness of the upholstery, as does the shining lacquer of the coffee table and the glass vases and objects.

Walls and ceiling: Off-white latex semi-gloss paint with a touch of green
Floor: Bleached and polished boards set on the diagonal
Window: Green matchstick blinds
Furniture: Glass and chrome round table; gray lacquered coffee table; unit seating and chaise with gray upholstery
Lighting: Recessed downlights; uplights in corners
Accessories: Plants; glass vases and dishes; poster; flowers; fruit

A LONG NARROW LIVING ROOM

The long narrow living areas which result from two rooms being knocked together limit variations in furniture arrangement. Since daylight seldom penetrates beyond the center of this area, much of it is in perpetual twilight, but by clever use of color and concealed lighting, it is possible to surreptitiously boost the ration of daylight. One scheme depends in a relaxed way on subtle colors; another turns the room into an extravaganza of red and exotic objects, and in the Op art scheme, an illusion of space is created by using arches and mirrors.

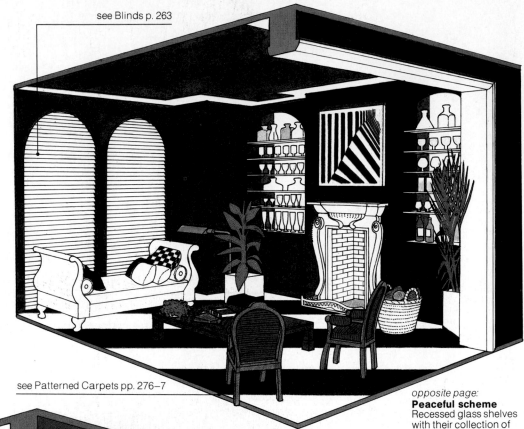

see Blinds p. 263

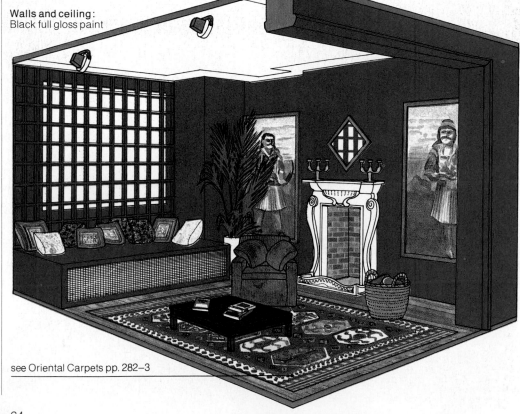

see Patterned Carpets pp. 276–7

see Oriental Carpets pp. 282–3

Op art scheme
To give a greater feeling of depth to the room, arches and diagonal stripes have been used together in a punchy, graphic scheme which plays with perspective. Diagonal stripes on the carpet sharply delineate the room as well as make it seem much wider. The space seems to have been further extended by the double arch in front of the window which has Venetian blinds behind it and is given substance by the Empire couch pushed in front.

Walls and ceiling: Black full gloss paint

Moldings and woodwork: White latex paint; white full gloss paint
Windows: White Venetian blinds
Floor: Black and white diagonally striped carpet
Furniture: Empire couch; black table; chairs
Lighting: Uplights under shelves; concealed strips underneath all arches; brass floor lamp
Accessories: Pillows; mirrored planters; plants; glasses, decanters; Op art painting; basket

Extravagant red scheme
The extravagant use of color here is meant to distract the eye from the real size of the room. Indian paintings with almost lifesize figures reinforce the oriental theme.

Walls: Scarlet semi-gloss paint
Ceiling: White latex paint
Moldings: White latex paint
Woodwork: Scarlet semi-gloss paint
Floor: Red Kelim rug
Window: Red screen
Furniture: Black corduroy armchair; black-painted table; built-in window seat covered in red cotton
Lighting: Framing projectors; uplights in corners
Accessories: Indian pillows; green glass-framed mirror; log basket; paintings; candelabra

opposite page:
Peaceful scheme
Recessed glass shelves with their collection of blue and white porcelain seem to push the walls out, making the room appear wider. The large mirror above the fireplace and the margin of polished wood floor around the area rug give a greater sense of depth to the room.

Walls and ceiling: White latex paint
Woodwork: White semi-gloss paint
Floor: Polished wood with an off-white area rug
Window: White drapes over a white roller shade
Lighting: Spots behind arches above glass shelves; table lamps (not seen)
Furniture: Armchair covered in blue and white cotton; round, white-painted table; cane and glass coffee table; painted occasional chair; side table below shelves
Accessories: Blue and white porcelain; pillows; plants; creamy pink flowers; log basket; glass objects; books; prints

A STUDIO APARTMENT

City studio apartments which are basically one room, with sometimes, the additional bonus of a separate bedroom, are invariably exercises in ingenuity with three aims in mind: to make the anonymous space look as interesting, seem as large, and hold as much as possible. The room on this page has much the same features – or lack of them – as the room opposite: the same large window at one end; the same shape, the same lack of basic detail. Here, however, although the aims are similar, the treatments are totally different.

Richly colored scheme
To divert attention from the actual space, this room is filled with color and pattern and collections of objects, and long, dark, velvet drapes accentuate the feeling of great richness. A neat geometric rug adds some discipline to the general luxuriance, while the mirrored uprights at the windows reflect light and color.

Walls: Dark coco-cola high gloss paint
Ceiling: Cream latex paint
Woodwork: Cream semi-gloss paint
Floor: Red and cream geometric rug on polished hardwood
Window: Long brown velvet drapes
Lighting: Table lamps; uplights
Furniture: Armchairs; occasional chairs; stool; Coromandel screen
Accessories: Plants; ceramics; cushions; books

see Paints pp. 210–11

see Plain fabrics p. 250

see Carpets p. 272

Platform scheme
A floating platform at the window end of the room makes the space seem much larger as well as creating another seating area. The floating effect of the platform is enhanced by colored fluorescent lighting fixed underneath. The grid screen at the window gives a feeling of extra depth to the space.

Walls and ceiling: Very pale pink latex paint
Woodwork: Matching pink low-luster paint
Floor: Off-white wool carpet
Window: Screen in rosy semi-gloss paint
Lighting: Ceiling-recessed wallwashers: colored fluorescent tubes under platform
Furniture: Pale parma violet seating units; pink armchairs; glass coffee tables; bookshelves; wooden side table
Accessories: Plants; books; objects

A NARROW STUDIO APARTMENT

The schemes on this page have the same aims as those opposite – to make the space seem as large and as interesting as possible. The first room is made crisp and pretty, simply by using clear-cut colors and extensive mirror to maximize light and space. The strongly-patterned vinyl floor and panels of wood and mirror give the scheme below a sturdy character where none existed before.

Mirrored scheme
Panels of mirror down one side of the room double the space as well as the light. The effect is enhanced by the predominance of pale colors and the variations on the same cotton print for the upholstery. Every bit of space is utilized, so there are storage shelves behind the drapes (not seen), bookshelves under the window sill behind the dining table, and the bed, skilfully fitted behind an arch in the corridor, is reflected in the mirrored wall.

Walls and ceiling: White latex paint; mirror panels
Woodwork: White low-luster paint
Floor: Blue haircord carpet
Window: White cotton drapes
Lighting: Table lamps; uplights; candles
Furniture: White cotton-covered sofa; cotton-covered armchairs; dining table and chairs
Accessories: Throw cushions; flowers; candles; books

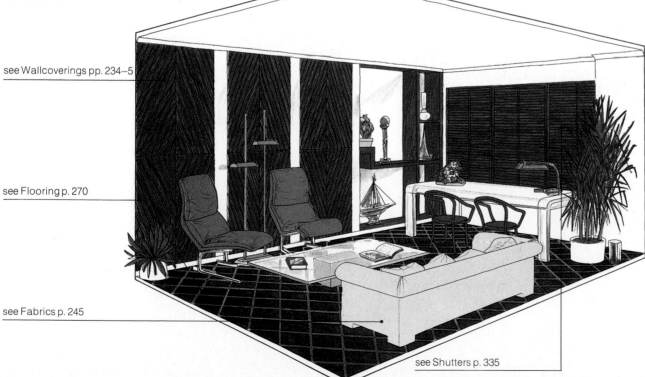

see Wallcoverings pp. 234–5

see Flooring p. 270

see Fabrics p. 245

see Shutters p. 335

Polished wood scheme
Geometric vinyl flooring and wood panels give this room quite distinctive character. The wood theme is continued by the shutters and the mirror-backed storage by the window. To avoid the space cluttering, the large table is in plexiglass.

Walls: Wood paneling with strips of mirror
Ceiling: White latex paint
Woodwork: White gloss paint
Floor: Leather finish vinyl tiles with wood intersections
Window: Wooden louvered shutters
Lighting: Uplights; table lamps; floor lamp
Furniture: Sofa in cream woven wool; leather chairs; glass coffee table; plexiglass dining table-desk; bentwood dining chairs
Accessories: Plants; books; ornaments

ONE-ROOM LIVING

In this large, well-organized space, sleeping, eating and working areas are kept separate. The bed, which is tucked away at the narrow end of the room, is partly screened by a worktable, and there is another table which can also be used for work or eating; the living area is in the foreground. The light, airy scheme opposite relies to a large extent on natural textures, with massive plants which act as room dividers. Bright color coordinates the different areas, right, and in the scheme below, subtle unity is provided by understated variations of one color.

see Fabrics p. 256

see Shades p. 263

Yellow and white scheme
The space is kept constantly light and sunny with these brightly colored walls, matching fabric and pale floor.

Walls and ceiling: Chrome yellow latex paint
Floor: White wool carpet
Window: White louvers

Lighting: Uplights; desk and reading lamps; umbrella light
Furniture: Divan bed with cotton spread; desks and tables; folding chairs; leather sofa and chairs
Accessories: Mirror; plants; books; typewriter; flowers; bookcase; mugs

see Carpets p. 274

see Blinds p. 262

Subtle gray scheme
To provide a luxuriously restful look and feel, one color is used here in various depths and textures. The subtle variations of emphasis and tone make this an especially suitable treatment for one-room living, and as effective by day as by night.

Walls: Dove gray smooth wallcovering
Ceiling: White latex paint
Woodwork: White semi-gloss paint
Floor: Dark gray wool-cord carpet
Windows: Black match-stick blinds
Lighting: Downlights; table lamps
Furniture: Double divan bed with quilted spread and gray flannel head-board cover; off-white canvas covered unit seating; coffee table; grand piano
Accessories: Mirror; plants; books; magazines; prints

see Smooth wallcoverings p. 230

opposite page:
Natural textured scheme
Each area of this room seems separate but all quietly merge together and are nicely complementary to the view. The mirror at the bed end of the room gives extra depth and light by reflecting the window.

Walls and ceiling: White latex paint
Woodwork: White semi-gloss paint or natural
Floor: Polished parquet; fur rug
Windows: White Venetian shades
Lighting: Uplights; reading and table lamps
Furniture: Double divan bed; leather and chrome chairs; folding chairs; work and dining tables; coffee table; cube side table
Accessories: Plants; flowers; books; typewriter

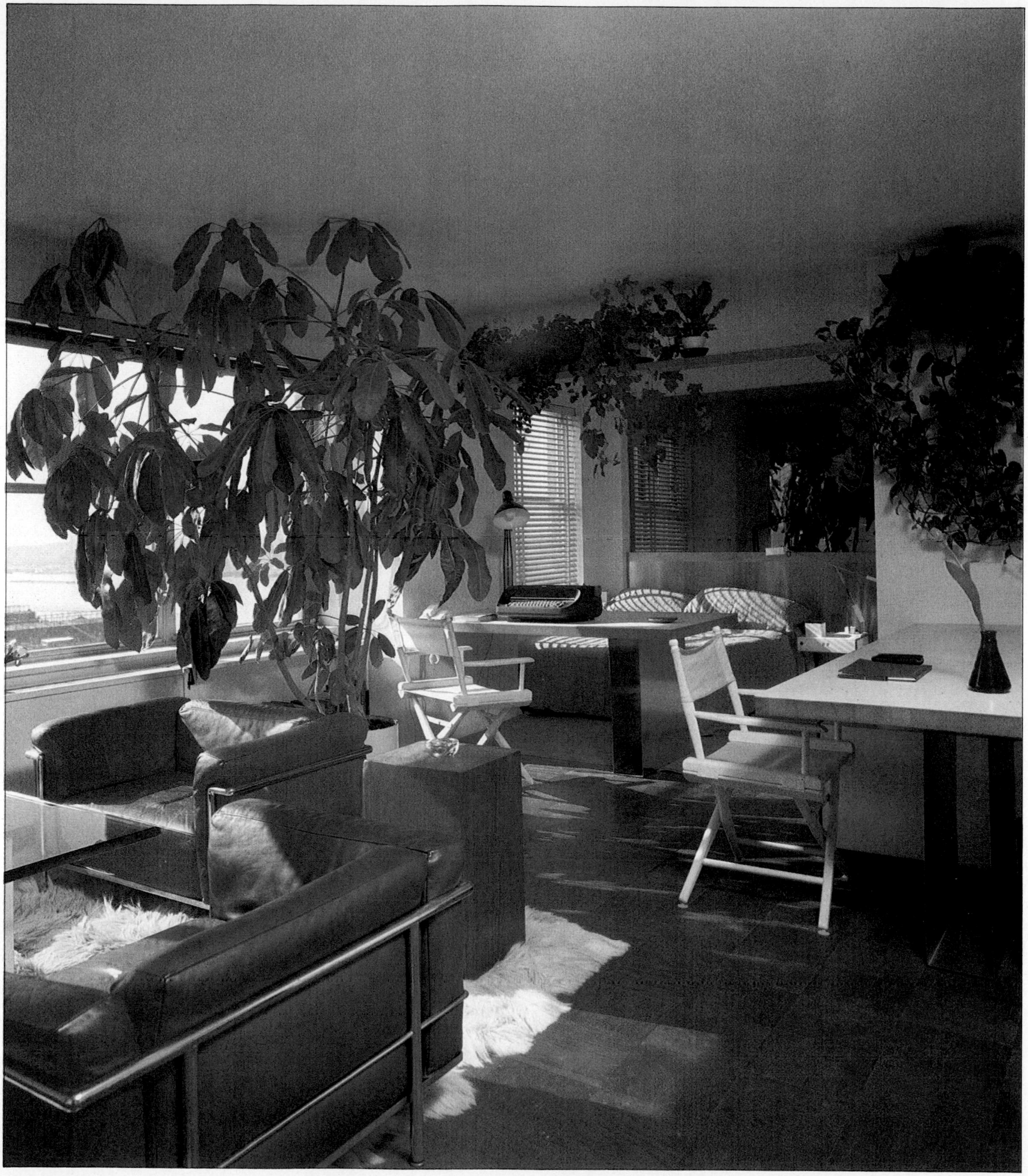

New York apartment of architect Luis Villa

A DINE-IN LIVING ROOM

As city space becomes increasingly rare, multi-purpose rooms become correspondingly more necessary. By thoughtful planning, living rooms can be used for dining as well as providing room for the occasional guest. Oblong rooms, often found in city apartments, lend themselves particularly well to just such treatment. The scheme opposite, with its eclectic use of prints and its eye-catching carpet, looks fresh and unstudied; the garden scheme uses a trellised arch to separate the living and dining areas, and the third uses Batik cotton to achieve a warm and mildly exotic effect.

see Paints pp. 210–11

see Matting pp. 278–9

Middle Eastern scheme
To achieve an oriental, mildly opulent look, Batik cotton is used here both as a wallcovering and again for the dividing drapes and floor cushions. The richness of the effect is balanced by the neutral floor, sofa and hamper.

Walls: Batik cotton stapled onto the walls
Ceiling: Reddish-brown latex paint
Woodwork: Reddish-brown semi-gloss paint
Floor: Basket weave coir matting

Furniture: Pine dining table; cane and chrome chairs; sofa bed; stool; wicker hamper which doubles as coffee table; banquette
Lighting: Overhead track with three spotlights; uplights
Soft furnishings: Batik cotton dividing drapes
Accessories: Plants; books; Indian print floor cushions

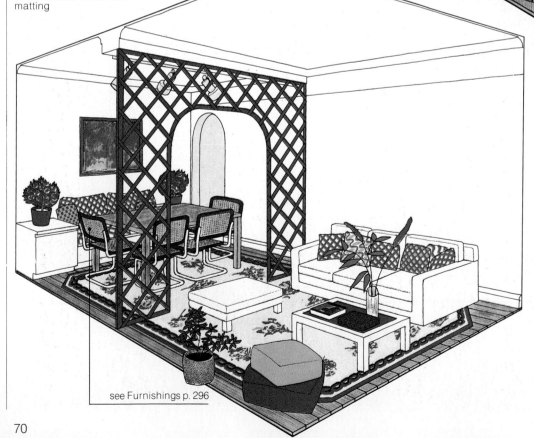

see Furnishings p. 296

Indoor garden scheme
By using a trellised arch to section off the dining area, the space has been turned into a garden room. The trellis motif is repeated in some of the fabric, and the colors of the carpet are echoed in the floor cushions and throw pillows.

Walls and ceiling: White latex paint
Woodwork: White semi-gloss paint
Trellis: Green painted wood
Floor: Stripped floor-boards; octagonal wool carpet
Furniture: Pine dining table; cane and chrome chairs; creamy white bed and stool; chrome and glass coffee table; banquette with trellis-patterned cotton cover
Lighting: Overhead track with three spotlights; uplights
Accessories: Plants; flowers; books and magazines; cushions; pillows

opposite page:
Eclectic scheme
It should be possible to achieve a cohesive room style by the gradual accumulation of possessions over a period of time. With its unusual carpet and mixture of prints and styles, this scheme demonstrates the effectiveness of just such an eclectic approach. While there is an overall unity to the room, there is still a degree of freshness to its unstudied look.

Walls and ceiling: Creamy white latex paint
Woodwork: Creamy white semi-gloss paint
Floor: Stripped and polished wood boards; octagonal wool carpet
Furniture: Pine dining table; cane and chrome chairs; creamy white sofa bed and stool; chrome and glass coffee table; banquette with striped cotton cover
Lighting: Overhead track with three spotlights
Accessories: Plants; flowers; books and magazines; candles; Indian print floor cushions; throw pillows

DINING ROOMS

Rooms used for the sole purpose of dining are getting rarer and rarer. Instead, people increasingly have living-dining rooms, kitchen-dining rooms, they have dining areas in the hall or the guest room. All are moderately easy to furnish since it is only necessary to fit a table and chairs which don't usually interfere with the other purposes of the room.

Planning a dining room

If you do have a proper dining room it is easier to decorate if you bear in mind that its main purpose is to provide an area for relaxed and enjoyable eating. This is an obvious, but nevertheless important point, for dining rooms have a woeful habit of looking formal and often stereotyped, as if eating was a duty rather than a pleasure. Colors, then, should be chosen as a background for the food, the china and glass. Dark rich colors are particularly successful, therefore, although more vivid colors can also look handsome.

Wherever you end up eating, what table you choose depends very much on the shape of the area. Round tables are usually more sociable and hold more people in less space. They can double up for use in a living room, study, or even guest bedroom. If you have a very narrow room, you could try placing a long table against the window or a wall with an upholstered bench running along that side and chairs along the other. This type of arrangement always makes it seem as if there is more floor space than there actually is. In a very small space, a table set up against a mirrored wall seemingly doubles in size.

It is often difficult to find just the right round table. One good solution is to fix a circle of blockboard, cut to the right size, to a base of the right height, which can then be covered permanently with a floor-length cloth. You can change the look of it with the help of a series of different overcloths. The same principle of improvization also applies when it comes to enlarging any table if you have the room to store a spare top. Remember that any money saved on such makeshift tables can be spent on better chairs, especially if you have a room solely for dining in.

On the whole, carpets are not a good idea in any dining area, particularly if you have children. Food gets dropped, drinks get spilled, candles leak melted wax. It is easier to have some surface that is easily cleanable and which will stand the strain of chairs being scraped back and forth. If your dining table is in part of the living room, you could position it on a rug which can always be cleaned more easily than an entire carpet. On the whole, though, more practical surfaces for a dining room floor would be stripped and polished boards, or ceramic, vinyl or cork tiles, all of which can be easily wiped or swept clean.

Storage in the dining room

Nowadays, few people have the space for a conventional sideboard. Many store glass and china in the kitchen or in closets or built-in storage in the living or dining room itself. Make sure that any surface you serve from is heat-resistant; if it isn't, protect it with a mat.

Lighting the dining room

Dining room lighting should always be subtle. Candles are flattering and romantic, but do keep them above or below eye level when seated, and since some other sort of light is necessary, boost the candlelight with uplights set in corners, or downlights set in the ceiling, either of which can be linked to dimmer switches. Or you may well prefer some sort of adjustable light fixture over the dining table.

You will need good light over the serving table, again on a dimmer switch, and accent light on any interesting objects in the room, or on paintings, since the dining room is invariably a good place in which to display possessions. In a dining area, the lighting can be so worked that all the light will shine on the table during dinner, leaving the rest of the room in comparative shadow. Fires or woodburning stoves are always a great success and a mixture of firelight and candlelight always puts people in a mellow mood. Plenty of mirror on the walls will refract the flickering light.

Window treatments

When it comes to window treatments, remember that very heavy fabric is inclined to pick up smells of food and to harbor them, and while velvet is still one of the most popular fabrics for dining room drapes, it is certainly impractical.

The dining rooms shown in this section range widely in size and in style, and the aim is to show how very different the same space can be made to look, by purely decorative means.

Opposite page:
Lacquered green walls, gleaming brass, silver and glass, and subtle candlelight combine to make an opulent, relaxed setting for dining. The plain carpet was hand-painted to achieve much the same feeling as the Indian temple wall hanging in this glamorous dining room.

This page, right:
Mirror can be used in a variety of ways, for a variety of effects. Here, a curve of mirror strips frames this dining area, giving a razzle-dazzle reflection of color and refracted light.

Below left:
A large mirrored panel placed opposite a door makes this light, but confined space seem part of a flowing series of rooms. A framing projector above the table exactly lights it at night, and upholstered chairs, plants and flowers repeat the colors of the painting.

Below right:
Food always looks especially good against a warm dark background. In this otherwise all-brown room, latticed screens lit from behind give an interesting filtered light by night or day and make an interesting, inexpensive wall treatment.

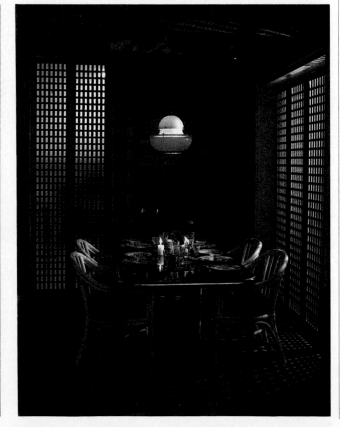

A SMALL, SQUARE DINING ROOM

Old country houses are often full of small square rooms leading from one to another. The problem is how to make them look as personal and idiosyncratic as possible without cluttering them up or being too clichéd. In the scheme opposite the ingredients are traditional, but interestingly arranged so that the room is a series of small vignettes. In the second, a patterned fabric wallcovering makes the room seem fresh and bright, while in the scheme below, a wash of color on the walls, striped cotton on the table, different chairs, accessories and plants make the room seem warm and comfortable.

Patterned fabric scheme
To make the room seem cool and airy, a colorful mini-patterned fabric is stuck on the walls (see page 198 for technique) and the woodwork is painted a strong contrasting color. The floor has been covered with pale tiles to make the room seem even brighter, while the patchwork cloth on the table co-ordinates with the walls.

Walls: Pale blue and lilac cotton

Ceiling: White latex paint
Woodwork: Blue semi-gloss paint
Floor: White vinyl tiles
Lighting: Recessed downlights and wall-washers; table lamps
Furniture: Refectory table with patchwork cloth; white painted chairs; hutch; side tables
Accessories: Collection of stoneware; tramp art; mirrored wall pockets; plants in baskets

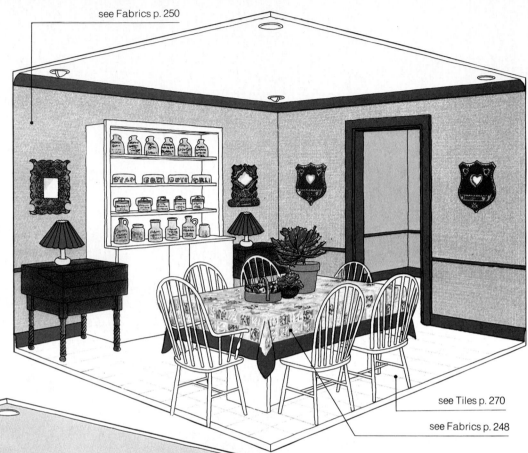

see Fabrics p. 250

see Tiles p. 270

see Fabrics p. 248

see Carpets p. 274

see Fabrics p. 252

Terracotta scheme
A wash of warm color on the walls, the freshness of plants and tablecloth, the cooler tones of ceiling and carpet and the matching tones of paintings all combine to make this a warm, welcoming room.

Walls: Dark terracotta latex paint
Ceiling: Warm cream latex paint
Woodwork: Warm cream semi-gloss paint
Floor: Warm cream carpet
Lighting: Concealed uplights; ceiling recessed downlights
Furniture: Table with long green and terracotta-striped cotton cloth; polished mahogany display cabinet; dark mahogany chairs; two carpeted blocks
Accessories: Large plants in old pots; paintings; glasses

opposite page:
Traditional scheme
The problem here was how to make an old-fashioned room full of traditional items: oriental rug, hutch, stick back chairs, a collection of old glass and silhouettes and miniatures still look new and interesting. The answer is in the arrangement and juxtaposition of colors and objects, so that there is a new view as it were in every part of the room.

Walls and ceiling: White latex paint
Woodwork: Black semi-gloss paint
Floor: Bare wood strips with ethnic rug
Lighting: 19th century candelabra
Furniture: Hutch; refectory table; stickback chairs; child's chair
Accessories: Old glass bottles, jugs and jars; wooden plates; baskets; silhouettes; prints

A SQUARE DINING ROOM

Rooms with distinctive characteristics (this one has long beams and a shallow window down one side) pose their own problems when it comes to redecoration. One solution is to focus on the distinguishing features themselves. The scheme opposite is kept very simple: a basically white space with a strongly-patterned end wall. But the two rooms on this page alter the mood radically, one with graphic use of color which effectively emphasizes the beams, and the other which uses a gamut of soft rose tones for a much more traditional feeling.

see Fabrics pp. 256–57

see Fabrics p. 250

see Plain carpets p. 274

Rose-colored traditional scheme

Soft, warm colors can be used to make a room appear welcoming. Here, the series of pastel tones for the walls, ceiling, floor and drapes also effectively changes the rectangular shape of the space, as do the built-in closets and the round dining table. The simple expedient of stapling fabric to walls is a reliable way of softening the overall effect.

Walls: Rose-colored rough cotton, stapled to the walls (page 198)

Ceiling: Pale and dark rose latex paint
Woodwork: Pale rose semi-gloss paint
Floor: Rose-patterned carpet
Windows: Multi-patterned cotton drapes
Lighting: Victorian globe lights; table lamp; light above glass shelves
Furniture: Round table with two-toned pink cloths; dark cane chairs with patterned squabs; side tables
Accessories: China; cutlery; collection of glass; books; plants

see Furniture p. 296

see Paints pp. 210–11

Beige and black scheme

Contrasting colors and good-looking modern furniture give this space a streamlined feel. The beams are painted to match the table and the storage units (which form a useful study area, if needed, as well as acting as a serving space), while the neat shades maintain the graphic effect.

Walls: Creamy-beige latex paint
Ceiling: Creamy-beige latex paint; black semi-gloss beams
Woodwork: Black semi-gloss paint
Floor: Creamy-beige deck-painted boards
Windows: Beige cotton Roman shades
Lighting: Recessed spotlights
Furniture: Black table; cane and steel chairs; black-stained wood wall units
Accessories: China and cutlery; books; plants

opposite page:
White and blue scheme

Although the rest of the room is kept deliberately low key (the simple furnishings and bleached-out tones providing a suitable background for dining), the patterned wall provides a needed focal point. The long sheers at the window filter any sharp light, while at the same time adding softness to the otherwise crisp lines.

Walls: Blue and white wallpaper; white latex paint
Ceiling: White latex paint
Woodwork: White semi-gloss paint
Floor: White carpet
Windows: Floor-length sheer drapes
Lighting: Pendant light over table
Furniture: Table; chairs; sideboard
Accessories: Mirror; china; cutlery; glasses; flowers and plants

A RECTANGULAR DINING ROOM

The problem here is how to give interest to the sort of characterless room which is often so difficult to furnish without monotony. In the scheme opposite, the room has been given a rustic feel, with brick walls and floor and old pine furniture. The scheme below is much more sophisticated and soigné, with soft, dark walls, an interesting floor, and a polished round table. In the third scheme, the room has been made a base for some splendid early furniture and portraits — although any interesting furniture would look good with this quiet background and subtle lighting.

Early furniture scheme
Against a muted background, the early furniture and formal portraits give this room a distinctive character. The natural burlap wallcovering, the color of sacking, and similarly colored, heavily textured matting on the floor are ideal, quiet foils for the paintings and furniture, which are given a special emphasis with subtle downlighting.

Walls: Natural colored burlap

Ceiling: Pale nutmeg latex paint
Woodwork: Stripped pine
Floor: Heavyweight coir matting
Window (not seen): Natural burlap drapes caught back
Lighting: Downlights; low voltage spots
Furniture: Early gate-legged table; chairs; armoire; side table
Accessories: Tableware; portraits

see Wallcoverings p. 228

see Matting p. 278

opposite page:
Rustic scheme
The natural brick walls (sealed to keep down dust), handsome, boarded ceiling and brick floor all add a definite rustic feel to this room. Further interest is provided by the china-filled bookcase, the pine table and chairs and the old oak furniture. A wall oven behind the door is a useful addition.

Sophisticated scheme
Felt wallcovering and thin gilt picture frames are used together here to create a paneled effect. The polished mahogany table becomes the focus of the space when lit exactly and dramatically from above center.

Walls: Deep blue felt wallcovering outlined in thin gilt picture frames
Ceiling: White latex paint
Floor: Blue and red patterned carpet
Window (not seen): Deep blue heavy cotton Roman shades edged with red
Lighting: Framing projector above table; lamps on sideboard; candles
Furniture: Polished mahogany library table; 19th century chairs; mahogany sideboard
Accessories: Tableware

Walls: Stripped and sealed natural brick
Ceiling: Tongue-and-groove pine boarding
Floor: Brick tiles
Window (not seen): Wood shutters
Lighting: Uplights; downlights (not seen); strip lights concealed inside bookcase
Furniture: Pine table; chairs and bookcase; oak corner closet and chair
Accessories: China; glass; glass rolling pins; tableware; plants; candlestick; wood carving; tableware

see Wallcoverings p. 230

see Carpets p. 276

A NARROW, LOW-CEILING'D ROOM

Lack of space in this room is further compounded by a low ceiling and the fact that one wall is entirely taken up by window. In the scheme opposite, the theme is uncompromisingly 20th century with almost *de rigueur* contemporary prints on the wall. Another plays on reds so effectively that it entirely distracts from constrictions of the area. And in the scheme below, a much more traditional feel is achieved, with painted paneling, polished floorboards and period furniture.

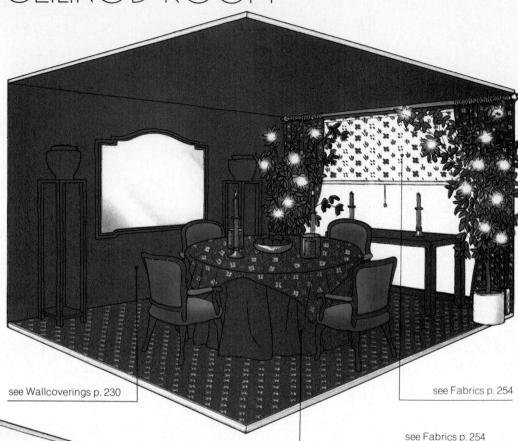

see Wallcoverings p. 230

see Fabrics p. 254

see Fabrics p. 254

One-color scheme
A single, strong color is used here to add distinction to the space, and mixed tones and patterns combine to turn the room into a blaze of warmth. The comfort of upholstered chairs and luxuriant foliage add to the effect, while candles and uplights combine to give a pleasant, underlying glow.

Walls and ceiling: Dark red felt

Woodwork: Dark red satin finish paint
Floor: Dark red patterned wool carpet
Windows: Red and white floral fabric with cotton shade in reverse pattern
Lighting: Uplights
Furniture: Red upholstered chairs; round table; red lacquered side and pedestal tables
Accessories: Large plants strung with small lights; candles; fruit; red lacquered mirror; tablecloth; jardinières

see Stencils p. 242

see Fabrics p. 253

see Flooring p. 265

Traditional scheme
A pretty old refectory table and chairs down the center of the room looks so attractive in this scheme that no-one is aware of its narrowness. Candelabra, shuttered windows and traditional colonial colored walls are in keeping with the general feeling of the space.

Walls: Mayflower blue latex paint
Ceiling: Off-white latex paint
Woodwork: Mayflower blue satin finish
Floor: Plain brick
Window: Painted shutters
Lighting: Uplights in corners; candelabra
Furniture: Refectory table; 19th century chairs; cabinet
Accessories: Prints; tablecloth; candles; plants; glasses

opposite page:
Contemporary scheme
In this room everything is clean-lined, white and gleaming to make the smallish space an experience, rather than the slightly constricted reality that it is. At night, uplights and indirect lighting from the ceiling give the room an almost ethereal glow. Mick Jagger prints, sleek, black place settings, glass and candles complete the effect.

Walls and ceiling: White latex paint
Woodwork: White semi-gloss paint
Floor: White ceramic tiles
Window: Left bare
Lighting: Uplights; concealed fluorescent ceiling light (not shown); candles
Furniture: White lacquered table; white wire-framed chairs
Accessories: Black place mats and place settings; glasses; candlesticks; prints; plant

A BEDROOM/DINING ROOM

The problem of fitting sleeping, sitting and eating space into one small area is a perennial one. This room is particularly small and so long and narrow that without care, the space could look hopelessly jumbled. In the scheme opposite, the section at the end of the room containing the bed can be screened off when not in use. In the second scheme, the walls are softened with fabric to distract the eye from the lack of space, and in the third, mirror is used extensively to push out the walls.

Soft fabric scheme
A space can be made to seem bigger by blurring the edges. Shirred cheesecloth attached to wires below the ceiling effectively softens these walls, and definition is now given to the space by the painted ceiling. A pale floor and minimal furniture make the space seem airier.

Walls: Shirred cheese-cloth
Ceiling: Blue semi-gloss painted beams and white semi-gloss boards

Floor: Off-white wool carpet
Windows: White cotton roller shades; cheese-cloth drapes in front of the bed
Lighting: Downlights between windows and over bed
Furniture: Bed with storage drawers under-neath; table; director's chairs
Accessories: Bowls; pottery; fruit; tablecloth; plants

see Sheers p. 260

see Wallcoverings p. 230

Mirrored scheme
Any space can be expanded by clever use of mirror. Here panels of mirror on one wall and in between the ceiling beams widen the room enormously. The richly colored felt wallcovering, the matting on the floor, the toning blinds and the wooden dining chairs all give warmth to the room.

Walls: Right-hand wall covered in mirror; opposite wall covered in apricot felt
Ceiling: Apricot semi-gloss painted beams mirrored in between
Floor: Coir matting
Window: Pinoleum blinds as in bed area
Lighting: Downlights set in between beams
Furniture: Bed with storage drawers under-neath; semi-circular table; beech chairs; floor
Accessories: Painting; prints; ceramics; floor pillows

opposite page:
Natural-textured scheme
To keep the room looking simple, but as interesting as possible, these walls are left unplastered and the rafters unpainted. In this scheme, the practical bed-storage-lounging area can be screened off with matchstick blinds when convenient. The large lacquered dining table, equally suitable for writing as for eating, forms a useful visual division of the areas.

Walls: White gloss-painted brickwork
Ceiling: White latex paint with natural rafters
Floor: Off-white wool carpet
Windows: Matchstick blinds
Lighting: Ceiling-mounted downlights
Furniture: Bed with storage underneath; black lacquered table; director's chairs
Accessories: Floor pillows; prints

KITCHENS

Kitchens are probably the most complicated rooms of all to plan, varying in function as they do from straight preparation, cooking, washing up and dining areas to general family rooms. Small spaces, *force majeure*, come into the first category, large kitchens tend to fall into the second. For most people, the decision about how actually to use the room is dictated by the existing design: equipment, once built-in, is difficult, and certainly expensive, to shift. But even if you are moving into a house or apartment in which the kitchen is already planned and full of equipment, you can still imprint your own personality on the area by changing the color of the walls, by altering window treatments, by adding accessories, and, if you can afford it, by replacing counter tops and floor coverings or finishes.

Planning a kitchen

If you are planning the room from the beginning and are not quite sure what equipment you will need, or what style of kitchen you prefer, these questions will help rationalize your thoughts on the subject: What kind of meals are you likely to cook, for how many, and how often? Will your present situation remain static as far as you can tell or will the family expand? Is the kitchen solely for meal preparation and cleaning up, or would you prefer to eat there for most, if not all, of the time? Do you work all day, or live far from stores so that you need more than the average amount of storage space? Are you happier with a warm country feeling, natural textures and everyday functional objects on open display, or do you prefer easy-care surfaces and enclosed storage? Or do you like a judicious mixture of both?

Ideally, the layout of a kitchen should follow a work program based on a logical sequence of operations, so think about your usual working routine. Give each task its own special area. Cooking usually involves a good deal of doubling back to and from the refrigerator, sink, stove and different preparation areas; each one needs careful planning so that all necessary equipment and foodstuffs are at hand. Try to plan for a work surface next to each appliance: so the sequence goes work surface then sink, work surface then stove, work surface, and so on. You should allow a minimum of three feet (915 mm) for each preparation area, and for dirty washing up; allow two and a half feet (762 mm) for draining clean dishware if you do not have a dishwasher; set aside two feet (610 mm) by the stove for dishing up and serving food, one and a quarter feet (381 mm) of free work area beside the refrigerator. The cook top should be no more than six feet (1m 829 mm) from the sink, and the passage width between fixtures at least four feet (1 m 219 mm). If you live alone, you can usually make do with one foot (305 mm) less room.

Kitchen walls generally take quite a battering, so they should be painted in washable semi-gloss or gloss paint. Or they can be covered in a vinyl or washable paper. Windows should have easily cleaned or washable shades.

Kitchen floors also have to withstand a great deal of wear and tear and should be tough, waterproof, grease- alkali-

and acid-rejecting, and easy on the feet. Vinyl (whether in sheet or tile form) and vinyl-covered cork meet most of these conditions and are easy to maintain. Terracotta tiles, brick, flagstone, slate, terrazzo and non-slip ceramic tiles are all durable, impressive and good to look at, but they are inclined to be expensive. They are also heavy and are therefore probably only suitable for use at ground-floor level or where floors are particularly strong.

Whether you choose to store all the paraphernalia of cooking hidden behind closed doors or prefer to have things out on display is a matter of taste. Some cooks like to have things within easy reach – pots and pans hanging from rails or butcher hooks; implements or ingredients on pegboard or metal grilles; plates, cups and saucers on open shelves – others like the streamlined clean-cut appearance of conventional kitchen units.

Two types of lighting are useful in kitchens: general area light, preferably controlled on a dimmer switch, and specific task light over work surfaces and tables. Spotlights on tracks, downlights and wallwashers make good background light, or general diffusing lights can be fixed to the ceiling. Fluorescent strips are always useful, concealed behind valances, under wall storage units, they shine light onto the work surface below, and strips can be fitted inside closets to light up automatically when the doors are opened. More information about lighting is given on pages 19 to 24.

The next few pages show a variety of kitchen styles for every shape and style of room, most of which can be adapted to suit most rooms. But whatever style you eventually decide upon, remember that first and foremost, it is a space for the preparation of food; the more the background serves to encourage and enhance this task, the better.

Opposite page:
Four very different styles of kitchen. Three can be used for eating as well, and one is streamlined for fast preparation of food.

Top left:
A casual, comfortable space used for kitchen-dining and living. The run of units is raised slightly from the living area to separate work and living spaces.

Right:
In spite of lack of width, this well-planned galley kitchen manages to fit in most appliances and generous work tops.

Below left:
A low-key, highly efficient working kitchen with neat pale floor and wall tiles, natural wood work tops and matching stool seats, and a capacious island unit. Anti-glare lighting above the glass extractor hood is an especially useful addition. Next door, a butler's pantry has been beautifully-fitted with cabinets and drawers for the organized storage of cutlery, china and glass, together with an extra sink for flower arrangement and glass washing. The golden Afghan rug on the floor adds softness to the area.

Right:
A magnificent, old-fashioned farmhouse kitchen. Modern appliances and contemporary flooring fit without jarring into the ancient framework, as indeed does the lighting slotted into track fixed to a beam above the table. Strings of herbs, baskets, pans, even an old wooden rake are slung on hooks, and the tiled wall neatly divides the cooking area from the table, which is used, quite clearly, for monumental chopping and mixing, judging from its load of raw ingredients for chutneys and pickles.

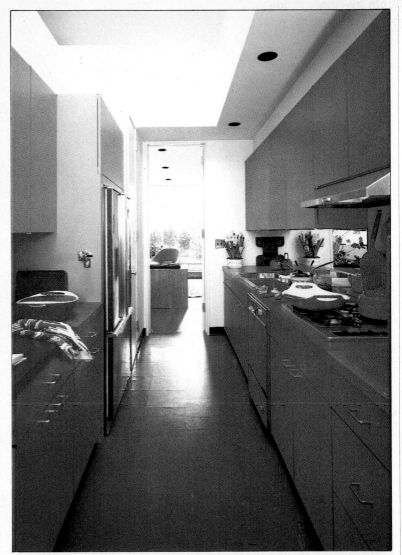

A RECTANGULAR KITCHEN

Faced with the problem of making a kitchen out of a rectangular room with one high window and a sloping ceiling, what are the alternatives? If the space is big enough for eating in, it should obviously be treated with maximum imagination to make it both esthetically and practically viable. The odd proportions of the space merge into the general whiteness of the scheme opposite and any color stands out with intensity. In another scheme, fresh, iris colors distract from the general awkwardness, and in the third, dark shiny paint and butcher-block tops give their own solidity and distinction to the space.

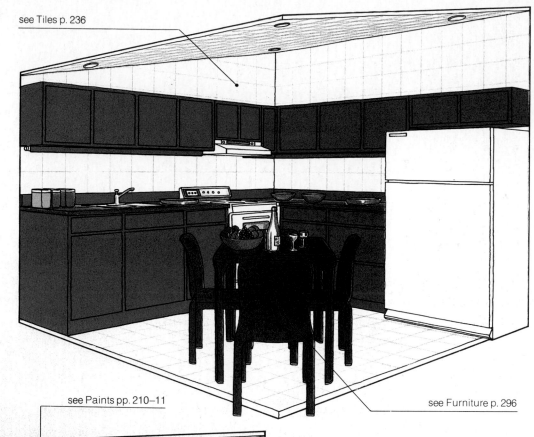

see Tiles p. 236

see Furniture p. 296

Dark green and wood scheme
A pleasantly cool, yet sophisticated look is used here to disguise the awkward shape of the room. The glossy units with tiled floor, ceiling and walls and the sturdy butcher block tops, all distract the eye from difficult proportions. The colors have the added advantage of making a good background for food and for eating. Dark blue units would look equally effective in this case.

Walls and ceiling: White ceramic tiles
Woodwork: White semi-gloss paint (not seen)
Floor: White ceramic tiles
Window: White cotton shade (not seen)
Lighting: Inset downlights; strip lights above units
Furniture: Shiny dark green units with polyurethaned wood tops; butcher block table; red chairs
Accessories: Wooden bowls; trays; chopping boards; jars

see Paints pp. 210–11

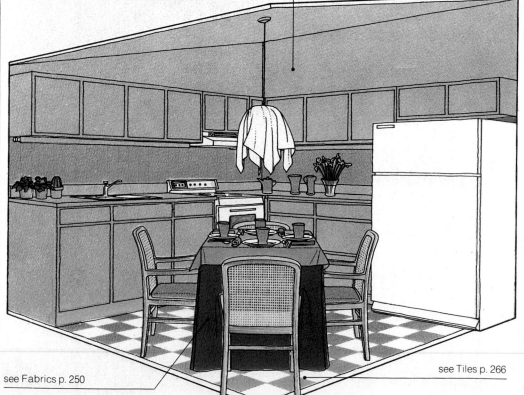

see Fabrics p. 250

see Tiles p. 266

Iris-colored scheme
Shape and proportion become a very secondary preoccupation in this scheme. Here, the soft, fresh colors are gently gradated to form a room of unexpected charm. Unusual enough in a kitchen, these shades distract from any awkwardness of shape.

Walls and ceiling: Pale blue-gray semi-gloss paint
Walls: Pale blue tiles
Woodwork: White semi-gloss paint (not seen)
Floor: Pale blue and white tiles
Window: Blue and pale mauve cotton roller shade (not seen)
Lighting: Strip lighting above work tops; handkerchief pendant shade
Furniture: Pale blue-gray units; cane dining chairs
Accessories: China and ornaments; napkins; tablecloth; plants, irises

opposite page:
All-white scheme
Any awkwardness of proportion is immediately lost here with walls, ceiling, floor, units and furniture all given the same treatment, enlivened by the spots of color in hardware and accessories. Against this pristine background, food and linens stand out with startling intensity.

Walls and ceiling: White semi-gloss paint
Woodwork: White semi-gloss paint (not seen)
Floor: White deck paint
Window: Left bare (not seen)
Lighting: Strip lights over work surface; pendant fitting from ceiling
Furniture: White units; white plastic table and chairs
Accessories: Enameled kitchenware; boards; napkins

A SPACIOUS KITCHEN

One wall that is really all window might sound ideal for a large family kitchen, but it does curtail preparation and storage space. This problem has been accepted in the scheme opposite, and the room treated as a good, old-fashioned kitchen-family room with preparation and work counter kept to one end of the room. The scheme below is much more of a working kitchen and part of the generous window space is sacrificed for more storage and preparation space including an island unit. In the scheme, right, the area is much more streamlined, but allows for eating space as well as providing ample work tops.

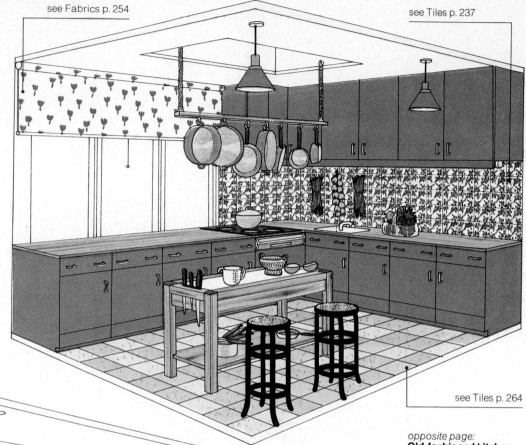

see Fabrics p. 254

see Tiles p. 237

see Tiles p. 264

see Blinds p. 262

see Tiles p. 266

Working kitchen scheme
Flush-fronted modern units provide cohesive storage space for this serious working – as opposed to eating – kitchen. A central island unit gives an extra preparation area.

Walls: Avocado and white tiles; green semi-gloss paint

Ceiling: White latex paint
Woodwork: White semi-gloss paint
Floor: Cork tiles
Window: Cotton roller shade
Lighting: Pendant lights; strip lights above work surfaces
Furniture: Wood and melamine units; stools; kitchen equipment
Accessories: Pots and pans; *batterie de cuisine* fruit; plants; herbs

Streamlined white scheme
Facilities for cooking and eating are provided in this scheme, in which the slick central island acts as an eating bar as well as a cooking area. An efficient extractor hood uses the skylight as a convenient outlet. Plants, lit from behind plexiglass panels, and the pretty floor tiles provide the only pattern in this sophisticated, yet eminently practical scheme.

Walls: White semi-gloss paint
Ceiling: White latex paint
Floor: Ceramic tiles
Window: White Japanese paper blind
Lighting: Downlights in extractor hood and recessed in ceiling; strip lights above work surfaces and behind plexiglass panels
Furniture: White units; stools
Accessories: *Batterie de cuisine*; china; glass; plants and herbs

opposite page:
Old-fashioned kitchen scheme
The large window has been given maximum impact in this room and treated as an asset not a problem. The work area is concentrated within and on top of an enormously long old hutch base, leaving space for eating, writing and just sitting around in nice, old-fashioned surroundings.

Walls: Stripped and sealed natural brick
Ceiling: Tongue and groove pine boarding
Woodwork: Stripped pine
Floor: Brick tiles
Window: Pine shutters
Lighting: Uplights; spots fixed below skylight; strip light over working surface
Furniture: Pine refectory table; chairs; hutch base; closet
Accessories: 19th century wooden plate rack; tableware; general *batterie de cuisine*

A SMALL EAT-IN KITCHEN

Windows set right up to one wall (often as a result of remodeling an old building) can look awkward. One way of overcoming this problem in a kitchen is to install slick, built-in units to restore the balance, as in the scheme opposite. Or the whole feeling of the space can be changed with clever use of color and pattern, as in the second scheme, so that any awkwardness is lost in the general design. The third scheme uses a sympathetic arrangement of collectibles and gently patterned fabric to distract from the less sympathetic proportions.

see Shades p. 263

see Matting p. 278

Striped scheme
A continuous frieze of diagonal stripes which covers the units and is repeated in the cottom shade lessens the impact of the awkwardly set window. Even the worktops, the table and the chairs take up the colors of the stripes. The floor is covered with coir matting to add a touch of softness to the area.

Walls and ceiling:
White and red semi-gloss paint; white tiles above the work surface

Woodwork: White gloss paint
Floor: Natural coir matting
Window: Red and white striped cotton shade
Lighting: Recessed downlights; hood light over stove (not seen)
Furniture: Folding table and chairs; red and white units with laminated top
Accessories: Kitchen equipment; casseroles; pans; clock

see Natural tiles p. 265

see Fabrics p. 253

Collectibles scheme
A mass of attractive old baskets on the wall effectively disguises the actual shape of this room. The stained oak units and the checked café curtains and matching tablecloth make a pleasing background for eating or cooking.

Walls and ceiling:
White latex paint; off-white tiles
Woodwork: Oak-stained to match units
Floor: Faded bricks
Window: Checked cotton café curtains and valance
Lighting: Recessed spotlights in ceiling; hood light above stove (not seen)
Furniture: Oak units; round table; bentwood chairs
Accessories: Old baskets; pottery; plants; kitchen equipment; tablecloth; china and glass; vegetable rack

opposite page:
Built-in scheme
What could be an awkward space is given a clean-lined harmony here with well-planned units and understated background coloring. A folding table and chairs fit neatly into this well-planned space. Cooking ingredients and accessories such as china and glass stand out with unexpected clarity against the prevailing monotones.

Walls: Parchment-colored semi-gloss paint; white ceramic tiles
Ceiling: White latex paint
Woodwork: White semi-gloss paint
Floor: Dark brown tiles
Window: White cotton roller shade
Lighting: Chrome wall light; hood light over stove
Furniture: Off-white units; white folding table and chairs
Accessories: Clock; kitchen equipment and ingredients; china and cutlery

A LARGE KITCHEN/DINING ROOM

Large kitchen-dining rooms seem an ideal, but it is important to have plenty of dumping space if the detritus of cooking is not to interfere with the pleasure of eating. In the scheme opposite, tiled walls and simple units make an inconspicuous background for the focal points of long refectory table and pots, pans and baskets hanging from the ceiling beams. The scheme on the right has a striking checkerboard theme, and in the third, neat matchstick blinds attached to beams can hide left-over cooking preparations.

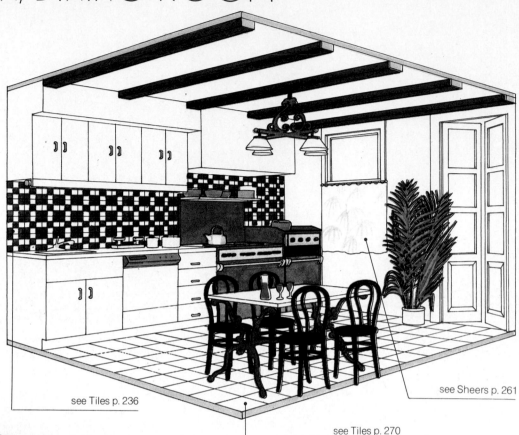

see Tiles p. 236

see Sheers p. 261

see Tiles p. 270

see Blinds p. 262

Checker-board scheme
The table and chairs are cleverly absorbed into this striking two-color composition. With crocheted curtains at the window, the overall effect is rather like nineteenth century French provincial café.

Walls and ceiling:
Black and white tiles with white semi-gloss paint
Woodwork: White semi-gloss paint; black gloss-painted beams

Floor: White vinyl tiles
Windows: Crocheted white cotton café curtain on brass pole
Lighting: Black iron and glass lamp over table; concealed strips over working surface
Furniture: White units; white marble table-top on black iron base; black bentwood chairs
Accessories: Plants; kitchen equipment

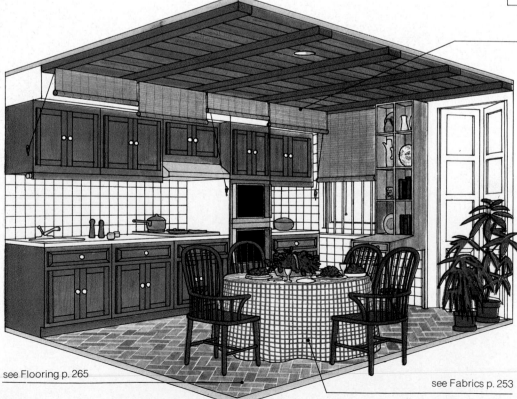

see Flooring p. 265

see Fabrics p. 253

Matchstick blind scheme
Blinds, which roll up neatly when not in use, are an ideal way of hiding dirty plates or cooking pots in a kitchen-dining area. The checked tablecloth provides a splash of color against the bricks.

Walls: Ocher latex paint (not seen); white tiles
Ceiling: Boarded and beamed
Floor: Herringbone bricks sealed with polyurethane
Windows: Matstick blinds
Lighting: Inset downlight over table; concealed strip light above working surface
Furniture: Dark wood units; kitchen equipment; round table; stick-back chairs; desk and shelf unit; stool
Accessories: Plants; tablecloth; pots and pans

opposite page:
Colorful, haphazard scheme
Simple units and shelves of cheerful cooking pans make an unobtrusive background for the handsome table and colorful collection of old pots and baskets.

Walls: Blue, red and white tiles; white semi-gloss paint
Ceiling: White latex paint; natural wood beams
Woodwork: White semi-gloss paint
Windows: Left bare to yard (grilled)
Floor: Polished wood
Lighting: Downlight above table; strip lights above working surface
Furniture: Kitchen units and equipment; refectory table; country chairs
Accessories: Pots and pans; china and glassware; plants

A NARROW KITCHEN-DINING ROOM

At first glance, this room seems to have a lot in common with the kitchen-dining area opposite, but the likeness is fairly superficial, since this space resembles a shoe-box in proportion, while the other is generously wide. Natural assets such as plenty of light and greenery are used to distract from any narrowness in the first scheme, while in the one below, every effort has been made to expand the space visually using most of the tricks of the trade (except expensive mirror).

Green and white scheme
Pale wood, plants and light, bright colors make this space seem so pretty that any narrowness of the room is effectively lost in the overall charm. The floor is only a few shades lighter than the pine of the furniture, and the tangle of greenery at the window makes it unnecessary to have any more of a window covering than a bamboo blind.

Walls and ceiling: White latex paint
Woodwork: Natural pine and white semi-gloss paint
Floor: Creamy quarry tiles
Window: Bamboo blind
Lighting: Pendant lights
Furniture: Pine units and settle; table and dark stick-back chairs
Accessories: Plants; tablecloth; mugs; plates; baskets; wooden bowl with fruit; dried flowers

Space-expanding scheme
Clever use of contrasting color and diagonal patterns seemingly doubles the width of this room. The diagonal boarding, suspended below a dark ceiling and lit with concealed spots, is echoed in the diagonally painted floor. Walls are tiled in small square aluminum tiles.

Walls: Aluminum tiles
Ceiling: White semi-gloss painted wood strips suspended below dark blue latex-painted ceiling
Floor: Deck painted wide white and thin mauve stripes
Window: Aluminum Venetian blinds
Lighting: Concealed spots
Furniture: Glass and white pipe tubing table; mauve canvas and wood chairs; mauve and white units; steel shelving above sink
Accessories: Plants; *batterie de cuisine*; china

see Blinds p. 262

see Tiles p. 233

see Paints pp. 210–11

A WIDE KITCHEN-DINING ROOM

A kitchen-dining room with a useful arched division like this one is a natural for the sort of comfortable, rustic feel achieved in the first scheme. But this space can equally well be given quite different, urban feeling as proved in the scheme below. Here, the combination of practical Hi-Tech components and everyday utensils chosen especially for their colors, makes for an interesting room with very definite panache.

Comfortable rustic scheme
Softly colored, shiny walls cast a kind of gentle, watery glow over the whole room in this scheme, making it relaxed and restful, in spite of its function. The effect is sharpened and perpetuated by the mass of foliage. The tones of the waxed pine furniture, the matchstick blinds and the baskets make an interesting build up.

Walls and ceiling:
Creamy-apple latex paint
Woodwork: White semi-gloss paint

Floor: White vinyl tiling
Window: Natural match-stick blinds
Lighting: Pearly shell light over dining table; recessed ceiling down-lights (not seen)
Furniture: Old pine chairs; round table; rectangular table; old pine hutch; kitchen units and equipment (not seen)
Accessories: 19th century ceramic jardinière; plants; baskets; pottery jars and plates; vegetables; herbs; tablecloths

see Paints pp. 210–11

see Flooring p. 270

Hi-Tech scheme
Practical ingredients which belong in the kitchen are used to make an interesting build-up of color here. The window is used as a strong focal point with its rows of massed, brightly colored glasses on glass shelves. Walls are covered with colored wire grids for easy open storage.

Walls, ceiling and woodwork: White low-luster paint
Floor: Rubber flooring
Window: Glass shelves
Lighting: Factory light; recessed downlights
Furniture: Formica-topped round table; red bentwood chairs, wooden stools, white filing cabinets with butcher block top; Kitchen equipment (not seen); wood and steel hospital trolley; industrial steel shelving
Accessories: Wire grids; steel rod; *batterie de cuisine*; plates; plants

A ROOF-TOP KITCHEN

Penthouses, which often have vast expanses of glass, present their own, very particular problems. The glass ceiling in this roof-top kitchen, for example, is both its main asset and main liability: the sun can beat down as fiercely in the summer as the rain and snow in winter; slide open the glass and city grime settles mercilessly. The scheme opposite plays it cool, filtering the elements with a diagonally-striped cotton shade which also visually expands the width. The scheme below with its trellis of plants treats the space like a proper greenhouse, while the third uses bright colors so that whatever the weather outside, the effect indoors is always bright and welcoming.

see Blinds p. 262

Strong colors scheme
Bold colors help make a room appear warm and cheerful, whatever the weather outside. Pivoting louvers are used across the ceiling to filter the sun where necessary.

Walls: Chestnut brown semi-gloss paint
Ceiling: Pivoting yellow louvered shades
Floor: Cream ceramic tiles
Windows: Yellow cotton roller shades
Lighting: Recessed spotlights (not seen); lights under units
Furniture: Chestnut brown units; glass-topped wicker table; wicker chairs
Accessories: Plants; kitchen equipment

see Shades p. 263

see Paints pp. 210–11

see Vinyl tiles pp. 270–71

Indoor greenhouse scheme
One obvious way to change the look of a roof-top room is to take advantage of the wealth of natural light and turn it into a greenhouse. Here a trellis is extended up the wall and across the ceiling and is massed with climbing and hanging plants (air conditioning keeps the temperature constant). Floor and ceiling are kept pale and the bamboo blind at the window adds to the garden effect.

Walls and ceiling: White semi-gloss paint with natural-colored single trellis
Floor: Black and white tiles
Woodwork: White semi-gloss paint
Window: Bamboo blinds
Lighting: Recessed spotlights (not seen); lights under units
Furniture: Black units; glass-topped table; molded white plastic chairs
Accessories: Plants; kitchen equipment

opposite page:
Cool, shaded scheme
There is no reason why shades should not be as attractive as they are functional. The cool, diagonal stripes of these cotton shades are used here to add width.

Walls: Cream semi-gloss paint; diagonal trellis
Ceiling: Green and white diagonally striped cotton shades
Woodwork: Cream semi-gloss paint
Floor: Cream tiles
Windows: White vertical louvered blinds
Lighting: Spotlights (not seen); lights under units
Furniture: Cream units; glass-topped table; molded white plastic chairs; round table with cotton cloth
Accessories: Plants; kitchen equipment

A LOFT KITCHEN

One of the more rewarding urban legacies of the late twentieth century must be the restoration of the upper floors of old commercial buildings for residential use. The decoration of such areas must be planned to cope with and divide up abundant space, without destroying the impact of natural details like wood floors, beams and natural plasterwork. Cooking, sitting, dining, working and sleeping areas are easily combined in this loft with no tangible barriers. The first scheme exploits spare, High-Tech components in a modern, but nonetheless warm treatment. The second divides up the space in a similar way, but uses built-in units to blur the edges and create a softer overall effect, while in the third, the area is transformed to resemble a country farmhouse by extensive use of wood and natural accessories like herbs and plants.

see Paints pp. 210–11

see Paints pp. 210–11

Smooth-edged scheme
While the areas of activity divide up in much the same way as in the High-Tech scheme, the overall effect here is tamer. The simple built-in shelves appear to smooth out the space, while the floor is softened with matting.

Walls: White semi-gloss paint
Ceiling: Pale corn latex paint
Woodwork: White semi-gloss paint
Floor: Sisal matting
Windows: Split bamboo blinds
Lighting: Semi-recessed wallwashers; angled light by bed
Furniture: Built-in shelves and units; butcher block tops; canvas and wood seating; plastic tables and tool chest; draftsman's table; bed; white desk
Accessories: Kitchen equipment; large plants; glasses; china; baskets

see Paints pp. 210–11

see Blinds p. 262

see Matting pp. 278–9

Farmhouse-style scheme
Even overtly urban surroundings can be given a country-style treatment. Here extensive use of rural-looking furnishings – a stripped pine table, old hutches, sturdy chairs, bare floor and a galaxy of drying herbs and flowers – all help turn a city loft into an Italian or Provençal farmhouse.

Walls and ceiling: Olive and white latex paint
Woodwork: White semi-gloss paint
Floor: Bleached boards
Windows: Left bare
Lighting: Pendant light over table; spotlights; candles
Furniture: Old hutches; old table; hob and sink unit enclosed in wood; beech upright chairs; armchairs; orange desk
Accessories: Kitchen equipment; plants; herbs; dried flowers; baskets; china

opposite page:
High-Tech scheme
With its factory lighting and shelves and its simple furnishings, this scheme still very obviously maintains the feel of a domesticated commercial building. The room is surprisingly flexible, nonetheless.

Walls and ceiling: White semi-gloss paint
Woodwork: White semi-gloss paint
Floor: Polished boards and area matting
Windows: Narrow slatted Venetian blinds
Lighting: Pendant factory lighting and semi-recessed wallwashers on a painted wooden track; angled light by bed

Furniture: Industrial wire shelving; restaurant range and extractor hood; long cupboard unit with butcher block work top; tool chest; plastic tables; canvas and wood seating; plastic drum table; melamine-topped draftsman's table; bed; orange desk
Accessories: Kitchen equipment; flowers; plants

A SMALL ISLAND KITCHEN

Restricted kitchen space is certainly not untypical in modern houses or apartments, so it is all the more important to be able to fit in the basic equipment. To save on the cook's energy, as well as decoration costs, the layout of this rectangular kitchen is planned around a peninsular unit for food preparation, cooking and eating, leaving a U-shaped walkway. The room is well lit, with windows on two walls for natural light, built-in overhead lighting and a range lit by a concealed spot under the ventilating hood. It is still possible to produce very different effects with decoration without going to the expense of changing the pine island unit. The three treatments given here are natural, French provincial and warm-toned.

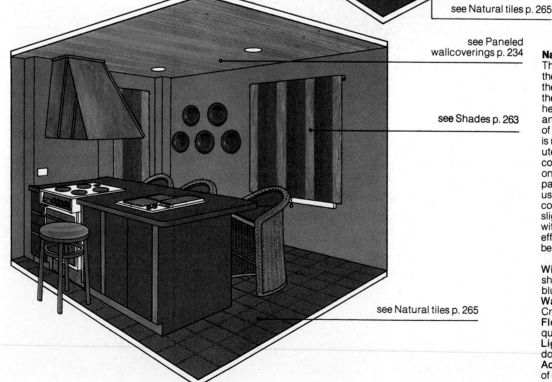

see Wall tiles p. 238

see Natural tiles p. 265

see Paneled wallcoverings p. 234

see Shades p. 263

see Natural tiles p. 265

French provincial scheme
By covering the walls from floor to ceiling with blue and white French ceramic tiles, the kitchen takes on a rustic look. The same tiles have been used to cover the ventilating hood, giving a modern fitting the look of an old-fashioned chimney breast. Unpainted rattan blinds hang at the windows and a collection of baskets covers the wall.

Windows: Natural-colored rattan blinds
Walls: Blue and white French ceramic tiles
Ceiling: Pure white latex paint
Floor: Terracotta quarry tiles
Lighting: Built-in downlights
Accessories: Collection of baskets

Warm-toned scheme
If you prefer a less somber atmosphere for cooking in, minimal changes can be made to produce a warm effect. The color of the walls blends well here with the window shades, whose flame color is picked out in the melamine work surface on top of the unit. A montage of different-colored plates adds wall interest.

Windows: Cotton shades in flame, brown and gold stripes
Walls: Nutmeg brown latex paint
Ceiling: Tongue-and-groove pine
Floor: Terracotta quarry tiles
Lighting: Inset downlights

Natural scheme
The natural textures of the chunky pine unit and the large quarry tiles on the floor are emphasized here by the pale walls and ceiling; the copper of the ventilating hood is repeated in the kitchen utensils and the collection of the plates on the wall. Vividly patterned shades are used to provide a contrast. To give a slightly warmer feeling without destroying the effect, beige paint could be used for the walls.

Windows: Roman shades in red, brown, blue and white pattern
Walls and ceiling: Creamy white latex paint
Floor: Terracotta quarry tiles
Lighting: Built-in downlights
Accessories: Montage of copper plates

A LARGE ISLAND KITCHEN

Generous window space, though good for natural light, can actually be rather a nuisance if a lot of storage space is required. In the room opposite which could be in town or country, closets and units are built right round the glass so that the window becomes an integral part of this pleasing, practical arrangement of white paint and natural wood with two-toned hexagonal tiles. In the scheme, right, rich, plum-colored walls and units are teamed with aluminum tiles and a dark slate floor for a much slicker look. In the scheme below, the space is made more traditional in appearance by the use of dark wooden units and café curtains at the window.

see Paints pp. 210–11

see Shades p. 263

see Tiles p. 265

see Miniprints p. 251

see Tiles p. 265

see Ethnic rugs pp. 280–81

Plum and aluminum scheme
Dark walls and ceiling teamed with gleaming tiles and a handsome slate floor make for a sophisticated space. Non-dirt showing surfaces like these are eminently practical in an urban environment, and not hopelessly out of place in a rural one.

Walls and ceiling: Plum low luster paint
Woodwork: Plum semi-gloss paint

Floor: Purplish slate tiles
Island and unit tops and tiles over counter top: Aluminum tiles
Window: Roller shade in plum woven cotton
Lighting: Recessed downlights in ceiling; strip lighting under closets and in extractor hood
Furniture: Polished chrome "tractor" stools
Accessories: Kitchen equipment; plants

Traditional, country-style scheme
Dark wood and brass handles paired with a tiled floor make a traditionally rural looking kitchen (which does not preclude it from the city). While the mellow walls, dhurrie rug and café curtains hark back to the past, the closets, island unit and lighting are unmistakably twentieth century.

Walls: Pale terracotta low luster paint with toning tiles
Ceiling: Pale terracotta latex paint
Woodwork: Pale terra-cotta semi-gloss paint
Floor: Terracotta tiles; dhurrie rugs
Window: Café curtains in provençal print cotton
Lighting: Recessed downlights
Units: Dark stained wood
Furniture: Breakfast stools
Accessories: Kitchen equipment; plants; pottery

opposite page:
White and natural wood scheme
By integrating the window into the run of storage, no space or light is lost, and the surrounding closets make a pleasing, deep frame for the glass. Pristine units and pale wood enhance the feeling of light and space, and the two-toned tiled floor is particularly practical for a country kitchen, with its constant traffic from the yard outside.

Walls: White, low luster paint
Ceiling: Tongue and groove board
Woodwork: White, low luster paint; butcher block on island unit
Floor: Terracotta and gray hexagonal tiles
Window: Left bare
Lighting: Square fluorescent in ceiling; strip lighting under closets and in extractor hood
Units: White
Furniture: Pine stools
Accessories: Kitchen equipment; flowers

A GALLEY KITCHEN

When a space is particularly small it is important to make it as appealing as possible and, of course, as functional. This room still manages to include all the amenities of a working kitchen without any sense of crowding. Horizontal beams across the ceiling in the scheme opposite make the room appear squarer than it actually is, while in the scheme, right, a streamlined effect is achieved with industrial wire shelving, butcher-block worktops; galvanized sheet metal splashbacks help exaggerate the width almost as much as mirror. All sense of boundaries is lost in the scheme below, in which walls, ceiling and units are all covered in the same dark, glossy paint. Against such a background, kitchen accessories and any other colors stand out with great intensity.

Pale and functional scheme
Open shelving teamed with pale walls and floor make for a sense of space here, as does the reflective quality of the metal splashbacks. Venetian blinds at the window continue the functional feeling. Pots and pans, baskets, and bunches of herbs hanging from the beams add a softening touch.

Walls and ceiling: White semi-gloss paint; galvanized metal splashbacks
Woodwork: White gloss paint
Floor: Cream ceramic tiles
Window: Aluminum Venetian blinds
Lighting: Recessed spotlights
Furniture: Industrial steel shelving; butcher-block worktops; stool
Accessories: Kitchen equipment; glass jars; baskets; plants; cookbooks; wine rack

see Paints pp. 210–11

see Blinds p. 262

see Ceramic tiles p. 236

see Blinds p. 262

see Ceramic tiles p. 236

Dark, shiny scheme
Many a cramped room can be pepped up with dark shiny paint. Here, the glossy, reflecting walls and ceiling, coupled with matching units and shelving are intended to blur the confines of the area. Good natural light and a pale tiled floor help maintain the dramatic feel, and keep the room from appearing dark and compressed. Any accessories stand out with great clarity and colors take on a special brilliance all their own.

Walls, ceiling, woodwork and units: Dark reddish-brown high-gloss paint with an extra coat of varnish
Floor: Cream ceramic tiles
Windows: Cream matchstick blinds
Lighting: Recessed spotlights; concealed strip lighting below shelves
Furniture: Red wooden stool
Accessories: Kitchen equipment; plates; wine rack

opposite page:
Wood-lined scheme
Warm-colored pine lining the walls and criss-crossing the ceiling gives a sense of comfortable unity to this confined space. Horizontal beams, open shelving and knee-hole spaces all contribute to the squaring off of an otherwise narrow space.

Walls: Polyurethaned tongue-and-groove pine paneling
Ceiling: White latex paint with pine beams
Floor: Cream ceramic tiles
Window: White paper blind
Lighting: Spotlights attached to beams; under-unit lighting
Furniture: White formica-topped worktops and units mixed with pine-clad units and open pine shelving; stool
Accessories: Kitchen equipment; glass jars; plants; wine rack

A SMALL IRREGULAR-SHAPED KITCHEN

Small apartments which are carved out of old houses and apartment buildings built for a more spacious age, often contain awkwardly-shaped rooms with cramped space and difficult angles. The major priority in decorating is to make those angles work, in whatever way is the most practical, without at the same time losing valuable floor area. The scheme opposite is purely cosmetic, almost emphasizing the angular character of the space and taking advantage of the greenery beyond the window. The second effectively loses the irregularity by clever use of color, and the third relies on the collection of kitchen accessories to distract the eye from the shape of the room.

Midnight blue scheme
One way of coping with any awkward angles in a room is by using a strong color, so that the basic shape is lost in the overall effect. Against this background, vegetables, fruit, flowers and foliage stand out with sharp intensity, as do the shapes of the pots and pans and china.

Walls and ceiling: Pale blue semi-gloss paint
Floor: Hardwood boards
Window: Painted shutters
Lighting: Recessed downlights in ceiling; warm white deluxe fluorescent strips under wall units
Furnishings: Fitted units; stool
Accessories: Hanging basket of fruit and vegetables; storage jars; chopping board; wine; pots and pans; picture

see Paints p. 210

see Blinds pp. 262–3

see Natural Tiles p. 265

Collector's scheme
The odd shape of the room is completely forgotten here thanks to the old colanders and bygones which are massed lavishly on every bit of spare wall space.

Walls and ceiling: White latex paint; tiles above units
Moldings and window frame: White and green semi-gloss paint
Floor: Terracotta tiles
Window: Matchstick blind
Lighting: Recessed spotlights; concealed fluorescent tubes above work surface
Furnishings: Scrubbed wood units; rush and wood stool
Accessories: Colanders; bygones; kitchen accessories

opposite page:
Simple cosmetic scheme
Making a virtue out of necessity, the asymmetric angles are deliberately delineated here by the use of wood strip to edge the working surfaces. A natural matchstick blind, matching cane wallpaper and terracotta octagonal vinyl tiles keep to the fresh, natural theme, while at the same time allowing the outdoor greenery to assume a major role in the scheme.

Walls: Woven cane wallpaper; white tiles
Ceiling: Cream latex paint

Woodwork and moldings: White shelves and window frame; dark cream moldings; natural wood edgings and shelves
Floor: Terracotta octagonal vinyl tiles
Window: Natural matchstick blind
Lighting: Fluorescent strips underneath wall-mounted cabinets; recessed spotlights in ceiling
Furnishings: Kitchen units; wooden stool
Accessories: Hanging vegetable baskets; pans; plates; prints; herbs; storage jars

BEDROOMS

The general consensus is that whether double or single, bedrooms should be restful rather than dramatic, capable of looking both warm and cool, depending on the season, and as personal as the occupants prefer. Many people consider comfort to be of key importance; for others, a certain spareness and simplicity may be the chief requirement.

Planning a bedroom

If the room is only to be used for sleeping, you will probably only need a bed and a system for storing clothes. On the other hand, if it is also to be used for relaxing or working in, you will need a space large enough for these activities.

An ideal main bedroom would be large enough to include a pair of comfortable chairs or a small sofa and there would also be room for an occasional table for books and magazines and, perhaps, the odd meal.

Ideally, a guest bedroom should be both welcoming and comfortable, interesting without being too strongly personal. If space is available, include a capacious dressing table, which can double for a desk, as well as a comfortable chair and good lighting.

It is obviously foolish to buy furniture for small children's rooms that will suit one age group admirably and be redundant the next, so look for sturdy pieces that will grow with the child. Fabrics should be tough enough to withstand childish onslaughts, yet cheerful enough to stimulate and satisfy the most color-conscious youngster. Flooring should be as soundproof and dirt resistant as it is possible to find.

Adolescents should have rooms of their own on which to impose their developing tastes. Let them choose the decoration and accessories for themselves as far as possible, or at least let them make some decisions in your presence. Their rooms should, if possible, include a bed, a worktable cum dressing table, at least one chair, shelves for books and other possessions, and good storage. If there is room, provide extra beds so they can entertain friends.

Bedroom storage

A bed can be built in with storage to seem all of a piece, or if space is very confined, drawers can be fitted under or bought with the bed. Built-in closets and small dressers or lowboys can be used instead of bedside tables. If there is no room for a separate desk or worktable, a long top placed across a pair of low dressers will give adequate writing, sewing and make-up space, and room underneath for extra storage.

The final touches

Choice of drapes, shades and blinds and accessories will depend on taste, budget and the style of the room. Soft pile carpeting, or at least one or two rugs by the side of each bed will provide an atmosphere of ease and comfort in a bedroom. The following pages show bedrooms of every style and description for every sort of situation. Most of the schemes can be adapted to suit different sized rooms.

Opposite page, far left:
Drapes attached to curved tracks on the ceiling give a handsome four-poster effect. Note the detail of the vivid print lining of the drapes repeated in the pillows.

Left:
Red and white in different proportions makes a fresh and cheerful impact in this room, which is as cool in summer as it is warm but pristine in winter.

This page, above:
Another red and white room with a quite different feeling. The coral walls make a sophisticated background for the striking lacquered screen bedhead and chest. The matchstick blinds and cane table and chair add to the Oriental feeling.

Right:
Soft blue and white seem to bring the ocean view outside right into this pleasantly cool room.

A BEDROOM/DRESSING ROOM

Sometimes it is necessary to try and get more or less separate sleeping and dressing room areas out of one space. In this case, a half partition wall is raised between bed-head and dressing space, leaving passage-way either side so that the room, though effectively divided, still maintains its feeling of spaciousness. The scheme opposite is somberly distinguished, with gray flannel, mirror and excellent lighting. Another takes as its cue the wooded view outside the window for a fresh green and white effect. And the third is rather more sumptuous, with moiré silk walls, a delicate sweet pea fabric and toning carpet border and accessories.

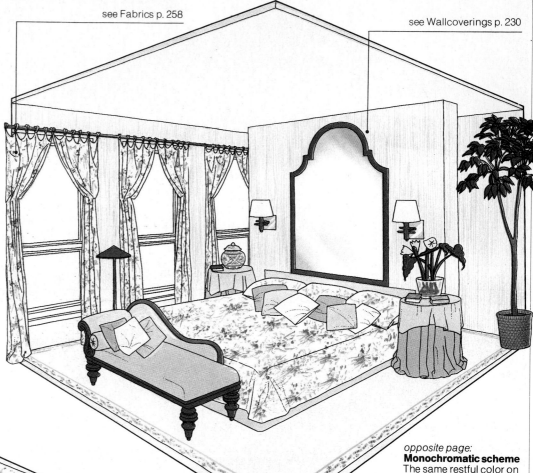

see Fabrics p. 258

see Wallcoverings p. 230

Sweet pea scheme
Moiré silk wallcovering and sweet-pea patterned Liberty chintz for drapes and bedcovering make this a sumptuously pretty room, which is finished off with a creamy carpet and toning pink border. A comfortable chaise-longue at the end of the bed adds to the general feeling of ease.

Walls: Oyster moiré silk wallcovering
Ceiling: Oyster latex paint
Woodwork: Oyster satin finish paint

Floor: Off-white Wilton carpet with pinky-red border
Windows: Liberty sweet pea glazed chintz drapes on thin brass poles
Lighting: Swing-arm wall lights; uplights; concealed spots attached to back of partition wall; reading light
Furniture: Bed; tables; chaise in creamy cotton
Accessories: Throw pillows; tablecloths; plants; books; mirror; ceramics; chintz bed-cover; plain dust ruffle

opposite page:
Monochromatic scheme
The same restful color on walls, windows and bed make this an especially peaceful room. The effect is further enhanced by the softness of most of the surfaces, and by clever use of mirror.

Walls: Gray felt edged with mirror
Ceiling: White latex paint
Woodwork: Dark gray satin finish paint
Floor: Off-white shag carpet
Windows: Open shutters lined with shirred gray felt
Lighting: Semi-recessed wallwashers over bed; swing-arm wall lights; track with cannister spots behind partition wall
Furniture: Bed; built-in mirrored bedhead with end tables; mirrored plinth for plants
Accessories: Gray flannel bedspread and pillows; plants and flowers; photographs; books; magazines

see Wallpapers p. 218

Green and white scheme
Here, colorful corn design wallpaper echoes the wooded outside view, which can be covered when necessary with white louvered shutters. The carpet adds to the general freshness, as do the plants along the window wall. The bed-covering takes up the pattern of the real ferns.

Walls and ceiling: Green and white corn design paper

Woodwork: White satin finish paint
Floor: Leaf green wool and nylon twist carpet
Windows: White painted shutters
Lighting: Recessed wallwashers; swing-arm wall lamps; track lighting
Furniture: Bed with built-in mirrored bedhead
Accessories: Plants; books; paintings; bed-spread; pillows; dust ruffle

see Carpets p. 275

see Sheers p. 261

A LARGE, WELL-PROPORTIONED BEDROOM

Turn-of-the-century rooms, with their graceful windows and good proportions, can absorb quite disparate pieces, and even if allowed to remain comparatively empty of furniture, they can still look interesting and sometimes memorable.

In the first scheme, the painted brass bed is a good vehicle for the chaste linen coverings; and in the second, the four-poster with sheer calico hangings makes a pretty, all-white, room within a room. In complete contrast, the third scheme uses brightly colored sheeting to transform the space into a warm, sophisticated area.

see Shades p. 263

see Furnishings p. 312

see Paints p. 211

White-on-white scheme
Minimum expenditure for maximum effect – the simple, home-made four poster bed with its calico hangings uses the space to good purpose, creating a white-on-white room within a room. Floor and walls are kept plain to tie in with the furniture, but relief from the monotone is provided by the foliage of the plants, and the wicker bedside tables.

Walls and ceiling: White latex paint
Woodwork: White semi-gloss paint
Floor: White deck paint
Windows: White shades
Lighting: White inset downlights; uplights in corners
Furniture: White painted four-poster with thin white calico drapes; wicker side tables; calico-covered couch
Accessories: Books; large plants

see Furnishings p. 311

see Carpets p. 275

Warm, sophisticated scheme
To create a desired effect and, incidentally, to cut costs, it is sometimes possible to adapt materials to uses other than those for which they were intended. Here, boldly colored sheets are used for wallcoverings as well as drapes, creating a warm, luxurious effect out of all proportion to the actual expenditure. Folding tray tables double as bedside tables, and the floor is covered with dark carpet to pick up the color of the walls.

Walls: Dark blue and white checked sheets
Ceiling: White latex paint
Floor: Blue wool carpet
Windows: Checked cotton drapes
Lighting: Downlights recessed in ceiling at corners; bedside lamps
Furniture: King-size divan with mahogany-stained frame and drapes attached to tracks on ceiling; folding tray tables; stools
Accessories: Comforter; pillows; flowers; books; pictures; mirror

opposite page:
Nostalgic scheme
The painted brass bed, with its Edwardian throw, lace pillows and old shawl, the gentle lace drapes, pine dresser, the comfortable old sofa and the cotton rug on a polished floor – all are used here to create what was the late Christian Dior's favorite sort of room. This "nanny decoration" as he called it, quite simply involves putting together a comforting collection of varied objects and fabrics, to form a nostalgic and in this case, inexpensive, unified scheme.

Walls and ceiling: White latex paint
Woodwork: White semi-gloss paint
Floor: Polished bare boards; cotton rug
Windows: White lace and cotton drapes hanging from wooden poles
Lighting: Japanese paper shade over central light; bedside lamp
Furniture: White painted brass bed with drawn linen throw and lace-covered pillows; pine hutch; cotton-covered sofa
Accessories: Pillows; shawl; clock; china; small round mirror

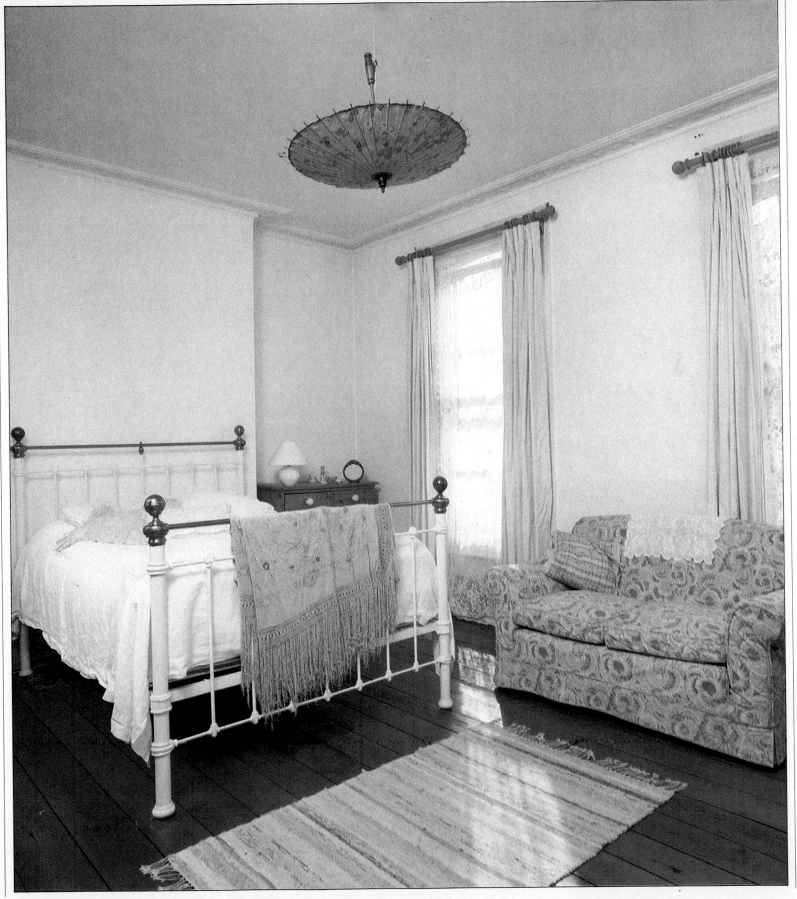

A RECTANGULAR BEDROOM

In most new blocks the bedrooms are often economically designed square or rectangular shapes with few natural assets except perhaps for the view, as in this room. To add internal interest, the scheme opposite depends on cleverly angled platforming; the second is based on a whim, centered around the palm motif, and the third turns the space into a prettily traditional room.

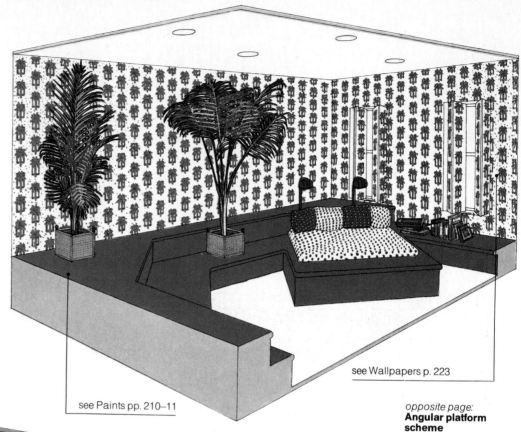

see Wallpapers p. 223

see Paints pp. 210–11

Whimsical scheme
Sometimes, a room can be designed around a whim – in this instance, palm paper was the starting point. Platform and carpet were kept as before, and the walls, shutters and closets covered with palm paper. The mattress and matching pillows continue the luxuriant, verdant feeling and large potted palms complete the scheme.

Walls and closets: Palm paper (page 223)
Ceiling: White latex paint

Platform bases and shelf behind bed:
Yellow semi-gloss paint
Windows: Palm-wallpaper-wrapped shutters
Floor: Off-white wool carpet
Lighting: Downlights in ceiling; strip light behind cornice above closets; two wide-angled reading lamps
Accessories: Large palms; books and magazines; spotted cotton bedcover and pillows

see Wallpapers p. 220

Traditional scheme
To give a less angular feel, the platform is dispensed with and a Provençal print paper used to cover the walls and closet. The pastels of the wallpaper are echoed in the fabric of the pillows.

Walls and closets:
Provençal paper in blues and pinks on cream
Ceiling: Cream latex paint
Floor: Cream wool carpet
Window: Shutters wrapped in fabric matching walls
Furniture: Brass bed; small armchair covered in cotton print to match walls; tables; mirror
Lighting: Strip light behind valance all around room; bedside lamps
Accessories: Plants in hanging baskets; Victorian prints in bird's-eye maple frames; books; cushions; matching cotton dust ruffle and pillows; cream blanket cover

opposite page:
Angular platform scheme
To break up the space, the bed is set out from the corner of the room into an angled platform, with a wide shelf behind and seating or dumping space to the sides. Colors are kept to monotones, set off by one bright, clear color. But a yellow, to match the box painting over the bed, or blue to match the other, could be used with off-white to create the same effect. The windows are simply shuttered.

Walls and ceiling: Off-white semi-gloss paint
Woodwork: As walls, or polished natural
Windows: Off-white shutters
Floor: Off-white twist pile carpet
Furniture: Mattress sunk into platform, row of closets
Lighting: Recessed downlights; two red reading lights; strip light behind cornice over closets
Accessories: Paintings; books; vases; red pillows

see Fabrics p. 250

see Fabrics p. 258

A BEDROOM WITH A "PROBLEM" WINDOW

Old houses often have unusual and sometimes difficult features to absorb. In this nineteenth century room, the wide window ledge, big enough to hold a mattress for a spare bed as well as making a generous window seat, is very high in relation to the floor. The first scheme, with wide carpeted steps, is dominated by a fern motif; in the second, traditional fabric covers boxes which serve as steps to the window seat, and the third scheme centers around a bookish theme.

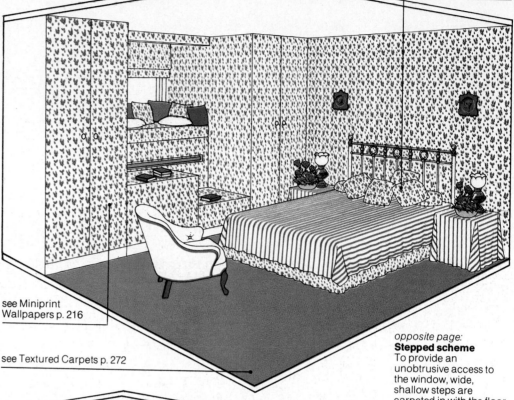

see Fabrics pp. 250–57

see Miniprint Wallpapers p. 216

see Textured Carpets p. 272

Strawberry scheme
Here, covered boxes (treated with poly-urethane to withstand the wear of feet) lead up to the windows. The strawberry design climbs over walls, windows, window seat and dust ruffle and pillows, its colors taken up again in the stripes of the blanket cover and the tablecloths.

Walls: Strawberry pattern paper
Ceiling: White latex paint
Woodwork: White semi-gloss paint

Floor: Moss green wool carpet
Furniture: Brass and white bedhead; cloth-covered tables; Victorian chair; covered boxes
Lighting: Converted brass oil lamps
Soft furnishings: Shades, window seat, dust ruffle, pillows in strawberry cotton; striped cotton blanket cover
Accessories: Pillows; books; flowers; wall plaques

opposite page:
Stepped scheme
To provide an unobtrusive access to the window, wide, shallow steps are carpeted in with the floor. In a predominantly cream and green room, the fern motif in printed burlap on the walls is taken up by the matching cotton of the shades, the dust ruffle on the bed and the window seat.

Walls: Cream burlap with fern motif
Ceiling: Off-white latex paint
Floor: Off-white wool and nylon thick pile carpet
Window: Fern-printed cream voile drapes
Furniture: Queen-sized bed; white painted brass bedhead; off-white and green Victorian armchair; round bedside tables
Lighting: Converted brass oil lamps
Soft furnishings: Fern-printed creamy cotton shades, window seat and dust ruffle; bedspread in creamy crochet with primitive fern over green cotton; bedside table-cloths in fern-patterned cream lace
Accessories: Cushions and pillows; ferns; mirror; wall plaques; books; baskets

Bookish scheme
A good non-structural way to reach a window seat would be to use library steps, and carry through the distinctly bookish effect by filling up the wall immediately below the window with bookshelves. The walls are covered in warm, dark felt.

Walls: Burgundy red felt wallcovering
Ceiling: White latex paint
Woodwork: White semi-gloss paint
Floor: Burgundy, pink and white geometric carpet
Furniture: Plain brass bedhead; two plain mahogany nineteenth century card tables; writing table; Regency chair; built-in shelving
Lighting: Brass oil lamps
Soft furnishings: Bed-cover and bolster in Burgundy felt; shades and window seat in Indian paisley cotton
Accessories: Books; pillows

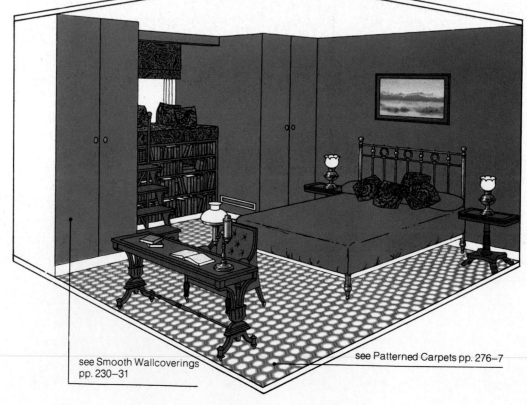

see Smooth Wallcoverings pp. 230–31

see Patterned Carpets pp. 276–7

A SIMPLE BEDROOM

Modern apartment buildings tend to contain anonymous rooms which have few, if any, architectural details or embellishments. Giving character to these spaces is a good exercise in cosmetic decoration: how best to use pattern, color and accessories. This is well demonstrated in the scheme opposite, which depends on horizontal and diagonal lines in crisp, fresh colors to achieve a bright, airy effect. In another, the pastel shades of both walls and fabrics add warmth to the space, while the third scheme uses the pale walls and floor as a backdrop for sculptural shapes.

Pale-colored scheme
Pastel shades go together naturally and are a useful way of giving a stark room intimacy. These gently colored walls provide a subtle background for the coordinating colors of the bedclothes which add warmth to the room.

Walls: Lavender latex paint
Ceiling: Cream latex paint

Floor: Lavender wool carpet
Window: Lavender cotton shade
Lighting: Inset downlights; concealed strip in shelf above bedhead
Furniture: Divan bed; rocking chair; side tables; bookshelves
Accessories: Rose pink sheets; rose and lavender reversible comforter; rose and cream pillows; painting; flowers; books

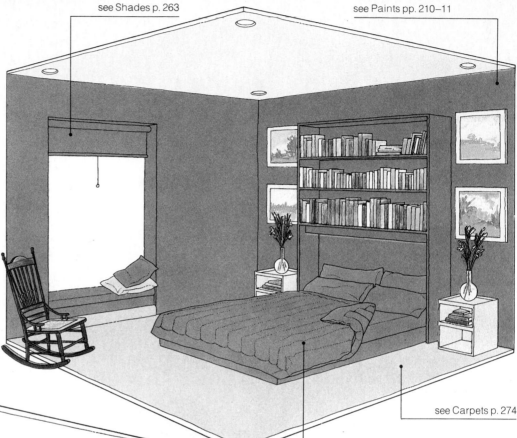

see Shades p. 263

see Paints pp. 210–11

see Carpets p. 274

see Fabrics p. 250

see Shades p. 263

see Wallcoverings p. 228

see Carpets p. 273

Natural textured scheme
Pale, finely woven linen with a daisy design freshens the walls in this design. Plain Berber carpet in the same background color maintains the sense of space. The tailored bed disappears into the general neutrality so that the accessories stand out like sculpture.

Walls: Off-white daisy-printed linen wallcovering
Ceiling: Off-white latex paint
Floor: Off-white Berber carpet
Window: Off-white cotton shade
Lighting: Recessed downlights; bedside lamp
Furniture: Divan bed; side table; pine armoire
Accessories: Bolsters; pillows and cushions; bowls; flowers

opposite page:
Cool, fresh scheme
Clever use of pattern is an ideal way to add interest to an otherwise undistinguished space. In this city bedroom a cool, striped carpet laid on the diagonal contributes to the feeling of space and calm, as does the measured arrangement of prints above the bed.

Walls, ceiling and woodwork: White semi-gloss paint
Floor: Moss green and white diagonal-striped wool carpet
Window: Green and white striped shades
Lighting: Inset downlights
Furniture: Mattresses; white bedside table; carpet-covered cube stool
Accessories: Pillows in sharper version of carpet and shade fabric; flowers; prints; books

A LARGE BEDROOM/SITTING ROOM

Large bedrooms are often quite big enough for relaxed sitting as well. This one is enviable for its generous proportions, its windows and balcony and splendid city view. Indeed, the only problem is how to make the most of its size and assets. One scheme is calm but idiosyncratic; another is cool and chic; the third is parrot-colored and bucolic, in direct contrast to the grays and browns of the view through the long windows.

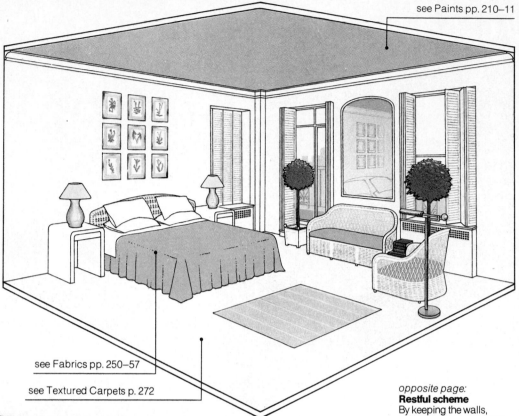

see Paints pp. 210–11

see Fabrics pp. 250–57

see Textured Carpets p. 272

Crisp, chic scheme
White louvered shutters are used here to create a crisp, clean effect. The walls and carpet are pale and the color of the ceiling is picked out in the matching cotton of the bed and upholstery. Two indoor trees standing in neat, white *Versailles* boxes in front of the windows add a touch of freshness. Prints in steel frames hang above the bed and additional lighting is provided by crystal lamps.

Walls: White latex paint
Ceiling: Sky blue latex paint
Floor: White wool carpet; dhurrie rug
Windows: White-painted louvered shutters
Furnishings: King-sized bed with blue cover; white cane furniture with blue covers; white tables
Lighting: Crystal table lamps with pink shades; polished steel floor lamp
Accessories: Polished steel framed prints; indoor trees in wicker baskets; books; mirror

see Paints pp. 210–11

see Textured Carpets p. 272

Parrot-colored scheme
A regular shaped bedroom can be transformed into an interesting living space by the bold use of striking colors. Here, walls and carpet contain the basic colors which are echoed and re-echoed in the plants, the striped throw and the wicker furniture.

Walls and ceiling: Apricot latex paint
Woodwork and moldings: White semi-gloss paint
Floor: Grass green shag carpet
Windows: White louvered shutters
Furniture: Bamboo bed with apricot and white striped throw and apricot dust ruffle; painted cane furniture; bedside tables
Lighting: Brass table lights; brass floor lamp; brass uplights
Accessories: Plants; books; cushions; mirror; paintings

opposite page:
Restful scheme
By keeping the walls, ceiling and carpet in pale colors an overall feeling of peace and calm is maintained. But stronger colors, the dark edging of the curtains, the chequered upholstery of the cane sofa and chair, echoed again in the striped rug, save the softness of the pastels from becoming too bland. The bed takes its cue from the painted wood construction above it.

Walls and ceiling: Pale yellow latex paint
Floor: White carpet, blue and white striped rug
Windows: White drapes edged dark blue
Furniture: King-sized double bed; white cane sofa and chair; white side tables
Lighting: Dark red pottery table lamps; brass floor lamp; uplights in corners
Soft furnishings: Bedspread; check upholstery and throw; sheets
Accessories: Painted wood construction; prints; magazines; plants

A DARK BEDROOM

Many houses and apartments contain dark, badly lit rooms which seem impossible to decorate with any sort of flair. But, while the light may be poor, the windows are often of a good shape and size and can at least be used as focal points. Rich, warm colors are used in two of these schemes, while the light, fresh colors of the one below make the space seem lighter than it actually is.

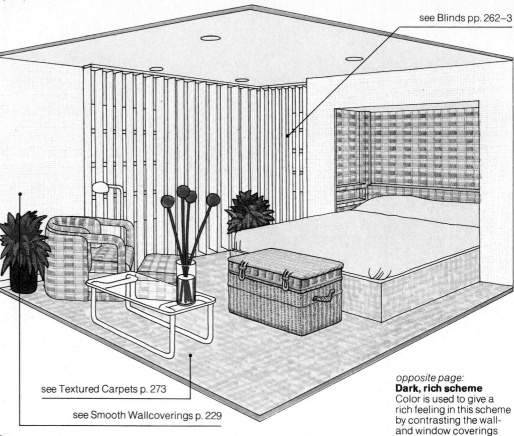

see Blinds pp. 262–3

Neutral, fresh scheme
Neutral shades make a room appear cooler, fresher and lighter. The gamut of milk and cream colors used here covers all different textures and tones: the window louvers are plasticized linen, the walls are wrapped in plain ribbed wool and the carpet is sculpted wool pile. The flowers and ferns stand out with great brilliance against the general pallor of the background. To keep the neutral emphasis without losing the interest of the varying textures, pale gray flannel or camel felt could be used instead of the cream-colored wool wallcovering.

Walls: Creamy wool wallcovering
Floor: Cream sculpted pile carpet
Windows: Plain white louvers in linen finish
Furnishings: Beige and gray checked upholstery on chair and ottoman; bed in cream slubbed raw silk
Furniture: Queen-sized bed; wicker chest; chair and ottoman
Lighting: Downlights; wallwashers; floor lamp
Accessories: Dried flowers; plants; paintings

see Textured Carpets p. 273

see Smooth Wallcoverings p. 229

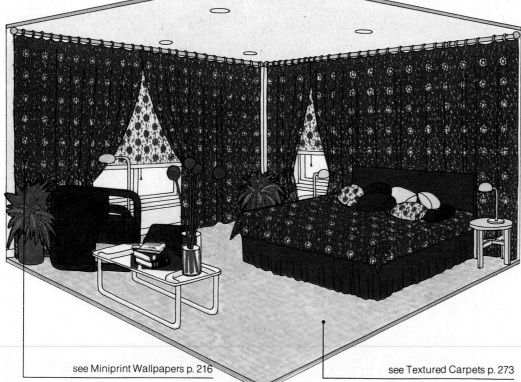

Mid-toned scheme
A soft, feminine feeling is achieved by using shirred fabric for the walls and dust ruffle, and by heaping pillows on the bed. The miniprint fabric hung around the room is caught back over the windows to form its own drapes.

Walls: Cream on dark rose miniprint cotton
Ceiling: Cream latex paint
Woodwork: Cream semi-gloss paint
Floor: Cream sculpted pile carpet
Windows: Printed cotton roller shades
Lighting: Downlights and wallwashers; floor lamp; two bedside lamps
Furniture: Queen-sized bed; two cream bedside tables; chair and ottoman
Soft furnishings: Deep violet heavy Indian cotton on chair and ottoman
Accessories: Pillows, flowers; ferns; books

opposite page:
Dark, rich scheme
Color is used to give a rich feeling in this scheme by contrasting the wall- and window coverings with those of the bed and carpet. An element of crispness is introduced with the vertical lines of the louvered blinds, the carpeted bed platform and the storage alcove. Built-in shelving and lighting around the bed form a canopy and provide a certain feeling of privacy as well as extra storage space. Alternative colors to the blue are plum or forest green.

Walls: Midnight blue latex paint
Ceiling: Off-white latex paint
Woodwork: Midnight blue semi-gloss paint
Floor: Cream sculpted pile carpet
Windows: Dark blue vertical louvers
Lighting: Downlights; wallwashers; floor lamp
Furniture: Queen-sized bed; basket; armchair; ottoman; table
Soft furnishings: Beige and gray checked upholstery on chair and ottoman; cream bedcover
Accessories: Dried flowers; ferns; paintings

see Miniprint Wallpapers p. 216

see Textured Carpets p. 273

A GUEST BEDROOM/STUDY

This is really an ideal bedroom—a good, airy space with an exceptionally high ceiling and long graceful windows: a country room, or a room in a large, old-fashioned apartment block. The scheme opposite, with its lavish use of muslin, is soft and deliberately feminine; another is cool and tailored, with shiny floor tiles and a play of grays; the third has fruit and flowers as its central design motif.

see Large Prints p. 219   see Textured Carpets p. 272

Fruit and flowers scheme

The use of striking fruit-and-flower patterned paper over walls and ceiling turns the space into a garden room as much as a bedroom. Colors in the paper are picked out again in the carpet, the bed cover, the window shades and the pottery base of the lamp on the side table. The wickerwork of the bedtable and the wicker stool add to the overall garden treatment. Additional light for reading and writing is provided by the brass floor lamp.

Walls and ceiling: Fruit and flower design paper
Woodwork: White semi-gloss paint
Floor: Leaf green carpet
Windows: Matchstick blinds (not seen)
Furniture: Divan covered in yellow heavy Indian cotton; bureau bookcase; white side table and cane bedside table; wicker chair
Lighting: Green table lamp; brass floor lamp
Accessories: Plants in wicker baskets; bowl of ceramic fruit; books; cushions; mirror

Cool, tailored scheme

Cool colors and clean lines create a thoroughly disciplined room. The textured suede covering on the walls contrasts nicely with the shiny dark of the floor tiles and the flannel divan cover. The functional low table by the bed, the large floor cushions and the crisp lines of the lacquered table and chair, all contribute to the tailored effect.

Walls: Pale gray suede
Ceiling: Pale gray latex paint
Floor: Large shiny gray tiles
Windows: White shades edged with gray (not seen)
Furniture: Divan covered in gray flannel; bureau bookcase; black lacquered table and chair; white plastic table; large floor cushions
Lighting: Uplights in corners (not seen); lamps on tables
Accessories: Plants; china; chessboard; books; photographs

see Natural Floor Tiles p. 265   see Smooth Wallcoverings p. 231

opposite page:
Deliberately feminine scheme

The overall softness of the effect has been exaggerated here by the extensive use of muslin—for bed and window drape, around the dressing table, and by the massed pillows on the divan bed, which also acts as a couch by day. Full advantage of the ceiling height has been taken by the high bureau bookcase. Rose pink or a soft, hazy print and lace instead of muslin could be used to achieve a similar effect.

Walls: White latex paint
Woodwork: White semi-gloss paint
Floor: Thick-pile white carpet
Windows: White muslin drapes (not seen)
Furniture: Blue divan; mahogany bureau; bookcase; chair and stool; dressing table
Lighting: Tall floor lamp; table lamps
Accessories: All shapes of pillows; flowers; porcelain; prints; china bust

A TINY, LOW BEDROOM

The charm of narrow country cottage rooms with their sloping ceilings sometimes fades when it comes to fitting in furniture. A minimal, uncluttered approach is generally wisest. The scheme opposite imposes focus on the space by treating the window like a painting, the primary color of the frame taken up and echoed elsewhere in the room. In the scheme below, a dimension is added to the room by the creation of a curtained alcove. The third scheme uses matching wallpaper and fabric to visually expand the space.

see Miniprints p. 216

see Matting pp. 278–9

Sprigged wallpaper scheme

By choosing a print small enough to be inconspicuous, yet colorful enough to retain a fresh effect, the wallpaper and matching fabric used here unify the scheme, blurring the awkward edges of the room. The ceiling and the furniture are kept plain, and all-over rush matting on the floor maintains the rural feeling and helps by seeming to visually widen the space.

Walls: Orange, yellow and green sprigged wallpaper
Ceiling: White semi-gloss painted boarding
Woodwork: White semi-gloss paint
Window: Roller shade
Floor: Rush matting
Lighting: Paper lampshade (not seen); bedside lamp
Furniture: White painted iron bed (with spread and pillows to match walls); white chairs and table
Accessories: Flowers; prints; books; plants

Alcoved bed scheme

Even in a confined space, it should be possible to alter the look of a room or create space by simple decorative means. Advantage is taken here of the oddly-shaped roof line by placing the bed under the window and curtaining the areas at either end. The walls and floor are kept plain, with the chairs, table and bedstead painted to match the bedspread and drapes.

Walls and ceiling: White latex paint
Woodwork: White semi-gloss paint
Floor: White deck paint on floorboards; cotton rug
Window: Trellis-patterned cotton shade
Lighting: Paper lampshade (not seen); bedside lamp
Soft furnishings: Green and white trellis-patterned cotton drapes
Furniture: Green-painted iron bed with green and white bedspread; green painted chairs and table
Accessories: Pillows; plants; painting; books

opposite page:
Framed window scheme

In skilful hands, sharply contrasting colors can be used to echo or delineate the shape of a room. By leaving a brightly painted window frame bare, a new focal point is created in this scheme, the walls, ceiling and dark floorboards acting as a foil for the vivid primary color. A skeletal iron bed frame takes up the color of the window, while the simple junk chair and table match the walls. The overall effect admirably suits the shape of the room and other bright colors like yellow or green could be used just as well.

Walls and ceiling: White latex paint
Woodwork: White latex paint; scarlet gloss paint on window frame
Floor: Black stained floor boards; red and orange mat
Window: Left bare to enhance the frame
Lighting: Central light (not seen)
Furniture: Scarlet-painted iron bed with patchwork quilt; white painted table and chair
Accessories: Flowers; mirror; painting

see Fabrics p. 251

see Paints pp. 210–11

A TINY WELL-PROPORTIONED BEDROOM

The height of a room has a considerable effect on the amount of furniture that will look good in the space. You can fit more, for instance, into a well-proportioned, tiny room, like this one in a summer home, than in a similar sized area with a high ceiling. The room also has deep windows overlooking a harbor and nice, battered old pine doors and shutters. The first scheme takes every advantage of these natural assets, while in the second, rather more sophisticated approach, the space is tinged with color and the view outside exaggerated by covering the window embrasures with mirror.

Natural-textured scheme

For maximum coolness in this summer home, the walls, ceiling, woodwork and brick floor have all been left quite plain. Use of color is deliberately subtle, with piping on the linen bedspread picking up both the predominant shades of the area rug and part of the abstract painting which hangs above the old chest. The overall effect is calm and relaxing.

Walls and ceiling: White latex paint
Woodwork: Left natural
Floor: Natural brick with area rug
Windows: Wooden shutters
Lighting: Lamps at night
Furniture: Bed with white linen cover piped with blue; small round table; chest; chair
Accessories: Abstract painting; ivory and china boxes; plant; books; earthenware pots

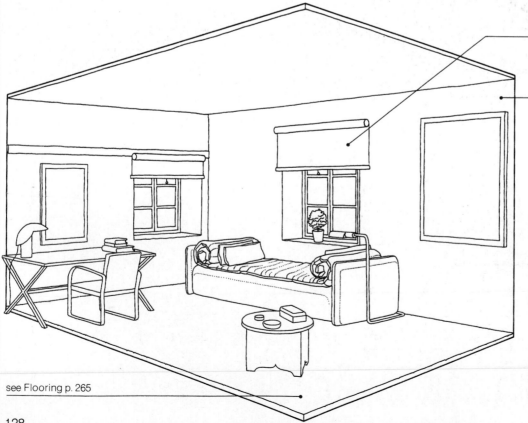

see Shades p. 263

see Paints pp. 210–11

see Flooring p. 265

Updated scheme

Natural assets should always be exploited. In this warmer scheme, the deep window recesses are covered with mirror to reflect other aspects of the harbor view. The walls and ceiling are tinged a sunset color, while the glass and steel of the mirror and table (which acts as both desk and dressing table) give the room a more modern, streamlined look.

Walls and ceiling: Pale pinky-apricot latex paint; window recesses lined with mirrors

Floor: Natural brick
Woodwork: White semi-gloss paint
Window: White roller shade
Lighting: Floor light at end of bed; table light
Furniture: Bed with apricot rolled mattress; glass and steel table; cane chair; white painted round table
Accessories: Plain steel-framed mirror; plant; books; ivory and china boxes; earthenware pots

A TINY, HIGH-CEILING'D BEDROOM

Small rooms with high ceilings may at first seem too cramped or badly proportioned either for any visual appeal or for real comfort. But even a tiny room can be given unexpected distinction by an interesting bed treatment to provide the focal point, plus minimal furniture and a good use of color. The first scheme centers on the cheerful colors of a pretty stenciled bed set against a background of quiet wallpaper. In the second, pale fabric is used lavishly all around the room, creating a softer, but no less interesting feel.

Stenciled bed scheme
An old bed was stripped, waxed and stenciled to provide the focal point of this simple room. Patchwork quilt, towels, sheets and rug all follow the colors of the stenciled flowers, and spotted wallpaper with a border at picture rail level helps to lower the ceiling height. The wicker hampers under and at the foot of the bed are good examples of improvised storage: an excellent solution in such a small space.

Walls: Green and white spotted wallpaper with coordinating border
Ceiling and woodwork: Cream latex paint
Floor: Striped cotton rug
Window: White roller shade
Lighting: Bedside lamp; ceiling lamp (not seen)
Furniture: Wooden bed with stenciled flower pattern; bedside cupboard
Accessories: Rose sheets and pillow cases; towels; patchwork quilt; embroidered wool pillows; hampers; plants

see Shades p. 263

see Paints pp. 210–11

see Sheers p. 260

Fabric scheme
To soften the edges of the room and distract the eye from the high ceiling, the walls here are hung with cheesecloth (the material hangs from a wire all round the room just below the ceiling). Floor and ceiling are kept pale to match, with pockets of color provided by the bedcoverings, the plants and the basket of mixed fruit.

Walls: White shirred cheesecloth
Ceiling and woodwork: White latex paint

Floor: White deck paint with small white rugs
Window: Pale blue roller shade
Furniture: Queen-size divan bed; wicker laundry baskets
Lighting: White bedside lamps
Accessories: Blue and white dust ruffle and tucked in cover with matching bolster and pillows; extra pillows; plants in pots; basket of fruit; books

A TEENAGER'S BEDROOM

Most teenage rooms need to have sleeping, sitting and studying space, and an area for listening to music and entertaining friends. There must, therefore, be some subtle, or not so subtle divisioning, so the space does not look too cluttered, and some attempt at soundproofing so that noise does not permeate the house. The scheme opposite is dominated by the supergraphics in the living part of the room; in another, the division is intensified by textural contrasts and crisp lines, and in the third, the paper in the sleeping part is contrasted with a solid color to break up the areas.

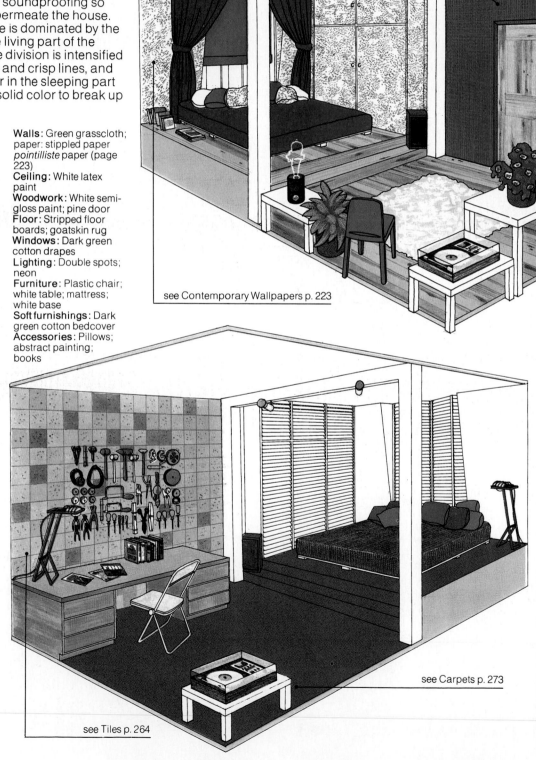

see Textured Wallcoverings p. 229

see Contemporary Wallpapers p. 223

see Tiles p. 264

see Carpets p. 273

Color break-up scheme
Plain, dark-colored grasscloth walls at the sitting end of the room give a study-like feeling which breaks up into a cloud of *pointilliste* design in the sleeping area. Plain curtains are looped back on either side of the window and the same fabric is used to cover the mattress. Closets for clothes on either side of the sleeping area have been cleverly disguised in the *pointilliste* wallpaper.

Walls: Green grasscloth; paper: stippled paper *pointilliste* paper (page 223)
Ceiling: White latex paint
Woodwork: White semigloss paint; pine door
Floor: Stripped floor boards; goatskin rug
Windows: Dark green cotton drapes
Lighting: Double spots; neon
Furniture: Plastic chair; white table; mattress; white base
Soft furnishings: Dark green cotton bedcover
Accessories: Pillows; abstract painting; books

Practical scheme
Tough, yet striking – the cork-tiled walls in the living end of the room act as an oversized pinboard for work, collections of tools and posters. A long desk top with drawers has been built along the wall opposite the door, and storage in the sleeping area is well concealed behind painted louvered doors.

Walls: Cork tiles; white louvered doors
Ceiling: White latex paint
Woodwork: White semigloss paint; stripped pine door (not seen)
Floor: Tobacco brown woolcord
Lighting: Red desk lamp; double spots; table light
Furniture: Long desk top on drawers; plastic chair; mattress covered in brown corduroy
Accessories: Pillows; tools; books; magazines

opposite page:
Supergraphics scheme
Rainbow-like supergraphics dominate this scheme. The vivid colors are taken up in the rug and curtains which hide clothes racks, and also serve to soften the sleeping end of the room. Pillows piled on the mattress repeat the coloring, but also turn the bed into a loungeing area by day. Bright-colored chairs and a white desk complete the build-up of color.

Walls and ceiling: White latex paint
Woodwork: White semigloss paint; stripped pine
Floor: Off-white ribbed wool and nylon carpet
Windows: Pink cotton Roman shades
Lighting: Neon; spotlights with filters
Furniture: Mattress covered in striped cotton cover on wooden base; plastic chair and table
Soft furnishings: Pink, lilac, apricot, blue and violet-striped rug; pink, green and white curtains
Accessories: Plants; pillows; hi-fi; guitar

A CHILD'S BEDROOM

Small children's rooms need both practical furniture that will see them through several stages of development and an adaptable treatment to suit their developing tastes. Color is among the most important elements to consider, and interesting schemes can easily be achieved with a paintbrush, paper cut-outs, and a little imagination. For younger children, vividly colored, yet robust furniture combined with bold decoration is ideal. The first two schemes are based on fantasy and use bright colors to great effect. The scheme below, with bunk beds, is suitable for slightly older children.

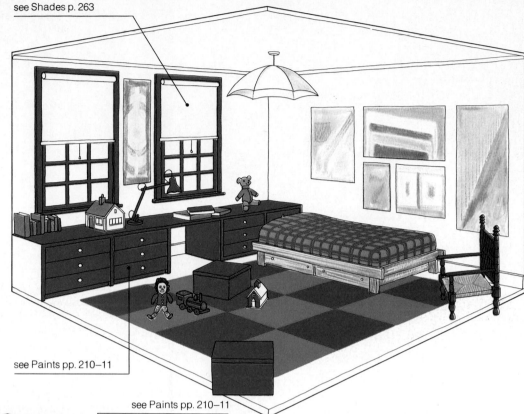

see Shades p. 263

see Paints pp. 210–11

see Paints pp. 210–11

Games board scheme
Deck paint can be used with care to quickly and cheaply transform any smooth-surfaced boards, linoleum or vinyl. The floor dominates in this scheme, the bold colors of its squares repeated in the bed cover and furnishings as well as the window frames.
Walls and ceiling: White semi-gloss paint
Woodwork: Red and white gloss paint

Floor: Red and yellow deck paint; white border
Windows: Plain white shades
Lighting: White umbrella shade; red articulated desk lamp
Furniture: Red painted shelves and top; red painted wooden chair; red cubes; wooden bed
Accessories: Yellow and red bed rug; toys; books; posters

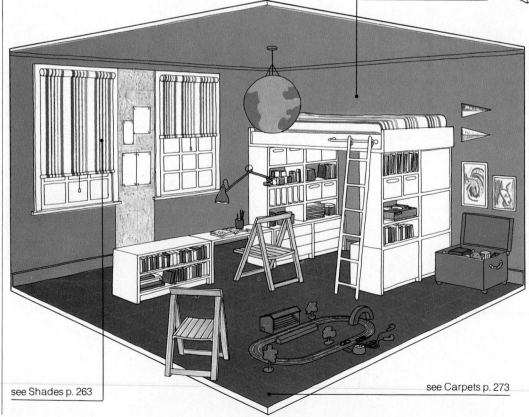

see Shades p. 263

see Carpets p. 273

Bunk bed scheme
Bunk beds are ideal for putting up slightly older children's friends. They are used here to form the basis of a tough, but light-hearted treatment in which bright colors still play a key role. The stripes of the window shades are repeated in the bed coverings and again matched in the carpet tiles on the floor and in the colors of the walls and woodwork.

Walls and ceiling: Apricot semi-gloss paint
Woodwork: White and apricot semi-gloss paint
Floor: Blue carpet tiles
Windows: Striped cotton shades
Lighting: Green clip-on articulated desk lamps; paper shade
Furniture: White bunk beds, desk and shelving system; folding chairs
Accessories: Cork pin board; paints; jars; books; bedspreads; toys; posters

opposite page:
Night and day scheme
In a largish children's room the imagination can be given quite a free hand. Here, a night sky with a large paper shade like the moon makes full use of extensive ceiling space. The cloudscapes adorning the window shades continue the sky treatment, while the vivid primary colors of the chair match the brightly decorative paper cutouts on the wall.

Walls and woodwork: White semi-gloss paint
Ceiling: Blue and white starry paper
Windows: Blue and white cloudscape shades
Floor: Beige haircord carpet
Lighting: White paper shade
Furniture: Wood-framed divan bed; yellow, red and blue striped painted chair; small cane chair; pine bedside table with drawers; painted table
Accessories: Blue and red bed rug; rocking horse; plants; false palm tree; paper kites and cutouts; aquarium

BATHROOMS

Clearly, the prime purpose of a bathroom is to be able to wash, bathe and shower in comfort. But, whether this means the room should be clean-looking and functional or luxurious and relaxing, depends on personal taste. A simple, well-lit, clean-cut tiled or wood-lined space suits one sort of person; a carpeted lounging space, possibly an extension of a bedroom, is the luxurious ideal of another.

Planning a bathroom
If you are starting to plan a bathroom from scratch, or going to make major changes in an existing room, the layout needs a good deal of thought, especially if the room is to be shared by several people of different generations. Given adequate space, you will probably want to include a bathtub and/or shower; a washbasin; a toilet, if it is not separate; a bidet; a well-lit mirror; storage; at least one chair or stool; a towel rail, preferably heated; practical flooring, such as tiling or water-resistant carpet; and a generous splash back area. You may well also plan to use the bathroom for laundry, in which case a space for a washing machine should also be considered.

Whatever the arrangement of equipment chosen, you should bear in mind the occasions when more than one person wants to use the bathroom at the same time. If there is space, there is no reason why you should not put in two basins (if they are side by side, they can share a large mirror) and two closets or cabinets.

Bathtubs come in many sizes and shapes, so it is worth shopping around to find the one that suits you best. Sunken baths can look dramatic and have a luxurious feel, but they are relatively expensive to install. Whirlpool baths are also becoming increasingly popular. They, too, are available in a wide number of sizes, shapes and colors and give the body a soothing massage with underwater jets. A free-standing tub looks good if the bathroom is really large. It could either be installed in the middle of the room or perhaps raised up on a platform. Or it could be centered against one wall with closets or shelves built either side, an arrangement which allows for interesting treatments with shower curtains.

Improving an existing bathroom
Even if you cannot afford new plumbing or radical rearrangement of fittings, it is quite possible to transform the smallest, dreariest, most badly planned space into a cheerful place of relaxation, for it is usually fairly easy to treat a bathroom cosmetically, that is, by purely decorative means.

On the simplest level, appropriately colored towels and shower curtains can improve a room that is totally tiled or laminated in an uninspiring color. A small, all-white bathroom can be given a totally different feel by massing it with plants, while a dark room can be enlivened with a contrasting trim and brightly colored towels. The trick is to take the base color and make it look more vibrant by spicing it up with sharper accent colors. Pastel-colored fittings are enlivened by bolder, richer tones of the base tone for towels, bathmats or facecloths. Tiles can be given a new look by painting them a more pleasing shade with a special tile or deck paint. Plain walls (even plastic-laminated ones) can be painted a warm, dark color and massed with prints, photographs, paintings, or china.

To make an immediate transformation, waterproof wallpaper can be used on ceilings, pasted on bathtub panels, and taken over flush doors and secured by beading (see The Sample Book pages 224 to 225 for ideas). Paper that is not already waterproofed can be over-painted with a clear lacquer or varnish. To make a space seem more luxurious, carpet or wood paneling is ideal for covering the side of bathtub or under-basin closets.

Storage in the bathroom
Open shelves can be stashed with neatly folded towels in good colors for decorative effect, or filled with collectibles for interest. Bathrooms used by children should definitely have extra storage space squeezed in, wherever practical, or the room will be in perpetual disorder. In a largish area, washbasins look better and are more practical surrounded by a vanity unit with storage space underneath.

Lighting in the bathroom
While small rooms probably only need a central ceiling light, downlights are effective in bathrooms, whatever the size, and one over the bath is worth considering. Good lighting for shaving and make-up is best provided by light at the sides or around the mirror rather than just above, but it should be backed by good general light. Additional information about lighting is given on pages 19 to 24 and pages 310 to 312.

Aim to avoid the problems caused by condensation by steady warmth and good ventilation. If a heated towel rail or radiator does not seem enough to heat the room, extra warmth can be provided with a wall-mounted fan or infrared heater.

The final touches
If your bathroom is overlooked, there are a number of alternatives to ugly, obscured glass in windows. Tightly-stretched voile screens suspended between narrow rods or wires can be fitted to the frame, or roller shades, or venetian blinds can be used to filter light and block out the view. Another alternative would be to fix glass shelves across the window frame and fill them with plants, or plants interspersed with collections of bric à brac. The walls can be massed with pictures and prints, collected absurdities or words of advice, for humor in decoration adds that extra levity that makes a room memorable. Long windows in a bathroom can be hung with drapes or given shades and full-length drapery. Use a practical fiber like toweling if the windows are near the tub or shower, ordinary cotton or some lightweight material, if not. Over the following 18 pages we give a variety of different schemes which can be adapted for bathrooms of all types and sizes to give some idea of the potential for decorating these spaces. None of these involve structural alterations or vast expense, but all succeed in modifying or transforming the existing rooms to a greater or lesser extent.

While these bathrooms are very different in concept, they illustrate well the various approaches to bathroom design. The first is cosmetic, its effect achieved with clever decoration; the second, with its new and varied equipment, was carefully planned from the begining, and the third, with its marble floor and sunken bath, is luxuriously sybaritic.

Left:
Dark, shiny walls and a matching bath panel are combined with the softness of creamy *broderie anglaise* in this two-color bathroom. The overall effect is pleasantly romantic.

Below left:
A useful panel inset with shelves for towels and wash cloths acts as dividing line between bathtub, bidet and toilet in this beautifully planned room with its separate areas for washing, exercising and resting.

Below right:
This sunken bath, which is more for relaxing in than washing, is inset into dark marble tiles. Similarly-toned ceramic tiles for walls are allied to paler surfaces for built-in closets and shades. A super-sized *Ficus* tree and mood lighting make for a softly romantic feel.

A SQUARE BATHROOM

see Shades p. 263

It is usually possible to decorate smallish bathrooms like this one without resort to structural alteration or enormous expense. In the scheme opposite, for example, indoor plants repeat the color of the carpet, and the collection of pictures echoes the lines of the bare window panes; the overall effect is simple and restful, yet effective. In the co-ordinated scheme to the right, patterned walls are teamed with a bright carpet and matching window shade. The brightly colored mosaic which dominates the scheme below is used to add a touch of grandeur to the small space.

see Plain carpets p. 274

Dark-painted scheme
To enrich this small space the walls are given the color and gloss of shiny egg-plants and teamed with a peppy carpet which continues up the side of the tub. The roller shade at the window matches the floor.

Walls: Eggplant semi-gloss paint plus a coat of flat varnish
Ceiling: White latex paint
Woodwork: Eggplant gloss paint

Floor: Red wool and nylon carpet, continued up the side of the tub
Windows: Red cotton Roman shade
Lighting: Recessed downlights
Furniture: Mahogany whatnot
Fittings: White bathtub, WC and basin
Accessories: Purple and red towels; cranberry-colored glass objects; plants; etchings; mirror

see Wallpapers p. 217

see Tiles p. 239

Wallpapered scheme
To give the room additional distinction, walls and ceiling are covered in a richly patterned wallpaper and this is teamed with a companion design which covers the sides of the tub and the basin.

Walls and ceiling: Dark blue, gray and white wallpaper plus a coat of semi-gloss varnish
Woodwork: White semi-gloss paint
Floor: Dark blue mosaic floor tiles
Bathtub and basin panels: Blue and white basket-weave paper plus a coat of semi-gloss varnish
Windows: Roman shade
Lighting: Recessed downlights
Fittings: White bathtub, built-in basin and WC
Furniture: White-painted cane stool
Accessories: Towels; plants; plates on wall; mirror over sink

opposite page:
Green and white scheme
Everything is kept very simple and clean-cut here and the overall effect is both pleasing and restful. The towels, the etchings, the plants and the shapes of the window panes each stand out in their own right, yet are also components of a collection of interesting objects

Walls and ceiling: White semi-gloss paint
Floor: Green wool and nylon carpet
Windows: Left bare
Lighting: Light above mirror (not seen)
Furniture: Mahogany whatnot
Fittings: White bathtub and basin with green marbled laminate top; WC
Accessories: Green towels; mirror; etchings; plants; shells

A LONG BATHROOM

A narrow room with a window at one end may tend to look tunnel-like – especially a bathroom, where equipment is standard and necessarily difficult to move around – unless decorated expressly to avoid this pitfall. In the room opposite, mirrors and striking tiles are used to visually expand the width. Another scheme uses geometric wallpaper and coordinating carpet, again to seemingly push out the walls as much as possible. And in the third, the eye is distracted from the general feeling of narrowness by edging plain paint with a border and adding a collection of pictures.

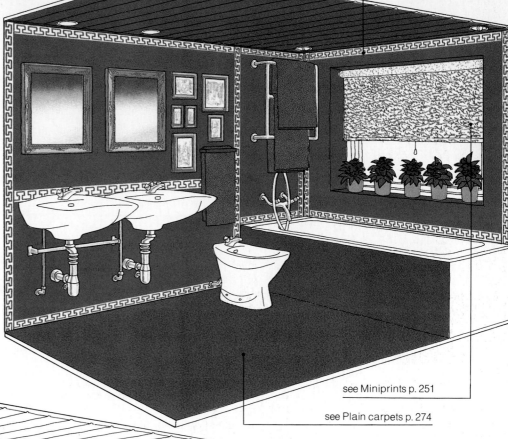

see Borders p. 213

see Miniprints p. 251

see Plain carpets p. 274

Painted scheme
The walls here are covered in prints, drawings and paintings to provide constant visual interest – thereby distracting the eye from the room's real shape. A neat wallpaper border and matching paint give a paneled look to the space and act as a good background for the art.

Walls and ceiling: Browny-red semi-gloss paint, Greek key border

Floor and bathtub panel: Red carpet
Window: Browny-red and white printed cotton shade
Lighting: Recessed downlights over mirrors; wallwashers
Bathtub, basins and bidet: White
Accessories: Gilt-framed mirrors; towels; paintings, drawings and prints; plants

see Geometric wallpapers pp. 214–15

opposite page:
Clear-cut tiled scheme
Large-scale tiles on the floor, the side of the bathtub and used as a border below the ceiling give a clean-cut, rather nautical look to what could be rather a forbidding space. The large, centrally-placed mirror apparently adds to the width, as do the pale walls and ceiling.

Geometric wallpaper scheme
This room is made to appear wider by the use of patterned wallpaper, which subtly alters the perspective. Carpet, towels and the frames of the mirrors are all chosen to match the paper, while the bathtub is boarded like the ceiling.

Walls: Washable red and white squared paper with a run of white tiles above basins and tub
Ceiling: Tongue-and-groove boarding painted white gloss
Floor: Red woolcord carpet
Bathtub panel: Tongue-and-groove boarding painted with white gloss
Window: White cotton shade with red border
Lighting: Recessed downlights
Bathtub, basins and bidet: White
Accessories: Red plastic-framed mirrors; towels; ceramics; plant

Walls: Large white ceramic tiles with blue and white tiled border
Ceiling: Tongue-and-groove boarding painted with white gloss
Floor and bathtub panel: Blue and white ceramic tiles
Window: White cotton shade
Lighting: White glass globes above small mirrors; built-in ceramic side lights beside big mirror
Bathtub, basins and bidet: White
Accessories: White, plastic-framed mirrors; towels; baskets; plant

see Textured carpets p. 273

see Paneling p. 234

A BATHROOM/DRESSING ROOM

The main problem with this practical bathroom cum dressing area was how to fit in plenty of storage while still keeping a sense of light and space. In the scheme opposite, in which the colors were kept fresh and light, the solution was a full-length closet one end of the bathtub. A more tailored, masculine scheme has matching closets both ends of the bath, while the scheme below is altogether softer and more feminine in effect, with its looped-back drapes emphasized by the mirrored wall at the back of the tub.

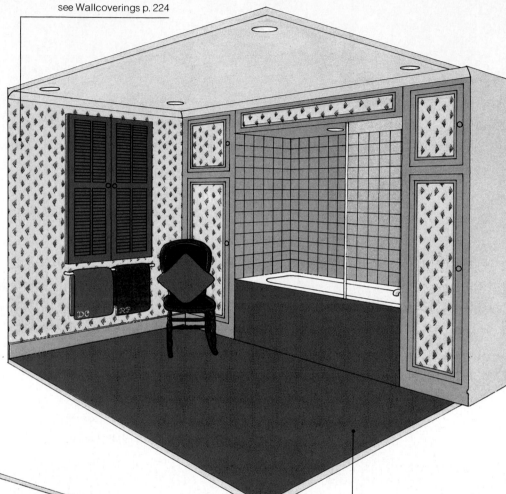

see Wallcoverings p. 224

see Carpets p. 274

see Fabrics p. 256

Tailored scheme
Distinctive vinyl wallpaper used in conjunction with toning carpet, tiles and painted shutters produces a tailored, rich-looking scheme. A floor-to-ceiling closet is built the window end of the tub to match the other one. A glass screen and tiled wall provide for a shower, and carpet is taken up the bathtub panel to give a slightly luxurious feeling.

Walls: Gray, red and blue crayon design vinyl wallpaper
Ceiling: Pale gray latex paint
Woodwork: Plain gray low luster paint
Floor: Dark red wool and nylon carpet
Window: Dark red gloss-painted shutters
Lighting: Recessed downlights
Accessories: Red and blue towels; red towelling throw cushion

see Carpets p. 274

Yellow and pink scheme
A soft, airy look is achieved here by the extensive use of pale colors and billowy fabric. An interesting color combination was built up with the fabric of the bath drapes also used for the window shade. For maximum impact, the wall at the back of the tub is entirely mirrored

Walls and ceiling: Off-white latex paint; mirror over tub

Woodwork: Off-white gloss paint with pink trim
Floor: Yellow ocher nylon carpet
Window: Yellow ocher, pink and off-white cotton roller shade
Lighting: Recessed downlights over bath and basin
Furniture: Small upholstered chair in pink towelling
Accessories: Bathtub drapes in fabric to match the window shade, lined with plastic; pink and yellow towels

opposite page:
Airy, comfortable scheme
Paneled bathtub, basin and closet give a certain solidity as well as practical storage in this light and airy scheme. A large mirror, plants, lace drapes and the pale wood rocking chair all add to the fresh and comfortable look.

Walls and ceiling: Off-white latex paint
Woodwork: Off-white semi-gloss paint
Floor: White wool and nylon shag carpet
Window: Long lace under-drapes; green and white cotton over drapes
Lighting: Downlights over bathtub and basin
Furniture: Stripped pale wood rocking chair
Accessories: Plants; large photograph; throw cushions; bathing accessories

A LARGE, PERIOD BATHROOM

Most turn-of-the-century bathrooms were really converted bedrooms where space invariably came second to the novelty of a working bath with running water. Today, the reverse is true and generous space is more of a luxury than the actual equipment. One design uses the sort of unpretentious furnishings that suit the young and impecunious; the second uses Edwardian colors and mahogany for an altogether more grand effect, while in the third scheme, the design on the bath is used as a base on which to build up the background colors.

see Paints pp. 210–11

Mahogany scheme
The effect here is rich and grand. Yet the luxurious mahogany treatment of the bath and basin paneling is inexpensively produced with stained blockboard. The handsome rug and chair and the primitive painting over the fireplace add just the right finishing touch.

Walls: Crimson semi-gloss paint with a coat of semi-gloss varnish; mirrors above basin; white tiles
Ceiling: White latex paint

Woodwork: Mahogany stain
Floor: Dark crimson nylon carpet; oriental rug
Window: Cotton pull-up shade
Lighting: Bulbs under valance
Furniture: Mahogany-surrounded bath and basins; 19th century chair
Accessories: Plants; toiletries; towels; towel rails; primitive painting

see Carpets p. 274

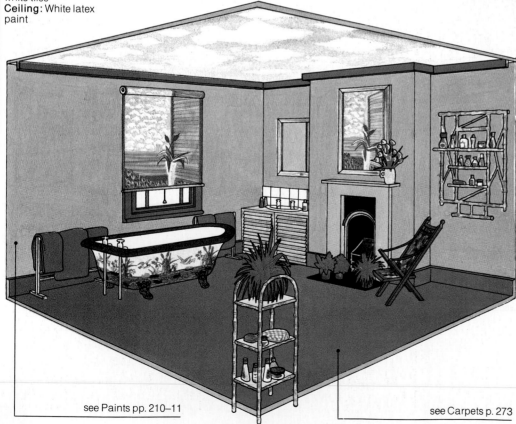

see Paints pp. 210–11

see Carpets p. 273

Painted bath scheme
One way of adding a personal touch is to improvise a design on one surface and enlarge upon it in the rest of the room. Here the bulrush motif on the old bath is taken up in the custom-painted shade at the window, and the replica of this shade in the painting over the fire-place provides an additional light-hearted flourish. The rest of the scheme follows suit: walls match the sand, ceiling matches the sky, and the carpet repeats the color of the leaves.

Walls: Ocher semi-gloss paint
Ceiling: Blue and white latex paint
Floor: Leaf green wool-cord carpet
Window: Painted roll-up shade
Lighting: Bulbs under valance
Furniture: Cast-iron painted bath; basin; bentwood chair
Accessories: Painting; mirror; towel rails; towels; plants; toiletries

opposite page:
Basic scheme
It is perfectly feasible to furnish an area over a period of time, so lack of funds need never be a real obstacle when it comes to decorating a room. This gentle scheme is based on individual components which cost very little — an old cast-iron bathtub, a Victorian jug and bowl, a junk shop towel stand, a bentwood chair. All help create an impression of space and ease while leaving plenty of room over the years to add shades and floor-coverings, or details like pictures and plants.

Walls and ceiling: White latex paint
Woodwork: White semi-gloss paint
Floor: Polished boards; area rug
Window: Natural matchstick blinds
Lighting: Pendant light
Furniture: Cast-iron bath; pine towel stand; washbasin stand; bentwood chair
Accessories: Bowl and jug; mirror; bath rack; flowers; plants; towels; toiletries

A SMALL SQUARE BATHROOM

Bathrooms in apartment buildings are usually far from large, and very little can be done to alter their structure without incurring enormous expense. The only way to improve these spaces is cosmetically – in general, there is little scope for change except in the ceiling and untiled areas of wall. This scheme uses coordinating paper and border to offset the hygienic effect of the white tiles. In the one below tongue-and-groove boarding and tiles create a neat, efficient space.

Simple papered scheme
Patterned paper and a coordinating border to edge the ceiling are used here both to temper the hygienic effect of the tiles and to define the shape of the room. Matching plain towels continue the two-color scheme. The same effect could be produced by using fresh green and white, or rose pink and white, to soften what is a basically utilitarian look.

Walls: White tiles; blue and white paper
Ceiling: White latex paint with coordinating border paper
Floor: White tiles
Window: White shade (not seen)
Lighting: Strip over mirror
Bathtub and basin: White
Accessories: Blue towels; mirrored cabinet; white shower curtain; plant; flowers

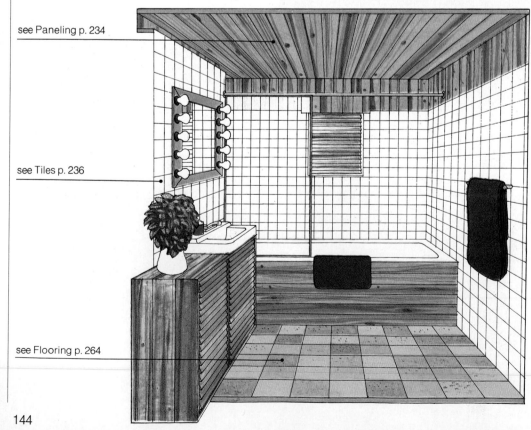

see Paneling p. 234

see Tiles p. 236

see Flooring p. 264

Wood scheme
To make a warm-looking bathroom, tongue-and-groove boarding, coated with polyurethane for protection, has been used over the ceiling, along the bathtub panel and the top of the walls (the rest are tiled). The wood shutters at the window, cork tiles on the floor, the glass screen and the boarded vanity unit which incorporates the basin all combine to create a neat, tailored scheme. Deep-dye towels are used to add a dash of color. This sort of scheme is, of course, immensely practical and therefore lends itself well to children, teenagers and any other rather messy bathers.

Walls: White tiles, tongue-and-groove boarding at top
Ceiling: Tongue-and-groove boarding with polyurethane seal
Side of bath: Tongue-and-groove boarding
Floor: Cork tiles
Window: Wood shutters
Lighting: Lights around mirror; central light (not seen)
Bathtub and basin: White
Other fittings: Vanity unit; louvered doors; glass shower screen
Accessories: Red and tobacco-colored towels; cream shower curtain; mirror; plants

144

A SMALL RECTANGULAR BATHROOM

This room is very similar in size and shape to the bathroom opposite. The strength of these small spaces is that they are usually inexpensive to redecorate: a little of anything goes a long way; their weakness is that they can easily look dreary and bedraggled. With its simple ingredients and minimal color, the first scheme manages to make the room look both gentle and glamorous; the one below expands the space into a kind of summer terrace, with clever use of mirror, wood and plants.

Milky white scheme
These gentle tones allow even the softest colors to stand out with great intensity, with the added advantage of making the space seem a good deal larger than it actually is. Walls, woodwork, fabric, chair and floor are all the same shade, softened by the lace drapes which frame the bathtub.

Walls: Milky-white ceramic tiles
Ceiling: Milky-white semi-gloss paint

Woodwork: Milky-white semi-gloss paint
Floor: Milky-white deck paint; striped rug
Window: Milky-white painted shutters
Lighting: Semi-recessed spotlight over bath; light around mirror (not seen)
Furniture: Milky-white painted chair
Bathtub and basin: White
Accessories: Lace drapes; towels; flowers; plants

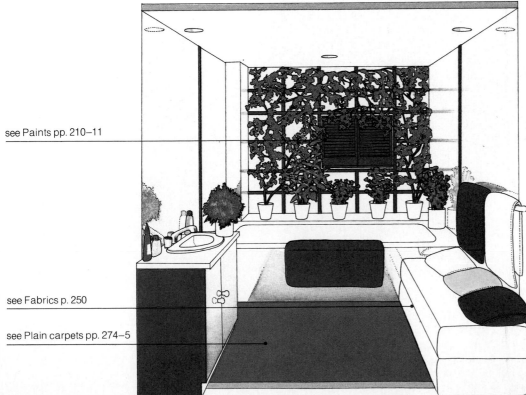

see Paints pp. 210–11

see Fabrics p. 250

see Plain carpets pp. 274–5

Mirror and plant scheme
Sheets of mirror glass cover the walls, bathtub panel and the front of the basin here, visually expanding the space as well as making it appear lighter. The green carpet underlines the mixture of plants, and the painted wood strips and shutters help the feeling of spaciousness, by giving a sense of depth to the area, and seemingly lengthening the perspective. The horizontal lines of the towelling-covered banquette under the towel rail and the gradation of colors in the throw cushions also help to seemingly extend the length of the space. Lighting is provided by spotlights recessed into the ceiling.

Walls: Mirror glass separated by strips of green-painted wood
Ceiling: White semi-gloss paint
Bathtub and basin panels: Mirror glass
Woodwork: White or green semi-gloss paint
Floor: Grass green nylon carpet
Window: Green-painted wood shutters
Lighting: Semi-recessed spotlights over bathtub and basin
Furniture: White toweling-covered banquette
Bathtub and basin: White
Accessories: Towels; plants; cushions

A BATHROOM UNDER A ROOF

Bathrooms often have to be fitted into the most awkward spaces and this cramped room with its sloping ceiling is no exception. The general feeling of pokiness is disguised well in each of the three schemes. One is a strong, two-color scheme which uses tongue-and-groove boarding for the panel of the tub as well as most of the walls; another fills the room with color by painting bold rainbow stripes on the walls, ceiling and bathtub. The third uses mylar wallpaper to make the space seem larger as well as to give it a certain dash of character.

Rainbow scheme
To fill the small space with unchanging light and color, the boards which cover most of the walls and surfaces in this room are painted in brilliant stripes.

Walls, ceiling and panel of tub: Stripes of turquoise, yellow, orange, pink, purple and blue semi-gloss paint; white semi-gloss behind tub
Other woodwork: Blue semi-gloss paint
Floor: Purple nylon carpet
Lighting: Center and mirror lights (not seen)
Window: White cotton roller shade
Bathtub and WC: White and creamy white
Accessories: White shower curtain; plants; toiletries

see Blinds p. 262

see Wallpapers p. 223

see Paints pp. 210–11

see Plain carpets pp. 274–5

Geometric scheme
A boldly-patterned silver mylar paper gives a feeling of much greater depth to this room. The reflective background of the paper is underscored by the mirrored panel of the tub and by the aluminum louvers which enclose the shower, while the carpet repeats one of the colors to give the scheme some solidity.

Walls, closet and ceiling: Green and yellow geometric silver mylar paper
Floor: Grass green nylon carpet
Window: Aluminum louvered blinds
Lighting: Center and mirror lights (not seen)
Bathtub and WC: White and creamy white; bathtub panel covered in mirror
Accessories: Aluminum louvered shower screen; toiletries; plant

opposite page:
Red and white boarded scheme
The regular lines of the wood, the diagonals of the shower curtain, and the darker wall behind the bath, all combine to give the illusion of a large area.

Walls and ceiling: White semi-gloss-painted tongue-and-groove boarding; red semi-gloss paint
Other woodwork: White semi-gloss paint
Floor: Red nylon carpet
Window: White cotton roller shade
Lighting: Center light and light over mirror (not seen)
Bathtub and WC: White and creamy white
Accessories: Striped shower curtain; plants; toiletries

A BATHROOM ON A LANDING

In old apartment blocks and buildings, bathrooms are often fitted in wherever they can be squeezed. Here, there is just room to fit a bathtub under the fine arched window with not a millimeter to spare. The scheme opposite achieves a casual elegance, while the paneled scheme, right, takes advantage of the window with a dramatic, plant-strung background for the tub. Painted glass is substituted for plain in the one below, to make the most of the window without loss of privacy.

see Stenciling p. 242

see Paints pp. 210–11

Wood paneled scheme
Pots of plants on the plate glass shelves stretching across the window obviate the need for a more conventional window covering. Extensive wood paneling on walls and ceiling and a tiled floor provide practical, hard-wear surfaces for this bathroom.

Walls and ceiling: Tongue-and-groove polyurethane-sealed wood
Woodwork: Stripped and waxed wood
Floor: Terracotta tiles
Window: Plate glass shelves
Lighting: Downlight above bathtub
Accessories: Towels; plants; bathing accessories

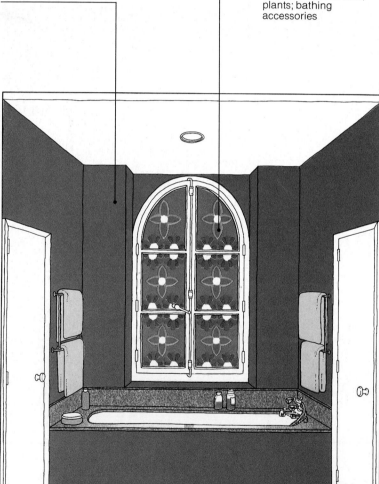

see Wood paneling p. 234

see Tiles p. 265

opposite page:
Casually elegant scheme
Vertical louvered blinds covering the arched window manage to make the elegant formality of the proportions seem almost throw-away. The warm coloring of walls and bathtub panel, added to the interesting tint of the marble, further the air of casual, rather dégagé elegance.

Purple and red scheme
Painted glass both emphasizes this window and provides privacy without hiding the graceful arch. The papered walls tie in with the carpet, which is continued up the side of the tub for extra elegance.

Walls: Plum-colored paper with a coat of clear varnish

Ceiling: White latex paint
Woodwork: White semi-gloss paint
Floor: Damson nylon carpet
Window: Purple, red and blue painted glass (see page 205 for technique using stencils)
Lighting: Downlight above bathtub
Accessories: Towels; bathing accessories

Walls: Sunset pink low luster paint
Ceiling: White latex paint
Woodwork: White low luster paint; sunset pink bath panel
Bathtub surround and floor: Purplish marble
Window: White vertical louver blinds
Lighting: Downlight over bath (not seen)
Accessories: White towels; prints; bathing accessories

A TILED BATHROOM

Even if the walls of a bathroom are extensively tiled, there are still ways of altering the look of the space. Quite reasonable changes can be effected by adding or changing the casing of the tub or basin; by replacing the floor covering and re-coloring any tiled areas with special paint; and by choosing different accessories. These three schemes illustrate how, despite the apparent lack of scope, comparatively inexpensive alterations can completely change the look of a bathroom.

Carpeted scheme
To soften the look of the space, the floor carpet is also used to cover the panels of the basin and bathtub.
Walls and ceiling: Beige ceramic tiles; beige semi-gloss paint
Floor: Gray cord carpet
Bathtub and basin panels and mirror recess: Gray carpet
Window: White and yellow checked shade
Lighting: Recessed ceiling light; light over top of basin behind valance
Accessories: Shower curtain; plants; towels; covered stool

see Shades p. 263

see Miniprints p. 251

see Tiles p. 236

see Carpets 274–5

see Laminates p. 232

Delphinium and beige scheme
To change the look of a bathroom without too much upheaval and expense, the bathtub and basin are paneled in with laminate that contrasts with the floor and wall tiles. Coordinating fabric is used for window shade and shower curtains. Given this treatment, the basic tiles take on an entirely new look. Chestnut could be used instead of delphinium.

Walls and ceiling: Beige ceramic tiles and semi-gloss paint
Floor: Beige ceramic tiles
Bath and basin panels: Delphinium laminate
Window shade and shower curtains: Delphinium and white printed cotton
Lighting: Recessed ceiling light; lights round basin
Bath and basin: Primrose yellow
Accessories: Shower screen; towel rail; towels

opposite page:
All-over tiled scheme
Low-key colors in a bathroom can look warm and inviting and certainly need never be dull. The subtle monotone tiling of most of this bathroom is gently pepped up by the livelier color of the bathtub, basin and shade.

Walls and ceiling: Beige ceramic tiles; beige semi-gloss paint
Floor: Beige ceramic floor tiles
Window: Rattan shade
Lighting: Recessed ceiling light; light over basin
Bath and basin: Primrose yellow
Accessories: Shower curtain; plants; stool; towels

A SHOWER ROOM

For those who prefer a straightforward shower, one major factor governs the choice of decoration: the space must be well waterproofed if the surrounding areas are to remain reasonably dry. This shower-room opens off a bedroom and the WC and basin in two of the schemes are tucked away behind a sliding door, designed to match the back of the shower itself. All three schemes aim to be practical and yet pleasing to the eye. The one opposite uses tiles and wood for visual interest; another aims for a more glamorous look with mosaic tiles and mirrors, while the scheme below, with its simple, contrasting colors, is clean-looking and timeless.

Mosaic and glass scheme
To achieve as romantic a feeling as possible in a not very romantic space, small, dark mosaic tiles are used here to cover both walls and floor. Mirrored glass on the sliding doors adds an extra, luxurious touch, and ceiling ventilation prevents the mirrored surfaces from misting.

Walls and floor: Deep sapphire blue mosaic tiles
Ceiling: White painted boarding
Partition wall: Sliding mirrored panel
Lighting: Recessed downlights (not seen)
Accessories: Plants; emerald green towels

see Wallcoverings p. 234

see Laminates p. 232

see Tiles p. 239

Black and white scheme
Classic contrasting colors give this room a clean-looking, ageless appeal. An interesting bordered tile is used with plain tiles for the recessed shower sink and covers the complete floor area of both shower and alcove. The walls are covered in contrasting laminate with a matching folding door between the two areas. The overall effect is clear-cut, yet stylish, nonetheless.

Walls: Black laminate with black bi-fold doors
Ceiling: White-painted boarding
Floor: Black and white bordered tiles with white tiled shower sink
Lighting: Recessed downlights (not seen)
Accessories: White towels; plants

opposite page:
Tiles and wood scheme
Practical, yet appealing, terracotta floor tiles are used here for both the surround and the lining of the sunken shower area, and converge on a step-out space formed from duck boarding. The boarding is poly-urethaned against damp.

Walls: White laminate in shower area; poly-urethaned boarding in inner room (not seen)
Ceiling: Polyurethaned tongue-and-groove boarding.
Floor: Terracotta tiles and duck boarding with cotton rug in inner area
Lighting: Recessed downlights (not seen)
Accessories: Shower curtain; plants; towels

see Tiles p. 237

POWDER ROOMS

Much the same basic rules apply to washrooms and powder rooms as to bathrooms, but in miniature, and quite apart from making them functional, the more interesting an otherwise dull little space can be made, the better. Since the area used is generally only a sliver of space, it is often possible to use wallpapers or coverings or tiles which would not normally be afforded in any quantity, if at all. The same can be said of floor tiles and especially carpeting, since it should almost always be possible to find off-cuts (reasonably-sized pieces left over from fitting carpets in bigger rooms) which will fit small spaces at minimum prices. Ask for these at carpet showrooms or any good department store.

Planning a powder room

Basically, a powder room is as much for guests as for family overflow and as such, should include a toilet, one or two washbasins, a generous, well-lit mirror with a shelf and/or closet for a clothes brush, boxes of tissues and cotton wool. If the room is to be used regularly by visitors, clean spare hair brushes and combs and, possibly, disposable toothbrushes and paste are a thoughtful addition. An electric razor point is always useful, so is a hook on the door for hanging coats, bags and purses, and if there is room, a long mirror. Again, if if there is a reasonable amount of space, it is worth considering the possibility of putting in a shower for overflow bathing, and even if it cannot be afforded right away, it will certainly be worth running pipes to the appropriate place against such times as it can be.

If there is an integral shower, or if the room is to be used mainly by men or children, it is usually practical to tile or mosaic walls and floors. Or if ceramic tiling seems too expensive – or too cold – use a hard-wearing, water-resistant flooring like vinyl tiles, or vinyl-veneered cork, and paint the walls with a shiny paint, or cover them with a washable vinyl or wallcovering, or plastic laminate. A handsome alternative would be to use wood panelling or veneer treated to resist water. Lighting should be as serviceable as possible. If the space is small, lights all round or over the basin mirror should be adequate, if the room is bigger, use a central light or peripheral light all round the space from under a cornice.

A showpiece for collections

As in bathrooms, powder and washroom walls can serve as a showing-off point for collections of memorabilia, cuttings from old newspapers and magazines, anything that seems humorous or of interest. Old postcards, cigarette cards, soap, cosmetic and dental advertisements, can all be framed, or just mounted and hung up, as can more conventional prints, drawings and photographs or small paintings or framed bits of useful, or useless, information. Pressed flowers, samplers, old record sleeves, school groups, certificates of awards and trophies, absurd bills, letters or fines are all grist to the mill. And it is often a service to leave a pile of old magazines or books around, laid out on a stool or put in a rack, if there is room. The main idea, as is shown in this section, is to combine function with interest and comfort.

Opposite page:
Vividly patterned walls
and roller shade, allied
to matching towels and
rug, effectively disguise
the real size of this small
space. The hanging
plant and the forsythia
add to the cheerful effect
and the spherical white
light above the mirror
repeats the circles on the
ceiling and painted
shade.

This page, right:
A collection of prints and
paintings clustered
together on panelled
wood walls adds con-
stant interest in any
small room. The mirror,
effectively recessed
behind the basin, adds
extra depth, and reflects
more art and objects.

Far right:
Two differently patterned
wallpapers in the same
coloring are cleverly
combined and juxta-
posed to make a match-
ing border, while the
narrow space is effect-
ively doubled by the
mirrored back panel.

Below:
In this practical and
capacious country
washroom, the contents
of the umbrella and coat
stand seem as decorative
in their way as the furniture, objects and prints.

A SMALL POWDER ROOM

The fact that a powder room is meant primarily for guests should not, of course, mean that the family is debarred from using it as well. It should include as many home-from-home facilities as is possible to incorporate in the space. In the scheme opposite, an already somber space is enriched by using soft, dark fabric for the walls and coordinating colors for the rest of the room. The distinguished effect of the Edwardian scheme is achieved with period-style tiles and more textured wallcovering. In the scheme below, flower-patterned carpet and pastel wallpaper create an altogether lighter effect.

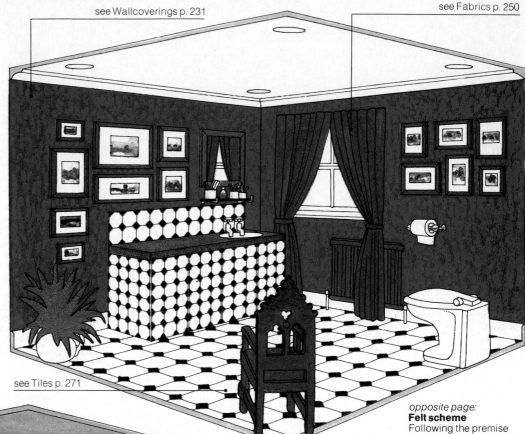

see Wallcoverings p. 231

see Fabrics p. 250

see Tiles p. 271

Edwardian scheme
To add a rather grand feel to the room, distinctive Edwardian-style tiles are the basis of this treatment. To keep the mood, the basin is incorporated into a wooden vanity unit, with matching tile-fronted closets below and tiled splash-back behind. Suede-finish wallcovering is used for the rest of the walls and with long drapes to match, make the room seem suitably distinguished.

Walls: Crimson simulated suede
Ceiling and molding: White latex paint
Woodwork: White semi-gloss paint
Floor: Black and white tiles
Window: Crimson drapes
Lighting: Inset downlights
Fittings: Wooden vanity unit incorporating white porcelain wash basin
Furniture: Gothic-style chair
Accessories: Gilt-framed mirror; toiletries; plants; pictures

see Carpets p. 277

see Wallpapers p. 212

see Sheers p. 260

Sprigged flower scheme
A flower-patterned carpet and toning, wash-effect plain paper combine here to give the room a feeling of lightness and clarity. The pale color of the vanity unit, the cane chair and its pastel cushion, and the filmy, gathered shade at the window complete the airy effect.

Walls and ceiling: Wash effect plain green paper
Moulding: White latex paint with a tinge of green
Woodwork: White semi-gloss paint with a tinge of green
Floor: Sprigged flower wool and nylon carpet
Window: Gathered shade in sprigged white muslin
Lighting: Converted grass oil lamps with etched glass globes
Furniture: White-painted cane chair with pink cushion
Accessories: Oval white-framed mirror; toiletries; plants

opposite page:
Felt scheme
Following the premise that it is often easier to make an already darkish space look rich rather than light, felt walls and a coordinating carpet make this space somberly distinguished. For overall unity, the Roman shade, towels and other accessories keep to the same color scheme. The shelf above the basin and the cane étagère are used for holding spare combs, brushes and toiletries.

Walls: Dark grey felt
Ceiling and molding: Off white latex paint
Woodwork: Off-white semi-gloss paint
Floor: Dove grey and terracotta geometric Brussels weave wool carpet
Window: Gray felt Roman shade edged with terracotta; white voile drapes
Lighting: Double spotlight on ceiling (not seen)
Furniture: Cane chair and étagère
Accessories: Cane mirror; towels; cushion; toiletries; plants; pictures

A LARGE POWDER ROOM

Lack of space can be a bonus. In the case of powder and cloakrooms, for example, it allows the use of materials and finishes that might otherwise be extravagant in a larger area. Remnants of luxurious carpets, small numbers of expensive tiles, a roll or two of costly wallpaper or wallcovering, a limited amount of wood, marble or slate – all can be used more with impunity than conscience. Low-key colors in the scheme opposite create a soft effect; in another, dark colors enhance the rich woodwork, and in the third, Dutch tiles and rush matting create a cooler effect.

see Plain Carpets p. 274

see Furniture p. 296

Turquoise scheme
Dark colors are used here to achieve an overall feeling of warmth. The slight sheen of the painted walls effectively complements the woodwork, enhancing the richness of the mahogany. To maintain the traditional feel, the surface above the basin is covered with prints, old photographs and other pieces of memorabilia. The warmth of the colors is relieved by the mirrors on both door and wall.

Walls: Dark turquoise semi-gloss paint with a protective coat of varnish
Ceiling: Cream latex paint
Woodwork: Polished mahogany
Floor: Dark turquoise wool carpet
Lighting: Brass wall lamps
Furniture: Regency chair with cane-backed seat
Accessories: Polished mahogany mirror; prints; photographs; *pot pourri*; decanter

see Matting pp. 278–9

see Wall Tiles p. 238

see Furniture p. 296

Blue and white scheme
The small, flower-patterned tiles on the wall are used here to give the space a light, fresh feeling. As well as providing a tough, practical surface, the tiles serve to accentuate the texture of the wood. The painted chair, covered only with a simple toweling cushion, adds a bright splash of color.

Walls: Blue and white Dutch tiles
Ceiling: Off-white latex paint
Molding: Stripped wood
Woodwork: Stripped wood
Floor: Coir matting
Lighting: Brass wall lamps
Furniture: Red painted bentwood chair
Accessories: Stripped pine mirror; decanters; cushion

opposite page:
Soft scheme
By using frosted glass and mirror together, a feeling of lightness and space is achieved here without sacrificing privacy. A simple miniprint wallpaper lightens the richness of the mahogany, as well as gently contrasting with the larger, space-expanding pattern of the carpet. To create a similar effect, the same sort of coloring could be used in reverse for walls and floors, or a green miniprint could be used in conjunction with a rose-patterned carpet.

Walls: Lavender pink and cream wallpaper with a protective coat of varnish
Ceiling: Cream latex paint
Woodwork: Polished mahogany
Floor: Blue and off-white Brussels weave carpet
Furniture: Victorian chair
Lighting: Brass wall lamps
Accessories: Rose cotton chair cushion; pictures; mirror; decanters; *pot pourri*

STUDIES AND WORKROOMS

It is rare to find a study on its own nowadays; rarer still to find the kind of study-library that figured so prominently as a male preserve prior to World War II and the feminist movement. Most usually, such rooms are either more of a den (which generally means a retreat from the family), or are part of a bedroom, guest room, dining room or hallway; often they are fitted into a corner at one end of the living room. All the same, similar principles for decoration can be used, whatever the placing. However small the area, it should be bookish, relaxed, comfortable, well-lit and decorated in the way best calculated to help the concentration as well as relaxation. This sounds obvious, but it is not so easy to achieve, especially with a study area in, say, a bedroom, or on a landing, or within a living room when some form of visual separation is necessary, even if it's only a screen or a change of level.

Workrooms, too, tend to be a luxury; adjuncts to the mainstream living areas. But, unlike studies with their rather comfortable connotations, these are essentially areas where specified functions can be carried out, with, hopefully, the greatest facility possible. Whether they are studios, music rooms, home offices, or what you will, they all share the premise that easy function rather than ambience is the prime factor.

Planning a study or workroom

If you are able to plan such an area from the start, make a list of priorities. Will you be likely to make any sort of noise (from music, to typewriters, machinery and saws), or smell (from varnish, glue, paint, clay) which will in any way disturb the rest of the household unless you insulate or ventilate with special care? Will you need special outlets for electrical equipment to avoid dangerous overloading or wires all over the place? What about a water supply; do you need any special surfaces, or services?

As a general rule, appropriate decoration can help the concentration and create a certain spirit. Clearly, in every case the actual function will dictate the way the room (or space, if functions have to be shared) is furnished and arranged. But whatever type of room you are redecorating, always allow more storage space than you think necessary. You will always manage to fill it. There should be plenty of deep shelves if there is space, either built-in, or in the form of storage units or a wall system (see pp. 316 to 317), and plenty of filing cabinets as well, although if space is tight, some sort of working surface can use filing cabinets as supports, thus doing away with the need for a separate desk or work table.

If the space is to be used as a studio, or in any event for sculpture, pottery, modeling or carpentry, you will need a good tough floor that is easy to clean and easy on the feet. Walls should be light colored, and any fabrics easily washable.

Whatever the room and its function, pay particular attention to the lighting for, in context, nothing will be more irritating than a badly lit desk, work surface, keyboard, drawing board or canvas. A good desk or work lamp, whether suspended over the entire surface, or casting light onto

relevant work, is the first essential. Provision for reading in an armchair, if any, or perhaps on a couch, is the next. In the case of bookshelves or massed wall units, light that falls on the spines of the books or files is the best. And general lighting in studies and dens should be provided by soft pools of light. Straightforward workrooms would do best with an even, all-over light backed up by the work lamps already discussed.

Multi-functional rooms

If you are including a study, or study area in some other room, closet space is especially valuable to take overflows of files and papers that would otherwise be stashed away in filing cabinets. For unless the latter are exceptional, or exceptionally well-integrated, they can look too utilitarian in multi-functional areas. In such areas too, decoration should tone in with the rest of the room, but in a study or den proper, warm dark walls often seem a better background for books than cool light colors. If the rest of the decoration is carefully thought out, as is shown in some of the rooms on the next few pages with their very varied alternatives, then it often happens that the study area will be integrated quite happily in the general scheme without jarring or seeming out of place.

Studies and work areas can be fitted into the most unlikely spaces. Above all, they should be conducive to work, but that does not necessarily mean they are dull.

Opposite page:
A study-bedroom in which the areas are neatly separated. The capacious desk is set on a raised platform built in behind the bed head. Overhead pendant fixtures provide light for bedtime reading and for work at the desk.

This page, right:
Classic shelf-lined study with a comfortable jumble of books, treen, odds and ends and plans. The general effect is calm and workable.

Far right:
The study end of this bathroom-dressing room makes a comfortable place in which to sit and read as well as work. Downlights grazing the spines of the books provide general background light.

Below:
An ingenious way of hiding clutter – simple roller shades conceal piles of samples and files in this neat, designer's workroom. Plasterboard fixed over the original paneling acts as a pinboard. For extra flexibility, filing cabinets fixed on rollers can be wheeled round to extend the already generous work surface. The chairs, posters and other daily objects provide colorful relief against the all-white background.

A DARK, NARROW STUDY

It is sometimes possible to distract the eye from the failings of a room by focusing instead on its assets. This narrow, rectangular study has a good high ceiling and a large bay window which divert attention from the fact that the space is rather dark. Studies should be restful, pleasing places, and in the scheme opposite, traditional, dark walls make a useful foil for good-looking furnishings. In the second, the aim is to enlarge the space with light colors; in the third scheme, the contrasting colors of wall and floor, teamed with glass and metal furnishings, produce a cool, urbane effect.

see Shades p. 263

Tawny scheme
Pale, lacquered walls and woodwork reflect the color of the matting here and automatically expand the apparent size of the space. The long, wool-upholstered chair is in keeping with the softness of the effect, and summer-sky shades seem to flood the room with sun.

Walls and ceiling: Creamy-beige semi-gloss paint with an extra coat of lacquer
Woodwork: Creamy-beige semi-gloss paint

Cornice: White semi-gloss paint
Floor: Herringbone coir matting
Window: Blue shades
Lighting: Recessed wallwashers; uplights
Furniture: Glass and plexiglass desk; white chair; tawny marble coffee table; beige wool-upholstered long chair
Accessories: Painting; club fender; books and magazines; bolster and pillows; plants

see Smooth Wallcoverings p. 231

see Matting pp. 278–9

Gray and white scheme
A cooler, more contemporary look, is conveyed here by a dark felt wallcovering and matching woodwork which contrast well with the light-colored carpet and upholstery.

Walls: Dark gray suede wallcovering
Ceiling and cornice: White latex paint
Woodwork: Dark gray gloss paint; fireplace in white gloss paint
Floor: White twist wool carpet
Window: Vertical louvered blinds
Lighting: Recessed downlights; uplights
Furniture: Glass and plexiglass desk (not seen); white calico-covered upholstered units; black rocking chair; smoked glass drum coffee table
Accessories: Large steel-framed mirror; low steel fender; plants; books and magazines

see Blinds pp. 262–3

see Textured Carpets p. 272

opposite page:
Eggplant scheme
To add a touch of spice to an otherwise conventional nineteenth-century study treatment (dark walls, mahogany woodwork, open fire), rich glossy walls provide an unaccustomed sheen which is taken up by the glass and plexiglass desk, the cane and glass coffee table and by the extravagant gilt mirror.

Walls: Eggplant super-gloss paint with an extra coat of varnish
Ceiling and cornice: Pinky-white latex paint
Woodwork: Polished mahogany
Floor: Herringbone coir matting
Window: Cotton Roman shades; cotton drapes, tied back
Lighting: Recessed wallwashers; uplights (not seen)
Furniture: Glass and plexiglass desk; white chair; cane and glass coffee table; leather-seated rocking chair
Accessories: Nineteenth-century mirror; candlesticks; busts; coal boxes; club fender; books and magazines; flowers

A NARROW STUDY

Narrow rooms are a common enough problem and each of these schemes seeks in a different way to overcome it by focussing attention away from any lack of breadth in the room. In the scheme opposite, the emphasis is on the high bureau-bookcase on one side and a tall run of bookshelves across the end of the room. The second scheme is so warm looking and rich in color and visual interest that the actual size of the area is forgotten, and in the scheme below, the space is given a fresh, country feel.

see Wallcoverings p. 228

see Fabrics p. 246

see Plain carpets p. 274

Warm-colored scheme
Any lack of width is lost in the rich coloring here and the overall effect is of the gleam of glass, mirror and mahogany. Arched tracks support looped-back drapes so as not to lose the prettiness of the windows.

Walls: Dark blue-green burlap
Ceiling: Duck-egg blue latex paint

Floor: Blue-green wool and nylon twist carpet
Windows: Drapes in reversible woven cotton
Lighting: Recessed downlights; floor lamps; miniature spots; strip over desk
Furniture: Chairs; mahogany desk and chair; mahogany stained shelves; side tables; upholstered stool
Accessories: Arched mirrors; books; plants

see Borders p. 213

see Matting p. 278

Countrified scheme
Pale walls, flooring and bookshelves have the combined effect of making this room seem both larger and more rural looking.

Walls and ceiling: White semi-gloss latex paint; wallpaper border
Woodwork: White semi-gloss paint
Floor: Sisal matting with red canvas border glued on all round
Windows: Arched drapes (fixed to a curved track) with double frill of red, emerald and green, tied back
Lighting: Uplights; ceiling-recessed spotlights and wallwashers; lamp on floor, desk and table
Furniture: Round table with floor-length cloth; bookshelves; wicker chair; pine desk and matching chair
Accessories: Plants and baskets full of books; throw cushions; magazines; mirror

opposite page:
Soft, muted scheme
Any lack of width is offset in this room by the height of the bureau-bookcase and the extensive shelving at the far end of the room. The rest of the space is kept pale, as befits a quiet study, except for the accent colors of the plants and books, and the throws, which exactly reflect the designs in the bleached cotton rug.

Walls and ceiling: Ivory semi-gloss latex paint
Woodwork: Ivory semi-gloss paint
Windows: Left bare
Floor: Dhurrie rugs on bare boards
Lighting: Recessed spotlights; uplights; desk lamp
Furniture: Pine bureau-bookcase; bookshelves; desk chair; chaise longue
Accessories: Throws and cushions to match rugs; plants; books

A RECTANGULAR WORKROOM/STUDY

Workrooms must, first of all, work for their occupants. This much might seem obvious, but the esthetically-minded are often inclined to put form before function, when in this case, it really must be the other way round. These schemes show one room used in three quite different ways. The one opposite is an essentially practical room for a designer; the one below, which works as a study/workroom/den and guest room, makes the best use of space by placing the furniture on the diagonal. while the third is a slick, study cum media room.

see Wallcoverings p. 230

see Fabrics p. 247

Study/media room
To keep this space calm and uncluttered, built-in modular units are used for storage. A glass and steel-framed desk looks insubstantial against the window, leaving ample visual space for the lounge chair and sleep sofa. The pattern of the carpet and the mirrored blinds at the window also help make the space look larger.

Walls: Dark green suede wallcovering

Ceiling: Off-white latex paint
Woodwork: White satin finish paint
Floor: Green and off-white wool carpet
Window: Vertical mirrored blinds
Lighting: Inset spots and downlights in ceiling; desk lamp; floor lamp
Furniture: White lacquered wall system; lounge chair; sleep sofa; coffee table; glass and steel desk; desk chair
Accessories: Books: stereo; plants; TV

see Fabrics p. 259

see Wallcoverings p. 230

see Carpets p. 276

see Carpets p. 273

Study/den/guest room
Maximum use of space is achieved in this scheme by setting much of the furnishing on the diagonal. The comparatively generous space in between could never have been achieved with a more conventional arrangement. The background color of the textured carpet, which also runs up the sides of the platform, is repeated in the smooth wool wallcovering to give a further illusion of space.

Walls: Camel wool wallcovering
Ceiling: White latex paint
Woodwork: White satin finish paint
Floor: Woolcord broadloom carpet (also used on the platform)
Window: Roman shade in printed cotton
Lighting: Uplights; downlights
Furniture: Built-in bed; storage units; desk and chair; side table; bookshelves
Accessories: Books: TV; stereo; cushions; plants; wool bedcover

opposite page:
Designer's room
Given enough space to absorb a certain amount of disorder, even a practical room like this, with tough surfaces and essential furnishings, can have a pleasing quality.

Walls: Cork tiles
Ceiling: White latex paint
Woodwork: White satin finish paint and natural wood
Floor: White vinyl sheet flooring
Window: Left bare
Lighting: Strip lighting behind valance; work lights
Furniture: Plan chest; drawing board; conference-work table; white chairs; tractor stool
Accessories: Posters; drawings; designer's paraphernalia

LEISURE ROOMS AND PLAYROOMS

Whether for children, adolescents or adults, playrooms and leisure rooms of every description are meant primarily for relaxation and enjoyment. And since, like studies and work-rooms, they are appendages to the main-stream living areas, and essentially luxury spaces, they can be treated away from the general feeling of an apartment or house, and often with a touch of fantasy. These are rooms where primary colors can be indulged and used in a way that can rarely be repeated in other areas – except by complete extroverts, so take advantage of the sudden freedom from constraints and play around with the space without inhibition.

Small children's playrooms that are separate from bed-rooms need to be as tough and bright as possible so that they can withstand the onslaughts to which they are inevitably subjected. If the room is not always to look a terrible mess, storage must be easily manipulable by even young children, and all electric outlets must be absolutely childproof. Games rooms, that is to say, rooms given over completely, or mainly, to indoor games like ping-pong, pool, billiards, shuffleboard and the like, whether for adults or children or both – are most often down in the basement of a house, though sometimes they are also to be found in the attic since there is seldom space in the house proper.

In the case of a basement, you will have to make sure that there is adequate ventilation, light and heat, and then see that the floor is damp-proof, sturdy and non-slip. Obviously, the sort of games that can be played in a basement games room depend on the space and money available, but lighting over pool, billiard and ping-pong tables should be bright, even and non-glare. Walls should be cheerful whatever the color chosen, and decoration here too, can be as uninhibited as taste and circumstances allow. It is useful to have casual seating for onlookers, and perhaps a refrigerator, hot plate and sink for casual entertaining as well as some sort of a bar or serving area, if there is room.

Attics are best for quieter games and relaxation unless you are sanguine about the whole house reverberating. Particular attention should be given to insulation here, for the space might be insufferably cold in winter and stifling in the summer, but the wood framing and the interesting shapes of an attic, could be capitalized on and picked out to great visual advantage. Space at the sides where the roof slopes down makes a generous storage area, and floorboards can be painted with deck paint, either all over or in stripes, to save money as well as to make the room look cheerful; or again, floorboards can be stripped, sanded and polished. If, however, noise is going to be a real problem, plan on some cushion flooring like rubber-tiling, or rubber-backed sisal, or tough wool or haircord with good quality, thick underlay to absorb as much sound as possible.

Rooms by swimming pools with changing rooms and perhaps a sauna attached, are different again in that they are obviously custom-built from the beginning. If the space is big enough, floors should again be surfaced for possible dancing and ping pong, yet be tough enough to be water repellant. Since they will obviously be all-round entertainment areas,

they should be equipped with the sort of storage that will encompass garden chairs, throw pillows, lilos, sun-bathing mats, airing cupboards, straw hats and sun umbrellas, as well as glasses, china and cutlery, drinks, a refrigerator, possibly a bar and minimal cooking facilities, and hi-fi equipment. Here, too, decoration can be as clean and fresh or as fantastic as is liked, with walls painted simple white or decorated with elaborate murals and *trompe l'oeil* decoration.

Media rooms – which are comparative newcomers to the leisure-room scene, should obviously be made as accoustic-ally perfect as possible using accoustic ceiling tiles and perhaps a textured wallcovering or panelling of some sort, comfortable seating, non-aggressive coloring, good carpet-ing and lights that can be dimmed right down to provide low background light. (It is never a good idea to sit and watch TV or movies in a totally darkened room.)

Whether or not a large screen is obvious or concealed is a question of taste and convenience. But if a room is especially geared for sight and sound it should be geared for comfort too, with well-designed and well-upholstered seating positioned advantageously for the screen, and in no way distracting for people listening to music.

While the group of rooms illustrated in this section vary wildly from each other, they share one thing in common. They have all been thoughtfully geared to their owners' require-ments and tastes, and all work well for them with the least possible maintenance.

Opposite page:
Divan beds set end to end in this teenager's room provide seating as well as sleeping space to leave room for all his various leisure pursuits.

This page, top:
The functions of this games and media room have been skilfully divided by ceramic-tiled blocks, upholstered in black for the cushioned lounging area, and carpeted in black for the pool table. The sleek chunkiness effectively matches the massive structure of the space, and the neat fitting-in of fireplace and log store, whilst shiny red, green and black pillows pick up upholstery, and pool colors.

Below:
Another kind of tiled surround effectively divides off the media-orientated sitting area from the rest of an open-plan apartment. Carpeted steps provide further seating as well as a convenient slot for projector and Hi-fi. Note how colored tubular lighting echoes the stepped tiling border.

A GAMES ROOM

Games rooms should be large enough to accommodate space-taking games like ping-pong and pool and still allow enough room for spectators. Two of these schemes center on the pool table (which doubles for ping-pong with an extra top), while the third also has a movie screen.

Green baize scheme
In a room with little or no natural light, it is important to make the framework as interesting and as cheerful as possible. The bright paintwork and pale ceiling and floor are used for maximum light reflection.

Walls: Billiard green felt
Ceiling: White latex paint
Woodwork: Brilliant red full gloss paint
Floor: White thermo-plastic tiles
Furniture: Pool table; white leather chairs
Lighting: Fluorescent tubes behind ceiling panel; pendant lamps over table; recessed downlights and wallwashers
Accessories: Posters; prints; balls etc.

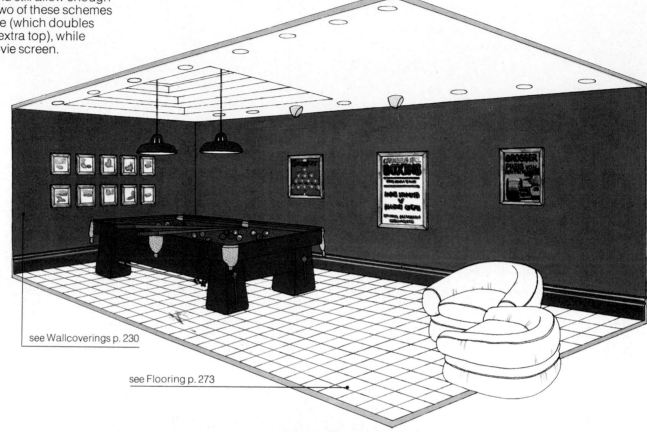

see Wallcoverings p. 230

see Flooring p. 273

Movie screen scheme
To transform the space into a media room, pendant lights over the pool table are replaced with recessed down-lights. A screen hangs on the end wall, and accoustics are improved by a matting floor which is tightly woven enough to stand up to vigorous footwork and soft enough to absorb sound.

Walls and ceiling:
Celadon green latex paint with mural
Woodwork: Celadon green full gloss paint
Floor: Coir matting
Lighting: Fluorescent tubes; recessed down-lights; wallwashers
Furniture: Pool table; corduroy chairs
Accessories: Screen; balls and cues

see Matting p. 278

see Fabrics p. 244

opposite page:
Mural scheme
An exotic painted mural is used to cover the walls here, distracting the eye and effectively transforming an other-wise claustrophobic area. Large fixtures cast direct light onto the table, which receives extra light from the concealed tubes above the ceiling panel.

Walls and ceiling:
Celadon green latex paint; mural
Woodwork: Celadon green full gloss paint
Floor: Industrial two-toned gray carpeting
Furniture: Pool table; two white leather armchairs
Lighting: Fluorescent tubes; pendant lamps; recessed downlights and wallwashers
Accessories: Pool balls and cues

A CHILDREN'S ROOM

Children's rooms usually have to be bedroom, playroom and workroom all in one. They also require tough surfaces to withstand childish ravages, and strong colors to please the childish eye. This long, narrow room has several windows which play a key role in the schemes. In two of the rooms, a ping-pong table top resting on desk and drawer bases provides clever space-saving, dual-purpose work and play surfaces. In the third scheme, the shape of the room is disguised so that the door, closet and windows are lost in the overall pattern.

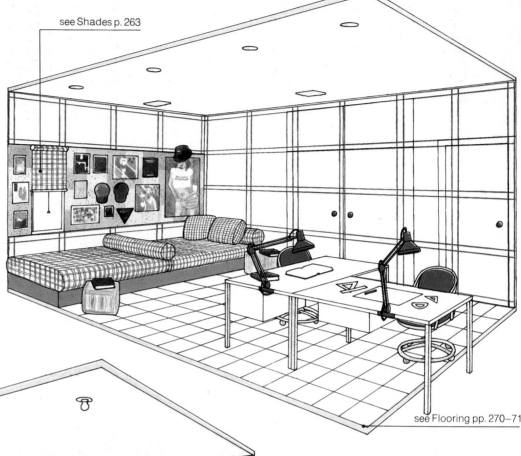

see Shades p. 263

see Flooring pp. 270–71

Grid scheme
The squares of color on the walls, and the windows, which are used here to form a pattern of their own, combine to distract the eye from the narrowness of this room. The palor of the ceiling and floor further enlarge the space as does the platform at one end of the room which is built to hold two beds. Conventional desks provide ample workspace, and the cork pinboards help absorb some of the clutter of papers.

Walls: Blocks of green and white satin finish paint; cork pinboard
Ceiling: White latex paint
Woodwork: White and green gloss paint
Floor: White vinyl tiles
Lighting: Recessed downlights; articulated desk lamps
Furniture: Long platform with two mattresses separated by bolster; desks; chairs; sidetables
Accessories: Throw cushions; pinboard; books; magazines; posters; pencils

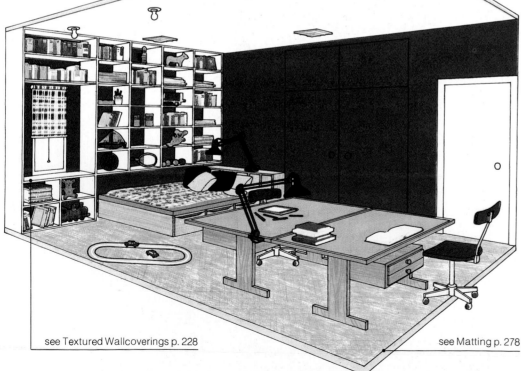

see Textured Wallcoverings p. 228

see Matting p. 278

Warm-colored scheme
Less garish colors are probably more suitable for adolescents. Here, the pale pine and matting colors are combined with grid-patterned cotton shades which echo the wall storage.

Walls: Warm red burlap
Ceiling: White latex paint
Woodwork: White gloss paint and natural pine
Floor: Bleached coir matting
Windows: Cotton roller shades with grid pattern
Lighting: Bare bulb lights on dimmer switch; articulated desk lamps
Furniture: Pine bed with drawers underneath; red desk chairs; pine side table; ping-pong table tops over desk bases; grid storage
Accessories: Grid-patterned cotton bedspread; books; throw pillows; toys

opposite page:
Blue and yellow scheme
Ping-pong table tops over desk bases are a brilliant space-making idea in a children's room, providing for both work and play. The wavy painted dado on the walls in this scheme helps make the room seem wider, while at the same time providing a scribble-proof surface.

Walls: White latex paint; dado in deep blue satin finish
Ceiling: White latex paint
Woodwork: White, red and yellow gloss paint
Floor: Gray haircord carpet
Windows: Yellow roller shades
Lighting: Round bulbs; articulated desk lamps
Furniture: Red-framed bed; red chair; ping-pong table top over desk bases; white table
Accessories: Throw pillows; games; books

GARDEN ROOMS

The first point to remember for any of these areas is to place the emphasis on plants, views or vistas, and a general merging with the outside. Not only is it a way of bringing the outside in – as in the case of a conservatory or garden room – but a way of taking some of the comfort of the inside out – as in the transitional way of decks, porches and terraces.

It is pleasant – but not essential – in a garden room to have as much glass as possible, although the illusion of a summery, conservatory type of room can be easily managed by hanging walls with garden trellis from any hardware shop, tiling the floor and having plants in baskets suspended from the ceiling and in front of windows, as well as massed on the floor and on different surfaces.

Planning a garden room

If you are lucky enough to have a conservatory proper (and many people are adding them on to their houses again as a passive heat source), walls *are* mainly glass since the whole point of the room is to be a kind of luxurious, habitable greenhouse with temperature control. Windows and roof can have filtering shades of one kind and another and lighting can be almost entirely provided by uplights shining through the plants, and reading lamps where necessary. Floors should be tiled with ceramic or quarry or terracotta tiles of some sort which will withstand water splashing on them – an important point in areas like these, in which plants have to be kept well dampened. Given enough space, any area like this will be as pleasant for eating as for sitting and even sleeping.

If a room runs out onto a deck, terrace or porch it will give the illusion of much more space if both areas are tiled in the same way – or at least use the same floor color, and this will also help the interplay of indoor and outdoor space. Of course, many decks and porches are duckboarded anyway, in which case chair fabrics and accessories could continue the colors. Sliding glass doors or French windows or a mixture of fixed glass panels and a glass door will all add to the sense of light, space and freshness. And if the same sort of planters are used indoors and out, the merging of the glossy green of house plants with the outdoor foliage will heighten the freshness and verdancy, as important in hot climates as in rather gloomier ones.

A terrace, deck and, of course, a glass conservatory can get unbearably hot in mid-summer unless it has some sort of shade or shelter system, and in bug-ridden areas it will certainly help if the area is flyscreened. In any case, roof and screen sides can make the area doubly useful because the space can then be used during fine days in the fall and early winter as well, with booster heating if necessary. There is special paint available which can be painted on conservatory roofs to alleviate the sun's rays, or else use shades or blinds.

Permanent outdoor furniture should be tough and waterproof as well as relaxing. Other furniture should be easily portable and storable, capable of being used indoors or out, hence the popularity of cane and whicker. Lastly, do not forget to install electric outlets on decks, porches and terraces for lighting and extra cooking facilities.

This page, above: Decks are pleasant indoor-outdoor spaces which can be used for dining and entertaining as well as just sitting and relaxing, and the aim here is certainly to bring the outdoors in. Slatted tables like this one can be left outdoors most, if not all of the time, without coming to any real harm. Indeed, the weather-beaten look of aged wood only adds to its appearance.

Opposite page, near left: Nature is only just held back by this porch whose furnishings look remarkably civilized in contrast to the tangled wilderness outside. All the same, the muted colors and natural textures underscore rather than overwhelm the background foliage. Since the area is obviously not closely overlooked, there is no real need for any sort of window treatment other than the dense trees just beyond the seating area.

Top right: A good old-fashioned conservatory with its *de rigeur* palms, marble floor and matchstick shades looks all set for sitting out the next dance in Edwardian splendor. The lily pool in the foreground adds to the sumptiousness of the general effect.

Below right: Curved, slatted blinds make a striking interplay of light and shade over the comfortable, button-backed upholstery in this covered porch. The bright aluminum is in restrained contrast to the soft green.

A SUN ROOM/SITTING ROOM

A room with a large expanse of glass enables people to enjoy all the feeling of the outdoors, indoors. It also permits the opportunity for alfresco schemes within a conventional room framework. With its minimal furnishings and disciplined planes, the room opposite has a Japanese feel to it, allowing little to distract from the greenery outside. For a more conventionally comfortable room, the one below is thoroughly western in approach; while the third, which has Moorish-style pierced screens to counteract the more untoward effects of the elements, uses sky and grass colors for the ceiling and floor in an attempt to bring the outside in.

see Blinds p. 262

see Fabrics pp. 256–7

Indoor plants scheme
In this scheme greenery both divides the inner space from the outer and connects it. To keep emphasis on comfort, the wicker chairs and banquette are covered in soft cushions, whose flower strewn fabric echoes the natural foliage and petals. The rattan shades can be lowered to block out inclement weather without losing the prevailing garden feeling.

Walls: Sliding glass; frames painted in leaf green gloss paint
Ceiling: White semi-gloss paint
Floor: White painted boards
Windows: Rattan blinds
Lighting: Uplights behind seating
Furniture: Wicker chairs and banquette; green-painted Parson's table; flower-patterned cushions and pillows
Accessories: Plants in baskets; books

see Paints pp. 210–11

Moorish scheme
To counteract bad weather or to filter strong sunlight, sliding Moorish-style pierced screens are placed in front of the sliding doors. The corners of the room are completely mirrored, reflecting the outside views and effectively expanding the space inside.

Walls and windows: Sliding glass doors covered with white painted wood screens; mirrored corners
Ceiling: Sky blue latex paint
Floor: Grass green carpet
Lighting: Uplights behind banquettes and plants; fluorescent strip lighting behind screens
Furniture: Upholstered banquettes in grass green and sky blue quilted cotton; off-white lacquered coffee table; floor cushions; chaise longue in off-white canvas
Accessories: Plants in baskets; books; candles

see Fabrics pp. 246–7

see Plain carpets pp. 274–5

opposite page:
Japanese-style scheme
Decoration and furnishings are both minimal in this Japanese-style room, so that the main feeling is of the greenery and light outside barred only by the large panes of glass. Seating is mainly kept at conventional Japanese floor level, so that anyone entering the rooms sees the expanse of wooden deck and the view before anything else.

Walls and windows: Glass sliding doors
Ceiling: White latex paint
Floor: Black polished ceramic tiles; white Flokati rug
Lighting: Uplights; outside downlights
Furniture: Low round glass table; dresser; rocking chair; chest; floor cushions
Accessories: Rug; tall grasses

A CONSERVATORY/DINING ROOM

Almost any enclosed area built onto the side of a house can be treated as a traditional nineteenth century conservatory and made into a comfortable, indoor greenhouse, available in all weathers and in all seasons for relaxing and dining. The glass doors on both sides of this long, narrow space leave very little wall area to decorate, but in the scheme below, a tented effect can be achieved by pulling the fabric shades across the glass roof and down the walls. The scheme opposite is kept simple, concentrating on the greenery, while the scheme, right, is more rustic in feeling, with natural textures and stripped woodwork.

see Blinds p. 262

Rustic scheme
Rattan blinds, stripped woodwork and floor bricks to match the wall lend a definite countrified air to this space. A scrubbed wood table and leather and willow chairs complete the buildup of natural textures.

Walls: Natural brick and unpainted trellis
Woodwork: Stripped and waxed pine
Floor: Brick
Windows: Rattan roller blinds
Lighting: Uplights concealed behind plants
Furniture: Scrubbed wood refectory table; leather and willow chairs
Accessories: Plants; baskets; china; glass

see Shades p. 263

see Natural tiles p. 265

see Tiles p. 266

Striped shades scheme
Patterned shades which can be rolled back or drawn across the ceiling and down the walls are a practical, yet attractive method of providing shade. Toning cotton is used for seat cushions and the tablecloth and china and glass are also chosen to match. Ceramic tiles make a pleasing, but practical floorcovering.

Walls: White latex painted brickwork and trellis
Woodwork: White gloss paint
Floor: White ceramic tiles
Windows: Striped cotton roller shades
Lighting: Uplights concealed behind plants
Furniture: Cane table and chairs
Accessories: Cotton tablecloth; cushions; plants; baskets; china and glass

opposite page:
Simple scheme
Trellised brick and plain painted woodwork are simple foils against which the patterned floor tiles and the complicated tracery of plants are allowed to form their own elaborate decoration. The cane dining table and chairs turns the space into an exotic year-round eating area.

Walls: Natural brick, covered in white semi-gloss painted trellis
Woodwork: White gloss paint
Floor: Yellow and off-white vinyl tiles
Windows: Left bare; frosted glass roof
Lighting: Uplights concealed behind plants
Furniture: Cane table and chairs
Accessories: Plants; baskets; cane screen

A SLEEPING PORCH

A sleeping porch is undoubtedly a romantic adjunct to a house, but it poses certain problems when it comes to decoration. Ideally, a porch should relate to the outside in feeling; it should be as comfortable for lounging by day as it is for sleeping at night; and it should be possible to maintain the airiness without letting in bugs, or drafts, or both. The scheme opposite subtly continues the wooded outdoor coloring with greens and browns and natural textures. The scheme, right, takes the cheerful juxtaposition of sunny sky and foliage as its theme, while the third achieves a more sophisticated effect with its design rather than coloring taken from nature.

see Paints pp. 210–11

see Paints pp. 210–11

Patterned scheme
For a lighter, brighter scheme, another aspect of the outside is taken up and repeated here. An abstract floral cotton stretched over the mattress and used as shades, together with toning pillows, bring a feeling of high summer to the space.

Walls, balustrades and woodwork: White semi-gloss paint
Ceiling: White semi-gloss painted beams
Shutters: Faded green semi-gloss paint
Window openings: Fine fly screens with printed cotton window shades
Floor: White ceramic tiles
Furniture: Cane chair; natural wood table; mattress with throw cushions
Accessories: Plants; woven cane planters

see Fabrics pp. 256–7

see Tiles p. 266

see Plain Cottons p. 244

opposite page:
Green and brown scheme
In this scheme the porch is very definitely an extension of the outside. The colors of the surrounding woods are repeated skilfully in the mattress covering and pillows, the shutters, paintwork and floor. The whole area seems to slip easily, almost dreamily into the landscape, each component subtly repeating another.

Walls: Cream semi-gloss paint
Ceiling: Dark wood beams
Shutters: Dark green semi-gloss paint
Window openings: Glass screens
Floor: Coir matting squares
Furniture: Mattress with quilted cotton cover; pillows; rattan chair; natural wood table
Accessories: Plants; woven cane planters

see Fabrics p. 248

see Matting pp. 278–9

Russet scheme
Although the coloring in this scheme does not overtly repeat nature, its burnt earth shades backed by flowerpots blend in well with the faded tones of the house and the occasional autumnal colors of the trees. The pale twigged motif on the cotton covers repeats the natural pattern.

Walls: Pink latex paint
Shutters: Faded blue semi-gloss paint

Balustrade and woodwork including shutters: Faded blue semi-gloss paint
Ceiling: Faded pink latex paint
Floor: Coir matting
Furniture: Heavy terracotta and off-white cotton on mattress; matching pillows; cane chairs with throw cushions; extra large, upturned flowerpot as table
Accessories: Plants; flowerpots

WHOLE HOUSE TREATMENTS

In the preceding pages, we have shown all kinds of alternative treatments for every sort of shape, type and kind of room. But the fact remains that the majority of homes are made up of a collection of rooms, and since most people prefer to have some sort of cohesive feel about their living spaces, it is important to know how to link these separate entities together in some way; how to give them a corporate and unifying identity of their own.

A feeling of unity or flow is especially important, of course, in a small apartment or house; the greater the sense of continuity, the greater the sense of space. But how do you manage to preserve individual interest and identity in a room, while at the same time making it feel part of the whole?

Using color

Sometimes color can provide the best link. A particular color, or different permutations of color in differing proportions, can be used from room to room. A particular shade of green, therefore, might be used as a solid block of color on the floor in one room; in throw cushions in another; in the pattern on a rug in the next, and in china or glass or paintings somewhere else. Or blue could be used, say, for a wall color in the hall, as a dominant note in drapes and some of the upholstery fabric in the living room, and as fabric for pillows and in paintings in the bedroom. Sometimes it works very well to take one combination of colors and to use them in quite different ways in different areas. This way, the house or apartment will look very varied, but there still will be a definite feeling of coherance and familiarity.

Following this approach, and using green, white, pink and apricot, for example, a possible approach might be to paint hall walls apricot (I use the entrance hall again, since this is obviously the first room to be seen in most homes) and put down a green carpet. In the living room, the green would be used as a felt wallcovering, the apricot would appear in a pink and apricot striped, rough-Indian-cotton upholstery fabric with matching Roman shades, and the carpet could be a toning green, apricot and white geometric. A bedroom might have pink, apricot and white wallpaper, used with a white carpet and pristine *broderie anglaise* bedcoverings; a generous number of plants would provide the greenery. The bathroom might be shiny white, with a green carpet and pink, apricot and white towels, while the kitchen could be white with apricot woodwork and matching cooking pots and pans, a tongue-and-groove pine ceiling and a terracotta floor.

For other ideas on how to use color, refer to The Principles of Design and the Sample Book.

Choice of furnishings

Another way of linking rooms is by the choice of furnishings. If you have an eclectic eye, the inevitable mixture of periods and objects in each room betrays this, but cohesion will be maintained by virtue of a sure, steady taste. If, on the other hand, you are a Minimilist, your floors will probably all be covered in charcoal haircord carpet with spare, black leather upholstery, carpeted platforms and shiny white walls. The

only color would be provided by plants and paintings, and the rooms will differ one from another by the obviousness of their functions; Modernists who believe wholeheartedly in Bauhausian concepts will keep sternly to furniture designed by Mies van der Rohe, Le Corbusier and Breuer, with a spicing of pieces by Eames and Saarinen; serious collectors of antique furniture might only use the best of a particular period, however uncomfortable, or pieces made only of one type of wood or decorated only with marquetry.

On the whole, though, people tend to furnish their homes in certain styles, choosing what they feel is appropriate to country or city, ocean or summer house. This does not, of course, mean that the homes in question *have* to be sited in the sort of environment that their style betrays. Many people enjoy having a country style in the city, an urban sophistication in the country, a rustic style by the ocean, or a Mediterranean look in the suburbs. As in most things, what seems comfortable is the style to choose.

To help formulate ideas, we have put together certain groupings taken from the Room-by-Room Guide to show various possibilities for creating a single, coherent style for your home. We have also given a summary of the various characteristics which seem most typical of the different groups to make them more easily recognizable.

These rooms, designed by Mary Gilliatt, show just what is meant by achieving a continuity of color or feeling. This hall, **right**, for example, sets the tone for much of the house with its eclectic approach and tawny colors taken from the golden Afghan rug. Coir matting is almost exactly matched to the stripped wood of the staircase, the semi-circular side table and pine mirror, while the darker wood of the bannisters matches the darker, border colors of the rug.

Far right and opposite:
The living areas continue the hall theme, with the same coir matting and walls which follow the ground color of the hall rug. Pine shutters repeat the wood in the entrance and extra visual interest is provided by the woodburning stove in one room and the fresh green of indoor trees.

Below left:
The same colors and different weights and textures are used in the dining end of the kitchen with its stripped brick walls and newer, diagonally set brick floor. The pine of the dining chairs, 19th century Irish bookcase (used for china storage), and ceiling boards contrasts with the dark oak of an early carved chair, the corner cupboard and the fragment of paneling. Like the living room, this space is spiced with green plants, and the green of the tablecloth border and wine glasses.

Below right:
The kitchen proper, not surprisingly, has much the same feeling as the dining area, with all its tawny tones contrasted with the colors of spices, herbs and the normal *batterie de cuisine* as well as the, by now *de rigeur*, greenery.

185

UPDATED TRADITIONAL STYLE

Traditional eclectic rooms are full of a mixture of objects and periods, often with no real rationale behind them other than all the possessions were chosen with pleasure by someone of catholic taste. Most contemporary rooms in this style mix comfortable modern upholstery with antique furniture and accessories, and graceful window treatments. Floors might be stripped and polished wood, with oriental rugs; or they may be comfortably, yet plainly carpeted, with the odd rug as an addition.

It is, of course, easier to instil this sort of feeling in a room with high ceilings and good proportions, with, if possible, interesting architectural details, but a grand space is not always necessary, since carefully chosen objects can often distract the eye from the actual background.

Choosing the right colors
Certain colors are more connected with traditional feel than others. Colors like dark red, crimson, dark green and brown all make good unifying backgrounds for a disparate collection of objects, while at the same time instilling a certain air of graciousness. Likewise, there are certain patterned wallpapers and coverings that

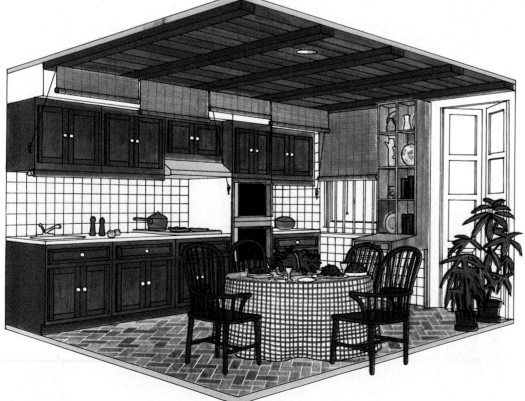

Left:
In the kitchen, much the same coloring is used but in quite different ways. Tablecloth and plants introduce the same red and green against a background of natural textures. And again the feeling is eclectic, with the traditional chairs and covered round table mixed with sleek but paneled kitchen units and objects displayed carefully on shelves.

Above:
Modern Italian armchairs and easilymovable, upholstered stools are mixed with 19th century furniture and cloth-covered tables in a room which is both traditional in feeling and proportion, and eclectic in possessions. The stools are covered in old oriental rug fragments, and the two-toned tablecloths are repeated by the red trim on the drapes, and the red and green upholstery of the chairs.

are more suited to a traditional approach than others. Flowers, fruit, birds and foliage would always be chosen above geometrics, crayon-like dashes and other uniquely contemporary designs; and stripes are more in keeping than squares. Windows usually sport drapes, or drapes and shades together, or long shutters, but never vertical blinds. Upholstery fabrics are generally velvets, linen unions, damasks, heavy cottons and leathers.

Mixing the old with the new

For a change of pace, updated traditional rooms – which are a style of their own – can be furnished with old chairs upholstered in tweeds, corduroys and washable suedes, or suedecloths. Updated traditional might also involve mixing plexiglass and steel pieces with a button-backed Chesterfield; lacquer and glass with a Regency chaise longue and a French bergère.

A traditional eclectic room will look both comfortable and interesting. While this sounds easier to achieve than it actually is in practice, once again, it is all a matter of observing what is pleasing elsewhere and adapting and adopting to suit one's personal requirements. Sureness of taste can only be achieved with time.

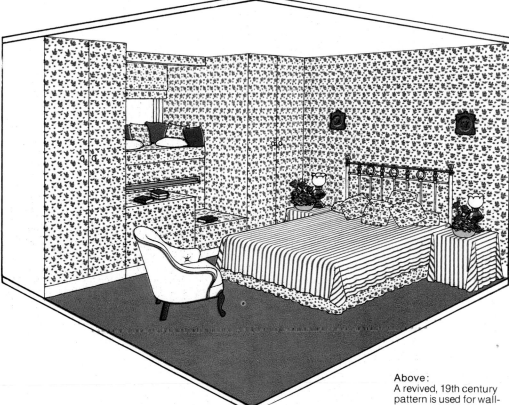

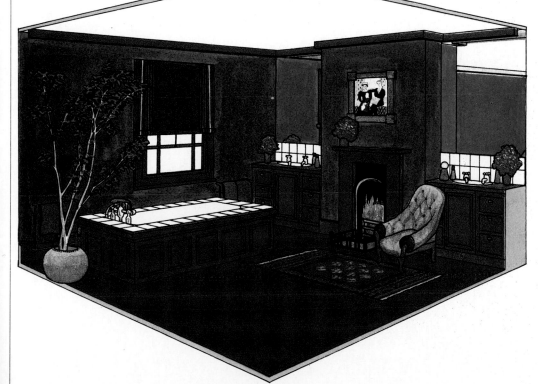

Above:
A revived, 19th century pattern is used for wallpaper and matching fabric in a bedroom that has a traditional feel, but nevertheless fresh look. The Victorian button-backed chair is covered with rough white cotton with a red trim to match the overall strawberry pattern and red and white stripes. Once again, the familiar red and green theme has been continued in yet another way, but with a totally different balance this time.

Left:
Warm red for the walls, floor and at the window give a thoroughly comfortable feel to this bathroom, while mahogany vanity units and bath paneling, Victorian chair, blazing fire and oriental rug add all the appurtenances of a traditional club feel. Nevertheless, the striped canvas window shade, neatly concealed lighting over the mirrored alcoves, rangy plant and heated towel rails make this a positively contemporary room – again with similar colors throughout.

COSMOPOLITAN STYLE

As comfortably international as it is comfortable to be in, this style is recognizable in every capital city in the Western world and could be transplanted from country to country without ever looking out of context.

The French have a useful word, *cossu*, which is often just translated as rich or well-to-do in dictionaries, but in fact means an amalgam of comfort, luxury, ease and well-tended care. Cosmopolitan style generally has all that about it, as well as a quiet sense of detail, so, for instance, bathrooms always seem to have room for a comfortable chair or chaise; storage is beautifully arranged and beautifully capacious; kitchens appear to have space for everything.

Appropriate in town and country

This internationally recognizable style is not, however, just confined to town houses and city apartments, since it is frequently found in carefully-tended suburban areas, and in large country or weekend houses. Yet it is in no way rural, and has nothing whatsoever to do with the simplicity of natural country style, even though it, too, is

Left:
White and sand tones accented here and there with copper pans and terracotta pots continue the understated look with its careful attention to detail. This is the sort of decoration which pleases first with its harmony and then by the obvious thought behind it all.

This page:
Subtle detailing and understated coloring provide a connective link to each of the spaces here.

Above:
Crisp lines of wall paneling, stripped wood floor and vertical louvered shades in the living room make an interesting background to comfortable seating. The ottomans are upholstered in tough white canvas, Scotch-guarded for added practicality. The elaborate mantlepiece and luxuriant foliage of the tall plant are in pleasing contrast to the deliberate simplicity of the rest of the room.

distinguished for its simplicity – the kind that takes a certain assurance to achieve.

Interestingly, in spite of easily recognizable hallmarks, cosmopolitan style almost always manages to escape seeming bland or derivative because of its clever juxtapositions and quiet contrasts, its air of certainty: colors are subtly repeated; scale is skilfully balanced; textures are played one against another; there is a strong and luxuriant plant life, and great attention is paid to flowers. There is not, on the whole, much pattern, but if there is, it is usually cleverly mixed or reversed, and there is a bias to the geometric in carpets, or plain carpets with borders.

Mirror is often used generously, with mirrors themselves, or with mirror glass on walls and sometimes ceilings to apparently extend space, sparkle and light. Walls might be covered in wood, or suede, or felt or some sort of thick wool wallcovering, or again they might be lacquered.

Choosing the furniture

Choice of furniture is usually fairly eclectic, with the emphasis on deep sofas, armchairs and ottomans, with one or two old pieces or at least old accessories. There is probably also a handsome sprinkling of modern classics – Saarinen pedestal tables and chairs, the Corbusier long chair, Mies van der Rohe's Barcelona chairs and stools. Coffee, occasional and side tables are made of glass or plexiglass and steel, lacquered wood and gun metal, marble and mosaic; art is always carefully chosen and carefully hung.

A cosmopolitan interior is usually conspicuous for its interesting collections of objects, which, like paintings, are carefully arranged and juxtaposed. Even when rooms have a touch of fantasy, they look simply executed and unforced.

Sometimes, components are deliberately understated. Floors might be covered in coir matting rather than obviously expensive carpet. Or they might be stripped and polished, or painted with deck paint and softened with rugs. Upholstery can be covered in calico or sailcloth, or plain or painted canvas. Solid brass door handles will be chosen to match other details such as uplights, set behind tall, indoor trees in deep, wicker baskets.

This sort of mixture can only be carried out by people with a sure knowledge of when to spend and when to save; it is impressive because it is not designed for outward show, but merely to please its owners. This style might break new ground, but it will very rarely look bold.

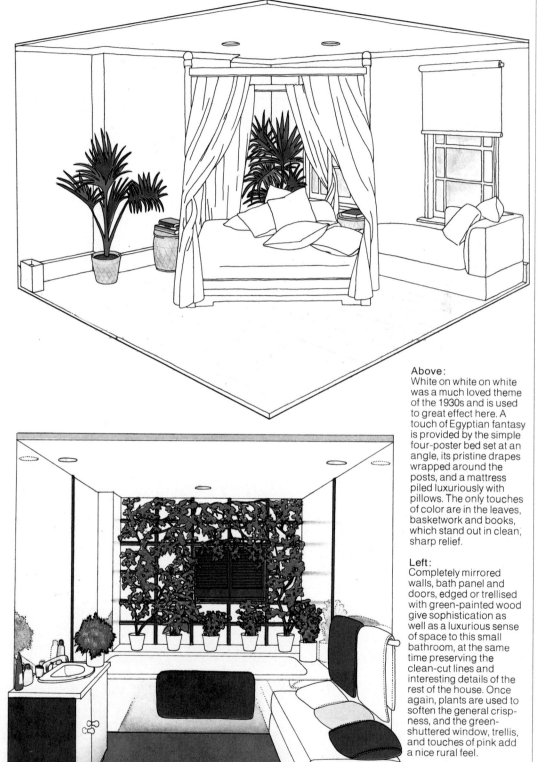

Above:
White on white on white was a much loved theme of the 1930s and is used to great effect here. A touch of Egyptian fantasy is provided by the simple four-poster bed set at an angle, its pristine drapes wrapped around the posts, and a mattress piled luxuriously with pillows. The only touches of color are in the leaves, basketwork and books, which stand out in clean, sharp relief.

Left:
Completely mirrored walls, bath panel and doors, edged or trellised with green-painted wood give sophistication as well as a luxurious sense of space to this small bathroom, at the same time preserving the clean-cut lines and interesting details of the rest of the house. Once again, plants are used to soften the general crispness, and the green-shuttered window, trellis, and touches of pink add a nice rural feel.

EASY CITY LIVING STYLE

The revival of the inner city has created a whole new sensibility to urban living problems and this, in turn, has resulted in a fresh, new style that is sensible, pragmatic and workable.

Rents, taxes, maintenance and mortgages are generally high and usually absorb a great proportion of people's incomes, so money that is left is spent on furniture and furnishings of maximum value, with a padding of improvized ideas, and junk or thrift shop finds. Natural light is not necessarily very generously apportioned through apartment windows, so background colors are kept crisp and neat, or warm and harmonious to compensate. And since most occupants of city apartments are at work most of the day, rooms are arranged to be as labor-free and uncluttered as possible.

City apartment or studio rooms are often box-like and uninspiring, with nothing very much in the way of natural features to give character or distinction. But interesting textures, enjoyable shapes, tailored window treatments and a judicious use of plants and indoor trees all can be used to over-

Left:
A reversible comforter matches either walls or sheets in the bedroom. When shades are closed the room becomes a comfortable wild violet-colored box with its paler carpet taken up to the bottom of the window seat. And the bookshelf fitting also acts as a bedhead with its practical lighting.

Above:
Interesting textural and color contrasts and minimal furniture are the dominant features in these rooms. Checked cotton covers on slabs of foam make for relaxed seating in the living room, and look well on the nubbly Berber carpet, which, in turn, contrasts with the parchment walls and bamboo shades.

Whole House Treatments/**Room-by-Room Guide**

come this anonymity. Furniture, which is often unconventional, might consist of nothing but modular seating and an improvized coffee table, or a series of covered foam blocks, carpeted platforms, or built-in seating units.

Soft carpets and discreet lighting
Because a lot of time is spent sitting and lounging on floors, much flooring consists of thick, shaggy carpet or rugs. Lighting is usually well thought-out and discreet, with careful attention to the right mixture of background, work and accent light.

Storage has to be especially well planned. Closets and bookcases can be fitted into improbable but always workable areas

Above:
The general effect of this kitchen is spare, practical and good-looking, with industrial shelving and aluminum backing to the walls above the counter-top contrast interestingly with the butcher block tops and pale quarry tiles. Beams are utilized as hanging racks for herbs and saucepans.

Left:
Neat charcoal carpeting both softens and distinguishes this other-wise all tiled bathroom, and the yellow checkered fabric used for shade and stool echoes the brown and white check on the living room seating units.

(like around windows or doors), however skinny the space. And to make them less conspicuous, they are generally painted to match the wall colors. Given that many city views are unspectacular, windows are often covered with vertical louvered shades or roller or matchstick blinds, or half-lowered Roman or Austrian blinds. Elaborate drapes are comparatively rare.

City-dwellers are generally aware of current vogues, and in contemporary interiors Hi-Tech ingredients like aluminum tiles, pressed tin sheets, industrial shelving or factory lights are mixed with practical surfaces like butcher-block worktops, quarry or mosaic tiles, mirror or extra shiny paint and polished steel.

In complete contrast, a *rus in urbe* country style can be created, depending on taste and space, with old Provençal or rustic pieces of furniture, fresh-looking wallpaper and spriggy muslin drapes.

The style for city living, then, is practical, no-nonsense; it is never extravagant, whether in terms of space or upkeep. It must, above all, be adaptable to people's needs and circumstances, for city spaces are generally small, and every inch of space must be used to its best advantage.

191

ONE-ROOM LIVING

One-room living has special needs and requirements that are quite different from single or even dual-purpose rooms. One-roomed studio apartments or lofts need usually to provide adequate space, or what passes for adequate space, for sleeping, living, lounging, studying, eating, and sometimes cooking, without making the place seem a hopeless muddle.

The difficulty here is almost always in the neat division and apportioning of space. Sometimes a room can be divided by a screen or a platform, sometimes by a large plant, sometimes by judiciously-placed large pieces of furniture; and sometimes rugs and furniture can be arranged so that each area seems like an island in itself. Or clever lighting can be used to cast pools of light onto different, isolated areas, leaving others in comparative obscurity.

It helps to keep to only a few permutations of colors in one-room living, so the eye is not distracted too much. In confined areas, anything that helps to expand the sense of space can only be advantageous. But with lofts, the reverse is true, for the aim here is to rationalize the area, to tame it.

Sleep sofas or large couches usually have to double as beds, unless these can be hidden in some sort of alcove, or put behind natural divisioning such as a bulky table or desk. In any event, in public a bed should look crisp and well-tailored, more like seating than lying space. Tables can often double as desks as well, and bookshelves of an appropriate height can also act as serving areas for eating.

Where space is minimal, it often makes sense to platform the room. This has several advantages, including demarcating different areas for sleeping, eating or studying, as well as providing extra seating space and sometimes storage as well. A platformed space generally looks neater and more comfortable if the whole area is carpeted. Strip lights concealed under the "lip" of a platform will make it appear to be floating at night (see page 21). Another advantage with platforming is that it can be designed for positioning at an angle, for the best possible use of space.

Straight or curved screens can also be used to divide areas effectively. Study space, for example can be hidden behind an eating area, or private sleeping quarters can be divided off from the more public entertaining area.

If the available space is planned with a modicom of common sense and quite a bit of imagination, this can be a both rewarding and economical way of dealing with multi-functional living areas.

Color is very much the connecting factor in these two rooms. The main living area, **above**, uses a strong, chrome yellow for ceiling, walls and sofa, and a yellow and white, zebra print for the bed. The same feel is then extended into the bathroom, **left**, with its similarly colored but darker toned carpet, zig-zag cotton shade and drapes and toning towels.

THE
SAMPLE BOOK

ALL ABOUT PAINT

Paint is the cheapest and simplest finish to apply to walls, and it provides a quick means of changing the appearance of a room. Paint can be used, not only to disguise faults, but also to change proportions. If, for example, a ceiling is painted lighter than the walls, it will appear higher, because light colors have a recessive effect. Conversely, if the walls of a very large room were painted a dark color, the space would appear smaller.

Eyesores, like a confusion of heating pipes or the converging beams and sloping ceilings in lofts, can be painted the same color as their background, effectively disguising them. Alternatively you can make a sculptural feature of them by painting them in contrasting colors to the walls.

Dull, featureless spaces can be edged or delineated with stripes of color by keeping the walls light, and painting the trim and baseboard in a contrasting shade.

Types of paint

Alkyd

A combination of natural and synthetic resins, color pigment, oils and white spirit. Although hard-wearing, these paints take a while to dry and smell strongly of paint. They should be thinned with turpentine. Gloss alkyds are the most suitable paints for hard-wear areas like halls, bathrooms and kitchens because they are scrubbable.

Painting sash windows
Stretch masking tape along the edge of the panes before painting, to guarantee a straight edge. Painting order:
1 Bottom meeting rail of pulled down top window;
2 Rest of window;
3 Entire bottom sash;
4 Window frame;
5 Runners, inside and out.

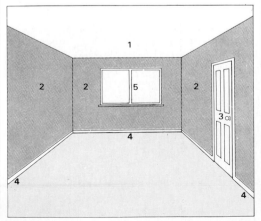

1 Ceiling; **2** Walls;
3 Doors; **4** Baseboards;
5 Windows.

Latex

A combination of resins and color pigment in a water suspension. Two frequently used resins are acrylic and vinyl. Although not as hard-wearing as alkyd paints, they are easy to apply (leaving few brush marks), dry quickly and leave little smell. They should be thinned with water. Latex are general purpose paints, but matt latex shows scuff marks and should be used in light-wear areas like bedrooms, living rooms and dining rooms.

Thixotropic

A non-drip paint with a jelly-like consistency, available in both water- and oil-based forms. Oil-based thixotropic paints are more durable than latex ones, and are ideal for hard-wearing areas.

Epoxy enamel

A tough paint with a hard, gloss finish which resists dirt, grease and abrasion. It can be used on masonry, metal, fiberglass, porcelain and high-glaze ceramic tiles. It is therefore ideal for re-coloring bathroom fittings and tiled walls.

Deck and floor enamel

Available in both latex and alkyd preparations, these hard-wearing enamels provide scuff-resistant surfaces. They are therefore ideal for re-painting floors.

Special-purpose paints

A number of other specialized paints exist. These include heat, mildew and damp-resistant varieties as well as paints for metal, rubber, glass and fiberglass.

Stains

Can be either water- or oil-based. They are produced in a number of colors, as well as the traditional "wood" finishes. Amateurs should use the water-based varieties.

Painting a door
Remove all fittings and wedge open. Work quickly to avoid join marks between sections. Painting order: **1** Moldings; **2** Set-in panels; **3** Center upright; **4** Horizontal crossrail; **5** Outside uprights.

Order of painting a room

Buying information

It can be hard to gauge the effect on the furnishings of a room from one small paint chip, but one way around this is to hold a similarly-colored piece of fabric up against the wall. Bear in mind that hard-wear areas will need a durable paint finish like oil-based gloss, for example. Also, remember to buy all your paint in one batch, especially if you are having it custom-mixed. A selection from the vast range of paints available appears on page 210. For information on how to measure up your walls so that you can estimate the quantity of paint required, and on the spreading capacity of paint, see The Design Kit.

Applying gloss paint
1 Before you start to paint, it is important to make sure that the surface is perfectly smooth. Then apply the paint in vertical strokes.

2 To smooth over the paint, draw the brush horizontally across your first, vertical strokes.

3 Now paint upwards again from the wet band into the body of the paint.

Painting a room

Before any type of paint is applied, both room and walls should be well prepared. Remove any pictures, accessories and fixtures, and cover floors and furniture with dropcloths. Any badly soiled walls, particularly in kitchens, should be washed with a detergent, both to remove dirt and grease, and to dull the surfaces, making them more receptive to painting. Fill in any fine cracks or dents with a ready-made patching compound and sand lightly when dry. Have all the tools you need near to hand, namely a roller for large areas and a small brush for corners.

If you plan to paint both walls and ceilings, always start with the ceiling to prevent any spatters falling onto newly painted walls. Paint in strips (this should eliminate any overlap marks which occur when you paint into a dry edge).

Special techniques

Apart from its straightforward use as a wallcovering, paint can be applied and treated to produce a variety of unusual finishes and textures. The techniques of lacquering, glazing, stippling, combing, dragging and scumbling are well-known to decorators, but are rarely used by amateurs. With practice, however, effects can be created which are almost indistinguishable from professional results. There is also the added bonus that an unusual finish can be produced with little extra effort or expense. However, it is always advisable to try out any new methods on primed pieces of board, using a variety of colors, before starting on your walls.

Lacquering

The technique described here is not lacquering in the strictly Oriental sense, which was generally used on furniture, but the finish is nevertheless deep, rich and durable. The surface must be prepared with particular care. Cracks and dents should be filled in, rough edges sanded down, and the surface painted with an undercoat. A perfect job usually needs six or more coats of semi-gloss or satin gloss paint, each of which must be allowed to dry thoroughly, then rubbed down carefully with steel wool before the next coat is applied. If the finish is to be very shiny, all coats should be of a high gloss paint with a final coat of clear varnish.

Glazing

This is a hard, almost transparent, colored finish that is often used in hot countries where its clear, light-reflecting, cool appearance is particularly appropriate. If, for example, you wanted a grass green effect, you would use a yellow paint for the first coat, and a transparent, blue-green one for the top coat. It is usual to finish off the surface with a coat of clear, protective varnish, which also gives a shiny finish.

Stippling

This is a good finish for a large area because it softens and breaks up the surface, as well as eliminating brush marks. The effect is produced by gently dabbing a stippler brush against the last coat of wet paint. The walls are primed in the usual way, but the final stippled coat is prepared more thickly than the first one. Ready-prepared cans can be bought, or existing paint can be thickened with semi-gloss. The stippler has to be pressed firmly but carefully into position, but not jabbed or an uneven surface will result. It is best to have two

people working at the same time, one to apply the main coat, the other to follow with the stippler.

Good effects can be produced by using contrasting colors in the top two coats of paint, so that the stippling reveals another color underneath. The ground coat must be absolutely dry and impervious to the stipple coat, and the colors of both should complement each other. A good apricot, for example, could be produced by painting a ground coat of red, with an orange cast. A buff-colored top coat should be applied, then stippled almost immediately.

Brush stippling   **Paper stippling**

Dragging

This technique is not unlike stippling. It requires a good base coat, which should be allowed to dry before applying the top coat. Do this with an almost dry brush in a slightly darker color than the first coat.

Combing

This technique produces a thick, coarse texture on the walls, and is achieved by dragging a steel, rubber or metal comb through a wet top coat. The thickness of the stripe will depend on the size of the comb, and the pattern – whether straight, crossed or circular – is a matter of choice. The base is painted first and allowed to dry. Then the top coat is put on and the comb dragged through it. If two different colors are used, for example, brown and cream, interesting optical effects will be produced.

Scumbling or rag rubbing

In this technique, the effect is produced by brushing or wiping off parts of the top, scumble color to reveal the coat beneath. The wall should be well primed, and an undercoat applied (never use gloss paint, or the top coat will not take). The top or scumble coat, which must be thicker than the original so that it will not spread or run, must be applied quickly. Special, thick paints can be bought from paint stores or made up with the addition of semi-gloss. Once the top coat has been applied, use either a well-worn brush, or a wad of cheesecloth or tissue paper to brush across the areas which are to be lightest. Then use a stippling brush to soften lines.

Murals

Many people shy away from producing their own murals, but when carefully planned and executed, they provide a wall-covering which is not only imaginative, but also cheap. The mural itself can be used as a decorative device. For example, a small, dark room can be made to appear larger by painting a 3-dimensional scene on one wall; a windowless room can be made to seem lighter by painting in a window; an old fire-place with a decorative alcove on one side only can be given a balanced look by using the *trompe l'oeil* effect of an identical alcove on the other side. If initially, you cannot trust your own design ability or skill, use pictures or postcards for inspiration.

The most suitable paints for murals are latex and artists' acrylic, and the manu-facturers' tint and mix ranges, especially, provide a wide variety of colors. Remember, too, that remnants of paint cans can be used up, provided they are sound. Use a standard paint brush for large areas and thinner artists' brushes for more intricate or detailed parts.

To draw up the design on the wall, first divide the mural area into a grid of one inch (2·5 cm) squares, using a soft pencil or charcoal. Measure the length of your original design and divide this number by the number of one inch (2·5 cm) squares along the bottom of the mural area. This figure will be the width of each square on your design grid. For example, if the width of the final mural is one inch (2·5cm) $\times$ 24 and the width of your original design is six inches (15cm), then the width of a single square for your design grid is 6 $\div$ 24 (15 $\div$ 24) $= \frac{1}{4}$in (6·2mm). You therefore draw up a grid of $\frac{1}{4}$ in (6·2mm) $\times \frac{1}{4}$in (6·2mm). Transfer the design onto the wall by carefully copying the original, one square at a time.

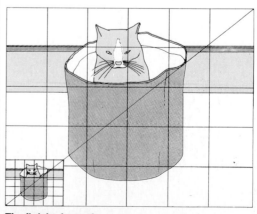

The finished mural
Shows the design scaled up square by square

ALL ABOUT WALLPAPERS

Wallcoverings can be divided into papers, fabrics, tiles, wood paneling, mirrors and laminates, and the prices within these groups vary from the cheap and comparatively cheap papers to the more expensive forms of wood paneling or silk wallcoverings. A cross-section of the styles and patterns available internationally is shown on pages 212 to 243.

Wallcoverings are chiefly used for cosmetic purposes. They are good disguisers, helping to change the apparent proportions of a room by visually enlarging or minimizing space. They can also be used to cheer up gloom, to turn the bleak into the comfortable, and to give a sense of style if none existed before. Each type of wall-covering includes such a wide range of colors and patterns that the difficulty is more one of narrowing down the choice than of finding something that is suitable within a given price range.

If you especially like a wallcovering but cannot afford it in quantity, do not despair. Consider buying, for example, only one or two rolls of paper to use as panels against a wall painted to match either the background or a predominant color in the paper. Alternatively, restrict the use of more expensive papers to small areas like bathrooms, washrooms and powder rooms, making sure that they are given a final coat of clear varnish to protect them. Some papers are inclined to run with varnish, so do test a small corner before using them.

General information on how to measure up for quantities is given in the Design Kit. Make sure that you order all your paper at the same time because there are sometimes color discrepancies in different batches which might show up on your walls.

Which pattern to use

The kind of pattern you choose depends entirely on personal taste and the proportions of the room. There are, however, certain general rules which are useful to know. For example, in a living room, it is preferable to use calm designs or plain papers with borders or friezes, since very strong patterns can be distracting and also make the choice of soft furnishings more difficult. Dark paper generally makes a room seem smaller; vertical stripes will make low ceilings seem higher, and horizontal stripes will seemingly broaden out a space (see illustrations for examples).

Miniprints, small geometrics, linear prints, small florals and gentle abstracts can all be successfully used in bedrooms. Miniprints are the best choice for small rooms, while more open patterns look

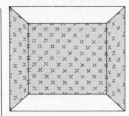

Miniprints: create a sense of space in small rooms

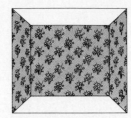

Large patterns on walls: plain ceiling helps retain sense of height

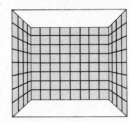

Large patterns on walls and ceiling: make room seem smaller

Geometric prints: give greater impression of space

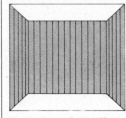

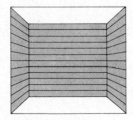

Vertical wood paneling: makes ceiling seem higher

Horizontal wood paneling: makes room seem wider

better in large spaces (see illustration). Scenic and geometric-patterned papers, plain papers with borders and friezes, large florals, abstracts, foils, mylars and trellis papers can all be used to great effect in halls, corridors and staircases. Any proportional faults in these areas can be hidden by clever use of the wallpapers.

All about Wallpapers

Wallpapers are available in a wide range of colors, patterns and finishes. They are machine- and hand-printed in a wide range of sizes, with plain, pre-pasted, or self-adhesive backings. In order not to be overwhelmed by the choice in a store or showroom, it is a good idea to work out exactly what effect you want a paper to achieve before making a final selection.

Apart from the standard paper varieties, there are a number of specialized types, often suited to a specific decorating problem; these are listed below:

Anaglypta and Lincrusta papers

These are very tough, washable papers and are ideal for hard-wear areas, or for covering old or irregular walls. Bear in mind, however, that no amount of cosmetic treatment will hide damp or peeling walls, which must first be treated at source. When carefully chosen both these types of paper can provide interesting textures.

Anaglyptas are made from wood pulp embossed with a texture or pattern and they invariably look better if they are painted (see page 211). Lincrustas consist of linseed oil, welded to a backing paper and then embossed with a burlap or tile-like texture. They too can be painted over.

Supaglypta and Vynaglypta papers

These hard-wearing papers differ in both texture and effect from Anaglyptas and Lincrustas, although they are used in the same situations. Supaglypta is a heavyweight, cotton fiber paper with a deeply embossed pattern; the equally heavy Vynaglypta is made of vinyl. Both can be used on badly cracked walls, but for the best effect they should be painted over with a latex or gloss paint.

Embossed and flocked papers

More suited to traditional styles of furniture, these papers are a practical choice for use on less than perfect walls. They also add an element of warmth. Although not usually appropriate to modern furnishings, some of the updated traditional patterns produced can look distinguished in formal living rooms and bedrooms. There are also geometric patterns available as an alternative to the old floral motifs.

Vinyl papers

These waterproof coverings are tougher than ordinary, washable wallpapers because they are made from backed polyvinylchloride rather than paper with a plastic coating. Vinyls stand up well to grease, fingermarks and cooking splashes, and are therefore ideal for use in kitchens, bathrooms and playrooms, as well as in corridors and staircases where the walls get a good deal of hard wear. Vinyls must, however, be stuck on with a fungicidal adhesive or mold will form underneath.

Foil and mylar papers

When used with lining paper, these steam-resistant wallcoverings are particularly useful in bathrooms and kitchens, as well as in dark areas where they will help lighten the space. Avoid using them on very uneven surfaces because they emphasize imperfections, or in very sunny situations where they will cause too much glare.

Wallpapering

Hanging wallpaper is more difficult than simply painting walls, but provided you use the right tools, and read and follow any instructions carefully, there should be no problems. The easiest papers to hang are obviously the plains, followed by the textured and woven varieties, then the striped, mini and all-over prints. Large repeating patterns are not so difficult, as long as you are careful about matching repeats. Bear in mind that if you have to work alone always use pre-trimmed light papers, and choose middle widths (between 24 and 30 ins (61 and 76cm)).

Preparing to wallpaper

Remove drapes and as much furniture as possible; cover carpets with cloths. Put up a pasting table, and have all tools, ladders and platforms that you require near at hand. Old wallcoverings should be thoroughly soaked with warm water and scraped off when soft. Any exposed plaster should be washed to remove all trace of paste; cracks should be filled in and the surface given a coat of size (usually a mixture of thinned wall adhesive). The same applies to newly plastered walls. Old vinyl should strip off in lengths, without needing to be soaked, and the backing that is left behind papered over directly. Latex- and alkyd-painted walls should be washed and dried prior to papering, and all glossy surfaces should be rubbed down with wet and dry paper.

Cutting wallpaper

Measure the length from the bottom of the wall to the top, and add 2in (5cm) cutting allowance. Cut out the first length to this measurement. If the wallpaper is plain, the whole roll can be cut into lengths at once. If, however, there is a pattern repeat, it is advisable to cut out and hang the first piece of paper before matching up the second against it. If you are pasting a large pattern always try to have a complete motif at the top of the wall. Keep all odd lengths as they may be useful for papering around doors or under windows.

Wallpaper has to be hung vertically, but do not rely on window and door frames to provide a straight guide – rely, instead, on a plumb line. To mark the vertical, either hang the plumb-line from a nail tapped into the masonry, or suspend it between thumb and forefinger. Whichever method used, make marks along the length of the plumb-line (having positioned it about 2in (5cm) short of the width of the wallpaper out from your starting point).

When hanging wallpaper it is usual to

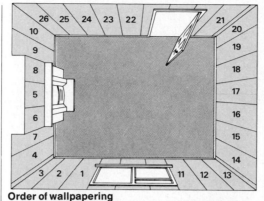

Order of wallpapering

1 Align long edge of first strip with vertical mark. Overlap at ceiling edge.

2 Brush over paper, from the center outwards, to remove air bubbles; trim top.

3 Unfold lower half, and brush it into position using the same technique as before.

4 Run scissors over paper, along baseboard to mark lower edge. Peel back and trim.

5 Measure and cut the length of paper before the corner, allowing $\frac{1}{4}$in (5mm) overlap.

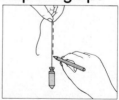

6 Paste next section on top of this so that its edges cover the overlap.

start by the window, so that any slight overlaps in the paper where two pieces join do not cast shadows and draw attention to the imperfect alignment.

Pasting wallpaper

Take your first length and lay it face down with the long sides parallel to those of the pasting table. To avoid pasting the table, let the long side of the wallpaper furthest from you overhang the table edge by about 2in (5cm). The paper must be thoroughly pasted or else bubbles will form under any dry patches, so paste the paper in two

halves. When you are satisfied that the first half is well covered fold the short edge to the center. Paste the left-hand half and fold over towards the center to meet the other edge. If any paste gets onto the front quickly wipe it off with a moistened sponge. The paper can either be draped over an arm and taken directly to the wall or, if the paste has to soak, it can be left over a chair back.

Hanging wallpaper

Take the first length of paper and gently unfold the top half. Position the top edge so that it overlaps the ceiling by about 2in (5cm). Take great care to align the long side of the paper with the plumb-line mark on the wall. When you are satisfied that it is in the right position, run a paper hanging brush lightly down the center of the sheet, then brush outwards to secure the rest of the paper. If any air bubbles appear, carefully peel back the paper before smoothing it into place. Any persistent bubbles should be pricked with a pin or sharp knife point, and then smoothed flat. Run the back of a pair of scissors along the line where wall and ceiling meet. Peel back the paper and trim off any excess. Smooth back into place. Unfold the bottom section of wallpaper length and repeat the brushing-in process. Take care to brush off any excess paste on adjacent sections. Pick up the second length of paper, unfold the top half and align it carefully with the one now in position. If you have pasted the first one correctly on the vertical, there should be no problems with consecutive lengths being straight. Brush out as before, and continue papering.

Papering tips

Plumb-line
Always use this to draw the vertical line prior to papering.

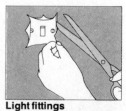

Light fittings
To expose fitting, cut a cross in paper; peel back and trim.

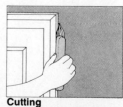

Marking (left image below)

Marking
1 Run scissors' back along overlap to mark a crease line.

Cutting
2 Peel paper back gently and trim excess. Brush remainder into position.

ALL ABOUT FABRIC WALLCOVERINGS

Wallcoverings in this group include both rough and smooth weaves, thick wools, burlaps, suedes, silks, felts, corduroys, flannels, and grasscloths. Although they are usually more expensive to buy than papers, they are well worth the extra expense in terms of practical and decorative appearance. Like papers they cover up imperfections in a wall, but more than this, they also act as sound and heat insulators and can be treated against dirt, spot-cleaned and vacuumed. They will also still look fairly pristine long after papers have faded and paint has become chipped and discolored.

Sticking fabric to walls

Most fabric wallcoverings are paper-backed for easy hanging but with care almost any unbacked fabric of reasonable weight and firm weave, like felt, can be stuck onto the walls. Try to choose fabrics which are stain- and mildew-resistant, as well as stretch- and fade-resistant. The important thing to remember when using unbacked wallcoverings is that the adhesive should be applied to the walls and not to the fabric. Any edges which have frayed during the process of hanging can be covered with braid or a trim of chrome or brass for a heater effect.

There are, however, two very effective alternatives to pasting, and these are battening and hanging.

Battening fabric to walls

Another way of using fabric as a wallcovering is to staplegun it directly to the wall, covering any raw edges with braid or trim. However, you get a better-looking, more professional and smoother finish if the fabric is stretched between battens. Laths or thin strips of wood are fixed horizontally along the top and bottom of

the wall, just below the ceiling or molding and just above the baseboard. Vertical strips of wood are then added at six feet (2m) intervals and then the fabric is seamed where necessary to join the lengths.

The first fabric panel is attached by centering it between the outside edge of the first vertical lath and the middle of the second one. With the top of the fabric level with the top of the horizontal batten, it is lightly tacked in the middle. The fabric is stretched to either side, tacked, then stapled into position.

To neaten the joins between two fabric panels, the trick is to use a piece of cardboard. Place the second panel, right side down, onto the edge of the first panel so that their two cut edges align. Lay a strip of cardboard over this join (see illustration), and staple through card and fabric onto the batten. Continue in this way. Any staple marks can be covered with lengths of matching or coordinating braid. This braid can also be used around doors.

If paintings or prints are to be hung on the walls it is important to work out where they are to go beforehand so that any battens can be positioned to hold the picture fixtures. Once the fabric is up, it is relatively quick to feel where the battens are and to hammer hooks or nails through.

Fabritrack

This almost foolproof system of attaching fabric to walls leaves the material neat and taut, without the need for battens or glue. Briefly, the system consists of long plastic strips with what the manufacturers call "jaws" to hide jagged edges, and an adhesive strip to hold the fabric tight.

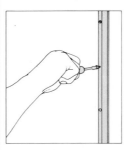

1 Decide at what intervals you want the strips to be. Following the manufacturer's instructions, screw them into the wall.

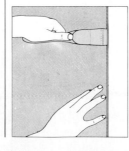

2 Using the special tool provided with the strips, push the fabric into the frame to secure it in position.

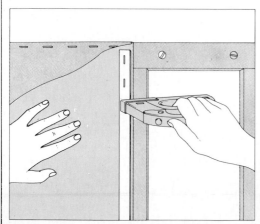

Staplegunning card for a neat, secure seam

Hanging fabrics on walls

The other way to cover walls with fabric is to hang the material. This is ideal for rentals because it does not damage the walls and the fabric can be taken away when you leave. Lightweight fabrics like muslins and cheesecloths can be shirred and hung between rods, wires or laths attached below the ceiling and above the baseboard, and slightly heavier fabrics like closely-woven linens or painter's cloths, can be suspended from rods or poles and left to hang free at the bottom (see Room-by-Room Guide, page 129). Whichever method you choose, the fabric can be neatly caught up and pulled back from windows and doors using fabric or cord ties.

Shirring

A lot of fabric is needed to produce a shirred effect (roughly three times the wall's width) which is why a relatively cheap fabric like muslin is ideal.

There are two ways to produce a shirred effect. In the first the fabric is gathered with shirring tape before it is put onto the walls. In the second the gathering occurs naturally as the fabric is slotted onto the rod or pole which is then mounted on the wall (for instructions, see below).

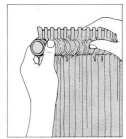 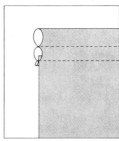

1 Make the casing large enough for the pole to slide into, but small enough to fit snugly.

2 Slide the fabric onto the pole, evening out the gathered material as you do so.

The finished wall, hung with tightly shirred fabric

ALL ABOUT HARD WALLCOVERINGS

Tile, wood and plastic wallcoverings are produced in a wide range of styles and colors, and are a tough, hard-wearing alternative to the usual fabrics, paints and wallpapers. A selection of them is shown on pages 232 to 241.

Ceramic tiles

These are the most popular of the hard wallcoverings, and are produced in a correspondingly wide range of sizes, shapes, colors and patterns. They are a functional, yet good-looking covering for walls in kitchens, bathrooms, utility rooms, powder and washrooms. There is no reason why they should not be used in general living areas as well, especially in hot climates where they look refreshingly cool. Remember that interesting effects can be produced by mixing patterns, colors and shapes, and by using plain tiles with borders; even broken tiles can be used to dramatic effect (see Accessories, page 345).

Ceramic tiles are comparatively easy for a beginner to lay in small areas, as long as each step of the process is planned out and the techniques are understood. For larger areas, it is more sensible to hire an experienced fitter. All tiles must be fixed to sound walls. Old walls should be stripped, flaking paint removed and cracks filled. Painted surfaces should be sanded and a coat of stabilizing primer applied to the newly-cleaned surface. A wall of old tiles actually provides a good surface for new ones, but they must be washed well first, and any loose tiles replaced.

Metallic tiles

These are usually either aluminum or stainless steel, both of which are washable, waterproof, heat- and fire-resistant. They are generally produced in squares (although other shapes and designs are available), and look very effective when used as a splashback behind a working area in a kitchen (see page 102). Despite being perfect for High-Tech schemes they are expensive, and they do show splash marks easily.

Cork tiles

These are produced in a wide range of natural colors, from light honey to rich chestnut, as well as in a number of lightly patterned styles. They are easily laid with glue, although some varieties are now self-adhesive. As cork is not naturally washable, it should only be used in kitchens and bathrooms once it has been coated with a vinyl sealer to make it moisture-resistant.

Mirror tiles and sheets

Tiles are much cheaper and easier to manage than sheets of mirror although they do not have the large unbroken look of the latter. Mirror tiles can be bought in plain and tinted varieties; sheet glass comes in a bigger range of tints and colors, from clear to near-black. Many mirrored surfaces are self-adhesive, and should be attached to a shiny surface. If you choose sheet mirror, do remember when measuring up, that it will have to be manoeuvered through doorways, and that the larger the unbroken areas of mirror, the more expensive the price and the more difficult the work of installation. Plastic mirror is another alternative, particularly for bathrooms, since it does not steam up so readily as regular mirror. It is much the same price, but less prone to breakages although it can crack or run like a stocking when being put up.

Acoustic tiles

These are used for ceilings rather than walls and are made to absorb sound. They have to be suspended from battens and are most often made from pre-finished, slotted insulation board, polystyrene or fiberglass.

Wood paneling

Boarding and paneling – now available in all sorts of colors and finishes – is specially manufactured for covering walls, and is as good an insulator as it is handsome. Tongue-and-groove is cheaper than the veneered paneling and can either be left natural, although sealed for easy-care, or painted over. It can be used vertically, horizontally or diagonally, and can even be covered with fabric.

If you are paneling a stud partition, you can fix it directly to the studs. A brick wall, however, will need to be battened horizontally at regular intervals. Vertical battens should be placed to correspond with the panel edges.

Plastic laminates

These come in almost as many colors, finishes and designs as ceramic tiles, and they are tough, durable and heat resistant. Laminated panels for walls are thinner than the hard-wear laminates used for work surfaces, but they are nevertheless useful in kitchens, bathrooms, shower rooms and corridors. They should be glued onto plywood or particle board, and can easily be cut with a fine-toothed saw. Although they are not cheap, they are generally less expensive than their equivalent area covered in ceramic tiles.

Tiling a wall

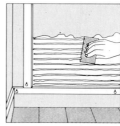

1 Fix horizontal and vertical laths. Spread adhesive.

2 Align tiles and press firmly into position on the wall.

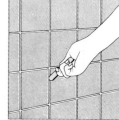

3 Allow adhesive to dry then grout the tiles all over, rubbing well into the joints.

4 Remove excess grout once it has set. Smooth down joints with a piece of rounded wood.

Decorative effects

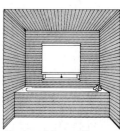

Diagonal paneling

Horizontal paneling

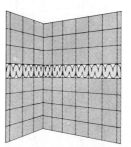

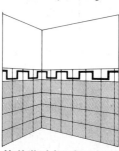

Fully-tiled, bordered wall

Half-tiled, bordered wall

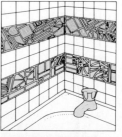

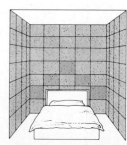

Broken-tiled borders

Decorative cork border

ALL ABOUT FABRICS

Fabric has an enormous number of uses in decoration, from softening hard lines and pepping up dull spaces, to covering seating, ceilings, walls, and even, on occasion, floors. Fabric can turn a dreary box of a room into a softly-draped luxury, add personality to an anonymous, rented space, and, in short, cover up a multitude of sins. In fact, much of the credit for improved standards in decoration is due to the variety of fabric designs and finishes now available (see pages 244 to 261). Identical designs can be printed on a wide range of different fabrics in a variety of colors, and many manufacturers now coordinate ranges so it is possible to mix and match furnishing fabrics in a room with the same infallibility as in clothing separates.

There are five main categories of fabric; four are natural (cotton, linen, wool, and silk) and one which is man-made includes synthetics like acrylic and nylon. The following brief guide may be of some help to a beginner, who may be lost amongst the number of fabric terms which exist.

Batiste
A fine, semi-sheer fabric, usually made of cotton; only suitable for delicate drapery.

Bouclé
Fabric made up from a tightly-looped yarn, which gives it its chunky appearance; it is used for drapery and upholstery.

Broadcloth
A hard-wearing, woollen fabric with a glossy finish; suitable for upholstery and occasionally for drapes.

Brocade
A heavy silk fabric with an intricate, raised design; used for drapery and upholstery.

Broderie anglaise
Cotton fabric, usually white, with a cutout design; suitable for bedspreads and tablecloths.

Burlap (hessian)
A coarse fabric with an open weave, made in both medium and heavyweights; it is used for upholstery, and occasionally for drapes.

Cheesecloth
Lightweight, gauze-like fabric, made from cotton, and used for drapery.

Chintz
A medium weight, cotton fabric with a glazed finish, frequently used for traditional drapery or light-wear upholstery.

Corduroy
A ribbed, hard-wearing cotton, ideal for heavy-duty upholstery.

Flannel
A soft, woollen cloth used for light upholstery.

Gingham
A crisp-looking cotton fabric, woven into stripes or checks, and traditionally used for drapes or tablecloths.

Lawn
A fine, closely-woven cotton used for drapery or bed linen.

Moiré
Any fabric with a watered appearance, usually made of cotton or silk; used for drapery or light upholstery.

Repp
Cotton or wool, with a prominent, ribbed appearance, used for heavy-duty upholstery.

Terrycloth
An absorbant cotton with a looped pile on both sides; used for bathroom drapery and light upholstery.

General buying information
When you go to buy the fabric, having decided what weight is most suited to your purposes and what color and pattern you want, ask to see the bale unrolled, and in daylight. Check that there are no flaws in the material, and that the dye is consistant throughout. Buy all the fabric required in one batch. It is very important that you check and double check the exact amount that you need. Ask what fabric care is required; whether it has to be machine-washed or dry cleaned and whether it is stain-resistant.

Fabrics for upholstery
When choosing any sort of upholstery fabric it is important to think of the use to which it will be put, and the amount of wear it will receive. Consider to what extent the fabric will come into contact with children, dogs and cats, sun, grease, mud, ink, ballpoint pens, cigarette and cigar ash, food and drink. For example, people who have children and pets are likely to need much tougher fabrics than people who don't; dining chairs will take a tougher beating than occasional chairs; houses in the sun will need fade-proof fabrics more than most city houses. This may all sound

obvious but it nevertheless needs repeating. Lightweight cottons or silks can be used for some upholstery, if you are prepared to replace them fairly often, but most people look for the more practical, hard-wearing fabrics for every-day use. The toughest upholstery fabrics are canvas, denim, duck, cotton, cotton repp, twill and corduroy, which are all cotton-based, and linen union which is linen mixed with cotton. Wool provides a hard-wearing but softer upholstery finish, and is the basis for tweeds, wool repps and jacquards.

Light-wear settee in air-brushed silk

Improvising a loose cover
One of the most simple and economic loose covers for sofas and chairs is this one using painter's cloths. Calculate fabric length needed by measuring up from the floor, moving up and over the seat to the crest of the back, and down behind, to the floor; measure the width in the same way. Then add 10in (25.5cm) for tuck-in and hemming and cut out cloth accordingly.

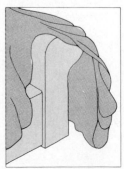 

1 Drape cloth over chair and tuck in to form basic shape. Gather excess of fabric on arms; mark tie positions behind these folds as you hold them.

2 Insert gromets into holes and hem cloth. Make cushion covers, then insert cord into gromets and tie to gather up fabric.

Fabrics for cushions

Not only do cushions add comfort to otherwise hard pieces of furniture, but they can also form an important part of a decorative scheme. Use cushions to provide splashes of color in otherwise monochromatic rooms (see Principles of Design, page 26), or consider them as a means of offsetting the seasons outside – choose warm, soft colors for winter and cool, sharp colors in summer. Cushions can be used to create an atmosphere in your room. For example, piles of neat, lace-covered cushions in different shapes will give a feminine effect while a single, firm bolster covered in a precise, geometric fabric will be much more masculine in appearance. Large floor cushions, which can even be used as adjuncts to seating, if necessary, will provide extra pattern, texture and color, and are also good in children's rooms.

Try experimenting with different cushion shapes – heart-shaped, shell-shaped, round, triangular – and consider decorating them with appliqué or even airbrushed paint or home-made stencils.

Delicate lace cloth, providing interesting contrast to old chairs

Fabrics for tables

Everyone uses tables in one form or another, whether for eating on, or displaying objects, or simply as dumping space. A round table covered with fabric makes the room look softer and prettier, although once again, the effect created will be determined by the fabric used. Lace has a gentle, delicate appearance, and will have a generally softening effect on most furniture. And an undercloth of lightly patterned fabric used with a small, plain overcloth or vice versa, will always introduce extra pattern and color to a room.

Fabrics for floors

Braided rugs have long been popular in both America and the north of Britain as attractive and economical household items. They are normally made in circular or oval patterns, and are most hard-wearing when made out of fairly thick, tweed-like fabrics. Braided rugs have a lovely, dappled appearance.

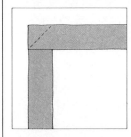

1 Wash all materials before braiding. Cut fabric into bias strips about $\frac{1}{2}$in (4cm) wide. Join across the bias, trim, then press open.

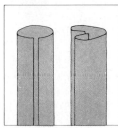

2 Lay strips right side down. Fold strip sides so they meet in the middle. Fold in half again, along the center line. Press.

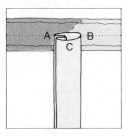

3 For a three-strand braid, join two strips together (A and B). Slot a third strip (C) in between the two at the center. Secure.

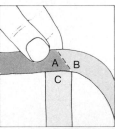

4 Begin braiding by moving A over between C and B. Continue braiding, always keeping your thumbs upwards, and the open edges to the right.

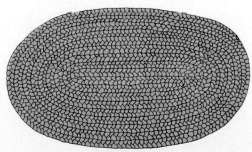

Finished rag rug

Care of fabrics

All fabrics will last a good deal longer if they are given regular attention – weekly if possible. Drapes and upholstery should be thoroughly vacuumed, cushions and pillows should be turned, and stains should be spot-cleaned as soon as they become apparent. Never saturate the fabric with the cleansing agent, and work out from the center of the stain to avoid leaving a ring mark. Always test chemicals and solvents on a hidden piece of fabric first, and for safety reasons, make sure that you keep all toxics out of the way of children. Remember to keep manufacturers instructions for care and cleaning filed along with all guarantee forms for easy reference.

Stain removal

Blood
Rinse with cold water until the stain is partly removed, then wash in warm, soapy water or water with an enzyme detergent.

Candle wax
Wait until the wax has hardened, then scrape off the excess. Lay a piece of blotting paper over the stain and press with a warm iron.

Chewing gum
Use carbon tetrachloride or methylated spirit to soften the gum, and then pick it off the fabric.

Coffee and tea
Treat stain immediately with a borax or peroxide solution.

Fruit and wine
Cover stains on wool and silk with borax and rinse in warm water.

Grease
Remove as much of the stain as possible with an absorbent like talc, then use carbon tetrachloride. Use eucalyptus oil on black oil and tar.

Ink
Rinse and wash as soon as possible. Soak indelible ink stains for three to five minutes in alcohol, then wash in warm, soapy water.

Milk
Rinse fresh stains with warm water but use a borax solution if dry.

Scorch marks
Wash in warm, soapy water as quickly as possible, or moisten the burn with a salt and lemon juice solution.

The range of window treatments for which fabrics can be used is shown on pages 332 to 333 and, as can be seen, it is varied enough to suit almost every decorative taste and budget. Here, we give simple instructions on how to make three of the more unusual types of shade. However, for specific details and measurements it is always advisable to consult an authoritative sewing manual.

Most fabrics, except very stiff, unyielding ones can be used at a window, but before you make your choice, there are two points to consider. Make sure, first of all, that the drapes or shades you choose suit the shape of the window (for problem windows, see page 336). It is equally important to choose appropriate fabric for the treatment, and to bear in mind how much, or how little light you want to let in. So, for general purposes choose from the wide range of plain and printed cottons and linens; where you want the room to be as light as possible, choose sheers or very light cottons; for heavy drapery use textured fabrics like slubs, bouclés or brocades; for formal drapes use velvets, silks or chintzes; for bathrooms and kitchens try plastic-coated fabrics; and for shades choose a tight weave but never a heavy fabric because it will not roll up well.

Buying information

Most stores stock a wide range of fabrics, so do shop around before you make a decision and don't be afraid to ask for advice. Your first consideration is bound to be color so, if possible, carry paint chips and fabric swatches around with you to compare the fabric with your walls and furniture. If you are in any doubt it is well worth buying a meter of the fabric to try out in the actual room (some stores even allow you to take home a bale of fabric which will give you a really accurate impression of the final effect).

Once you have made a choice, unroll several meters and drape it in your hand. It is most important that the fabric hangs well. Check that the fabric does not stretch. If it does, it will pucker when sewn and will not look right. For the same reasons, check the fabric's straight grain. The crosswise threads must run perpendicular to the lengthwise ones; if they are obviously out of alignment, don't take the fabric.

Finally, there is the cost. When choosing drapery fabric, for whatever room, do remember that it is far better to use yards and yards of cheap material (smartened, if needs be, with a braid or border edging), than to skimp on the amount of more expensive material.

Roman shades

These good-looking shades hang down almost as flat as roller types (see page 263), but as they are pulled up to the top of the window, they concertina into folds. They are particularly well suited to tailored, uncluttered rooms. While the fabric need not be as stiff as that for roller shades, it should be of a firm enough weave to fold well. Felts, heavy cottons and linen unions are therefore ideal for this window treatment.

Making the shades

First measure the window's width and length. To estimate the amount of fabric required add 4in (10cm) to that width and 10in (25cm) to that length. Cut out both fabric and lining to these measurements, and stitch together. Roman shades fold the way they do because of a series of cords threaded through rings on the wrong side of the fabric. These rings can be bought ready sewn onto tape, so you just cut the tape to the right length and stitch it at regular intervals along the shade.

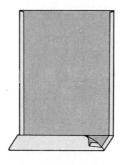

1 With right sides together, pin, baste and sew down both sides and along the bottom. Turn right side out and press. With lining side up, fold in two 1in (2.5cm) side hems. Turn up bottom edge by 4in (10cm); press. Stitch slat pocket 1½in (3.8cm) from this fold. Fold up another 4in (10cm) and press.

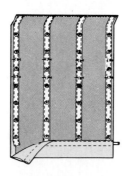

2 Mark the parallel lines for the tape. The first and last tapes should be 1½in (3.8cm) in, and the bottom rings on the tape should be at the top of the hem. Leave 1½in (3.8cm) at the bottom of each tape. Cut upper end of tape level with the top of the shade; stitch. Position other tapes, aligning rings. Insert slat and stitch up opening.

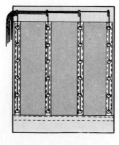

3 Attach shade to wooden heading board. Insert screw eyes (which will hold the pull-up cords), to align with the top of each tape. Insert cords from the bottom of the tape, securing each one firmly. Thread through each of the rings to the top of the tape and along the top of the shade.

Festoon or Austrian shades

These delicate-looking shades work on the same principles as Roman shades, but the fabric is shirred vertically so that the shade falls in a series of soft scallops. Take the window measurements. The width of fabric is determined by the number of scallops and a general rule is to double the desired finished width. The average length is 2½ times that of the finished shade.

1 Take the window measurements and calculate the fabric required (remember that the scallops should be no wider than 12in (30cm) each). Mark the parallel lines (1) on which the shirring tape will be stitched.

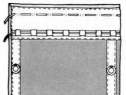

2 Hem the fabric and stitch the tape in place, following the same instructions given for Roman shades. Sew drape heading tape to the top of the shade, following the manufacturer's instructions.

3 Pull the cords of the heading tape until the fabric is the correct width for the window. Thread cords through the tape rings (see Roman shades), and mount the shade on the heading board.

Pull-up or balloon shades

These soft-looking shades are not unlike Austrian shades, although there is no shirring involved. The effect is created by deep, inverted pleats, which cause the shade to puff out along its base when the shade is pulled up. Measure length and width of window. Decide on the number of "balloons" to have. Divide the finished width by this to get each "balloon's" width.

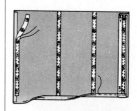

1 The fullness of this shade comes from the pleats – 2 singles each side; the remaining ones double. Add 6in (15cm) to your finished width per single pleat, and 12in (30cm) per double one.

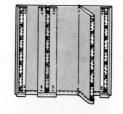

2 Hem both sides, and mark tape positions (these should fall in the center of double pleats). Sew on tapes, as for Roman shades. Make a 1in (2.5cm) double hem at the bottom.

Fabric for ceilings

Ceilings can be softened with fabric in much the same way as walls (see page 198). The most elaborate method is to tent them by attaching fabric from a central point and allowing it to fall in shirred folds to a selected level on the walls where it is caught and secured by some sort of border – as in the bedroom below. Here ceiling, window and bed treatments all combine to create a deliberately sensuous atmosphere (the pillars, by the way, are cardboard packing rolls covered with fabric). Alternatively, the fabric can be draped from hooks and wires (see right).

Luxurious room makes an imaginative use of fabric

Scalloped ceiling treatment

This is an ideal treatment for long, narrow rooms and corridors, and for lowering high ceilings. If a reasonably lightweight material is used, for example a stretch of dyed gauze, or a lightly-printed cotton, the effect created will be light and airy.

How to make

Measure the length and width of the area to be covered. Decide how many panels of scalloped fabric you want, and how deep they should ideally be. Divide the finished length by the number of panels and this will give you the number of hooking-up points, and the length between them. To make the finished treatment look neater, aim to seam the panels together at these points. Multiply the number of panels by the room's width, and add 4in (10cm) to get the total amount of fabric required. Cut out the fabric. Hem the two short sides of each panel (these will be the sides running the length of the walls). Next, join the panels together. With right sides facing, stitch a line 1in (2.5cm) deep across the widths.

Form the casing for the twine by making a second row of stitches $\frac{1}{4}$in (6mm) in from the edge. Insert the twine into the casings. Insert the hooks into the ceiling at the required intervals. With someone to help you, thread the twine onto the hooks, pulling it so the fabric lies close to the wall.

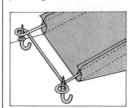

Scalloped ceiling
Essentially, fabric panels are joined together in a strip then threaded onto twine (left). This is then hooked onto the ceiling at regular intervals, to produce the draped effect, below.

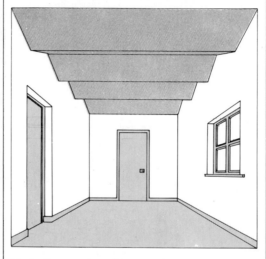

Fabric on beds

Fabric is used, not only for pillows and sheets, but also for comforters, head-boards and canopies (examples of the more elaborate bed treatments are shown on pages 348–9). On the whole, firm upholstery fabrics are best for tailored bed treatments, while lighter cottons, ginghams, chintzes and muslins are more suited to the softer looks. One new fabric – the pre-quilted variety – is ideal for making up comforters, as it keeps both its shape and finish and does not become rumpled (see Sample Book page 247). Don't be afraid to experiment with different patterns, scales and textures on the bed fabrics. So, for example, one scale of pattern can be used for the dust ruffle, with a plain or coordinating fabric for any side or back drapes (see Room-by-Room page 112). Similarly, reverse patterns can be used, or miniprints can be combined with geometrics (see page 116).

If you want to change the look of a bedroom one of the cheapest ways of doing it is to change the pillow covers or comforter and this little trick, along with an extra plant or two, can revive a room in a quite startling way. Many people automatically change pillows and slip covers on upholstery with the seasons, switching pastels and primary colors in the summer to richer, darker prints and colors in the winter. Some pillows are sold with different patterns and colors on either side to make the change of mood even easier. Sometimes, too, I have seen an unexpected color in a room, say a sweater over a chair, or even a shopping bag, which suddenly seems exactly right.

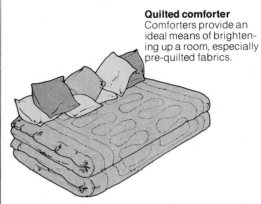

Quilted comforter
Comforters provide an ideal means of brightening up a room, especially pre-quilted fabrics.

The easiest way is to emulate it with a pillow or two.

Fabrics can also be used to make a feature out of a canopy or bedhead (see pages 348 to 349). Choose the fabric for your canopy according to the effect you want to create (a soft lace or a lightly-sprigged cotton for a soft feminine effect, or a heavy brocade or geometric pattern for a traditional effect). If you have an old bedhead which you want to re-vamp, try padding and covering it with a fabric to coordinate the bedcovering. Remember, too, the decorative device of framing the bedhead with a similar pattern to the wall. This is very effective if you use felt on the walls, to match the colors on the bedhead,

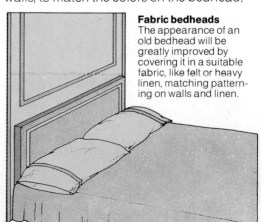

Fabric bedheads
The appearance of an old bedhead will be greatly improved by covering it in a suitable fabric, like felt or heavy linen, matching patterning on walls and linen.

ALL ABOUT HARD FLOORING

Floors take a tougher beating than any other surface, and are correspondingly expensive to cover. In terms of appearance and durability it is, as always, worth buying the best that you can afford.

Do not make any decisions about new floor coverings before you have decided whether you can revitalize the old in any way. You may, for example, try painting or dyeing your old carpets. Old timber floors, if they have no gaps, splits or splintered ends, need only be polished for a totally new appearance. Even if they are in bad condition they can easily be sanded down then sealed and polished. Another alternative is to paint them, either with deck paint, or with ordinary gloss paint with a finishing coat of clear varnish.

If you want to re-vamp tiles or stones, they can be painted over (see pages 242–243); even ordinary concrete slabs can be rubbed with shoe polish and crayons, then waxed to take on a battered flag-stone look.

Buying information

Before you decide on the floor covering, consider what room it is to be used for and what kind of wear and tear it will have. For example, kitchens are hard-wear areas and should have correspondingly tough flooring. Tiles are therefore ideal, not only because they are resilient but because they are easily-cleaned, stain-resistant, non-scuff surfaces. They would not, however, be generally acceptable for bedrooms, where people prefer the warmth of a carpet.

Other factors governing the choice of what floor to lay, especially in apartments, will be building regulations and requirements. Concrete floors can be covered with any kind of hard flooring like wood or parquet, composition tiles, marble, slate and even brick. However, with suspended floors, care has to be taken against stress. Carpet can be laid on almost any surface, although it is easier to lay on wood.

When you go to buy your floor covering, take samples of your wallcoverings and upholstery with you to get an accurate idea of the color and pattern combination. Bear in mind that while lightly polished floors reflect light, they show dirt more quickly, so if you have a large family, a patterned flooring might be more practical.

Tiled flooring

Although floors using brick, slate, marble, mosaic, terrazzo, ceramic and quarry tiles are expensive and hard on the feet, they provide a handsome surface, particularly useful in areas like kitchens. For examples, see pages 264–271.

Ceramic tiles

Made of clay, these hand- or machine-made tiles are fired at high temperature, and glazed; they are most useful for floors when they have a non-slip surface. They come in an enormous range of colors, designs, textures and shapes, for use both indoors and out (frostproof, vitrified tiles should be used for decks, terraces and patios). Like all other hard tiles, they can be tough on the feet and noisy, but they are invariably good to look at and easy to maintain. Tiles require a solid floor, and can either be laid on a concrete sub-floor with a cement or sand screed, or on any other smooth sub-floor with a latex screed. Like wall tiles, they can be used in conjunction with borders, wood or metal strips, and even differently patterned tiles. They should be cleaned with soap and water.

Mosaic tiles

There are three types of mosaic tile: glass silica, clay and marble. Available in a wide range of colors with varying textures, they are manufactured with peel-off sheets for easy laying. This elegant flooring should be laid on a screeded sub-floor base where a mixture of colors can be used to make up interesting patterns. Mosaic tiles can be washed, and cleaning is easier if the flooring is continued up the walls by about six inches (15.2 cm).

Quarry tiles

These are made from unrefined, well-fired high silica alumina clays. They are usually square or rectangular in shape and are available in various sizes and colors, ranging from beiges and browns to dark blue and black; there are also blended colors which look pleasingly mellow. They are impervious to grease and liquids, and are therefore both practical and hard-wearing for kitchens, halls and country rooms. Quarry tiles should be laid on a screeded sub-floor and sealed like slate; they wash easily.

Bricks

Special types of hard-wearing brick (or pavers) are available for use indoors, and are produced in shades of red, blue, brown, purple and yellow. They should be laid on concrete, and can be sealed for a stronger finish. Wash them gently.

Marble tiles

This natural stone flooring, generally imported from Europe, is available in colors including white, pink, green, gray, brown and black. The size of tiles is usually between twelve inches (30.5 cm) and eighteen inches (45 cm) square, although slabs can be specially ordered. This attractive flooring should be laid either on a cement bed on a concrete sub-floor, or on very flat block or particle board. Either lay a solid block of color or one main color with a border. Marble can be swept, washed and scrubbed, but never with acid cleaners.

Terrazzo

This flooring consists of marble chips set in a concrete base, and is available in tiles and slabs of varying colors. It should be laid on a screeded sub-floor, but care should be taken as it is expensive to lay and finish in small areas. The surface should be swept and washed but not polished.

Slates

This hard, impervious and expensive stone flooring is available in gray, green and blue-gray colors. It frequently has a lightly sculpted, rippled base. Since it is rather a tailored stone it looks best in squares or rectangles and can be used in conjunction with a different surround, like wood, for example. It should be laid in a cement bed. Slate floors should be swept and washed.

Vinyl

This flooring usually consists of a layer of vinyl backed with either latex or asbestos. Asbestos backing is useful for basement floors, or for any rooms, like bathrooms or utility rooms, which get damp. Latex-backed vinyl gives a softer feel to concrete or wooden floors; it is also a good sound reducer. Both types are produced in sheet and tile form, and are easy to care for.

Positioning tiles for laying

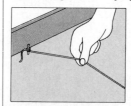

1 Mark room's center with two intersecting pieces of string.

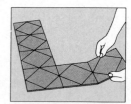

2 Lay out two rows of tiles from the center to the walls.

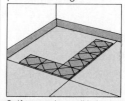

3 If space by wall is less than 3 inches (7.5cm), move center line out by half a tile's width.

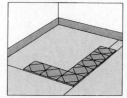

4 Fix the two center tiles and work outwards until the tiles reach the walls, and fit properly.

Tile patterns

A tiled floor will be visually more interesting if it is laid in an imaginative way. Try either using tiles which are unusually shaped, or combine different shapes and colors. If you want to enlarge a space, lay them on the diagonal.

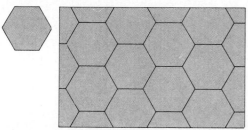

Pentagons

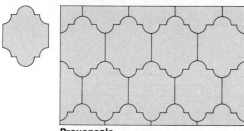

Provencals

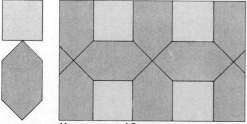

Hexagons and Squares

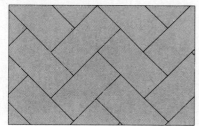

Rectangles

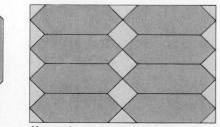

Narrow hexagons and squares

Wooden flooring

Wooden floors are usually divided into soft- and hardwood, although plywood, chipboard and hardboard can also be used in various ways to make inexpensive surfaces.

Softwood

These boards are generally made from spruce, fir and pine and should be finished with polyurethane or oleo-resinous sealer, then polished. Softwood provides a warm and handsome background for rugs, but if it is butt-jointed instead of tongue-and-grooved, beware that it does not shrink and leave gaps.

Hardwood

This is a high-quality flooring, available in oak, maple, afrormosia and teak, among others. Parquet is a form of hardwood and can be laid individually, or in panels already mounted on ply. It is resilient, warm, and hard-wearing and, like leather, seems to improve with age. Heating may cause shrinkage, so seal it like softwood.

Plywood

This is often produced to look like parquet, but in areas of heavy wear its appearance deteriorates rapidly. If being laid over floorboards it should be placed on a plywood base first. It must be sealed.

Particle board

This wood composite looks like cork when clear-sealed since it is made from different-sized wood chips, mixed with resins, and bonded under pressure. It can be used as a covering for concrete, prior to carpeting, or as a base for higher quality wooden floors. It is a cheap and efficient sound insulator but must be sealed immediately and the seal maintained as it stains badly.

Hardboard

This makes a cheap, short-term flooring which can later be covered with carpet or tiles, so it is good for people on a tight budget. It should be cut to order and sealed, or stained and sealed, when in place.

Corks

These are made of compressed and backed pieces of cork. Produced in both tile and sheet form, their color range is narrow — from light to dark brown. If used with a polyurethane sealer both provide a quiet, resilient surface which looks good in kitchens, bathrooms and children's rooms. They should always be laid on an even sub-floor. If they have been sealed they can be washed gently; stains are hard to remove.

Stenciling

With the popular Romantic revival, the work of men like Lambert Hitchcock and Louis Comfort Tiffany, both of whom designed and produced pieces of stenciled furniture, is once again of interest. Even more important, stenciling also provides a relatively cheap way to decorate walls, floors and furniture imaginatively.

Stencils, which are designs cut out of waxed paper or acetate, can be applied to most surfaces, including wood, plaster, plasterboard, wallpaper, metal, terracotta, brick, stone and fabric. Vinyls, ceramic tiles, glass, and other high-gloss finishes should be avoided because the paint will not adhere to their surfaces.

How to make a stencil

To make your own stencil you will need waxed paper (if you are uneasy about designing a stencil you can easily buy a pre-cut one), a utility knife for cutting the stencil, pencils for transferring the design, and stencil brushes or spray cans of paint to fill the design in.

Having drawn and cut out your design attach the stencil firmly to the surface in question. If using a spray can, fill in the stencil in light, circular movements, both clock and anti-clockwise. Do not concentrate on one small area; instead, build up a surface of color. If using a stencil brush, hold it vertically and dab the paint into the holes, starting top left and working inwards. Whichever method used, remove the stencil carefully to avoid smudging.

How to stencil

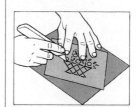

1 Draw up the design on stiff waxed paper. Cut it out carefully using a sharp knife.

2 Attach the paper to the surface being painted. If using a stencil brush, dab the color into the holes.

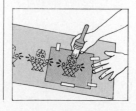

3 Where a series of designs is being applied, allow paint to dry, then remove and re-position each stencil.

ALL ABOUT CARPETS

As its name implies, soft flooring is the term used to describe the less resistant flooring surfaces like carpets, rugs and matting. The various piles or surfaces, and a good many patterns, are shown on pages 272–279. There follows a brief description of the types of carpet and matting currently available; specific terms are also included, to avoid any confusion:

Axminster
Like Wiltons (q.v.), Axminster carpets derive their name from the loom on which they are woven but unlike Wiltons, the loom positions the pile tufts at the same time as it weaves the backing. The surface is a cut pile, and because of both the size of the loom and the fact that the threads are not carried along the backing of the carpet, it is possible to weave in a great variety of colors. Quality depends on the type of fiber used. The best wearing is usually 80 per cent wool and 20 per cent nylon, but weaves made from acrylics, rayons or blends are also available.

Berbers
Carpets with a dense, looped pile, made from natural, undyed sheep wool. They are available in white, cream, beige, fawn, gray and dark brown.

Body carpet
A term for narrow widths of carpet, either 27 or 36 inches (68·5 or 91·5cm) wide. This is generally used for stairs, passageways and awkwardly-shaped rooms, where there will be less wastage than from broader widths. The denser, smoother, more expensive piles are often only available in body carpet.

Bouclé (or loop)
Pile formed by uncut loops of yarn, as in Brussels weave carpets.

Broadloom
The term for broader widths of carpet, woven on looms more than 6ft (1·85m) wide. The common widths are 6ft (1·85m); 12ft (3·7m); and 15ft (4·6m). Obviously, the more nearly a room approximates to these widths or their multiples, the less wastage there will be.

Brussels weave
The term for tightly looped rather than cut pile. Such carpets have a neat, crisp appearance which is ideal for clear-cut and geometric designs. However, like sweaters, they can snag, so ends need to be snipped off from time to time to keep it good looking.

Carpet tiles
Squares of carpet made from animal hair and viscose, wool and rayon, or cord. Usually quite inexpensive.

Coconut matting
Coarse matting used for doormats and runners. It has a rough, hairy finish which is ideal for absorbing excess dirt from boots and shoes.

Coir matting
A superior version of coconut matting. Coir comes in carpet widths in a good range of natural colors (although it can be dyed), as well as in different weaves. The more expensive qualities are backed with vinyl to stop dirt falling through and to provide a cushioned surface.

Cord
Although much cheaper, cord carpeting is woven in the same way as plain Wiltons, but it has an uncut pile that makes it look rather like corduroy.

Cut pile
As its name implies, the strands of yarn are cut not looped. The pile can be either short, long, or mixed with a looped weave to produce a sculptured effect. Axminsters and Wiltons both have cut pile.

Felt
This is sold in a special carpet thickness, in a very good range of colors, and is a cheap flooring for short-term rentals or infrequently-used rooms like guest and summer house bedrooms.

Indian carpet
This can be bought in both rug and broadloom widths, and is always off-white. The wool pile is looped and knitted into the backing so that it wears well. It is also comparatively inexpensive.

Looped pile
Uncut loops of pile; can be shaggy or smooth. Cords, some tufteds, Wiltons and Brussels weaves are available with a looped pile.

Low pile (plush or velvet)
A short, dense, deep and smooth cut pile finish, found in Wiltons and Axminsters.

Rush matting
Rushes can be woven into thickly-textured or plaited lengths or sold in squares. It can be laid loose over concrete and other hard floors, and is comparatively cheap.

Shag pile
Luxurious, one to two inch (2·5 to 5cm) long, cut pile carpet, best used in living rooms or bedrooms, but never stairs since heels can get caught in its surface. It gets dirtier more quickly than short pile carpets, and the cheaper varieties tend to flatten.

Sisal
A tough, durable white fiber which can be dyed successfully. It can be used in halls, passageways and other hard-wear areas.

Tufted
Non-woven carpets, made by needling individual fibers into the base material which is then coated with latex bonding to anchor the tufts. The pile can be cut, looped or mixed, and although the cheapest qualities should only be used in light-wear situations, the best tufteds can last as long as woven carpets.

Twist
A sturdy, hard-wearing finish, less likely to "shade" than the more luxurious velvets.

Wilton
Like Axminsters, Wiltons derive their name from the loom on which they are woven. In their case the yarn is woven in one continuous length so that surface pile and backing are woven together for extra durability. The number of colors in any one design is limited to about five, and as a result, patterned Wiltons are relatively rare: most people choose from the wide range of plain colors which are produced. The carpets are available with cut, looped and mixed piles or a short, velvety finish.

Carpet weaves
1 Gripper Axminster
2 Spool Axminster
3 Wilton
4 Tufted carpet
5 Bonded

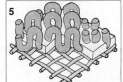
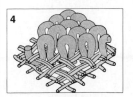
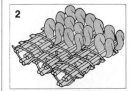

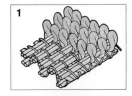

Planning

Most homes have a mixture of hard and soft flooring, so it is all the more important to remember the vistas that are constantly opened up in an apartment or house. Doors that lead off a corridor or hallway are often left open; glimpses of upper floors can be seen from stairways, and one room can often be seen when standing in another. Make sure that the feeling of space flows naturally by ensuring that floor coverings are coordinated, at least by color, if not by texture. A small space, such as an apartment, will seem much larger if there is a spread of one color throughout, and in large areas, where different flooring textures or colors meet at doorways, the effect is neater if a metal threshold strip is inserted between the two.

Which quality carpet to choose

The wearing qualities of all carpeting depend on the fibers used, and on how dirt-resistant they are. Although some fibers are particularly hard-wearing they might attract more dirt than others, hence the experiments with fiber mixtures to find good formulas. Wool carpets are comparatively dirt resistant, are luxuriously soft, and when mixed with 20 per cent nylon they are very hard-wearing, although expensive. Man-made fibers are improving all the time and non-static nylons, which are extremely tough and easily cleaned, are now being produced at attractive prices. The polyesters like Terylene and Dacron, which are soft and hard-wearing, are also fairly waterproof and are ideal for bathrooms.

Where to use which carpets

Since different areas of the home get more wear than others, it is sensible to put down different qualities where appropriate. For example, stairs, passages, hallways and living rooms get rougher use than bedrooms, while holiday houses and guest rooms get less wear than permanently lived-in areas. Adults' rooms usually get more gentle treatment than children's rooms, and any rooms near water (kitchens, bathrooms and utility rooms) need tougher surfaces than dry areas.

Hard-wear areas should have the best quality that you can afford. Rather than put down an inferior quality, it is better to start off with some sort of compromise treatment (like painted, stained or stenciled floors) until you feel that you can afford the right quality. Light-wear areas such as bedrooms can be covered with more luxurious, less hard-wearing flooring, like shag carpets.

Whichever carpet you choose, have it measured up (and laid) by experts, and check their estimates carefully to prevent over-ordering (a common fault). Remember that you will need to order more of an elaborately patterned or bordered carpet to guarantee that all patterned repeats match up.

Caring for your carpets

Neither carpet nor matting should be allowed to get too dirty. Although good quality wools, and wool and nylon are reasonably dirt-resistant they will look much better and have a longer life if they are vacuumed at least once a week. Shampoo them with a proprietary cleaning preparation once or twice a year (or whenever they look as if they need it), and spot-clean any stains as soon as they occur, making sure that in the process you do not over-wet the flooring.

Rugs

Rugs are useful in many different ways. They provide a comfortable surface for lounging on, by a fire or stove, they add extra color or texture to a room, and soften the effect of wood, tile or matting floors. In addition to oriental rugs (discussed on page 208 and illustrated on pages 282 to 288), there is also a wide variety of considerably less expensive, but no less distinctive, ethnic rugs. Produced by weavers throughout the world, these include flat weaves, deep, shaggy piles and hooked and braided rugs.

Care is much the same as for carpets. Deep-piled rugs need to be shaken and combed occasionally, and they need regular vacuuming. Any rug on a wooden or tiled floor should be secured to prevent it slipping using, for example, a slightly tacky mesh backing or Velcro which can be cut to the appropriate size. This same sort of backing can also prevent the irritating habit of "walking" when rugs are laid on top of carpets. Take care when cleaning skin rugs as some harden when wet.

The effects of carpet design

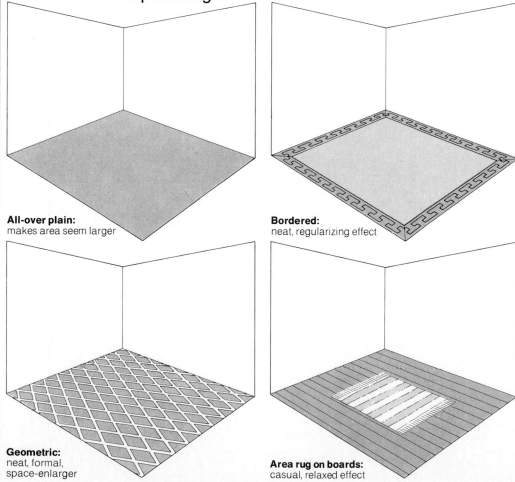

All-over plain:
makes area seem larger

Bordered:
neat, regularizing effect

Geometric:
neat, formal,
space-enlarger

Area rug on boards:
casual, relaxed effect

ALL ABOUT ORIENTAL RUGS AND CARPETS

The rugs, carpets and kelims made by village and nomadic craftsmen in Iran (Persia), Turkey, the Caucasus, Turkmenistan, China and India are generally known under the umbrella term of oriental carpets. Rugs and carpets are produced by *knotting* short lengths of wool around the warp threads of a loom; kelims, however, are made by *weaving* long threads in and out of the warp and weft, using much the same technique as for embroidery. In international usage, the term "carpet" is applied to any piece over forty square feet (four square meters); "rug" applies to anything smaller. In America, however, all handmade pieces are referred to as rugs (machine-made items are called carpets).

Whether the rugs are village, nomadic or factory-made, their designs are all based on traditional patterns and reflect the life and culture of the Islamic and Far Eastern worlds. It is usual for carpets to have a central "field" or "ground" which is surrounded by a border, and the designs in the center of the rugs range from the geometric and abstract to the figurative and floral.

Persian rugs and carpets

Although evidence suggests that rugs and carpets have been made in Persia for at least one thousand years, the earliest complete examples, including the famous Ardebil carpet now in London, England, date from the middle of the fifteenth century. Persian rugs are almost always rectangular or elongated rather than square, and are generally woven in wool using the *Senneh* knot. Their coloring is rich, and often has a central field of crimson or indigo, with figurings in warm browns, greens and yellows. The majority of designs are based on floral motifs, and some of the most popular are used in the "garden" rugs and carpets, so called because they are laid out in the form of a garden with paths, flowerbeds, pools and streams. "Vase" carpets are a more formal version of floral motifs, with vases holding flowers or plants. Occasionally figurative or geometric designs are used. The figurative "animal" carpets and rugs often show hunting scenes, while the geometric "medallion" pieces have a central geometric motif which may or may not be repeated.

Carpets made before the eighteenth century are usually classified according to their design, and are only attributed to specific towns (such as Herat, Heriz, Isfahan, Joshaghan, Keshan, Qum, Shiraz or Tabriz) after this date. However, if you see an early "animal" carpet there is a

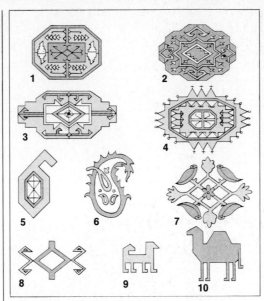

Traditional Islamic motifs: 1, 2 Guls; **3, 4** Tekkes; **5, 6** Botehs; **7** Herati; **8** Tarantula; **9** Dog; **10** Camel

reasonable chance that it was made at Isfahan, just as "vase" carpets probably came from Joshaghan, and "medallion" carpets from Herat.

Turkish rugs and carpets

Most Turkish rugs come from the Anatolia region of the country, hence the term Anatolian rug used by dealers. These rugs were popular in Europe long before the Persian varieties, so much so that until the eighteenth century, any hand-knotted piece was known as Turkey Work. They do, however, differ from Persian rugs, not only in design, but also in the type of knot used, which is generally the *Ghiordes* knot.

The most usual background colors are red and blue although Turkish prayer rugs are sometimes woven in green, a sacred color. Most Turkish rugs avoid the depiction of figures for religious reasons, and the most usual design has a pointed prayer arch or *mehrab*, at one end. This is sometimes flanked by two pillars of wisdom, or has a holy lamp hanging from it. In the more sophisticated workshops the design is elaborated with Arabic script.

The major rug-producing areas (including Bergama, Ghiordes, Hereke, Kula, Kum-Kapu, Mudjur, Panderma, Ushak and Yuruk) also developed their own individual designs and color combinations over the years. Ushak, for example, has a star design with rows of large stars filled with abstract flowers, worked in yellow or white on a deep blue base, surrounded by a white outline in contrast to the central ground.

Caucasian rugs and carpets

Caucasian rugs are very distinctive and brightly colored in red, blue, green and beige. The designs, although varied, are always severely rectilinear. Stylized figures, animals, birds, flowers, crabs, beetles or medallions are composed in geometric arrangements, with elaborately decorated borders of stars, rosettes or running dog patterns (the Caucasian equivalent to the Greek key pattern). The principal rug producing towns are Chi Chi, Kuba, Daghestan, Derbend, Karabagh, Kazak, Shirvan and Sumak.

Turkoman rugs and carpets

The Turkoman group includes rugs and carpets from Turkmenistan, Uzbekistan, Afghanistan and Pakistan. All use red as the predominant color, although different tribes and areas can be identified by the hues that they introduce into their designs. For example, rugs from the Beshire area of Afghanistan use yellow and green as well as red; Baluchis use a lot of dark blue with rust reds, bluish mauves and occasional touches of cream, ivory and camel. Their designs, like those of their Caucasian neighbors, are geometric and almost always feature the octagonal "gul" or rose motif.

Chinese rugs and carpets

Unlike most Islamic rugs, Chinese pieces were woven in organized workshops or factories, in much the same way as today, and it is quite clear that their design is based on totally different traditions. The ubiquitous reds and greens of Islam are almost unknown in China, where a preference is shown for more subtle blues, yellows, peaches and apricots. Their designs use the motifs common to most Chinese art. Buddhist and Taoist symbols are used extensively – animals, especially dragons, and flowers like the lotus, the peony, daffodil and pomegranate, are used extensively.

Indian rugs and carpets

Although the design of Indian rugs and carpets is generally in the Persian tradition, they have definite native characteristics, originally introduced to suit the tastes of the Indian merchants and princes who set up the various workshops. Abstract floral designs were replaced by animals, birds, trees and flowers, and colors became lighter than those in the Persian rugs, resulting in the extensive use of pink. Indian rugs are also notable for their long, relatively coarse pile.

HOW TO USE THE SAMPLE BOOK

One of the major hindrances to successful decoration in the eyes of most people is actually making the time to see what is currently available. Even when people do have the time, most have no idea where to go for what, or the scope of the choice available, and in many cases, of course, so many fabrics, wallcoverings, floorcoverings and tiles can only be seen in trade showrooms when accompanied by an interior designer.

In this Sample Book we try to obviate these difficulties by showing as many examples of the styles available in all the various decorating fields, as is possible in 96 pages. Almost everything shown here, or its near counterpart, is available internationally, and in the Directory of Sources on pages 355 to 359 we quote sources and showrooms in key centers. Even if a particular product is only available in one country, it is now perfectly possible to order merchandise from virtually anywhere in the world, and to pay for it by international credit card, bank draft, or even personal check (if you are prepared to wait several weeks for it to be cleared).

A portable department store

This section, then, can be treated like a portable department store with the most comprehensive stock that it is possible to buy; a concise catalog of almost everything that is good-looking, typical, and generally available. But the Sample Book is also much more than this because as well as being a guide to every sort of furnishing material, it also serves as a kind of visual dictionary of trade terms and definitions. How often in stores are we put off by salespeople (particularly in the carpet and fabric fields) who may, perhaps, use terms with which we are less than familiar and which we do not like to admit have no meaning for us. Terms like Wilton, Axminster, broadloom, Brussels weave, linen union, kelim, dhurrie, Afghan and Shiraz, for example, are all in common parlance in the trade, but they are not necessarily universally known. With the Sample Book you can familiarize yourself with terms and styles which will give you confidence when shopping.

The first part of the Sample Book gives a detailed appraisal of the best, as well as perhaps the more unexpected, uses of paints, wallcoverings, wall tiles, fabrics, shades and drapes, hard flooring (wood, and tiles of every kind), and soft flooring (carpets and rugs of every description), along with a brief introduction to the intricacies of oriental rugs.

The following pages illustrate actual samples from each of the above groups, and by showing the best of the sort of styles available may well provide definite ideas for schemes and will certainly save hours and hours of looking around. Obviously, it would never be possible to show examples of everything that is good in such a huge and constantly changing field, but we have tried to show the most classic examples or styles from each group of merchandise. And by classic, I mean examples that should have a life of over several years and will not suffer from any built-in obsolescence.

Used in conjunction with the Room-by-Room Guide and the Design Kit, it should be possible to use the Sample Book to work out exactly how your room will look, without any additional trouble or expense.

Sample Book scales

For an idea of the scale of each sample shown, see the instructions given, and to see how most samples would actually look in a room-setting, look carefully through the Room-by-Room Guide (pages 34–192) where many have been illustrated in the alternative schemes. Think about how each sample works, and how it can be adapted to your own personal requirements. And remember that most designs come in a good range of colors – quite apart from the examples illustrated.

Scale 2
The Scale 2 grouping includes the larger print wallpapers, fabrics, blinds, shades and carpets. To guarantee that a good enough idea was given of the pattern, the samples were photographed and reproduced as if they were *actually* seen at a distance of 12 feet (3·70m).

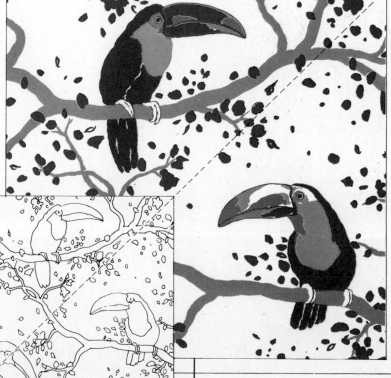

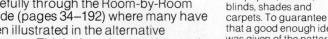

Scale 1
Samples reproduced at Scale 1 are the approximate size of the *actual* object when viewed at a distance of six feet (1·85m). Scale 1 covers the majority of our samples, and, more especially, small-print wallpapers, fabrics and plain carpets.

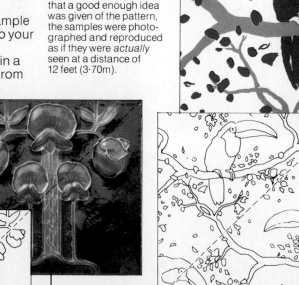

PAINTS

Although they can be applied to achieve a number of different effects (see page 194), paints are basically divided into oil-based alkyds, and water-based latex paints. Both types are available in flat, semi-gloss and full-gloss finishes. Oil-based paints take longer to dry, but are tougher and more easily cleaned than latex paints and are more suitable for use in kitchens and bathrooms.

Color combinations

These color combinations can be used with white or in varying permutations for walls, floors and accessories.

See page 26

See page 42

See page 68

See page 48

See page 58

Color range

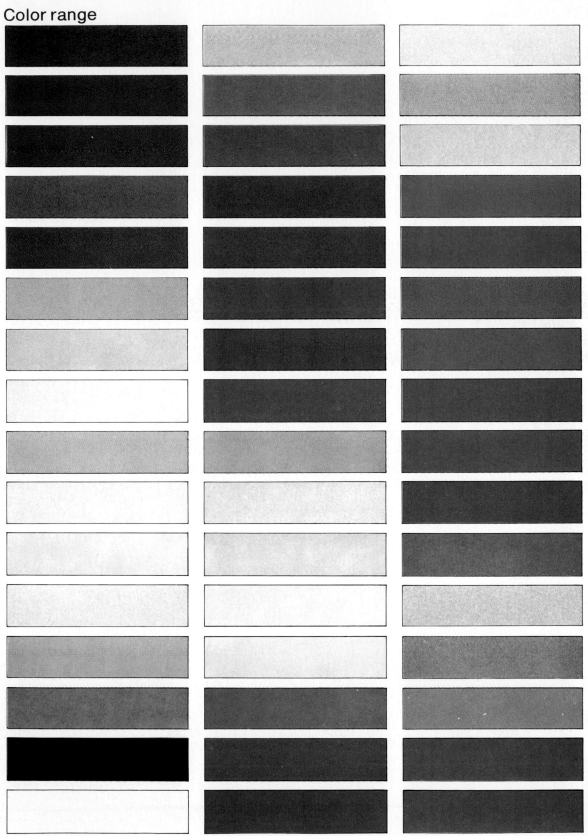

The uses of paint

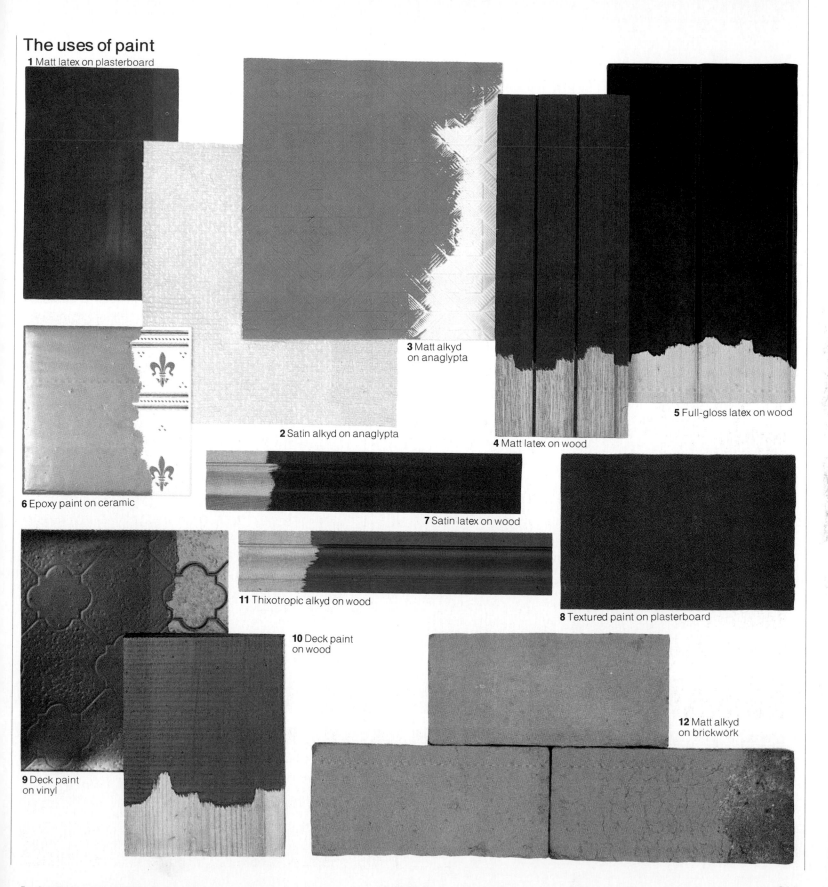

1 Matt latex on plasterboard

2 Satin alkyd on anaglypta

3 Matt alkyd on anaglypta

4 Matt latex on wood

5 Full-gloss latex on wood

6 Epoxy paint on ceramic

7 Satin latex on wood

8 Textured paint on plasterboard

9 Deck paint on vinyl

10 Deck paint on wood

11 Thixotropic alkyd on wood

12 Matt alkyd on brickwork

PLAIN WALLPAPER AND BORDERS

Usually placed along the top of a plain papered or painted wall, borders add distinction to otherwise featureless halls, corridors or rooms. Although they are usually produced in single strips, they are also available as part of a wallpaper design so that paper and border are manufactured in one piece. In this way they coordinate with the pattern and provide a neat finishing touch.

Stippled

1 Leaf Green

8 Sky Blue

Plain

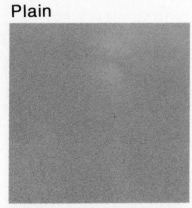
2 Beige

3 Blue

10 Dusky Pink

9 Elephant Gray

11 Pinky Apricot

4 Rust

5 Yellow

12 Tobacco

13 Midnight Blue

6 Field Green

7 Pink

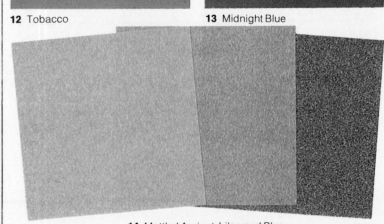
14 Mottled Apricot, Lilac and Blue

All items at Scale 1 reduction; see page 209

Geometrics

15 Parallels

16 Tramlines

17 Key Motif

18 Greek Key

19 Diamonds

20 Zigzag

Classical Motifs

21 Odeon

22 Art Deco

23 Scallop

24 Songbird

25 Bullrush Motif

26 Mackintosh

27 Art Nouveau

28 Tulip Motif

29 Twenties Motif

Florals

30 Tangleweed

31 Tulips

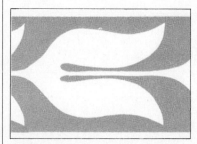

32 Lily

33 Ivy

34 Fans

Bordered Papers

35 Clover

36 Spanish Border

37 Provençal

38 Butterfly

GEOMETRIC WALLPAPERS

Geometric papers, which are a comparatively new departure in wallpaper design, are becoming increasingly popular because they can be successfully used to alter the perspective of rooms and disguise faults in their proportions. They also provide a neat, graphic finish to any space. These papers can be teamed with abstract prints, florals or plains, as their patterns rarely dominate.

Linears

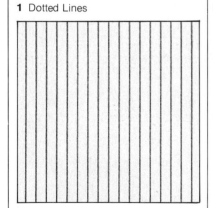

1 Dotted Lines

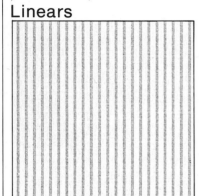

2 Narrow Lines

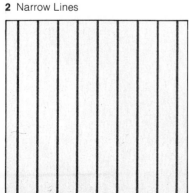

3 Wide Lines

Squares

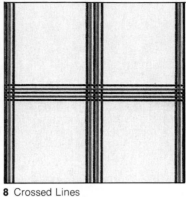

Grid

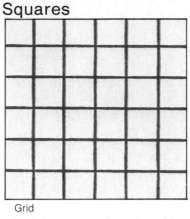

5 Wide Squares

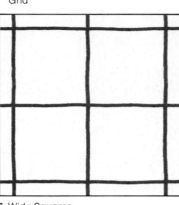

6 Plus Two

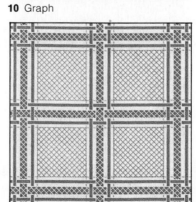

7 Mondrian

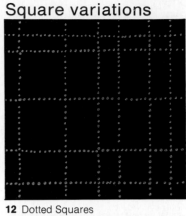

8 Crossed Lines

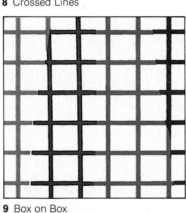

9 Box on Box

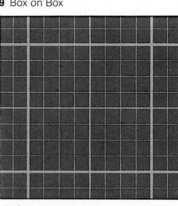

10 Graph

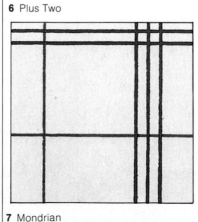

11 Bordered Squares

Square variations

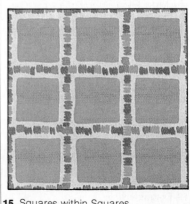

12 Dotted Squares

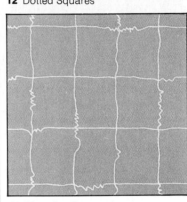

13 Wavy-line Rectangles

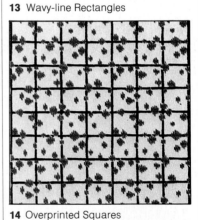

14 Overprinted Squares

15 Squares within Squares

All items at Scale 1 reduction; see page 209

Diagonals

Key patterns

Openweaves

16 Patterned Diagonals

20 Basketweave

24 Woven Keys

28 Art Deco

17 Trellis

21 Chevrons

25 Links

29 Web Weave

18 Patterned Trellis

22 Striped Diagonals

26 Diagonal Keys

30 Triangles

19 Diagonal within a Diagonal

23 Flying Arrows

27 Random Keys

31 Fan and Square

MINIPRINT WALLPAPERS

Patterned wallpapers are ideal for brightening up an otherwise dull room, and delicate miniprints are especially useful in small spaces, or for providing interest in rather dreary areas. Miniprints are available in a variety of patterns and colors, and because of their wide price range, are suitable for all budgets, as well as all tastes and types of room.

Diamonds

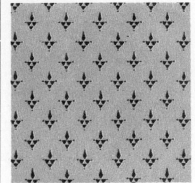

1 Trefoil

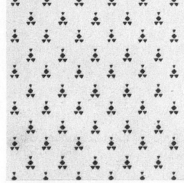

2 Triangles

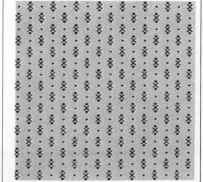

3 Crossed Diamonds

Sprigs

4 Small Flowers

5 Bellflowers

6 Daisies

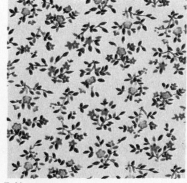

7 Nosegay

Dense Florals

8 Strawberry

9 Butterflies and Flowers

10 Clover

11 Rosehip

12 Dahlias

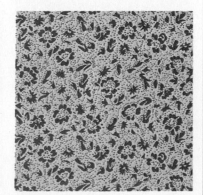

13 Flower and Seed

14 Tangleweed

All items at Scale 1 reduction; see page 209

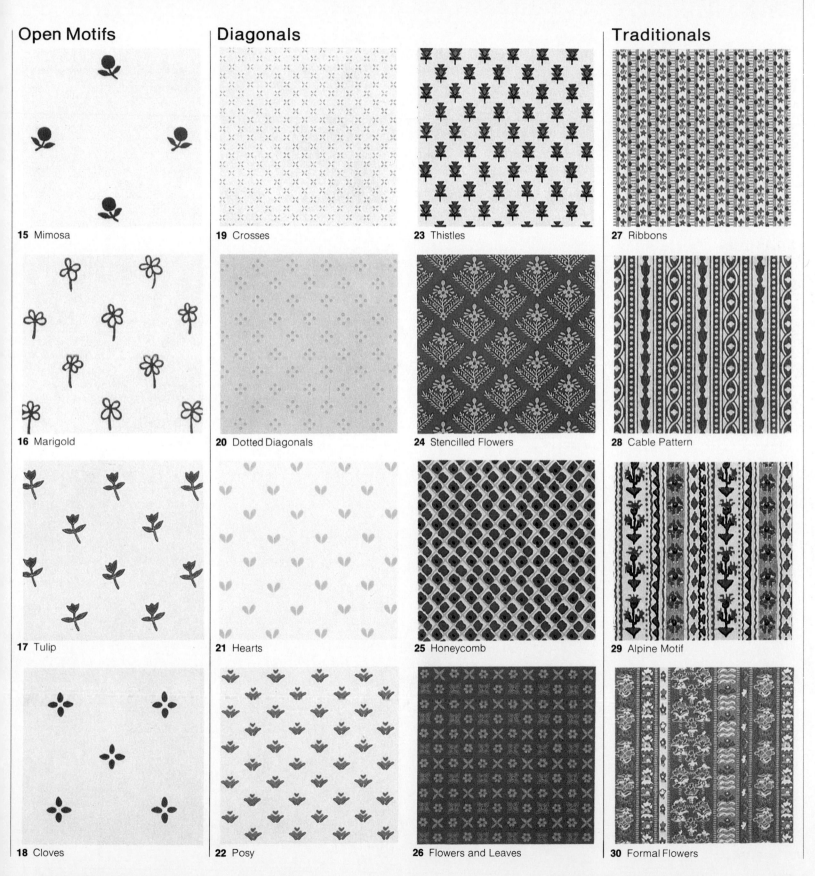

Open Motifs

15 Mimosa

16 Marigold

17 Tulip

18 Cloves

Diagonals

19 Crosses

20 Dotted Diagonals

21 Hearts

22 Posy

23 Thistles

24 Stencilled Flowers

25 Honeycomb

26 Flowers and Leaves

Traditionals

27 Ribbons

28 Cable Pattern

29 Alpine Motif

30 Formal Flowers

LARGE PRINT WALLPAPERS

Large designs are obviously best suited to big rooms, but they can also be used to great effect in a small room where they will blur the confines of the space, giving the illusion of a much larger area. Choose simple furnishings and link them to the wallcovering by using fabrics which either pick up the brightest colors of a bold print, or ones which contrast with the monotones of a subtler print.

Grasses

1 Grain *

2 Water Weed

3 Green Bamboo

Leaves

4 Falling Leaves

5 Oak Leaves

6 French Parsley

7 Outlines

Florals

8 Poppies *

9 Spring Bulbs *

Fruits and flowers

10 Strawberry Runner

11 Quince

12 Crocus

13 Buds and Flowers

Trellises

14 Pansy Stencil

15 Flowered Trellis

16 Exotic Flower

17 Tea Rose

Wildlife

18 Toucan *

19 Zebra Stripe *

TRADITIONAL WALLPAPERS

Old-fashioned prints remain perennial favorites for many people, particularly in bedrooms, where they look especially fresh and soft if used with co-ordinating fabric and matching paint. Traditional designs look surprisingly modern when printed in unusual color combinations and can be used with plain, textured upholstery, cotton or bamboo shades or blinds, and matting on the floor.

Nineteenth Century Prints

4 Posie

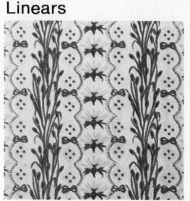

5 Climbing Flower

Linears

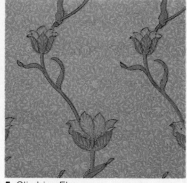

12 Colonial Motif

Chintzes

1 Roses

6 Tiger Lily

7 Ivy

13 Floral Motif

2 Garlands

8 Fire Flower

9 Thistle

14 Leaf Motif

3 Dog Rose

10 Poppy Motif

11 Camelia Motif

15 Floral Motif

Florals

Updated Traditionals

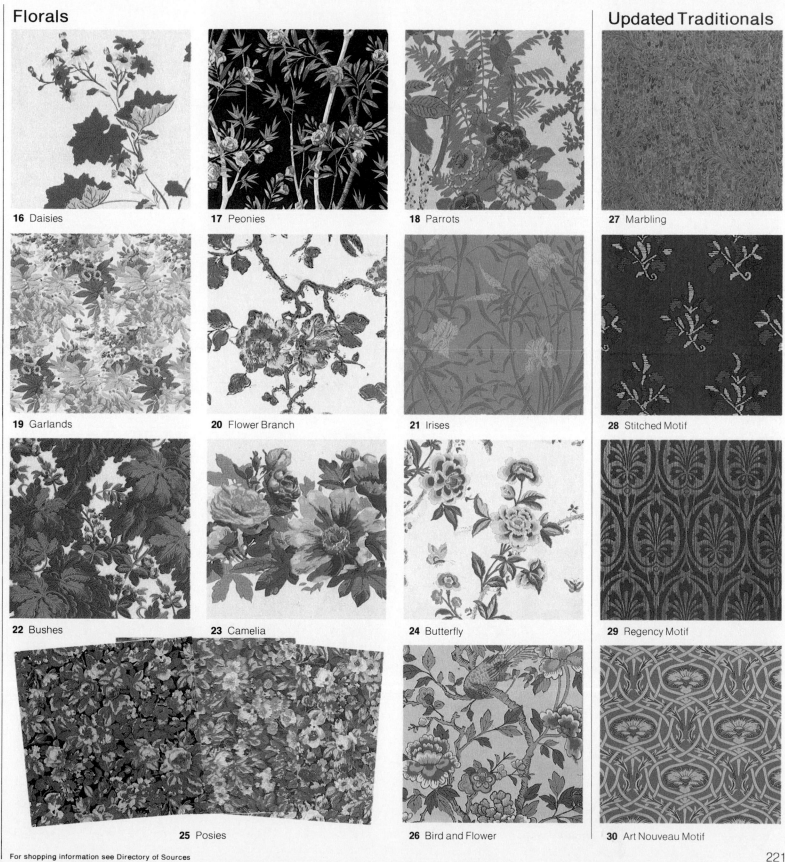

16 Daisies

17 Peonies

18 Parrots

27 Marbling

19 Garlands

20 Flower Branch

21 Irises

28 Stitched Motif

22 Bushes

23 Camelia

24 Butterfly

29 Regency Motif

25 Posies

26 Bird and Flower

30 Art Nouveau Motif

CONTEMPORARY WALLPAPERS

Modern prints reflect a variety of designs ranging from simple geometrics to abstract impressions; from softly-colored, dotted designs to bold, clearly-drawn pictures. Simple but vividly-colored designs are also reproduced on foil and mylar and because of the way they reflect light they can be used to give the impression of depth to a room. Remember, more manufacturers are now producing coordinating fabrics.

Linears

1 Spirogyra

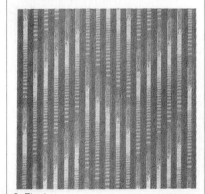

2 Streamers

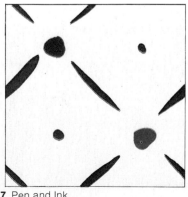

3 Flash

Florals

4 Tulips

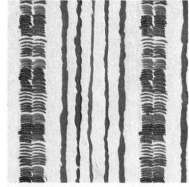

5 Daisies

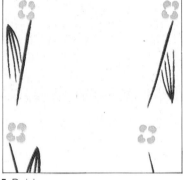

6 Carnations

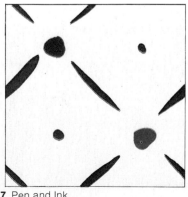

7 Pen and Ink

Abstracts

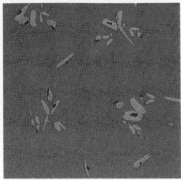

8 Mimosa

9 Posies

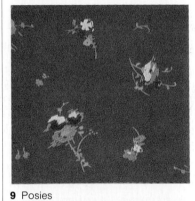

10 Grasses

11 Jungle

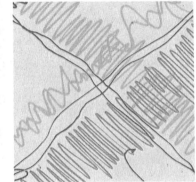

12 Jumping Beans

13 Doodles

14 Aerial

15 Leaf and Flower

Stipples

16 Spatterware

17 Lichen

18 Frost

19 Floral

Figuratives

20 Bunnies

21 Hens

22 Ducks

23 Palms

24 Passing Clouds

25 Stars

26 Autobus

Mylars

27 Frozen Fronds

28 Tiger Leaf

29 Ice Diamonds

30 Golden Chevrons

VINYL WALLPAPERS

Made of cloth- or paper-backed PVC, vinyl papers are tougher than normal wallcoverings and come in a variety of designs, colors and finishes. They are water- and steam-proof, washable and scrubbable and are therefore useful for kitchens, bathrooms, utility rooms and playrooms. Being impervious, however, they can easily form a mold underneath, so attach them with fungicidal adhesive.

Geometrics

4 Diamond Motif

5 Grass Motif

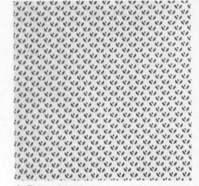

6 Flower Motif

7 Broken Diamond

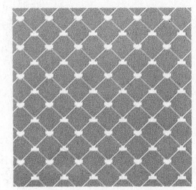

8 Diagonal Motif

9 Broken Diagonal

Plains

1 "Linen"

10 Linear Motif

11 Squares

12 Linear Squares

2 "Burlap"

13 Basketweave

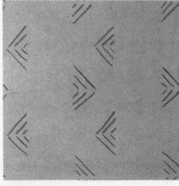

14 Triangles

15 Broken Squares

3 "Textured Paint"

All items at Scale 1 reduction; see page 209

Traditionals

Contemporaries

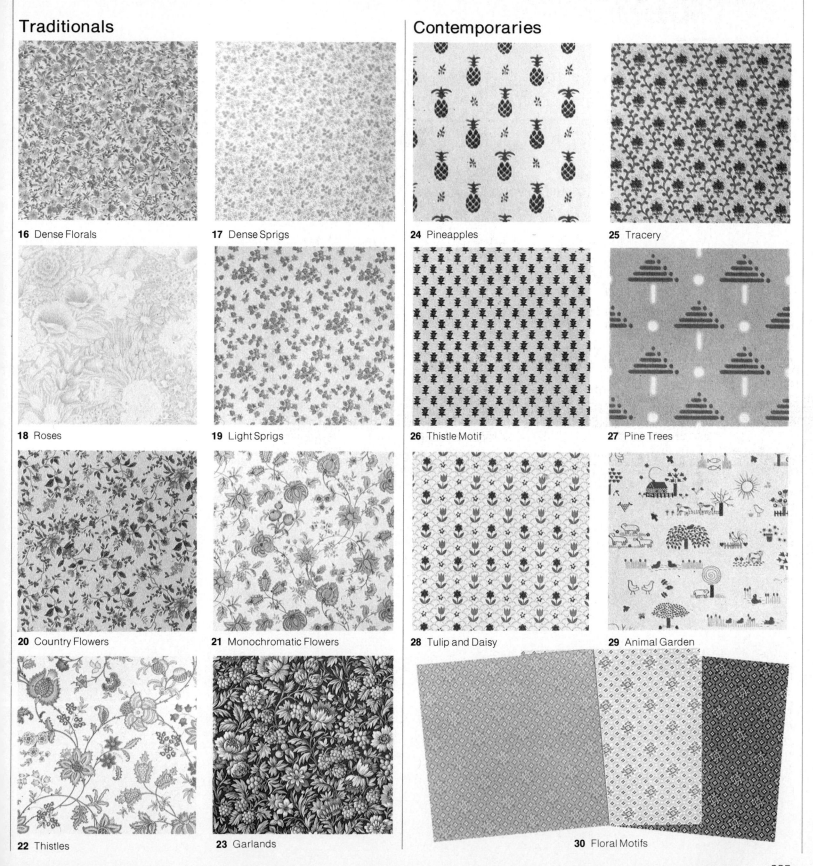

16 Dense Florals

17 Dense Sprigs

24 Pineapples

25 Tracery

18 Roses

19 Light Sprigs

26 Thistle Motif

27 Pine Trees

20 Country Flowers

21 Monochromatic Flowers

28 Tulip and Daisy

29 Animal Garden

22 Thistles

23 Garlands

30 Floral Motifs

FLOCKS

Flock wallpapers, so frequently used on late 18th century and early 19th century walls, as a substitute for wallhangings and tapestries, are not much favored today. Nevertheless, the traditional designs and colors can look suitably sumptious in an elaborate period room, and there are now quite interesting modern variations on rather more restrained lines. They are made with either a wool or nylon pile.

Geometrics

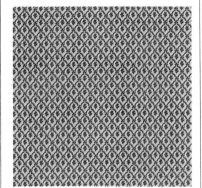

1 Fleur de Lys

2 Geometric Motif

3 Diagonal Squares

Florals

4 Flower and Shield

5 Flowers and Feathers

6 Regency Urn

7 Pineapple Motif

8 Thistle

9 Fan

10 Gold Motif

11 Posy

12 Sprigs

13 Acorn Leaf

14 Artichoke Leaf

15 Large Spray

All items at Scale 1 reduction; see page 209

RELIEF PAPERS

Relief papers, especially the neat, geometric patterned ones, are once again becoming popular, both for the textural interest they can add to a wall and because they are heavy enough to hide irregularities and faults. They are made of embossed cotton fibers or wood pulp, and their appearance is greatly enhanced if they are painted in deep, rich, or bright, clear colors, depending on the feeling of the room.

Anaglypta

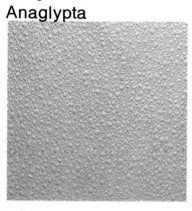

1 Bubbles

2 Seeds

3 Circular Motif

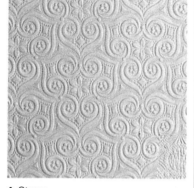

4 Stars

5 Floral Motif

6 Victorian Motif

7 Geometric

Vynaglypta

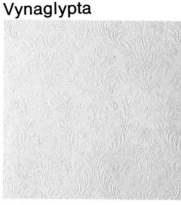

8 Ferns

9 Oval Motif

10 Interlocking Motif

11 Textured Motif

Supaglypta

12 Burlap

13 Linear Motif

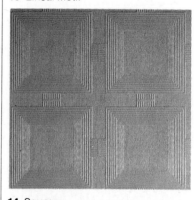

14 Squares

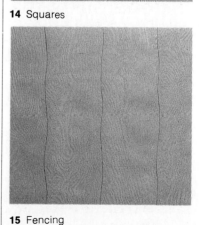

15 Fencing

TEXTURED WALLCOVERINGS

Wallcoverings, such as linens, burlaps, wools and grasses, are especially useful for disguising any irregularities in a wall; the thicker wools in particular help with both sound and heat insulation. Burlaps and linens, which provide a neat, regular finish, are produced in patterned and plain designs and in a wide range of colors. The finer textures are best suited to sophisticated schemes.

4 Open Lines

Jutes

8 Fleck

10 Diagonal

Linens

1 Close Weave

5 Cross Lines

9 Arrow

11 Crosshatch

2 Medium Weave

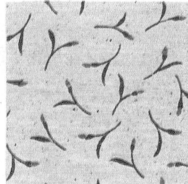

6 Flowerbud

Burlaps

12 Plain burlaps

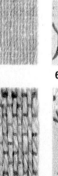

3 Coarse Weave

7 Daisy

13 Crossway

14 Print

All items at Scale 1 reduction; see page 209

Wools

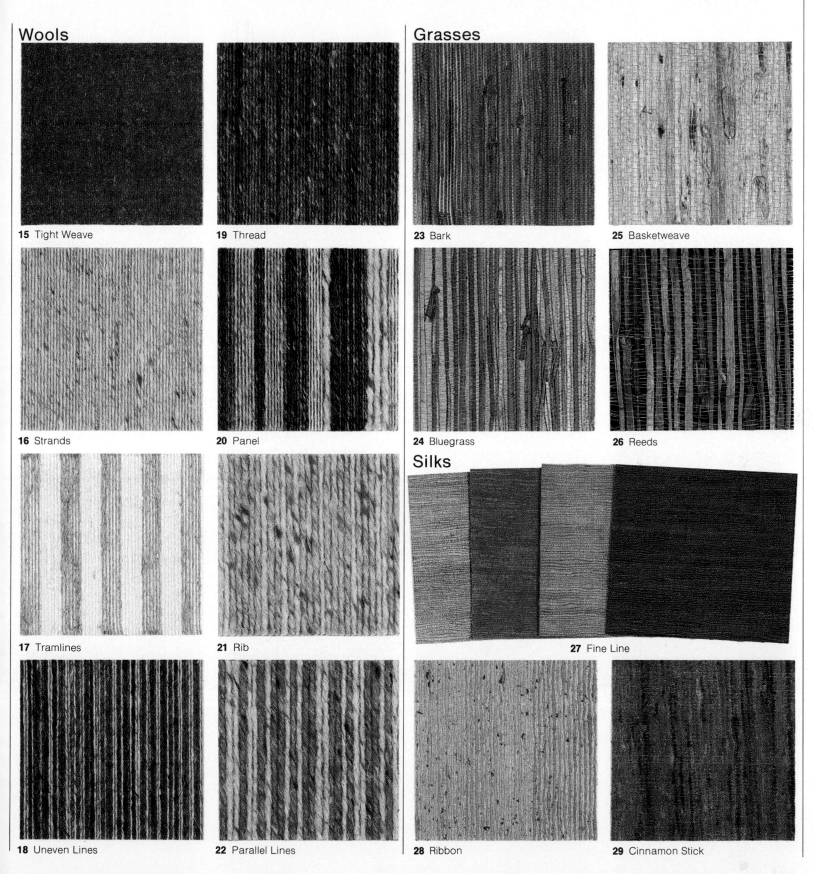

15 Tight Weave

19 Thread

16 Strands

20 Panel

17 Tramlines

21 Rib

18 Uneven Lines

22 Parallel Lines

Grasses

23 Bark

25 Basketweave

24 Bluegrass

26 Reeds

Silks

27 Fine Line

28 Ribbon

29 Cinnamon Stick

SMOOTH WALLCOVERINGS

Materials such as wools, suedes, felts, silks, moirés, foils and corks are a richer, softer and longer-lasting alternative to traditional paper wallcoverings. The more practical versions are either paper-backed, or specially treated for easy hanging, and despite their luxurious appearance, most fabric coverings can be spot cleaned.

Felts

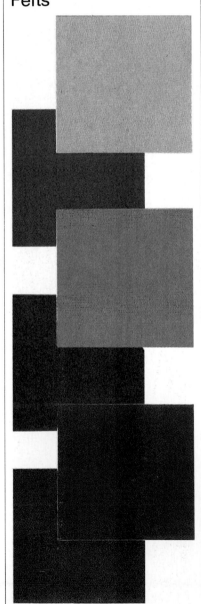

1 Various Colors

Wools

2 Gray

3 Light Beige

4 Beige

5 Brown

Silks and Moirés

6 Plain Silks

7 Lightweight Moirés

8 Medium weight Moirés

9 Heavyweight Moirés

All items at Scale 1 reduction; see page 209

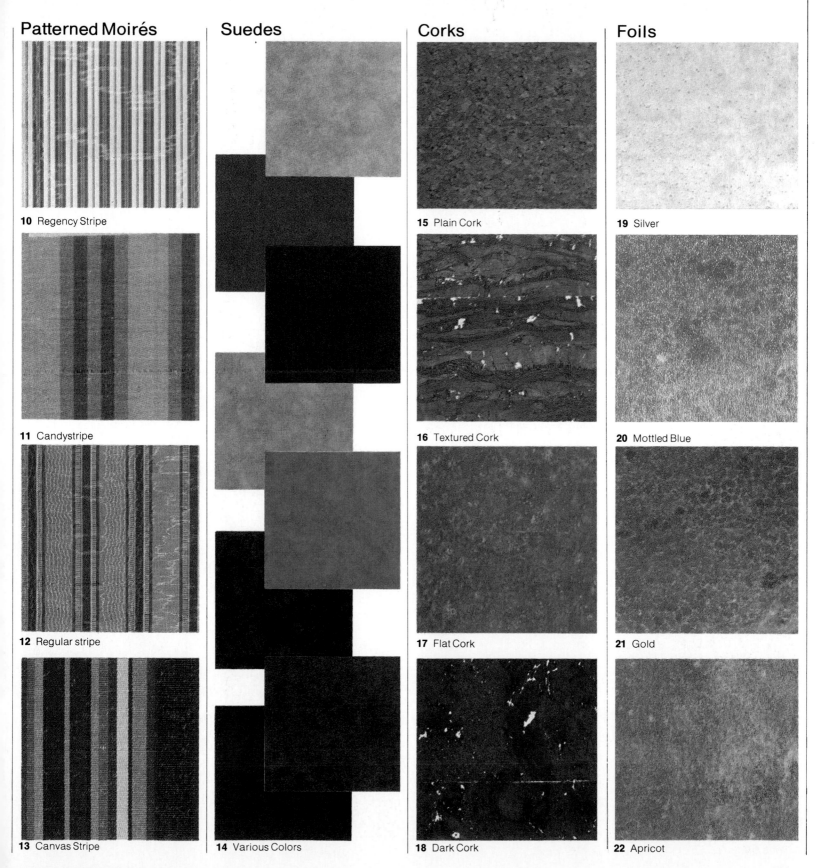

Patterned Moirés

10 Regency Stripe

11 Candystripe

12 Regular stripe

13 Canvas Stripe

Suedes

14 Various Colors

Corks

15 Plain Cork

16 Textured Cork

17 Flat Cork

18 Dark Cork

Foils

19 Silver

20 Mottled Blue

21 Gold

22 Apricot

LAMINATES

The major point about laminates is that they provide a tough, practical, easy-to-clean surface for both walls and worktops and this makes them ideal for use in kitchens, bathrooms, children's rooms, workrooms, powder rooms, and washrooms. They are produced with both plain and textured surfaces and are generally cheaper than the natural materials they are designed, so realistically, to emulate.

Plain

1 Sea Green

2 Terracotta

3 Midnight Blue

Patterned

4 Fine Burlap

5 Burlap

6 Leaves

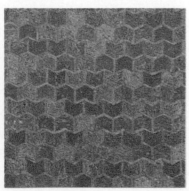

7 Brickwork

Marble

8 Adriatic Marble

9 Smoky Marble

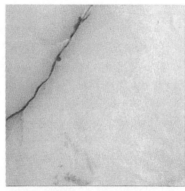

10 Beige Onyx

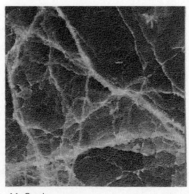

11 Sepia

Wood

12 Light Pine

13 Inlaid Mosaic

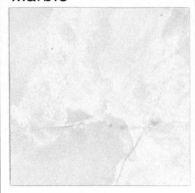

14 Sapele

15 Rosewood

All items at Scale 1 reduction; see page 209

REFLECTIVE TILES

All reflective surfaces exaggerate the available space and light, and mirrored and aluminum tiles tend to be cheaper than panels of the equivalent material. In general, they can be fixed on much the same surfaces as ceramic tiles, but it is important to remember that mirrored tiles should only be fixed to walls first treated with a shiny paint. Mirror and aluminum tiles are ideal for use in small spaces, or along work surfaces.

Plain mirror

Patterned mirror

Plain and textured aluminum

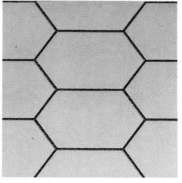

4 Lozenge

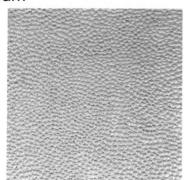

8 Plain

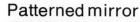

12 Relief

1 Plain

5 Diagonals

9 Semi-circles

13 Squares

2 Smoky

6 Bronzed Leaves

10 Circle

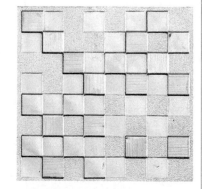

14 Checkerboard

3 Bronzed

7 Tracery

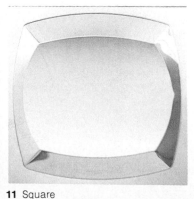

11 Square

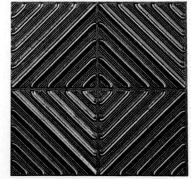

15 Square Patterns

PANELED WALLCOVERINGS

The clean-cut appearance of wood paneling, combined with its acoustic and insulating properties, make it a practical as well as an attractive alternative to other wallcoverings. This is especially true of the tongue-and-groove variety, with its wide range of tones and graining. Paneling looks good in general living areas but is equally suited to kitchens and bathrooms.

Plain

Plain tongue-and-groove

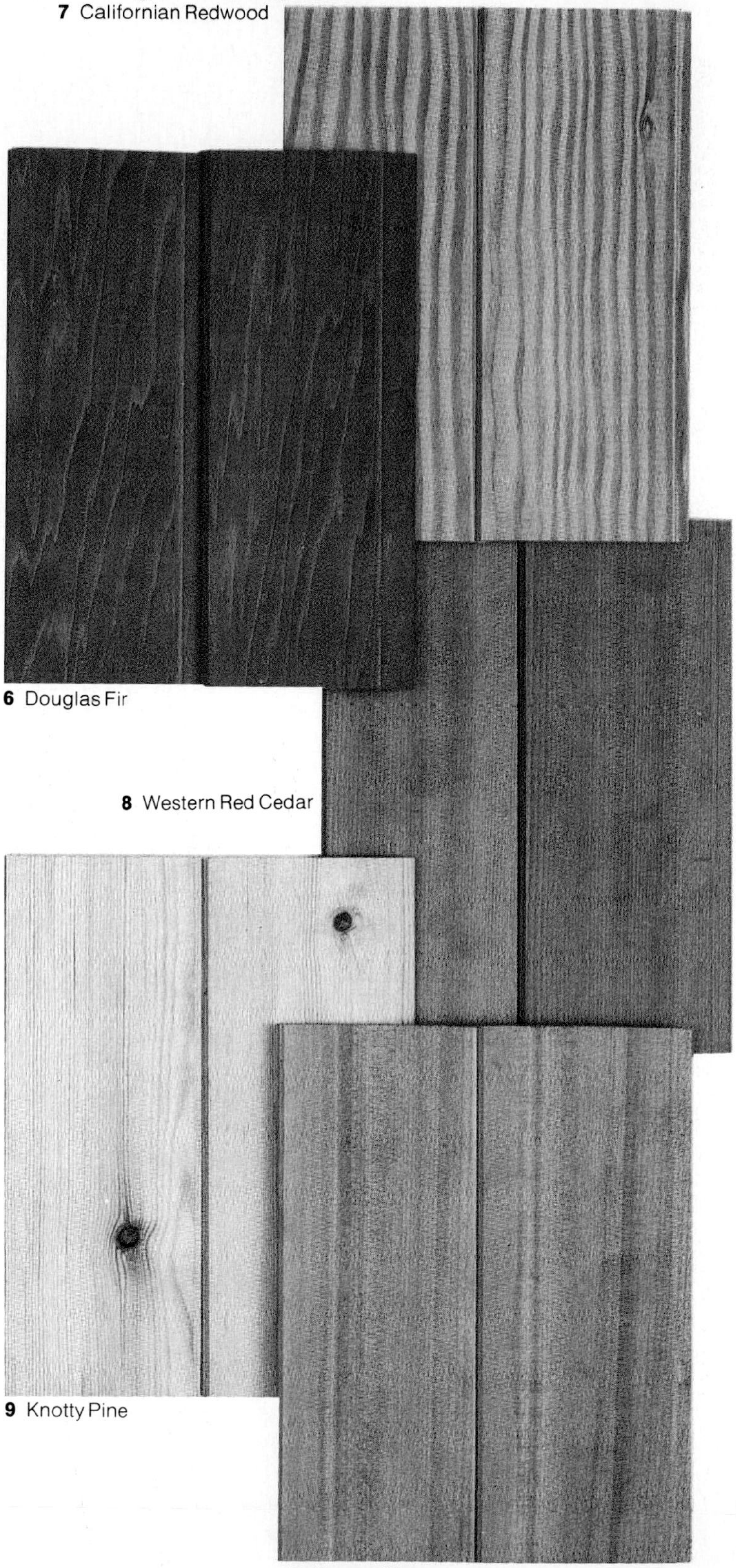

7 Californian Redwood

6 Douglas Fir

8 Western Red Cedar

9 Knotty Pine

10 Parana Pine

1 Elm
2 Brazilian Mahogany
3 Stained Ash
4 Ash
5 Black Walnut

All items at Scale 1 reduction; see page 209

Channeled tongue-and-groove

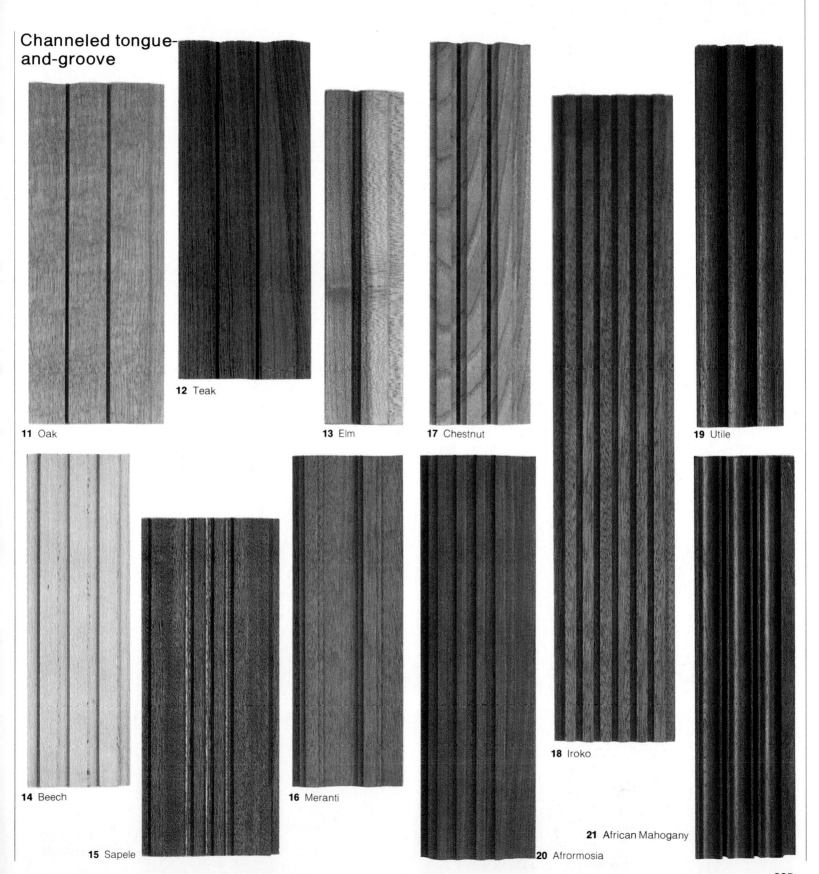

11 Oak

12 Teak

13 Elm

17 Chestnut

19 Utile

14 Beech

15 Sapele

16 Meranti

18 Iroko

20 Afrormosia

21 African Mahogany

CERAMIC WALL TILES

Produced in many distinctive styles, ceramic wall tiles are available in a wide range of colors and patterns. Apart from using them on bathroom or kitchen walls, they can be put behind sinks and stoves, as well as on work surfaces, table and window sill tops. Even broken tiles, whether glazed or unglazed, can be carefully grouped together to form a handsome mosaic.

Geometric

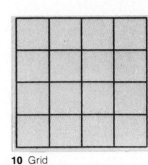

5 Stripes

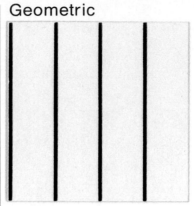

10 Grid

1 Smoky Plains

6 Quadrants

11 Shaded Squares

Plain

2 Matt Plains

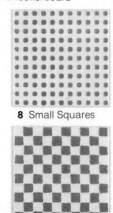

7 Checkerboard

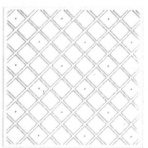

12 Dots and Diamonds

8 Small Squares

13 Blazes

3 Striped Plains

4 Dappled Plains

9 Checks

14 Diagonal Stripes

All items at Scale 1 reduction; see page 209

Bordered

Figurative

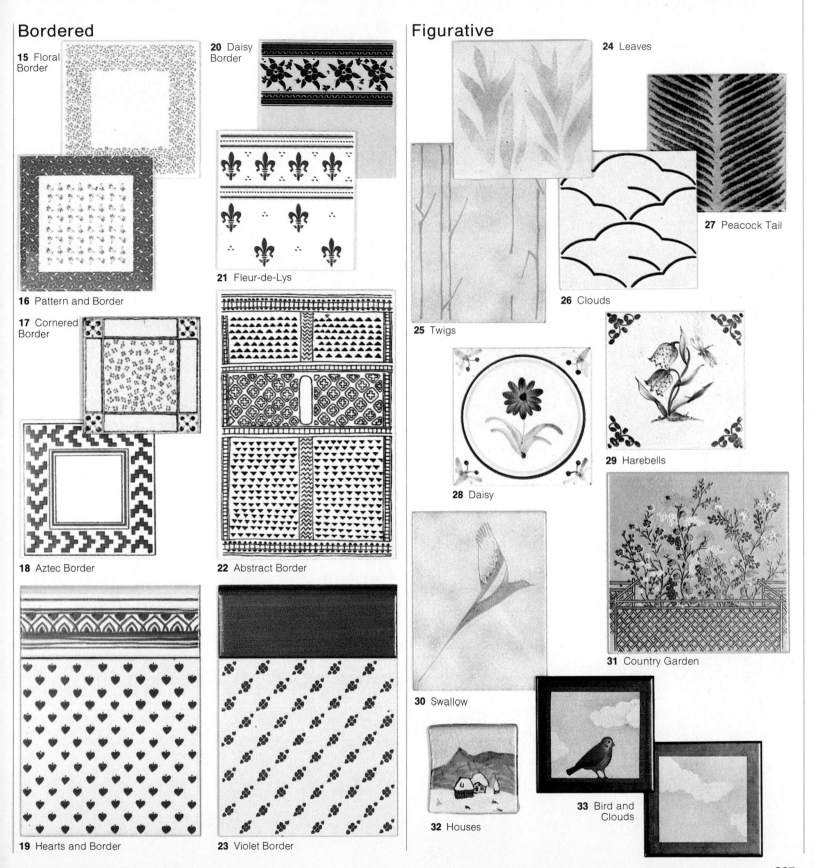

15 Floral Border

20 Daisy Border

16 Pattern and Border

17 Cornered Border

21 Fleur-de-Lys

18 Aztec Border

22 Abstract Border

19 Hearts and Border

23 Violet Border

24 Leaves

25 Twigs

26 Clouds

27 Peacock Tail

28 Daisy

29 Harebells

30 Swallow

31 Country Garden

32 Houses

33 Bird and Clouds

CERAMIC WALL TILES

Mexican style

1 Plains

2 Bordered

3 Pinwheel **4** Garland

5 Sprig **6** Posy

7 Daisy **8** Strawberry

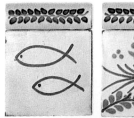

9 Fish and Border **10** Bird

11 Cross and Border

Dutch style

12 Hunter **13** Stick Game **14** Woodman **15** Leopard

16 Bull **17** Ball Game **18** Porter **19** Fruit Bowl

French style

20 Plain **21** Field Scene **22** Girl **23** Ship

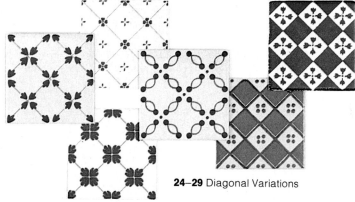

24—29 Diagonal Variations

30, 30a Star Variation

31 Fleur-de-Lys

32—35 Maze Variations

36—39 Figurative Variations

40—41 Borders

Mosaic tiles

42 Circles

43 Textured Hexagonals

44 Provençals

45 Squares

46 Hexagonals

47 Mottled Squares

48 Octagonals and Diamonds

49 Quarry Mosaics

50 Provencals

51 Lozenge and Squares

Mural tiles

52 Dotted Trees

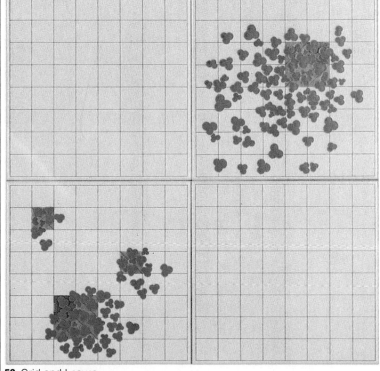

53 Grid and Leaves

TILE MURALS

Modern tile murals are widely available in most countries, produced by both manufacturing concerns and individual artists. Additionally, turn-of-the-century pictorial sets are occasionally to be found in old stores, markets and commercial buildings about to be pulled down or remodeled. Demolition contractors can often be persuaded to remove them quite cheaply for setting up elsewhere.

1 Cranes

3 Hunting Scene

2 Oasis

4 Home Scene

5 Horseman

6 Steam-packet

All items at Scale 1 reduction; see page 209

ART NOUVEAU TILES

"That strange decorative disease", as the English designer and esthete, Walter Crane, called the *Art Nouveau* movement, has left its curvilinear mark as much on tiles as on every other aspect of the applied arts. As with the tiled murals opposite, individual *Art Nouveau* tiles can still be found decorating the walls of old buildings, but perhaps the easiest way to collect them is in junk yards and antique shops.

1 Rose Motif

2 Tulip

3 Dog Rose

4 Winged Motif

5 Open Tulip

6 Scabious

7 Daisies

8 Lily Motif

9 Red Flower

10 Thistle Motif

11 Pelican

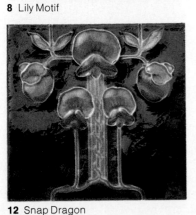

12 Snap Dragon

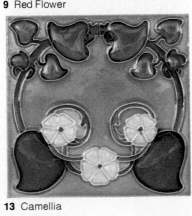

13 Camellia

14 Feathered Leaf

15 Floral Ring

STAINS AND STENCILING

Wood stains can be bought in a variety of colors and are useful for cheering up white or plain wooden furniture, as well as stripped floors; unlike paint they do not hide any graining. They are either water or spirit-based, although the water variety is more versatile in that it can be thinned down and mixed. Both types should be finished with a compatible sealer. Stencils, like stains, will enliven any surface and can be bought ready-cut, as below.

Stains

1 Full-strength Green; **2** Yellow Beech; **3** Golden Oak; **4** Hazel; **5** 80% Blue; **6** Full-strength Blue; **7** Mahogany; **8** Cherry; **9** Walnut; **10** Teak; **11** Full-strength Gray; **12** Birch Gray; **13** Black Oak

Stencils

Garlands, Posies and Fruit Basket

All items at Scale 1 reduction; see page 209

PAINT TECHNIQUES

An interesting alternative to simply painting your walls is to use one of the special techniques shown here. General information on how to produce them is given on page 195, and good results can easily be achieved by the amateur, so long as he or she is prepared to practice and experiment on primed boards before embarking on larger areas like walls or ceilings.

1 Stippling

2 Dragging

3 Scumbling

4 Rag Rubbing (with muslin)

5 False Marbling

6 Rag Rubbing (with paper)

PLAIN FABRICS

Plain and textured cottons

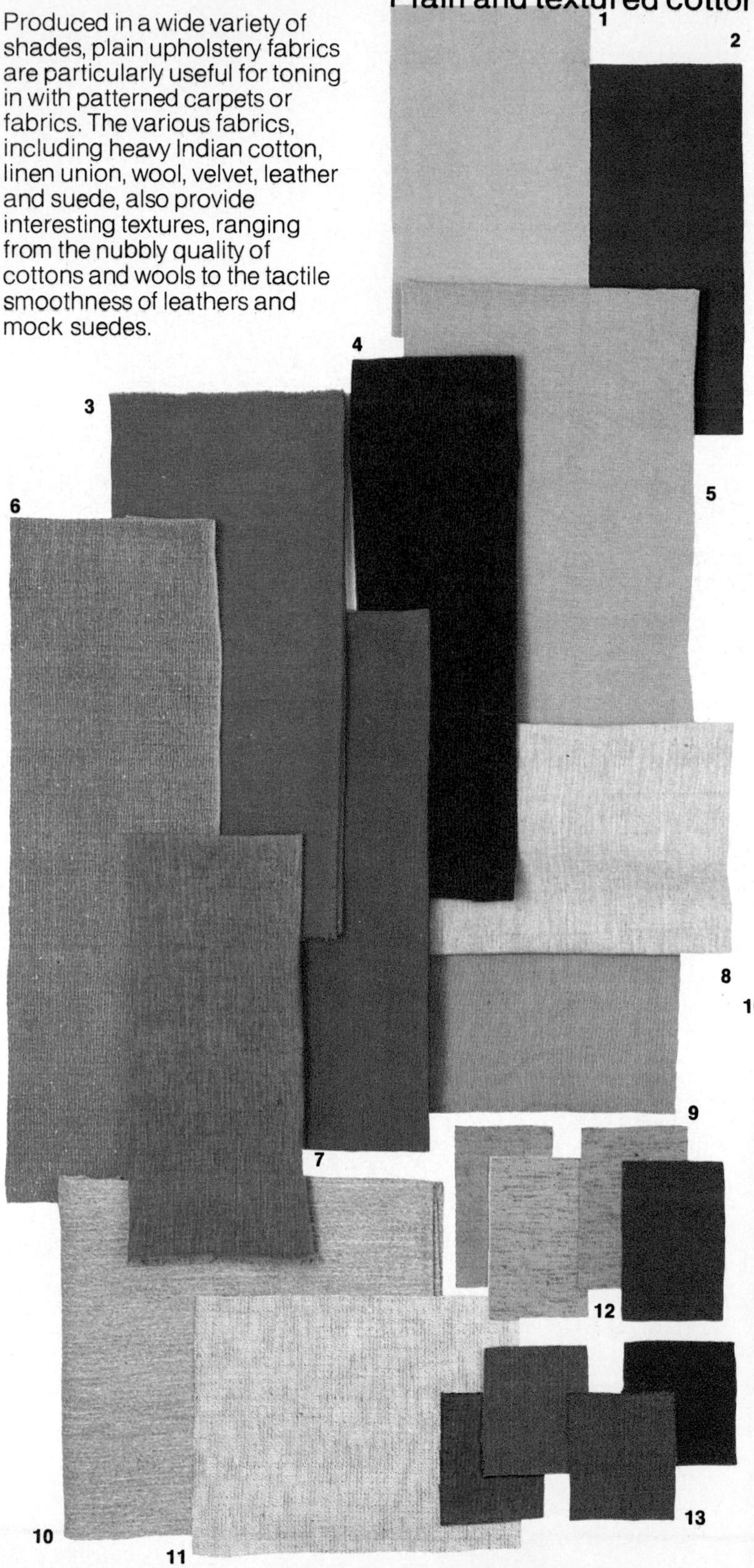

Produced in a wide variety of shades, plain upholstery fabrics are particularly useful for toning in with patterned carpets or fabrics. The various fabrics, including heavy Indian cotton, linen union, wool, velvet, leather and suede, also provide interesting textures, ranging from the nubbly quality of cottons and wools to the tactile smoothness of leathers and mock suedes.

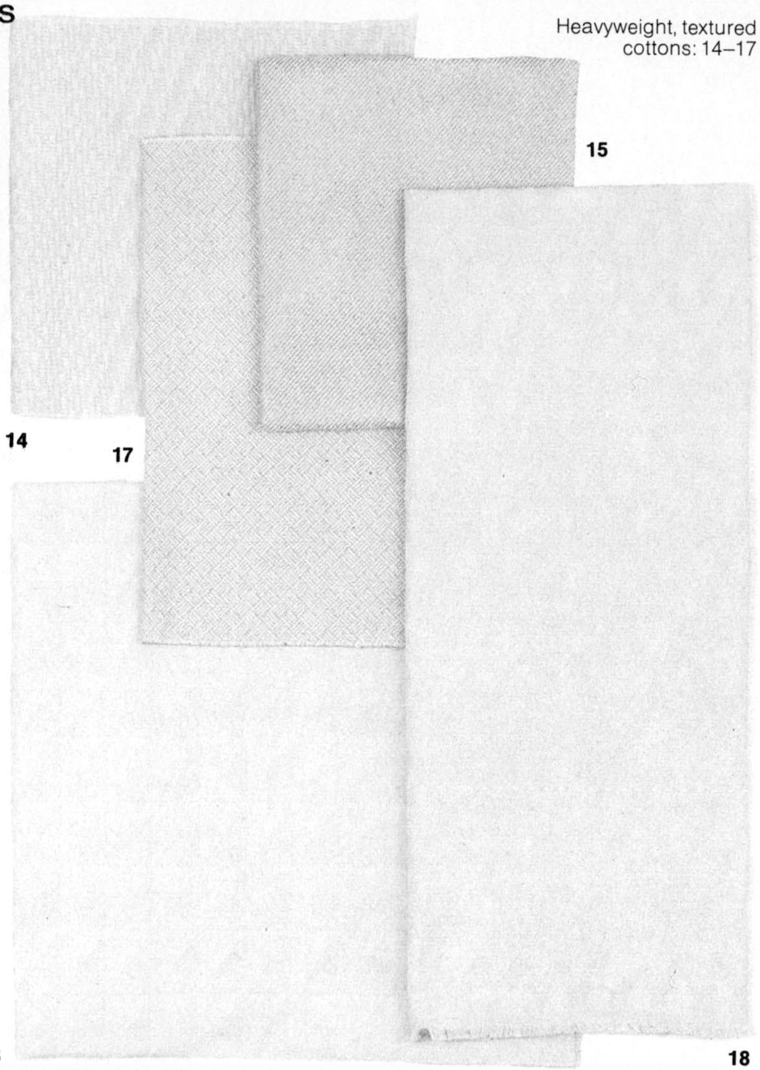

Heavyweight, textured cottons: 14–17

Velvets, corduroys, and leathers

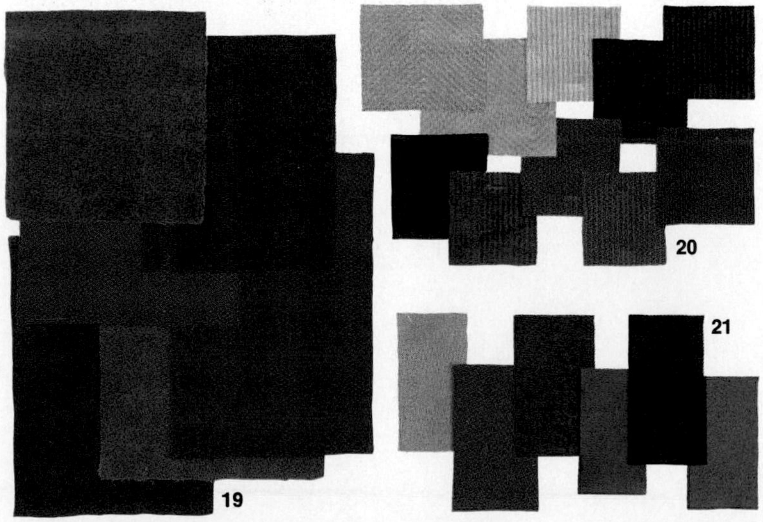

Smooth cottons: 1; 2; Plain linens: 3–9; Lightweight, textured cottons: 10–13

Velvets: 19; Corduroy: 20; Leather and Suede: 21

All items at Scale 1 reduction; see page 209

Wools

Plain wools: 22; Textured wools: 23; 24; 28; 29; Patterned wools: 25–27; 30–34

Silks

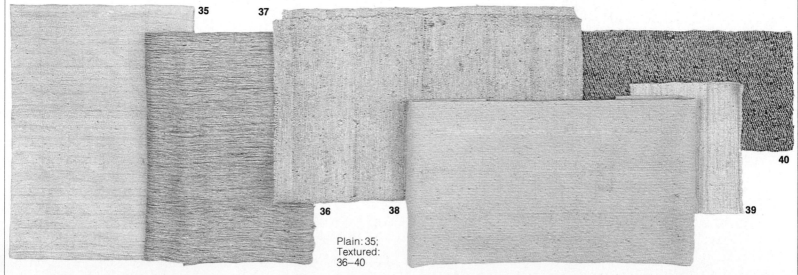

Plain: 35;
Textured:
36–40

HEAVY PATTERNED FABRICS

These fabrics are available in linen unions, velvets and woven mixtures. Because of their strong design they are best combined with plain colors, or with smaller scale prints in much the same coloring to avoid a conflict of patterns. All patterned furnishing fabric is more practical than plain fabric in that it does not show wear and tear as quickly.

Geometrics

Cottons: 1–4
Wool-mix: 5; 6

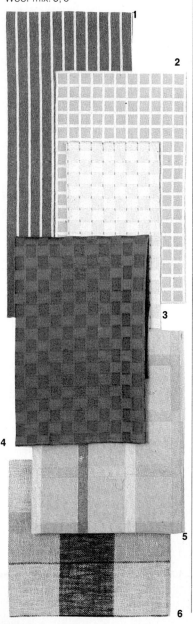

Patterned cottons

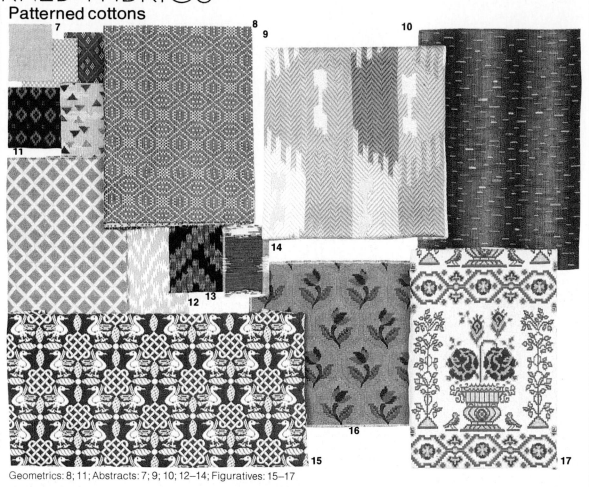

Geometrics: 8; 11; Abstracts: 7; 9; 10; 12–14; Figuratives: 15–17

Velvets

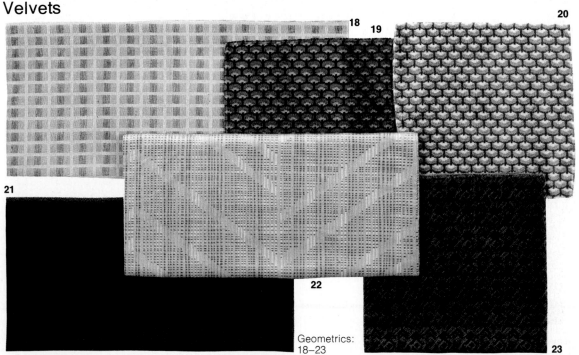

Geometrics: 18–23

All items at Scale 1 reduction; see page 209

QUILTED FABRICS

The process of quilting automatically makes a material stronger and firmer, so that it becomes particularly practical for covering bedspreads, sofas and chairs. Many fabrics can now be bought ready-quilted, and apart from the more conventional cottons, silks, satins, and linen weaves, there are some unexpected finishes like flannel or tweed, sometimes in very intricate designs.

Plains

Patterned

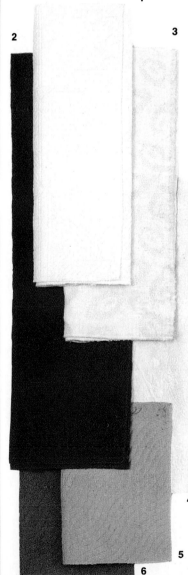

Medium weight cotton: 3; 5; 6
Heavyweight cotton: 1; 2; 4

Wool: 7; 8; 13; 35
Silk: 9; 15; 19–22; 24; 26–29; 31; 32; 37–39
Cotton: 10–12; 14; 16–18; 23; 25; 30; 33–34; 36

For shopping information see Directory of Sources

LARGE PRINT FABRICS

Large-scale patterns are best suited to large-scale furniture: sofas, modular seating, day beds or chaises longues; they can also be used as wallcoverings. Large-scale geometrics, used judiciously, can make a space seem larger, but too much of a large print, especially on smaller pieces of furniture, will tend to look quite overpowering.

1 Swirls; **2**, **3** Celtic Motif; **4** Keys;
5 Tadpole; **6** Chinese Motif; **7** Trellis;
8 Strawberry; **9**, **10**, **11** Fronds;
12 Indian Motif; **13**, **14**, **15** Ink Prints

All items at Scale 2 reduction; see page 209

CANVAS FABRICS

Tough canvas, ducks, sailcloths and coarse cottons, are all suitable for chairs and sofas. They are available in natural colors, or with hand-painted or specially printed designs, which seem to suit them especially well. These painted or patterned varieties look handsome on large-scale seating, or they can be used on walls as interesting backcloths. Whichever way they are used, they provide textural interest as well as a sturdy finish.

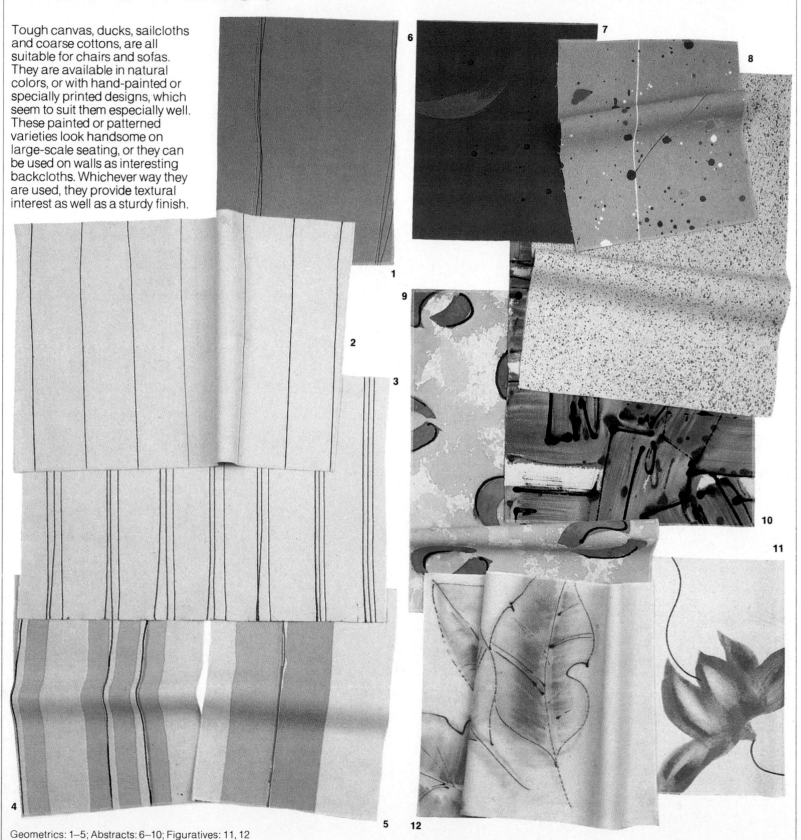

Geometrics: 1–5; Abstracts: 6–10; Figuratives: 11, 12

PLAIN FABRICS

Plain drapery fabrics include
woven and smooth cottons,
linens, silks, moirés, velvets and
wools. They can be teamed with
patterned upholstery fabrics of
similar coloring, or used to pick
out dominant tones in a carpet,
rug or painting. They can also be
matched with a patterned shade,
or used in conjunction with
patterned drapes. Bright colors
can fade and should be used
with protective linings.

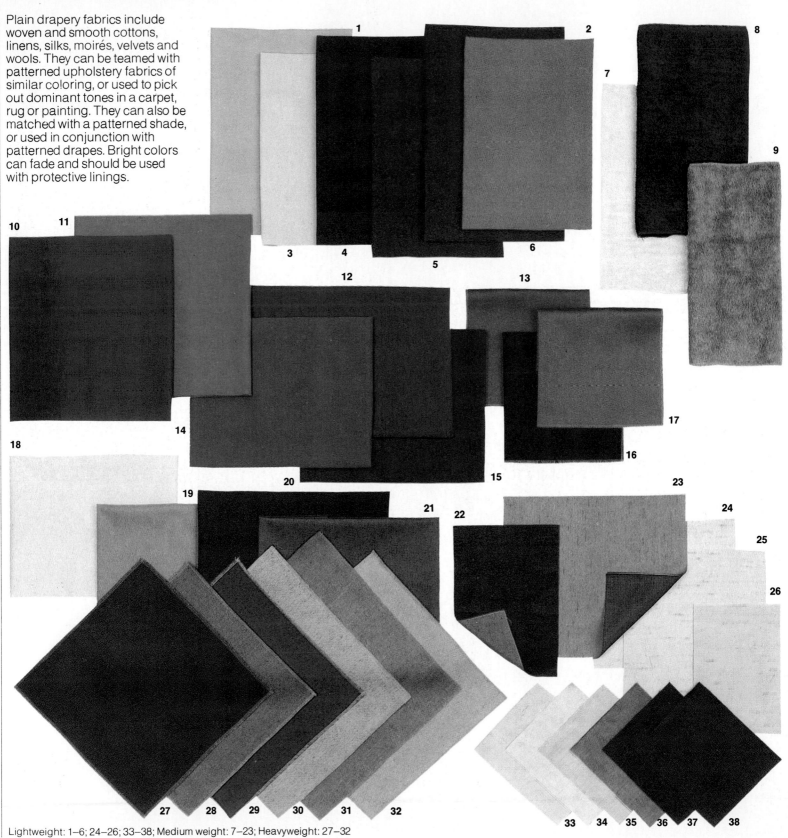

Lightweight: 1–6; 24–26; 33–38; Medium weight: 7–23; Heavyweight: 27–32

All items at Scale 1 reduction; see page 209

MINIPRINT FABRICS

"Miniprints" is an umbrella term for any small, all-over pattern whether geometric, floral or abstract. Miniprints are best used in comparatively small rooms as they tend to look blurred in large spaces, especially if they are pale in color. They can be successfully mixed and matched with large-scale patterns in the same tones or used to good effect with matching wallpapers or contrasting fabrics.

Florals

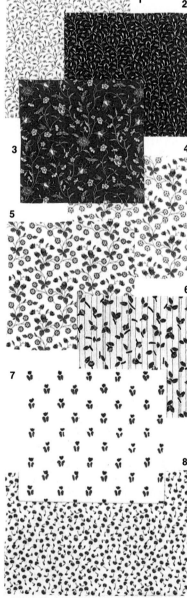

Lightweight: 1–8

Geometrics and abstracts

Lightweight: 9; 10; 13; 14; Heavyweight: 11; 12; 15; 16

Medium weight: 20–23;
Heavyweight: 17–19

GEOMETRIC FABRICS

A crisply-tailored look can be given to a room by using geometric or diagonally-patterned fabrics; diagonal prints, particularly, will increase the feeling of space in a room. Such effects are easily achieved by using the fabric for window shades, as a wallcovering, or simply as bed covers, throw cushions and tablecloths. Geometric prints often look good in conjunction with miniprints.

Linears

Lightweight: 1; 3; 5–9; 11; 15; 17; Medium weight: 2; 4; 10; 16; Heavyweight: 12–14

All items at Scale 1 reduction; see page 209

Squares

Lightweight: 1; 2; 4; 7
Heavyweight: 3; 5; 6; 8

Diagonals

Lightweight: 4; 8
Medium weight: 1–3; 5; 7
Heavyweight: 6

CONTEMPORARY FABRICS

The superabundance of choice in contemporary fabrics is one of the best things to happen to decoration in this century. The fact that in one way or another most of the best of these designs are available throughout the western world is another. Some contemporary designs are essentially of the 1980s, others are free adaptations of earlier ideas; all are strong enough to make good starting points for schemes.

Florals

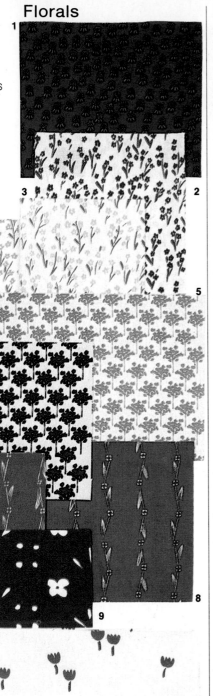

Ethnics

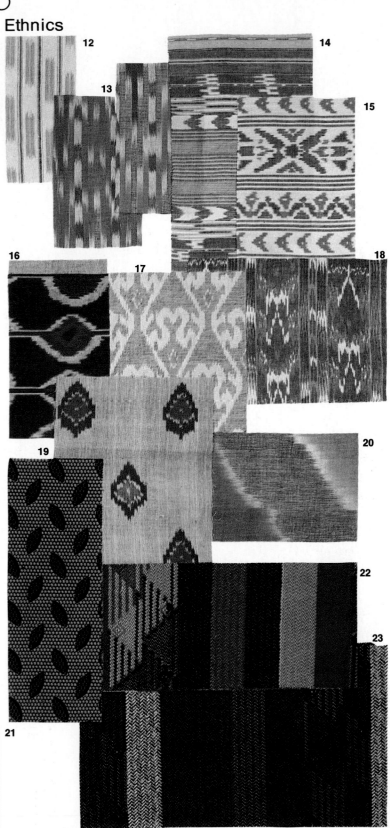

Lightweight: 1–10; Medium weight: 11

Lightweight: 12–20; Medium weight: 21–23

All items at Scale 1 reduction; see page 209

Abstracts

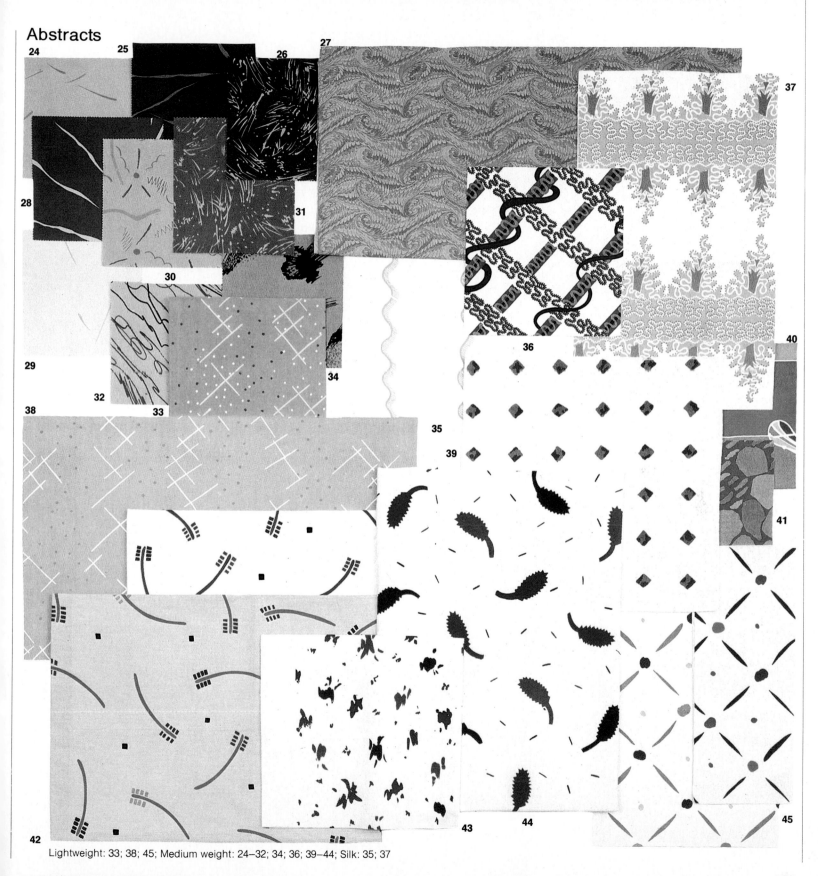

Lightweight: 33; 38; 45; Medium weight: 24–32; 34; 36; 39–44; Silk: 35; 37

LARGE PRINT FABRICS

The same basic rule of scale
(that a large pattern should be
used in large areas) applies to
drapery as well as to upholstery
fabrics or wallcoverings. Unless
the print is very abstract, it
should be hung so that the full
repeat of the pattern is shown.
Large prints can be used
successfully with plain or small-
scale designs.

Lightweight: 2; 3; 6
Medium weight: 1; 4; 7; 8; 9; 11
Heavyweight: 5; 10

All items at Scale 2 reduction; see page 209

Lightweight: 1; 3; 4; 5; Medium weight: 2; 6; 7; 9; 11; 12; 13; 14; Heavyweight: 8; 10

TRADITIONAL FABRICS

From the vantage point of the late twentieth century, it is comparatively easy to pick out the best designs of the past, and to re-color and re-edit them for modern use. These two pages of designs have, in one guise or another, been selling happily for a hundred years or more. Some are colonial designs, some are early Liberty, some are traditional crewels; all look good.

Colonials

Nineteenth Century Prints

Medium weight: 1–3; 6
Glazed lightweight: 4–5

Lightweight: 15; 19–20
Glazed Lightweight: 14
Medium weight: 7–9; 11; 13; 17–18
Heavyweight: 10; 12; 16

All items at Scale 1 reduction; see page 209

Large Scale

21

22

23

Medium weight: 21–23
Glazed medium weight: 24; 25

Crewels

26

27

24

25

28

Medium weight: 26; 28; Heavyweight: 27

SHEER FABRICS

Produced in a wide variety of finishes, sheers range from the cheaper cheesecloths and muslins, through nets and synthetics to the more expensive laces. They filter light beautifully, and prevent outsiders from looking in without much loss of natural light. As well as being used as drapes, either on their own, or as under-drapes for heavier fabrics, they can be used on tables, beds and walls.

Loose weaves

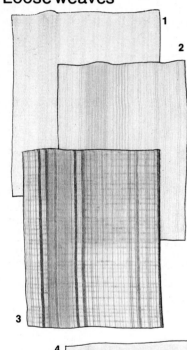

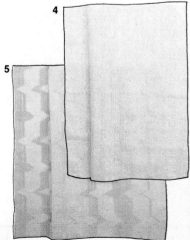

Openweaves: 1–3
Muslins: 4–5

Cheesecloths

6 Stripes

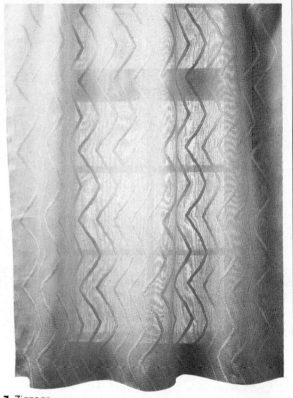

7 Zigzags

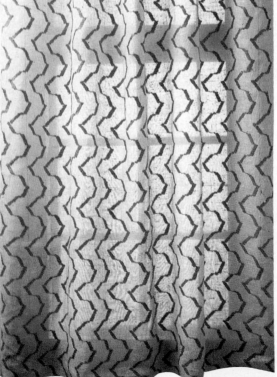

8 Wavy lines

9 Furrows

All items at Scale 2 reduction; see page 209

Laces

10 Singing Birds

11 Butterflies and Birds

12 Flowers and Fronds

13 Ferns

Nets

14 Waves

15 Palms

Synthetics

16 Wisps

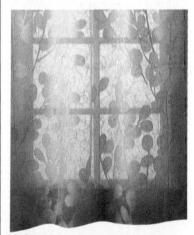

17 Seed Pods

18 Branches

BLINDS

Made in a variety of widths to fit most window and door shapes, blinds range from comparatively cheap matchstick, bamboo and paper types to the more expensive wooden, aluminum and fabric louvers, and slatted Venetian blinds. As well as filtering light, which some blinds do automatically, stiffened fabric louvers can also be used effectively as room dividers.

1 Plain Venetian Pull-up

2 Patterned Venetian Pull-up

3 Paper Pull-up

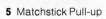

4 Slatted Wooden Pull-up

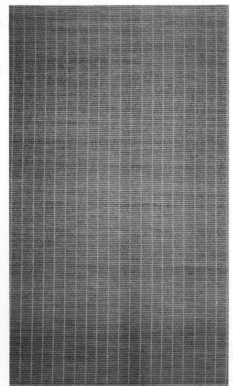

5 Matchstick Pull-up

6 Painted Pinoleum Pull-up

All items at Scale 2 reduction; see page 209

SHADES

There are many advantages to fabric shades. They use less fabric, take up less space and block out less light than drapes, and are therefore ideal for small windows and dark spaces. Shades also come in many styles, ranging from plain roller types, which give a "finished" look to a room when used with drapes, to the more extravagant Roman and festoon shades, which fold up with varying degrees of fullness.

1 Plain Roller

2 Sun-patterned Roller

3 Sheep-patterned Roller

4 Scenic-patterned Roller

5 Light-reflecting Pull-up

6 Vertical Louver

WOODEN FLOORING

Plain

Strips, tiles and blocks of hardwood flooring can either be laid in traditional patterns like herringbone and basket weaves, or arranged in an original design to fit the space. Parquet can be laid in a similar way or glued down in pre-mounted panels. Cork is warmer, quieter, has good insulating qualities and is easy to clean, but tiles are inclined to fade in strong sunlight.

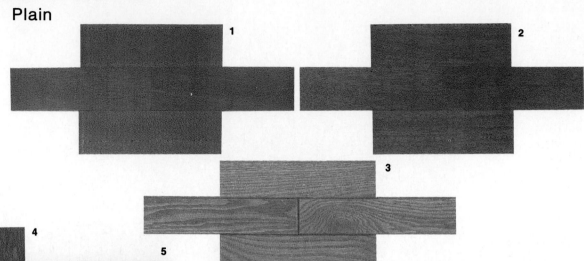

1 Stained Oak; **2** Strip Oak; **3** Ash

Patterned

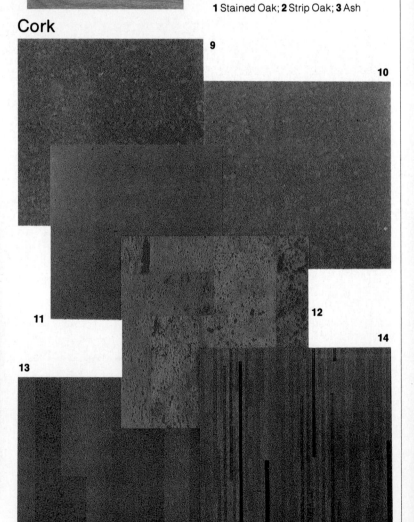

Cork

4, 5 Plank style; **6** Square with oblongs;
7 Pine basketweave parquet;
8 Oak parquet

9, 10, 11 Plains; **12** Paint-backed cork;
13 Columns; **14** Thin linear

All items at Scale 1 reduction; see page 209

NATURAL TILES

Natural tiles: quarry, brick, stone and expensive slate come in beautiful subtle colors, and for the most part, are very hard-wearing. The first four resist damp and are easy to care for but are hard on the feet and hard on dropped china and glass. Nevertheless they are so good-looking, that their esthetic virtues outweigh more practical considerations.

Plain

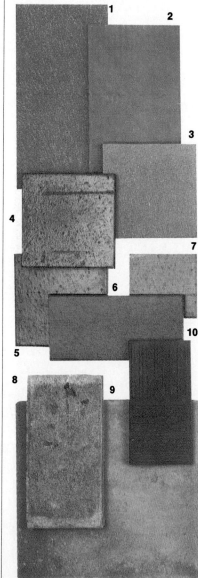

1, **2**: Slate; **3–7**: Quarry; **8**, **9**: Natural Stone; **10**: Brick

Shaped

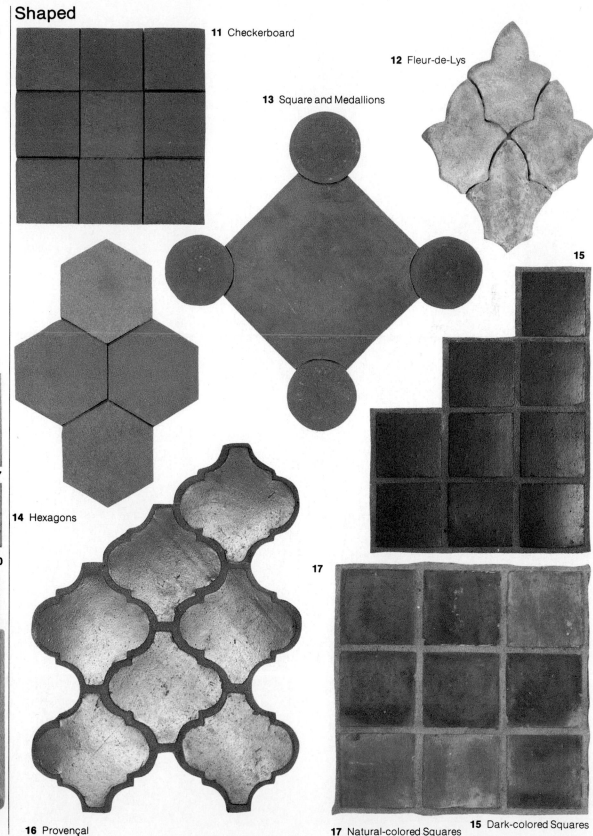

11 Checkerboard

12 Fleur-de-Lys

13 Square and Medallions

14 Hexagons

15

16 Provençal

17

17 Natural-colored Squares   **15** Dark-colored Squares

CERAMIC TILES

Ceramic tiles are produced in a wide variety of shapes, sizes and colors and provide a hardwearing, easy-to-clean surface. The effect created by this versatile flooring will vary according to the style and pattern. Plain Italian tiles, for example, are ideal for a sophisticated, classically decorated room, while rougher, rustic-looking French tiles are better suited to the simpler styles of room.

Classical Italian

Alternative shapes

4 Corners

8 Shaded

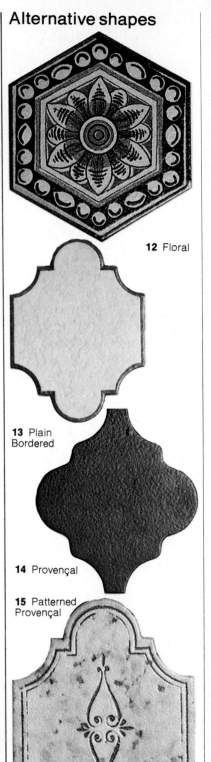

12 Floral

13 Plain Bordered

14 Provençal

15 Patterned Provençal

1 Four-leaf Clover

5 Textured

9 Bordered

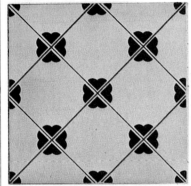

2 Mosaic

6 Checkerboard

10 Flowers

3 Patterned Motif

7 Fronds

11 Grapes

266

Rustic French and German

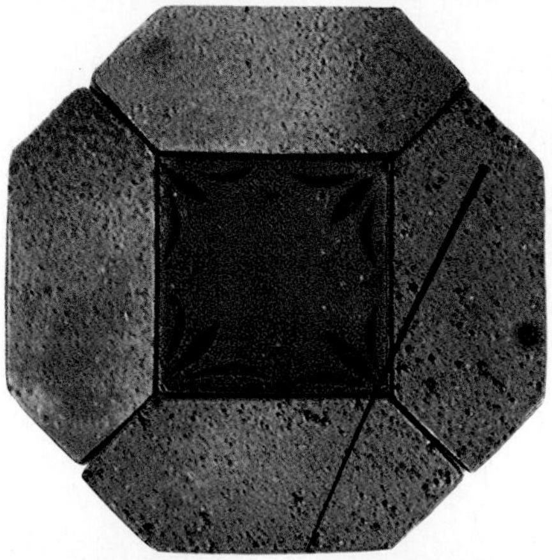

16 Square and Lozenges

17 Mottled

18 Flower

19 Plain

20 Plain

21 Border

22 Rose

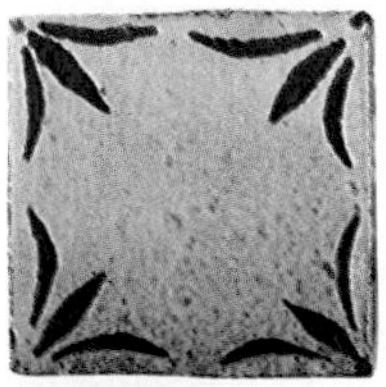

23 Fleur de Lys

24 Bird

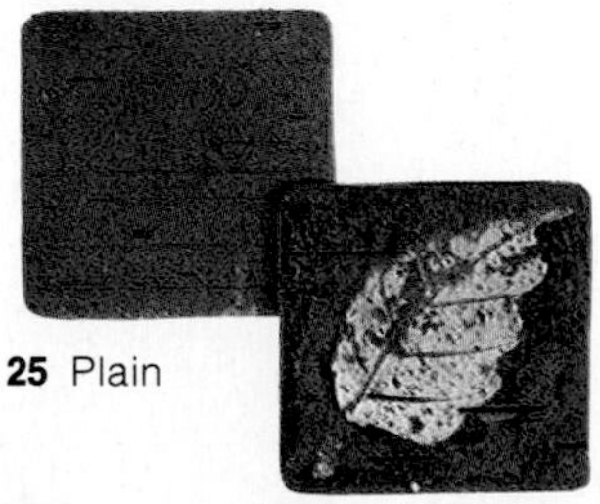

25 Plain

26 Leaf

27

28

29

30

31

32

27–32 Plain and Textured Oblongs

Traditional Mexican

33 Bordered Flower

34 Daisy

35 Sunburst

36 Flower

37 Squared Flower

38 Lace

39 Cross

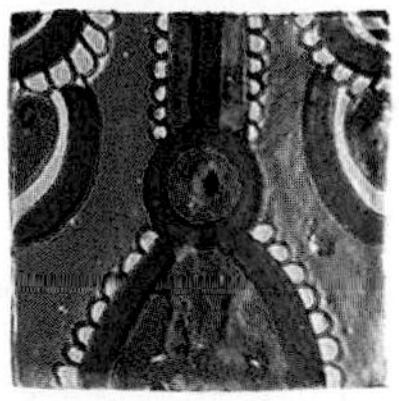

40 Indian Motif

41 Bordered Cross

Modern Spanish

42 Plain

43 Floral

44 Plain

45 Fan

LUXURY TILES

Marble, in its various forms, is one of the most luxurious floorings: luxurious to look at and luxuriously priced. Although expensive to buy, it lasts a long time, is practical in hard-wear areas like hallways and kitchens, and suits any style of furniture. Tiles are equally well suited for use in hot climates or in cooler countries when they can be safely used with underfloor heating.

Terrazzo

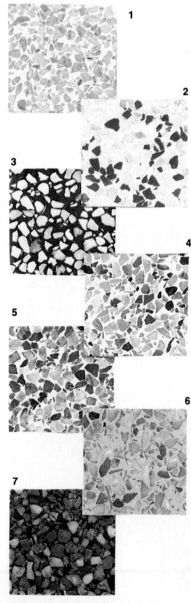

Compound

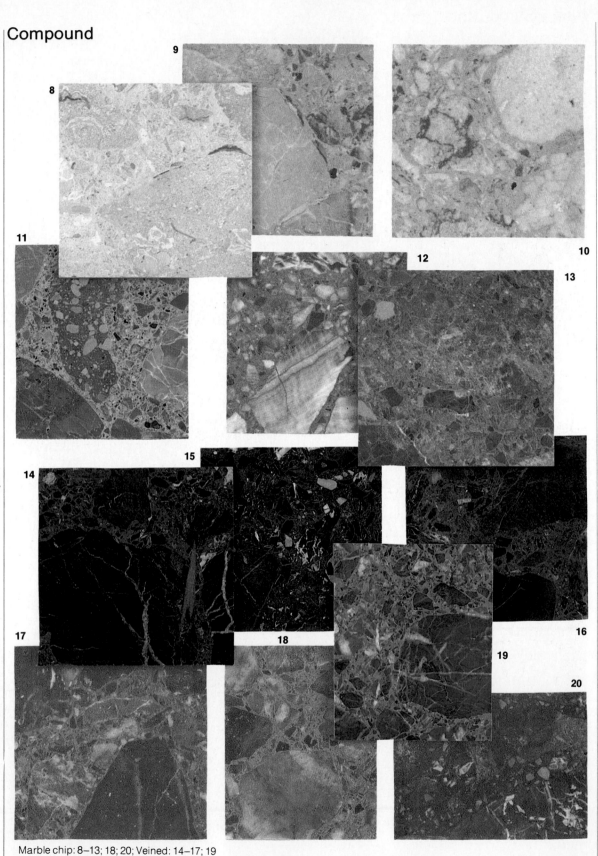

Open chip: 2; Dense chip: 1; 3–7

Marble chip: 8–13; 18; 20; Veined: 14–17; 19

All items at Scale 1 reduction; see page 209

Pure, open-grained

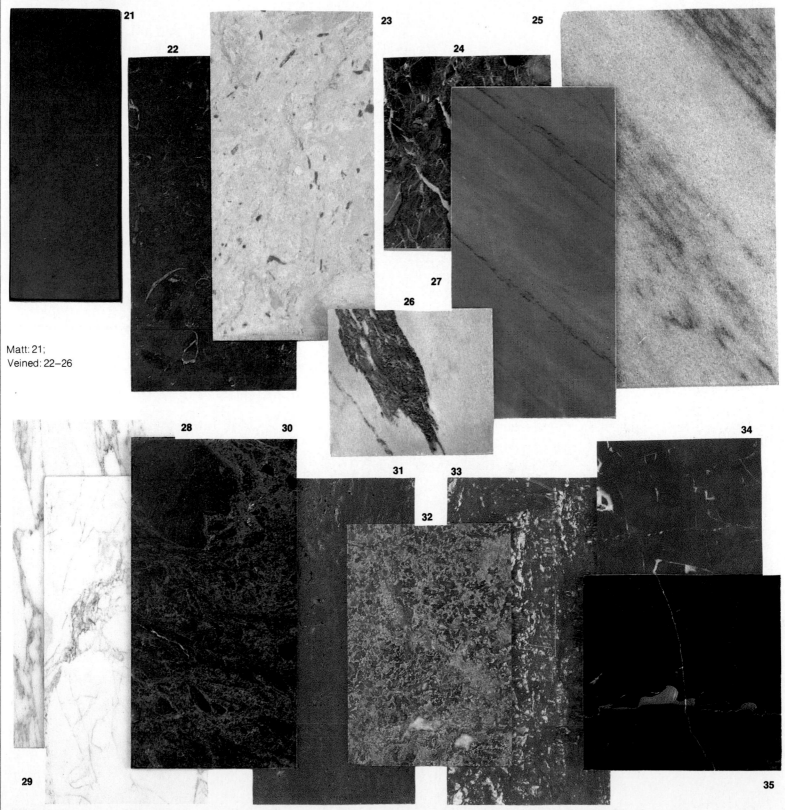

Matt: 21;
Veined: 22–26

Veined: 27–30; 34; 35; Textured: 31–33

COMPOSITION FLOORING

Plain

Linoleum, rubber, thermo-plastic, vinyl, vinyl-cork and vinyl-asbestos tiles all come under this category. Vinyl is by far the most durable material for domestic use although the techniques of producing thermoplastics and linoleum have greatly improved. Composition flooring is available in sheet and tile form, both of which are produced in many patterns, colors and textures.

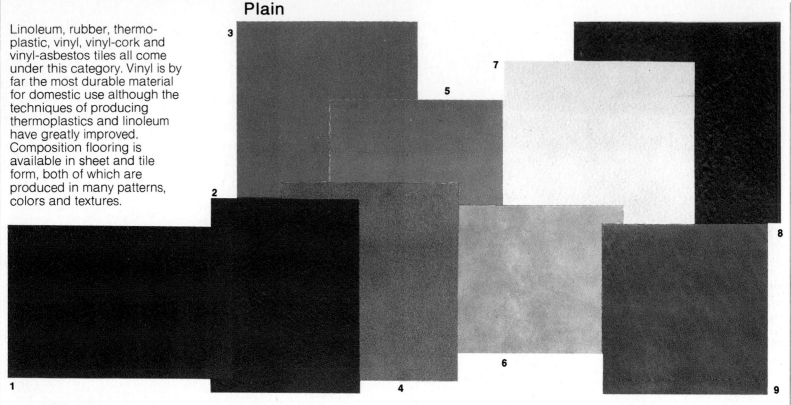

Leather-look: 1; 2; 4–9; Matt: 3

Patterned

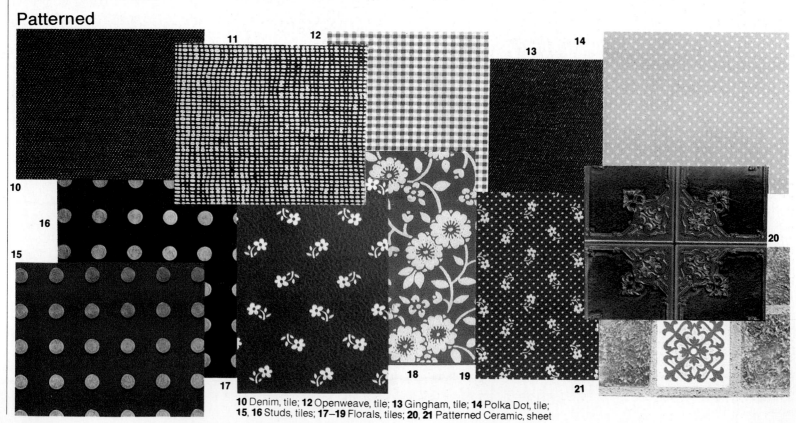

10 Denim, tile; **12** Openweave, tile; **13** Gingham, tile; **14** Polka Dot, tile; **15**, **16** Studs, tiles; **17–19** Florals, tiles; **20**, **21** Patterned Ceramic, sheet

All items at Scale 1 reduction; see page 209

Brick, Stone and Wood

22 Basketweave Brick, tile

23 Squared-up Brick, tile

24 Herringbone Brick, tile

25 Strip Oak, tile

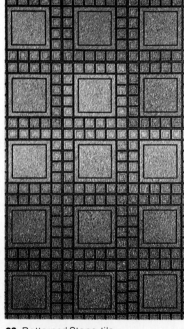

26 Patterned Stone, tile

27 Parquet, tile

Marble

28 Bordered Marble, tile

29 Travertine, tile

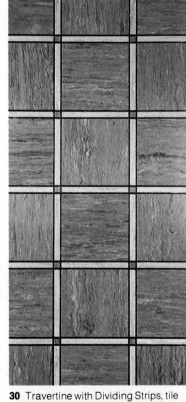

30 Travertine with Dividing Strips, tile

31 Squares with Dividing Strips, tile

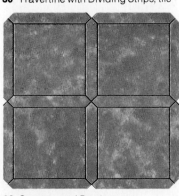

32 Squares and Borders, tile

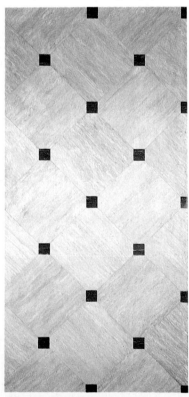

33 Diamonds and Squares, tile

TEXTURED CARPETS

When choosing a carpet for a specific room setting bear in mind that the effect created will differ according to weave and texture. The luxurious pile of a shag carpet gives an opulent effect but is impractical for heavy use, whereas the coarse loop pile of a haircord carpet gives a rough, flat surface capable of much hard wear. They both provide a unifying background for an eclectic collection of furniture.

Velvets

1 Fine pile

2 Medium pile

3 Thick pile

Twists

4 Fine pile

5 Medium pile

6 Thick pile

7 Extra thick pile

Shags

8 Fine pile

9 Medium pile

10 Thick pile

11 Extra thick pile

Fine loops

12 Fine pile

13 Medium pile

14 Thick pile

15 Extra thick pile

All items at Scale 1 reduction; see page 209

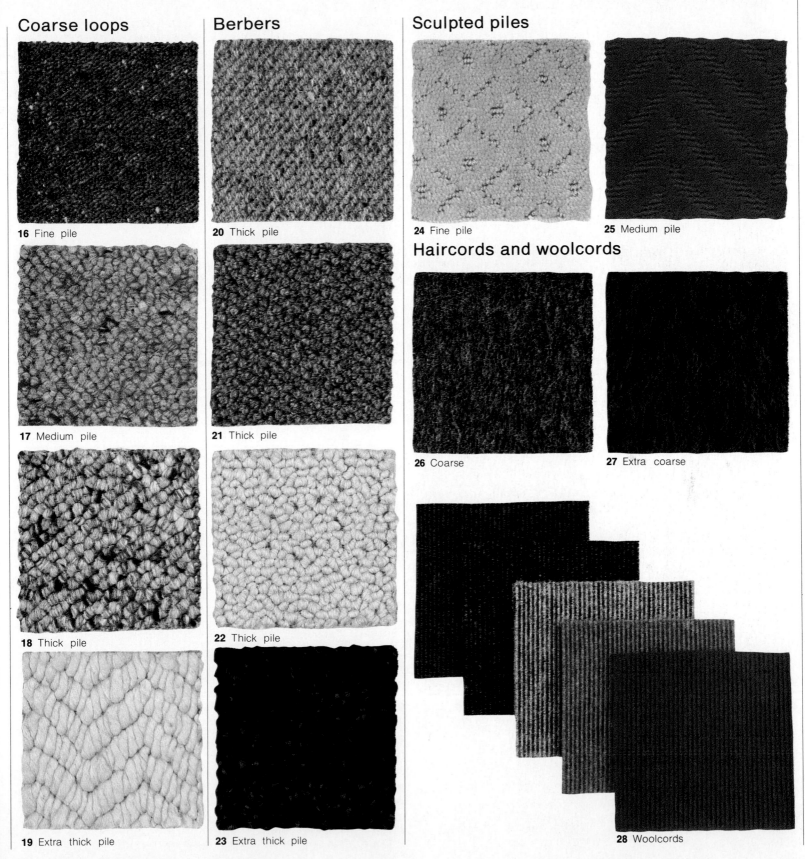

Coarse loops

16 Fine pile

17 Medium pile

18 Thick pile

19 Extra thick pile

Berbers

20 Thick pile

21 Thick pile

22 Thick pile

23 Extra thick pile

Sculpted piles

24 Fine pile

25 Medium pile

Haircords and woolcords

26 Coarse

27 Extra coarse

28 Woolcords

PLAIN CARPETS

Although most plain carpets are woven using the Wilton method (see page 206), they are also available in tufted and Brussels weaves. However, the effect created by the carpet depends more on the type of pile than on the means of construction. Smooth or tight loops provide a neat, regular finish well suited to border patterns, whereas shags and velvets give a more luxurious effect.

Plains

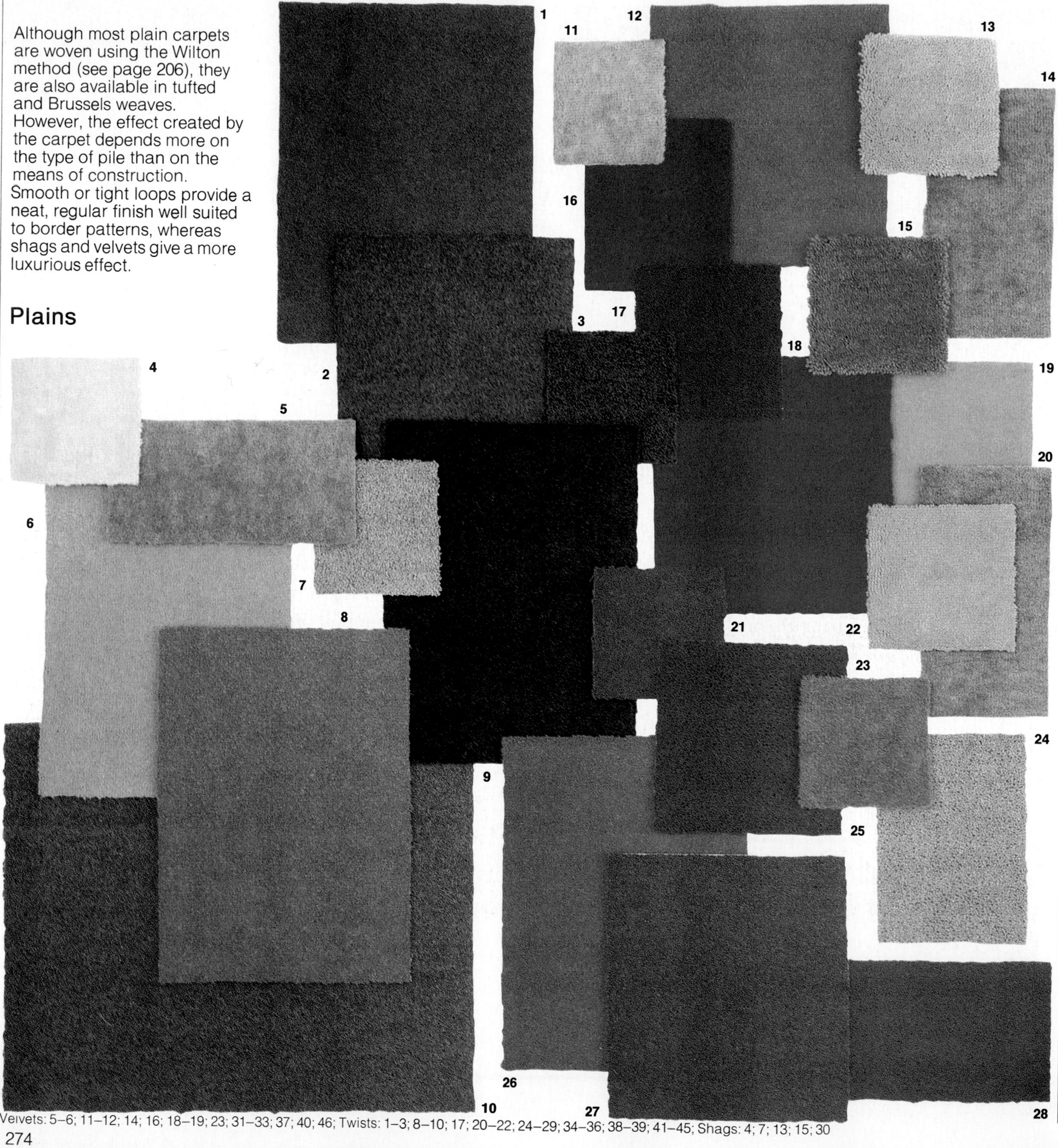

Velvets: 5–6; 11–12; 14; 16; 18–19; 23; 31–33; 37; 40; 46; Twists: 1–3; 8–10; 17; 20–22; 24–29; 34–36; 38–39; 41–45; Shags: 4; 7; 13; 15; 30

All items at Scale 1 reduction; see page 209

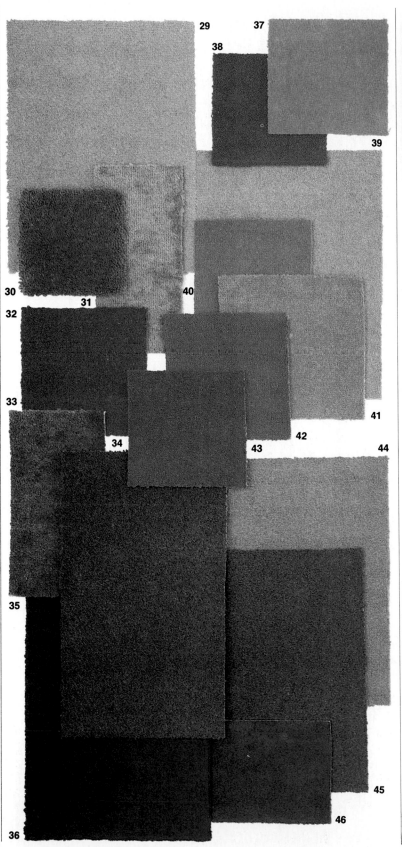

Borders

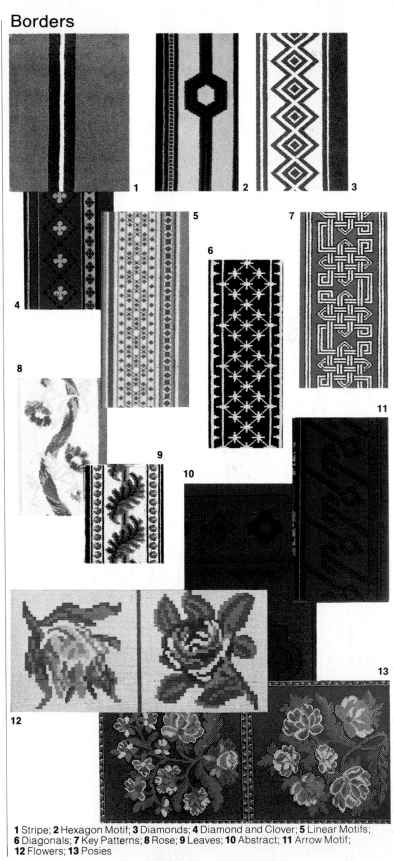

1 Stripe; **2** Hexagon Motif; **3** Diamonds; **4** Diamond and Clover; **5** Linear Motifs;
6 Diagonals; **7** Key Patterns; **8** Rose; **9** Leaves; **10** Abstract; **11** Arrow Motif;
12 Flowers; **13** Posies

PATTERNED CARPETS

Patterned carpets, whatever the weave, are practical in that they do not show dirt as readily as plain carpets. They can be bought in geometric, abstract and floral designs, in a wide range of color combinations. Geometric patterns have a regularizing effect on rectangular-shaped rooms, while abstract patterns are useful for disguising irregularly-shaped ones.

Geometrics

1 Broad stripes; 2 Dots and Squares;
3 Squares; 4 H-Motif; 5 E-Motif;
6 Netting; 7 Diagonals; 8 Diagonal
Flower; 9 Stepped Diamonds;
10 3-D Motif; 11 Key Pattern;
12 Pentagon; 13 Square Diamond

All items at Scale 2 reduction; see page 209

Florals

14 Flower Basket; 15 Cherries; 16 Sprig; 17 Leaves; 18 Tendrils;
19 Star Motif; 20 Lily Motif; 21 Cross Motif

Chains

22 Ribbons; 23 Links; 24 Regency Motif; 25 Trefoil Motif

MATTING

Made of rush, coconut or coir, matting makes an interesting and comparatively cheap flooring. It also provides a neat surface for modern furniture, as well as making a good, unifying background for a mixture of old and new pieces. Matting usually comes in natural colors, but can be dyed. Dust and dirt usually fall through the rush variety which can be lifted up for cleaning; coir can be scrubbed lightly.

Basics

Crossweaves: 1–4
Basketweaves: 5; 6

Firm weaves

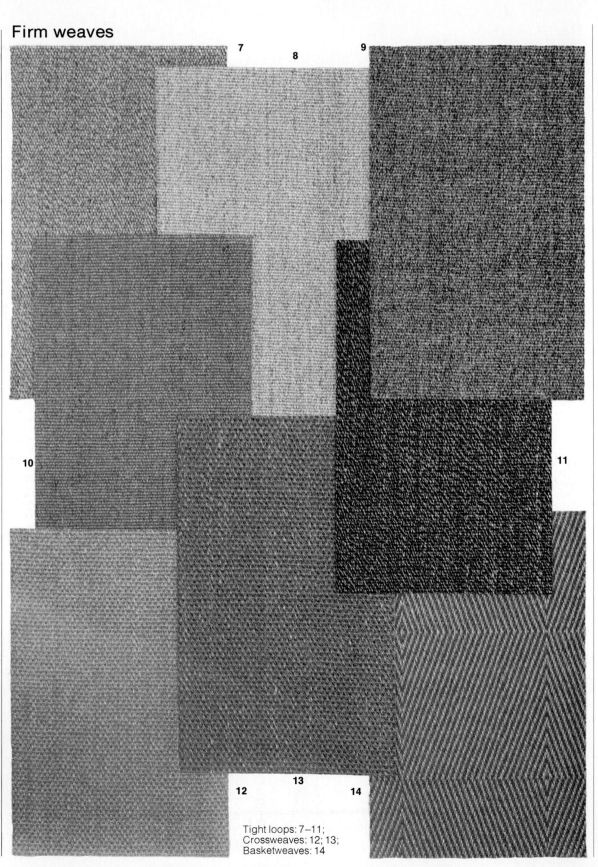

Tight loops: 7–11;
Crossweaves: 12; 13;
Basketweaves: 14

All items at Scale 1 reduction; see page 209

Berber styles

Patterned

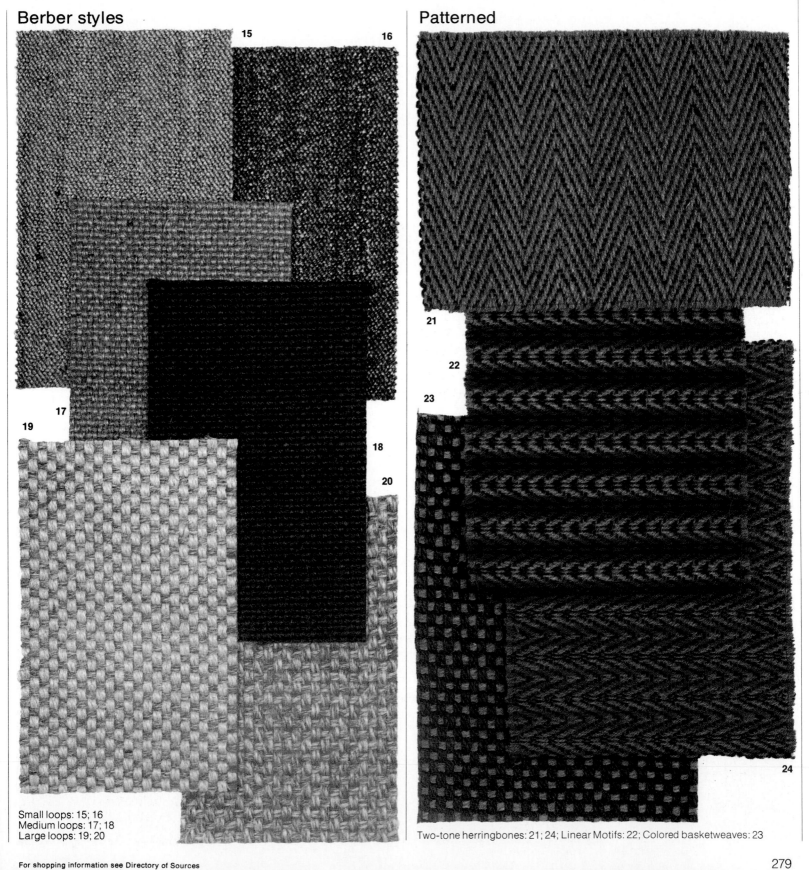

Small loops: 15; 16
Medium loops: 17; 18
Large loops: 19; 20

Two-tone herringbones: 21; 24; Linear Motifs: 22; Colored basketweaves: 23

ETHNIC RUGS

Ordinary rugs fall roughly into three categories: ethnic cottons, like traditional Moroccan or Greek weaves and Indian dhurries; dense, woollen piles like the Finnish rya and Greek flokati; and the luxurious woollen Spanish, Portuguese, South American and Irish varieties. As well as looking good on polished floorboards (when they must be safely secured with a non-slip backing) these rugs can be used as wall hangings.

Unusual weaves

The textured rugs below are produced using techniques other than those on the right.

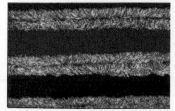

Greek Flokati. Shag Pile

Irish V'soske. Sculpted Pile

American Rag Rug. Woven or Braided

Finnish Rya. Tufted Pile

European, Indian and African

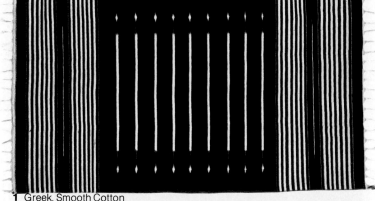

1 Greek. Smooth Cotton

2 Greek. Coarse Cotton

3 English. Wool

4 Indian Dhurrie. Wool

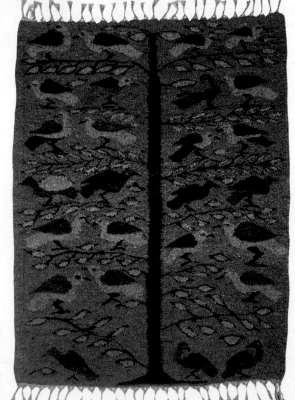

5 South African. Goat Hair

All items at Scale 2 reduction; see page 209

North and South American

6 Navajo Tribe, Arizona. Wool

10 Ayacucho, Peru. Wool

11 Ayucucho, Peru. Wool

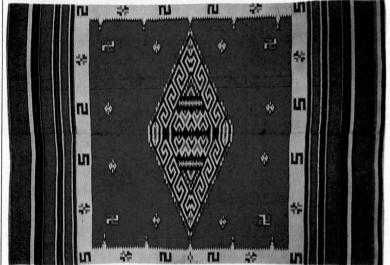

7 Rio Grande, New Mexico. Wool

12 San Pedro de Cajas, Peru. Wool

8 Navajo Tribe, Arizona. Wool

9 Navajo Tribe, Arizona. Wool

13 San Pedro de Cajas, Peru. Wool

TURKISH

Turkey has a rug-making tradition as old as Persia's, but since most Turks are Sunni Muslims, they observe the Koranic prohibition against the depiction of people and animals rather more strictly than their Shiite neighbors. For this reason their designs are based on geometric motifs, frequently of a prayer niche design (see the Yuruk and Mudjur rugs). Less rigid designs also exist. For example, the rugs from Hereke, one of the finest carpet-making towns, often use calligraphy as a motif. Turkish rugs also tend to be more coarsely woven than Persian rugs, and are always woven with the Ghiordes knot. The colors most frequently used are red and blue; green, their sacred color, is used on prayer rugs. For further information, see page 208.

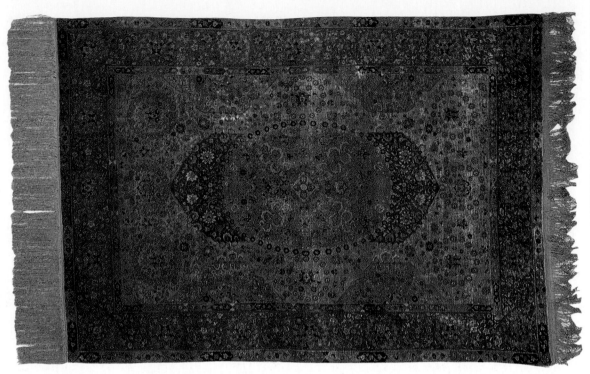

1 Kum-Kapu 6′ 9″ × 4′ 9″ (2.01m × 1.45m)

2 Mudjur 6′ × 4′ 5″ (1.83m × 1.34m)

3 Nomadic rug 5′ 8″ × 4′ 10″ (1.77m × 1.47m)

4 Mudjur 5′ 7″ × 3′ 9″ (1.75m × 1.22m)

5 Hereke 6′ 4″ × 4′ 4″ (1.93m × 1.3m)

6 Hereke 6′ × 4′ (1.85m × 1.25m)

7 Yuruk 6′ × 3′ 7″ (1.85m × 1.17m)

PERSIAN

For many people the term "Persian rug" is synonymous with oriental rugs in general. Certainly the variety, from the sophisticated larger versions made by master weavers to the smaller but no less charming nomadic rugs, is extraordinary. The colorings are invariably rich and deep, usually with a ground of crimson backing symbolic, figurative or naturalistic motifs. The most usual material for carpets and rugs was, and is, wool, but particularly fine silk rugs are now much sought after. In fact, there is an old Persian saying: "The richer the man the thinner the carpet", which refers to the superb quality of the finest silk rugs. For further information, see page 208.

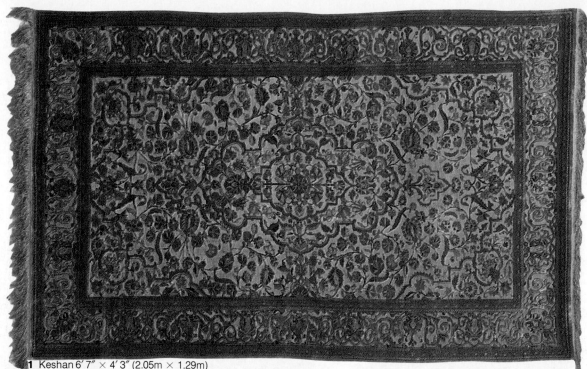

1 Keshan 6′ 7″ × 4′ 3″ (2.05m × 1.29m)

2 Qashga'i 10′ 5″ × 5′ 8″ (3.66m × 1.78m)

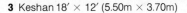

3 Keshan 18′ × 12′ (5.50m × 3.70m)

4 Baktyar Dozar 6′ 11″ × 4′ 8″ (2.11m × 1.42m)

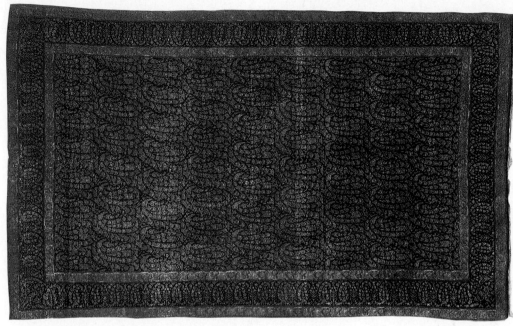

5 Teheran 7′ 6″ × 4′ 7″ (2.27m × 1.40m)

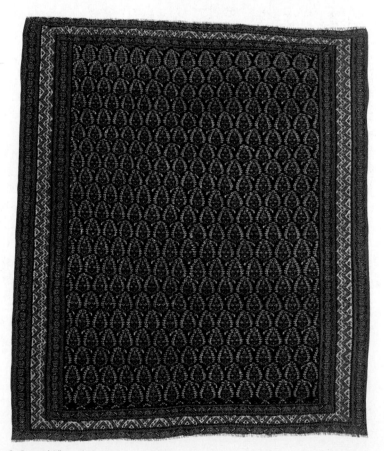

6 Keshan 10′ × 5′ (3.05m × 2.08m)

7 Teheran 2′ 5″ × 2′ 1″ (0.74m × 0.64m)

8 Sine 5′ 2″ × 4′ 5″ (1.57m × 1.35m)

CAUCASIAN AND TURKOMAN

Two major rug producing areas in Central Asia are the Caucasian and Turkoman regions, which are justifiably famous for the high quality weaves of their nomadic tribes. The Caucasus is a difficult mountain area between the Caspian and Black Seas and, although the region now belongs to the USSR, it has been home to many different tribes from Turkey, Armenia and Persia, all of which have contributed to its heritage. Carpets produced in this area are strongly geometric, with figures, birds and flowers reduced to straight lines. Turkestan covers the region between the Caspian and north-western China, and the rugs made by the various Afghani, Baluchi and Beshir tribesmen all have a similar geometric style. For further information, see page 208.

1 Chazli (USSR) 13′ 2″ × 3′ 3″ (4m × 1m)

2 Kazak (USSR) 7′ 3″ × 5′ 4″ (2.20m × 1.62m)

4 Kazak (USSR) 8′ 8″ × 6′ (2.64m × 1.85m)

3 Kazak (USSR) 7′ × 5′ (2.08m × 1.52m)

5 Gendje (USSR) 8′ 9″ × 4′ (2.67m × 1.24m)

All items at Scale 2 reduction; see page 209

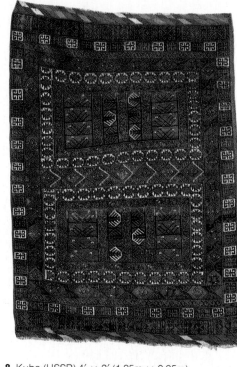

6 South Caucasian (USSR)
7′ 3″ × 3′ 8″ (2.20m × 1.11m)

7 Hila (USSR) 4′ 9″ × 3′ 3″ (1.45m × 1m)

8 Kuba (USSR) 4′ × 3′ (1.25m × 0.95m)

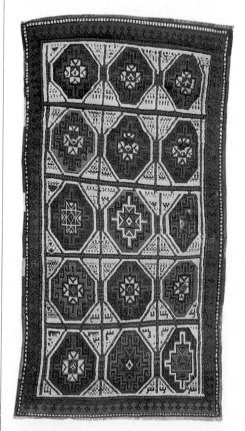

9 Kazak (USSR) 10′ × 4′ (3.04m × 1.25m)

10 Gendje (USSR) 4′ 4″ × 2′ 10″ (1.32m × 0.86m)

11 Beshir (Afghanistan)
10′ 4″ × 4′ (3.31m × 1.50m)

CHINESE AND INDIAN

While rugs were being woven in China two thousand years ago, there was not a real industry until the mid-eighteenth century. Chinese rugs differ radically from their main Islamic counterparts by using traditional Buddhist and Taoist motifs, and blue, apricot and yellow as their main colors. Early Indian carpets were based originally on Persian models, but soon developed their own styles and colors (see page 208 for further information).

1 Tinsin 3′ × 2′ (0·92m × 0·61m)

2 Tinsin 6′ × 4′ (1·83m × 1·22m)

3 Peking 5′ × 3′ (1·52m × 0·92m)

4 Amritsar 5′ 11″ × 4′ (1·8m × 1·22m)

5 Srinagar 6′ 2″ × 3′ 11″ (1·86m × 1·20m)

6 Jaipur 6′ 6″ × 4′ 1″ (1·98m × 1·25m)

All items at Scale 1 reduction; see page 209/For shopping information see Directory of Sources

FURNITURE AND FURNISHINGS

THE DEVELOPMENT OF FURNITURE

There is a great deal more to furnishing a house than simply choosing the furniture. It sounds elementary enough, but you have only to analyze all the aspects of a room, from floor to ceiling, to realize that "furnishings" is, in fact, an umbrella title which includes any or all of the following: architectural elements (like staircases and doors); fireplaces and freestanding stoves; light fittings; bathroom and kitchen appliances; hardware; shelves and storage as well as furniture and accessories. All contribute to the general feeling of the home, and the way furnishings are chosen and put together forms its eventual style.

General background information on design, with tips about balance, scale and use of color is given on pages 10 to 32, while everything you need to know about arrangements and accessories is dealt with on pages 322 to 352. Below, we deal with the development of furniture, from its early beginnings to the present.

Up to 1600

Early medieval furniture tended to be crude and functional with very little decoration. Seats consisted mainly of plain benches or stools; beds were simple frames, topped with a straw mattress; tables were trestle style – long and easily dismantled. With the exception of chests, which doubled for storing goods and for seating, few early pieces have survived from the period prior to the fifteenth century.

The Renaissance and Reformation Period

Domestic furniture in Italy, France, Spain, Portugal, Germany, Austria, Scandinavia and the Low Countries became much more sophisticated as a result of the Renaissance. This fifteenth century movement, which began in Italy and spread throughout Europe, aimed to return to classical styles and ideals and it led to a great flowering of the decorative arts. Although furniture was still bulky, carving became increasingly elaborate as the century progressed, and the functional rustic stools which began the period evolved into lavishly decorated chairs.

Renaissance ideas were never fully assimilated by English designers, and following the Reformation English craftsmen were increasingly influenced by their northern contemporaries. Oak was most commonly used, with low relief carving, bulbs, and inlays. Richly upholstered chairs and draw tables, which extended to twice their length, were the other developments.

1600–1830

Although the European countries all produced national variations up to, and following the Renaissance, the predominant style was definitely Italian. Between 1600 and 1830, however, this influence was completely eclipsed by France, to the extent that Europe, and on occasion America, accepted and assimilated all that was Gallic.

France 1600–1830

Louis XIV and the Baroque (1643-1715)

The great influence of France on the development of furniture really began in 1663, with the establishment at Gobelins of the *Manufacture Royale de la Couronne*.

State bed in florid Baroque style, c. 1680

The prevailing influence on the arts at that time was Italian and now the Gobelins craftsmen began to adopt the lavish, ornate Baroque style. The furniture was well-balanced, but floridly decorated, with elaborate carvings and intricate mirror arrangements. Veneering and marquetry using pine, walnut and ebony became increasingly popular and a new inlay technique using tortoiseshell, pewter and brass instead of wood was developed by André Charles Boulle (1642–1732). The principal new pieces introduced during this period were the chest of drawers or *commode*, the writing table or bureau, and the closet or *armoire*.

One important development was the opening up of trade routes to the East, resulting in increased interest in oriental designs, especially lacquered chests.

The Style Régence (1715-25)

Louis XV was only five years old when he came to the throne and for almost a decade France was ruled by a regent. This period is seen as a bridge between the heavy Baroque period and the elegant Rococo which developed in the 1720s and 1730s.

Without the pomp and ceremony of Louis XIV's court, Baroque-style furniture now seemed out of place and it was gradually replaced by lighter, smaller, more delicately-designed pieces. The furniture was still highly decorated with elaborate wooden marquetry, with overlaid *ormolu* mounts, or with geometric inlays.

Louis XV and the Rococo (1725-74)

The style promoted by Louis XV's craftsmen was essentially a development of the *style régence*. The Rococo owed much to the influence of oriental art and is characterized by an excessive use of curves, with asymmetrical surface carvings of rocks, shells and waves. Console tables, occasional chairs and beds are pieces which best reflect this style. Veneered woods continued to be popular, and marquetry and even paint were used for decoration.

Towards the reign's end a number of small pieces were specially designed for women. These included the writing table or *secretaire, bonheur du jour* desks and the dressing table or *bureau toilette*.

Louis XVI and Neoclassicism (1774-93)

By 1774, when Louis XVI came to the throne, there was a growing reaction against the floridness of both the Baroque and Rococo movements which resulted in a return to simple classical forms and motifs.

Following formal classical lines, furniture design became more rectangular, and chairs and tables were given straight as opposed to curved legs. Plain woods, particularly mahogany, were used as veneers and were then decorated with either geometric marquetry, porcelain adornments, or white and gold paint. New styles of the period were the corner commode or *encoignure* and the side cupboard (with curved doors) or *demi-lune*.

The Directoire Period (1795-99)

Increasing social unrest led eventually to the French Revolution of 1789 and the establishment of the short-lived French republican government or *Directoire*.

One of the most successful cabinet-makers of the period was Georges Jacob

(1739–1814) who had been an important craftsman under Louis XVI and who now continued to promote the classical style. Jacob worked principally in mahogany and for decoration often used ebony, satinwood and pewter marquetry, occasionally patinating the wood so that it resembled bronze. Chairs were frequently modeled on English designs, with carved and pierced splats or with scrolled and saber-curved legs. Two new tables introduced during this period were a round table with a central pedestal, the *guéridon*, and a pedestal bedside table, the *somno*.

The Empire Period (1800-1815)
Stability once again returned to France in 1799 when Napoleon Bonaparte (1769–1821) overthrew the *Directoire* government and was elected First Consul of France.

Designs became more sober after the fanciful styles of previous eras and the oriental influence waned, possibly because its rather florid style was not in keeping with the strict, militaristic feeling of the period. Napoleon's military triumphs were often echoed in interior designs, so walls and beds were festooned in drapery to resemble tents while stools were made to resemble drums. A typical Napoleonic piece was the rectangular console table – with a classical fauna-motif support. Scroll-backed chairs were replaced by upholstered rectangular-backed ones.

England 1600–1830

The Early Stuart Period (1603-49)
During the period of the early Stuart kings (James I, *reigned* 1603–25 and Charles I, *reigned* 1625–49), furniture styles were slow to change and most pieces were adapted from earlier Elizabethan designs. Formed mostly of oak, furniture was still rectangular and sturdily made, although less exuberently decorated. Innovations of the period include chairs without arms, called *back-* or *farthingale stools*, and chests of drawers with two drawers in the lower section and a chest on top.

The Restoration Period (1660-85)
Furniture produced during the Commonwealth (1649–60) had reflected the sobriety of the period but the developments in furniture design which occurred in France during the reign of Louis XIV were now paralleled in England during that of Charles II. Restoration of the monarchy heralded an elegant period of furniture making, for Charles' exuberant court adopted many of the Baroque styles popular throughout contemporary Europe. Walnut

was now in common use and the solid parts of the furniture were frequently carved. Chair legs were now either plain-turned, twist-turned or scrolled; chair backs often had a caned panel or seat. The *chaises* and upholstered stools of the day reflected the growing desire for comfort. During this period more small pieces such as writing and card tables were produced.

The William and Mary Period (1689-1702)
The Revocation of the Edict of Nantes in 1685 outlawed the Protestant religion in France and resulted in the influx of Huguenot craftsmen to England. One of the most influential refugees was the cabinetmaker Daniel Marot (1663–1752) who interpreted the florid styles of Louis XIV's craftsmen and produced much more subtle, restrained designs, better suited to the sober attitudes of William III's court. By 1690 the French-style chair, with its upholstered back and seat, had replaced the cane-paneled chair, so popular in the Restoration period.

Lacquered furniture was in increasing demand and when supplies from the East began to run out, they were replaced with native imitations, made using the technique of japanning. Chests and cabinets were the most popular items made in this way; the other items in great demand were writing desks, tea tables and bookcases.

Furniture in graceful Queen Anne style, 1708

The Queen Anne Period (1702-14)
The process of adapting the Baroque into an English style, which had begun under William and Mary, was continued by Anne's craftsmen and produced the happiest and most graceful of English designs. Typical of the period were small, elegantly curved walnut pieces with French-style, cabriole legs embellished with scallop shell, bracket, hoof, pad, club, or claw-and-ball feet. Elaborately carved chair backs were now tall and hooped to accommodate women's hairstyles of the time. In 1700, the upholstered wing chair was introduced and this was followed by the settee.

The Early Georgian Period (1714-60)
Under George I a return to classical ideals and values was promoted by the Palladian Movement. The chief designer of this group was William Kent (c.1685–1748), the first architect to design furniture specifically for his houses. Mahogany now replaced walnut as the basic raw material and although the Queen Anne style of furniture continued to be produced, it was in considerably modified form. The hoop-backed chair, for example, was replaced by a square-backed design with decorated legs.

The Age of the Designers
The development of furniture from 1725 until the end of the century, while still coming under the general heading of Georgian (whether early, middle or late), depended significantly on a handful of outstanding architects and craftsmen. They undoubtedly deserve praise for the skilful way they interpreted prevailing Rococo fashions.

Thomas Chippendale (1718-79)
Typical Chippendale chairs were made of mahogany, with carved cabriole legs and scrolled claw-and-ball feet; their backs usually had a serpentine-shaped top rail with a fretted and carved splat. Some Gothic-style Chippendale chairs had fretted legs with splats forming pointed arches; Chinese Chippendale was based on imported oriental forms.

Robert Adam (1728-92)
The Neoclassical revival, again imported from France, began in the 1760s and was encouraged in Britain by Adam, a Scottish architect who exercised total control over his interiors. His romantically elegant designs were frequently made up by contemporary craftsmen, including Chippendale. Adam worked extensively with satinwood and fruitwoods and used both marquetry and inlays for decoration, with very delicate carving.

George Hepplewhite (died 1786)
The Hepplewhite period is generally considered to cover the years 1770–90 (his date of birth is unknown). Hepplewhite's book, *Cabinet-Maker's and Upholsterer's Guide* was to influence the development of many types of furniture, including bedroom and dressing room pieces. Like Chippendale, Hepplewhite worked with mahogany, but he also decorated furniture with satinwood or other hardwood inlays. Hepplewhite chairs, of which the shield-backed chair is the most famous, were much lighter and less curved than Chippendale's and usually had tapered legs; in most cases the heart- or oval-shaped shield enclosed a splat.

Thomas Sheraton (1751-1806)
Chair design reached its peak of refinement with Sheraton, and his *Cabinet-maker's and Upholsterer's Drawing Book*, which was produced between 1791 and 1794, filled the gap between the Neoclassical and Regency periods. Sheraton, too, worked with mahogany, and for decoration he used thin strips of wood or brass inlay, building up patterns of oval or circular bandings. His chairs were light and delicate, frequently with striped upholstery, and he also produced painted chairs with plain cane seats.

Delicate, classically-styled pieces, c. 1780

The Regency Period (1760-1830)
Spanning the reigns of George III and George IV, this period derives its name from the years when the Prince of Wales (later George IV) was regent (1811–20). The most famous English furniture designer of the time was Thomas Hope (1769–1831), whose influential *Household Furniture and Interior Decoration* included French *Empire* and *Directoire*-style pieces.

In spite of classical, Egyptian, oriental and even Gothic details, early Regency furniture was simply made and elegantly decorated. Notable exceptions were the oriental-style pieces which were used for the opulent interiors of the Royal Pavilion, Brighton. Faux bamboo was in common use for Regency Chinoiserie, as was rosewood.

America 1600–1830

The Early American Period (1620-1700)
The earliest surviving American-made furniture dates from the mid-seventeenth century. The early colonists began by importing furniture from their native countries, but this was less than successful since the imported pieces cracked and shrank in the new climate.

Instead of continuing to transport furniture (a lengthy business in those times) both skilled and unskilled men began to adapt original designs, basing them on the pattern books they had brought with them and using available tools and materials. The results were less ostentatious than their European counterparts, but had a simplicity and vitality all their own.

Most of the early pieces, which date from 1650–70 were bulky, though well-proportioned, carved chests. Like the better-looking court cupboards, presses, chests and chests of drawers, these were made from native oak or maple. Brewster and Carver chairs (named after two of the Pilgrim fathers), made mostly of hickory, ash, maple or elm, were the most popular. Three-legged armchairs, wainscot chairs, high-backed Charles II chairs and some cane-backed day beds have also survived.

The American William and Mary Period (1700-25)
William and Mary "Dutch" furniture reached America just before the beginning of the eighteenth century and immediately became popular. Walnut was the favourite wood of that particular time in Europe, and it was used by American craftsmen to produce much lighter pieces than the heavy, bulky styles of the earlier period. Furniture became more ornamental now, both in form and decoration. Legs, which had been straight, were now curved with the introduction of the cabriole leg. The use of marquetry, painting and lacquering was widespread.

One of the most interesting developments was the tall chest of drawers, or highboy, which had five or six tiers of drawers on a six-legged stand. The stand on its own, with one layer of drawers, was known as a lowboy. The new "butterfy table", with hinged supports, also became popular.

The American Queen Anne Period (1714-60)
Queen Anne designs reached America after her death in 1714 and remained in fashion until 1755–60. Mahogany was increasingly used, although walnut, pine and maple were ever popular. Formal William and Mary-style furniture was rejected in favor of graceful, curving styles; cabriole legs with rounded or claw-and-ball feet finally replaced straight legs and became the predominant feature of furniture design.

The American Chippendale Period (c. 1755-85)
Chippendale-style furniture, which succeeded Queen Anne designs in America, includes a variety of imported styles ranging from early Georgian to the Gothic, Chinese and Rococo styles of mid-eighteenth century England. Chippendale-style furniture was elaborately developed by Philadelphian cabinetmakers and although theirs was the most luxurious furniture to date, it was still much purer and more restrained than the English prototypes. Key features of American Chippendale were Rococo-style, complex forms such as the cresting "crossbow" backs of chairs, and cabriole legs with claw-and-ball feet. Mahogany was the most commonly used wood and pieces had carved decoration.

The American Hepplewhite, Sheraton and Phyfe Period (1785-90)
Adam-style furniture never became popular in America, largely because Adam only produced his furniture for wealthy patrons and as a result published no pattern books that people could copy. Thus, by 1784 when communication was re-established after the War of Independence, the predominant influences on English design were Sheraton and Hepplewhite; the Americans adopted features of both. Mahogany continued to be used, with satinwood or maple inlays.

Sheraton's delicate designs reached their zenith in the hands of cabinetmaker Duncan Phyfe (1768–1854) – so much so that American Sheraton is often called Phyfe-style furniture. Lowboys and highboys began to be replaced by waist-high dressers or bureaux, and more side tables were produced.

The Federal Period (c. 1790-1810)
After the period of English influence, Americans began to look towards France for artistic inspiration. They assimilated the neoclassical influence of the French *Directoire* and *Empire* styles into their own, Federal style (named after America's adoption of a federal government). The *Directoire* influence was especially clear in the design of chairs and couches. Made from mahogany, their backs, sides, arms and legs were concave, with saber-shaped curves. Empire styles were typified by larger, bulkier furniture, traditionally using veneers of mahogany and rosewood.

1830–1900

This was a curious transitional time for furniture design. Ironically, mechanical improvements, which had been developed as a result of the Industrial Revolution, were mainly used to reproduce historical revivals. In America, John Henry Belter, for example, used his innovative laminating machine to produce Rococo copies. But there were also many genuine improvements. Inventors like Samuel Spratt in London revolutionized upholstery with his wire springs, patented in 1828, and in Vienna, Michael Thonet discovered techniques for bending beechwood with steam.

Two distinctive styles emerged. First there

was a spontaneous reaction against poor, mass-produced copies of established styles, in favour of functionalism. Secondly, there was the popular Art Nouveau movement known as Jugendstil in Germany, Secessionism in Austria, Art Nouveau in England and Le Style Anglais in France.

France 1830–1900

The Restoration and the Second Empire 1814–70

This period, covering the restoration of the Bourbon monarchy (1814–48), and Napoleon III's declaration as Second Emperor of France (1852–70), coincided with the rise of the middle classes. Their increasing demands for furniture were met by new, mechanized production techniques. However, no consistent style emerged from this period, which was notable for the number of copies produced.

The Art Nouveau Period 1870–1905

The inevitable reaction against industrialization and the stagnation of designs came towards the end of the century when Comte Léon de Laborde applied the principles of his contemporary, William Morris, and founded schools of applied art to educate craftsmen.

This esthetic revolution, which began in the 1870s, paved the way for the international Art Nouveau movement whose influence applied to both fine and general arts. In France, the main designers were Louis Majorelle, Alexandre Charpentier and Emile Gallé; the other exponents included Arthur H. Mackmurdo in England, Charles Rennie Mackintosh in Scotland, Henry van der Velde and Victor Horta in Belgium, Joseph Hoffman in Vienna and Louis Comfort Tiffany, who was the guiding light in America. Their designs showed the influence of Japanese and Celtic art, and were typified by sweeping, curving shapes, sinuous lines and flowing, naturalistic curves.

England 1830–1900

Victorian Styles

The keynote of Victoria's reign was a sense of tradition, and furniture manufacturers quickly interpreted the market by producing copies of classical, Rococo and Tudor styles which the rising middle classes could afford.

Yet despite revivalism, new styles did emerge. The first was a revised and purified version of the Gothic style, produced by the influential designer A. W. N. Pugin in the early years of the reign. The second style reflected the willingness of designers to

experiment with new materials. Samuel Spratt's invention of wire springs in 1828 led to the production of the first fully upholstered, fully sprung "naturalistic" seating.

Victorian bedroom in Chinese style, c. 1860

The Arts and Crafts Movement 1861–1900

In 1861, as a reaction against the factory-produced furnishings of the period, William Morris set up the firm of Morris, Marshall, Faulkner and Co. Influenced by Pugin, Morris and his colleagues sought a return to the standards of craftsmanship which they felt had been destroyed by capitalism and mass production. But the furniture produced, although beautifully made, and on occasion lavishly decorated, was not mass-produced and as a result could only be afforded by a small, wealthy minority.

During the 1870s and 1880s, many designers supported the views of Morris' esthetic movement, and men like A. H. Mackmurdo, E. S. Prior, C. R. Ashbee, C. F. A. Voysey and R. N. Shaw were inspired by him to set up the Arts and Crafts Movement. They advocated simple pieces in which form would follow function.

The Art Nouveau Period 1890–1910

This movement grew out of the Arts and Crafts Movement. Although influenced by their European contemporaries, British designers retained a simplicity and solidity of design more in keeping with Morris. The major influence was the Scottish architect Charles Rennie Mackintosh, whose distinctive, but outrageously uncomfortable pieces were well-received abroad, especially by the Vienna Secessionists.

America 1830–1900

The Historical Revival Period

Influenced by trends in Europe, and aided by improved production techniques, American manufacturers began making home-produced imitations of Gothic, Elizabethan, Rococo, Renaissance and Oriental designs. The best of these were made by John Henry Belter whose Rococo copies of the 1850s were produced by

pressing steam-heated, laminated rosewood into shape.

Indigenous American Styles

At the same time as the manufacturers were producing these copies, indigenous styles (or those complementary to them) were being developed and promoted. One successful manufacturer of these was Lambert Hitchcock, who used factory methods to make simple, stenciled chairs.

Another important development was the folk furniture produced by the Shaker religious sect. They reduced design to its barest essentials, stressing functionalism by making pieces in plain, undecorated wood.

The style of furniture produced by the English Arts and Crafts movement was introduced into America in the 1880s, when William Morris' contemporary, Charles Eastlake, published his *Hints on Household Taste*. Eastlake's simple designs were immediately popular with Americans. The growing taste for rural-style functional design was also reflected in the popularity of the Mission furniture of the 1890s, which was based on ethnic Indian furniture.

Innovative American Styles

American designers, like their European counterparts, were aware of the new techniques and innovations, and this led to a greater flexibility of design. With the introduction, for example, of the wire spring came the Turkish frame, coil-sprung, upholstered chair. Metal was now increasingly used to produce beds, rocking chairs, reclining chairs, and wire chairs. Because of the improved production techniques, both in lamination and on the conveyor belt, Thonet-style bentwood chairs were offered in most manufacturers' catalogs.

The Twentieth Century

This period marks a radical break with traditional furniture design. At the beginning of the century the prescient recognized that the machine would play an increasingly important part in modern life, and that the final results of mass-production would depend on a strong original design tailored for the machine, and not on the skills of the craftsman/cabinetmaker.

Two separate exponents of late nineteenth century Art Nouveau, Louis Sullivan in Chicago and Van der Velde in Belgium, were so moved by the changes in urban society (the demand for social equality; the technological advances; the growing demand for functional design and improving communications between countries) that they became founder members of what came to be called the *Modern Movement*. This aimed to create lighter, brighter environments where form would follow function, and it is interesting to note how many of the designers in the first third of the century were in fact architects.

Sinuously-curved Art Nouveau bedroom suite, 1903

It should also be noted that various countries played different parts in the development of production techniques, and at different times. And just as the balance of innovation has always switched from country to country, so has the amount of influence exerted on various neighbors.

With hindsight it is possible to discern a growing reaction against the harsh simplicity of modernism. Communications today are so easy, mass-production is so sophisticated, and taste is now so universal that it is possible to buy the same piece of furniture in almost every country in the world, so now people often express their individuality by taking up facets of old styles.

Germany

The Deutscher Werkbund (1907)
Germany's great contribution to modern furniture design came in the first third of the century when many designers moved away from the ideals of Art Nouveau. As early as 1907, an association of manufacturers, architects and craftsmen, called the *Deutscher Werkbund*, was formed. It intended to improve furniture production by encouraging artists, craftsmen and manufacturers to work closely together; this, in effect, was the start of industrial design.

The Bauhaus (1919–33)
The German-born architect Walter Gropius founded the Bauhaus School at Weimar in 1919, basing it on the same fundamental principles as the *Werkbund*. The school rapidly became the focal point of the Modern Movement and the light, austere and, above all, functional designs which emerged, animated design between the wars and remain influential today.

A fundamental development was the use

of new materials for the construction of furniture. In 1925, the outstanding German designer Marcel Breuer produced the first tubular steel chair made in one continuous piece, allegedly inspired by the curves of his bicycle handlebars. He followed this with a series of designs for tables, chairs and stools, combining steel with fabric, glass and wood, culminating in 1928 with his famous cantilevered chair. This prototype "S" chair was adapted for mass-production in Thonet's factory, and is still marketed world-wide today. Breuer's innovative use of steel encouraged several other architect/designers, notably Mart Stam and Mies van der Rohe, to experiment with the material and van der Rohe's "Barcelona" chair of 1929 has become a classic.

With the Bauhaus' closure by the Nazis in 1933, the principal designers fled abroad to Switzerland, France, England and America and now the Bauhaus ideals and teaching methods have been adopted and adapted throughout the western world.

Modern Designs
Germany, like all its contemporaries, has been influenced by other countries' trends in furniture design. However, what remains an identifiably "German Look" is functional, solid, well-made furniture: the principles of the Bauhaus linger on. Designers and manufacturers, above all, are now renowned for their efficient storage systems whether for the living room, bedroom or kitchen.

Holland

De Stijl (1917)
Although Germany was the major source of innovative design at the beginning of the century, Holland briefly became its center through the work of the *de Stijl* group. Greatly inspired by the painter Mondrian, *de Stijl* aimed to create simple, geometric designs, with an emphasis on purity of form and structure. The group's most distinguished furniture designer was Gerrit Rietveld, famous for his angular "Red-Blue" chair of 1917. The simplicity of Rietveld's approach greatly influenced his German contemporary, Breuer, who was working at the time in the Bauhaus workshop.

Modern designs
The influence of the *de Stijl* movement, with its clear-cut, geometric lines was very strong, and even now, the style of furniture which is produced is distinguished by the same characteristics. Furniture producers may import, or adapt, foreign styles to provide variety in the home market, but functional designs are still the most popular.

France

Art Deco (1920–*c.* 35)
France had been one of the centers of Art Nouveau at the turn of the century and, to an extent, the spirit of that decorative, romantic style was retained in Art Deco.

The movement's most famous exponent was the interior designer, Emile-Jacques Ruhlmann, whose expensive pieces were admired for their impressive craftsmanship. Typical Art Deco pieces are notable for the absence of sharply right-angled edges and for geometric decoration.

The Modern Movement in France
While Art Deco could be said to follow the fashionable preoccupations of the period and in many ways to capture its spirit, the complementary development of modernism followed important international movements in art and design. In France, modernism was primarily represented by two ex-patriots: the Swiss-born architect Le Corbusier and his French associate Charlotte Perriand, and Irish-born Eileen Gray.

Le Corbusier followed the modernistic principles of his Bauhaus contemporaries and developed sleek, tubular steel chairs with leather, skin or canvas upholstery. His most notable and popular piece was an updated version of the *chaise longue*.

Eileen Gray's early lacquered furniture showed the influence of Art Deco as well as the Orient. Later she progressed into sleek functionalism, with furniture of great originality, especially her sofas and chairs.

Modern designs
As in Germany, all this great individual talent was eclipsed by World War II, yet two distinct movements in French furniture production emerged. The first reproduced old-established, historical styles for the mass-market; the second catered for slightly more adventurous tastes with up-to-date pieces based on international contemporary styles like High-Tech and Scandinavian.

Britain

By the beginning of the century designers like Charles Rennie Mackintosh, A. H. Mackmurdo, Philip Webb, Norman Shaw and C. F. A. Voysey were creating a new, simple style of domestic architecture and furnishings. Their original designs were produced on a commercial basis by Ambrose Heal, at the same time as other manufacturers were promoting the Art Deco style.

The Utility Scheme
The British adoption of modernism arose initially out of necessity with the establish-

ment of the Utility Scheme and plain, standardized furniture.

The war also encouraged the development of new manufacturing processes, and enabled Robin Day to produce his polypropylene, stacking chairs.

Modern designs
"Fun furniture" had a brief hey-day in the 1960s, but more important, was the mass-marketing of good-looking, functional furniture by Terence Conran. Like their European contemporaries, British designers now adopt and adapt many styles fashionable elsewhere, and the range of choice is large. Thus, Italian-style sofas, American High-Tech lamps, German storage units and Japanese floor cushions, are all assimilated into traditional English style.

America

The Modern Movement in America
The functional style promoted throughout Europe was also gradually adopted during the first part of the century, and the attraction of simple design is well-illustrated in the pieces from Elbert Hubbard's workshops.

Two early exponents of the Modern Movement were the architects Louis Sullivan and Frank Lloyd Wright. As early as 1904, Wright was designing the metal swivel chairs – an integral part of office furniture everywhere.

Office designed by Frank Lloyd Wright, c. 1924

The influence of the Bauhaus on American designers became more direct when the German exile, Mies van der Rohe, came to work in America. With Hans and Florence Knoll he founded Knoll Associates, the firm which mass-produced not only van der Rohe's own work but also that of new designers. Hans Bertoia, for example, produced his famous wire seating range for them in the 1950s.

Eames and his contemporaries
However, it was not until the 1940s that America's unique contribution to modern design really began, stimulated by the aviation industry's new ways of bending wood and laminates. In 1940 the Finnish-

born architect Eero Saarinen and the American Charles Eames won a furniture design competition at the Museum of Modern Art in New York. Their collaboration produced a chair with a spartan, shell-like body made of a laminate of veneer and glue strips, covered with fabric; the legs were spindly, aluminum spokes. Eames improved on this chair design and in 1948 produced his famous molded fiberglass version, later manufactured by the Herman Miller Company. A further eight years of experiment produced yet another classic chair – the 670 chair and ottoman – made from laminated rosewood on a swivel metal base with comfortable leather cushions. Another breakthrough, in the 1950s, was Eero Saarinen's "tulip" chair, made from molded fiberglass on a slender aluminum pedestal, again manufactured by Knoll Associates.

Modern designs
But it is probably in occasional and upholstered furniture that America really excels today. Simply-shaped Parsons' tables, elegant glass and plexiglass tables and desks, neat, comfortable upholstered unit seating, sofas, armchairs and day beds – all look good and are well made.

"American style" has become synonymous with the advance of minimalism and High-Tech, which is basically the adaptation of institutional hardware – like steel lamps, trolleys and laboratory glass – for use in the home. The idea is practical and cheap to put into operation, and as a result has been rapidly adopted throughout Europe. There is, however, a growing swing against the harshness of this style, via the Neo-Romantic movement, which promotes much gentler lines and colors, in furniture and upholstery fabrics.

Scandinavia

Scandinavian designers, who had previously produced native versions of European styles, started to make their own simple designs in pale wood as early as the nineteenth century. A Swedish *Werkbund*, advocating functional furniture, was established in 1910, and the Swede Carl Malmsten, and Dane Kaare Klint both attracted attention for their similarly simple ideas.

Aalto and his contemporaries
Two of the most innovative Scandinavian designers were the Finnish architect Alvar Aalto, and the Swede Bruno Mathsson, both of whom were experimenting with the lamination of birch before World War II. In 1935 Aalto produced a cantilevered chair which, although inspired by van der Rohe's

and Breuer's basic designs, used the strength and resilience of bentwood instead of steel. Aalto went on to produce stacking chairs and stools, an innovative concept in the light of the modern need for space-saving devices. Simple, unpolished and uncarved wooden pieces continued to be made by Scandinavian designers, and were much in demand after World War II.

Modern designs
By the 1960s the Swedes were acknowledged as the best and most reliable source of uncompromisingly modern furniture, and their contribution served to raise design standards in general. Although no longer the main center of design, the styles promoted within Scandinavia remain simple and well made. This straightforward approach is reflected especially well in their industrial furniture, produced by architect/designers like the Danes Hans Wegner and Poul Kjaerholm, and the Swedes Borge Lindau and Bosse Lindekrantz.

Italy

Italian furniture design in the nineteenth century followed the general European trend of revivalism, but unlike other European countries, Italy was not greatly influenced by Art Nouveau (known there as *Floreale*).

In fact, Italy did not make any significant contribution to design until after World War II when the death of Mussolini, and the ensuing freedom of rule, seemed to act as a catalyst for designers. In 1959 Gio Ponti produced his delicate, but strong, ash chair with woven cane seat and it, too, has become a modern classic alongside the American, French and Scandinavian pieces.

Over the past twenty years Italian designers have produced revolutionary techniques and designs in furniture and decoration. The Scandinavian-style bare woods, once so popular in Europe, have been gradually replaced by rich, lacquered surfaces, glass, steel and molded plastics.

Modern designs
Unlike most countries over the last decade or so, Italy has produced several giants of furniture design. The most famous include Mario Bellini, Tobia Scarpa, Jo Colombo, Vico Magistretti and Gaie Aulenti. Their distinctive designs range from elegant occasional chairs and deep, comfortable upholstered furniture, to functional storage units and sculptural lighting. Indeed, the Italian combination of esthetic zip and deep comfort has been one of the happiest mixtures of twentieth century design.

CHAIRS

Chairs reflect the slow evolutions and regular recurrences of certain styles of furniture over the centuries better than any other piece of furniture. It is fascinating to see, for example, the sophisticated designs of the early Greeks and Egyptians resurrected in nineteenth century classical revivals like the Trafalgar chair. No less interesting is the interaction of ideas from country to country, and the designs inspired by new materials.

Dining Chairs

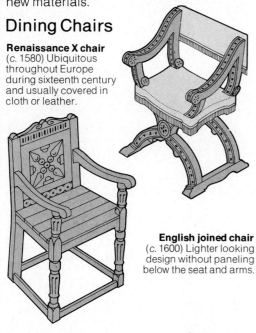

Renaissance X chair
(c. 1580) Ubiquitous throughout Europe during sixteenth century and usually covered in cloth or leather.

English joined chair
(c. 1600) Lighter looking design without paneling below the seat and arms.

American Brewster chair
(c. 1650–75) Elaborate example of Windsor, or stick furniture, with turned, upright spindles both above and below the seat.

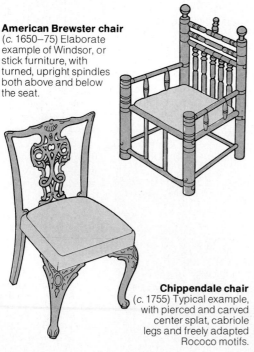

Chippendale chair
(c. 1755) Typical example, with pierced and carved center splat, cabriole legs and freely adapted Rococo motifs.

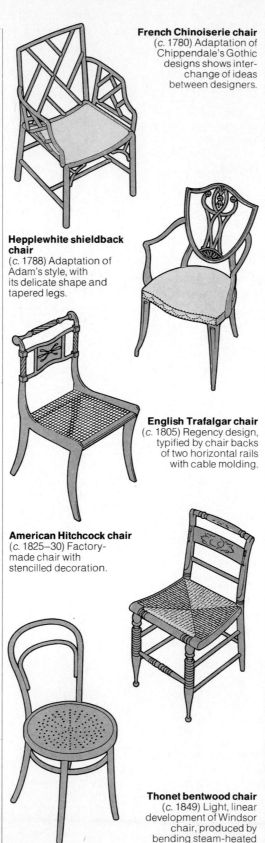

French Chinoiserie chair
(c. 1780) Adaptation of Chippendale's Gothic designs shows interchange of ideas between designers.

Hepplewhite shieldback chair
(c. 1788) Adaptation of Adam's style, with its delicate shape and tapered legs.

English Trafalgar chair
(c. 1805) Regency design, typified by chair backs of two horizontal rails with cable molding.

American Hitchcock chair
(c. 1825–30) Factory-made chair with stencilled decoration.

Thonet bentwood chair
(c. 1849) Light, linear development of Windsor chair, produced by bending steam-heated sections of wood.

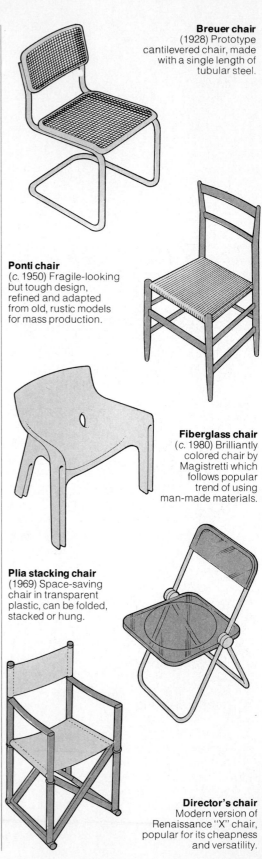

Breuer chair
(1928) Prototype cantilevered chair, made with a single length of tubular steel.

Ponti chair
(c. 1950) Fragile-looking but tough design, refined and adapted from old, rustic models for mass production.

Fiberglass chair
(c. 1980) Brilliantly colored chair by Magistretti which follows popular trend of using man-made materials.

Plia stacking chair
(1969) Space-saving chair in transparent plastic, can be folded, stacked or hung.

Director's chair
Modern version of Renaissance "X" chair, popular for its cheapness and versatility.

Occasional Chairs

English turned chair
(*c.* 1610) Solid oak chair with triangular seat and turned support.

Louis XIV Baroque chair
(*c.* 1680) Velvet-covered chair with gently sloping, high back; shows growing desire for comfort.

American slat-back chair
(*c.* 1680–1710) Sensitively-turned New England chair, typical of the sturdy finesse shown in early American furniture.

Louis XV Rococo chair
(*c.* 1710–60) Good example of sinuous, relaxed contours and florid decoration so popular throughout Europe.

Transitional Queen Anne chair
(*c.* 1710–30) Legs in the William and Mary style with a gracefully curved splat, typical of the Queen Anne period.

Danish Louis XVI-style chair
(*c.* 1775–85) French Neoclassical-style chair although decoration is simpler, using fewer curved lines.

Bergère chair
(*c.* 1810) English adaptation of French bergère style, using cane instead of upholstery.

French Restoration chair
(*c.* 1830) Typical style throughout Europe, with boat-shaped back and cabriole legs.

Early Victorian, English chair
(*c.* 1835) Revival of Gothic style, in gilt beech, with arched decoration.

Late Victorian, English chair
(*c.* 1875) Mass-produced, Georgian-style chair reflects technological advance and revivalist fashion.

Le Corbusier chair
(1929) Dramatic new use of tubular steel, reflects Bauhaus group's insistence on functional design.

Barcelona chair
(1929) Innovative design by Mies van der Rohe, combining intersecting steel bars with leather upholstery.

Eames chair
(1948) Molded plastic chair, designed using techniques developed during World War II.

Modern Gothic chair
(1980s) Simplified version of traditional Gothic style in black laquer and cane.

Light rattan chair
Lightweight, adaptable design resulting from an increasing emphasis on cheapness and maneuverability.

UPHOLSTERED CHAIRS

Until comparatively recently, comfortable chairs for relaxing in were seen as a badge of rank. The imposing look was important; the actual comfort only sketchily considered. There were sporadic and sometimes successful attempts to produce more comfortable chairs from the late seventeenth century on, but until the invention of the metal coil spring in the mid-nineteenth century, elegance rather than comfort usually prevailed; later designs reflect a general desire for comfort.

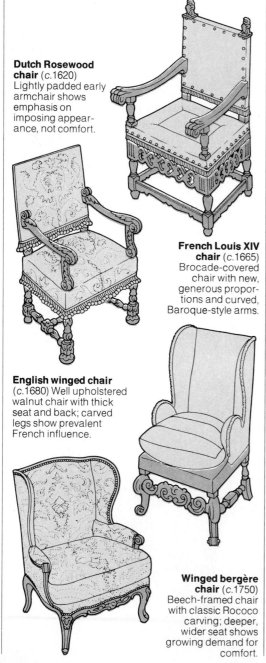

Dutch Rosewood chair (c.1620) Lightly padded early armchair shows emphasis on imposing appearance, not comfort.

French Louis XIV chair (c.1665) Brocade-covered chair with new, generous proportions and curved, Baroque-style arms.

English winged chair (c.1680) Well upholstered walnut chair with thick seat and back; carved legs show prevalent French influence.

Winged bergère chair (c.1750) Beech-framed chair with classic Rococo carving; deeper, wider seat shows growing demand for comfort.

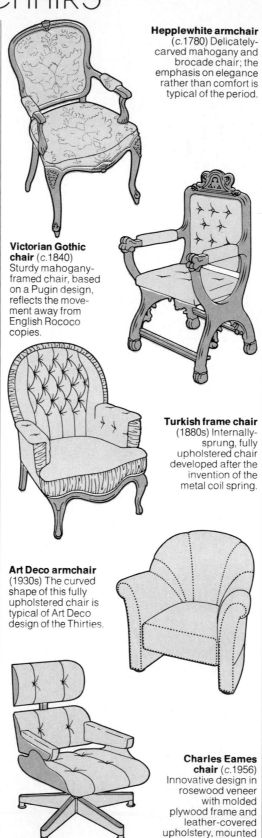

Hepplewhite armchair (c.1780) Delicately-carved mahogany and brocade chair; the emphasis on elegance rather than comfort is typical of the period.

Victorian Gothic chair (c.1840) Sturdy mahogany-framed chair, based on a Pugin design, reflects the movement away from English Rococo copies.

Turkish frame chair (1880s) Internally-sprung, fully upholstered chair developed after the invention of the metal coil spring.

Art Deco armchair (1930s) The curved shape of this fully upholstered chair is typical of Art Deco design of the Thirties.

Charles Eames chair (c.1956) Innovative design in rosewood veneer with molded plywood frame and leather-covered upholstery, mounted on a metal pedestal.

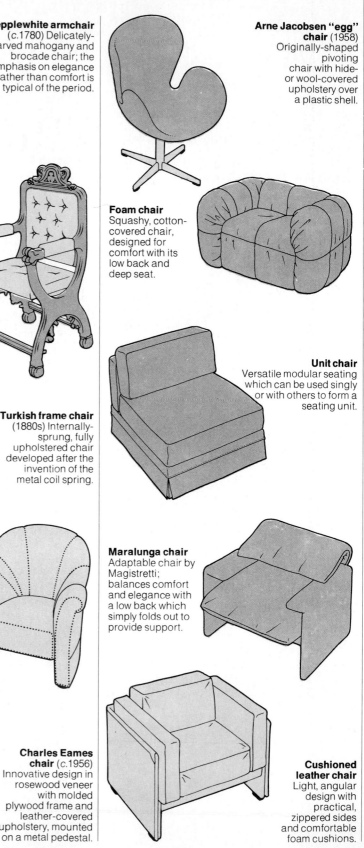

Arne Jacobsen "egg" chair (1958) Originally-shaped pivoting chair with hide- or wool-covered upholstery over a plastic shell.

Foam chair Squashy, cotton-covered chair, designed for comfort with its low back and deep seat.

Unit chair Versatile modular seating which can be used singly or with others to form a seating unit.

Maralunga chair Adaptable chair by Magistretti; balances comfort and elegance with a low back which simply folds out to provide support.

Cushioned leather chair Light, angular design with practical, zippered sides and comfortable foam cushions.

SETTEES SOFAS AND CHAISES LONGUES

Although a form of couch or day bed existed in earlier civilizations, it was not until the eighteenth century that the settee, with its hard back and arms and semi-upholstered seat, appeared in Europe and America. Later models, although handsome to look at, were hard to sit on and it was not until the mid-nineteenth century when sprung-upholstery or "marshmallow on legs" was introduced, that settees or sofas became really comfortable.

Settees and Sofas

Early Georgian settee
(c.1725) Walnut settee with gently curved serpentine back, cabriole legs and shepherd's crook arms, typical of the period.

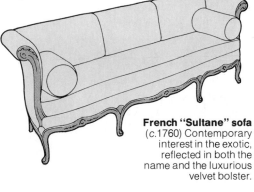

French "Sultane" sofa
(c.1760) Contemporary interest in the exotic, reflected in both the name and the luxurious velvet bolster.

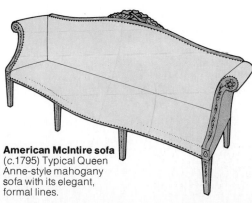

American McIntire sofa
(c.1795) Typical Queen Anne-style mahogany sofa with its elegant, formal lines.

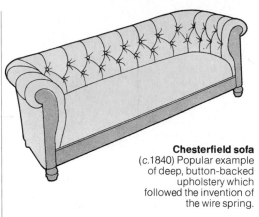

Chesterfield sofa
(c.1840) Popular example of deep, button-backed upholstery which followed the invention of the wire spring.

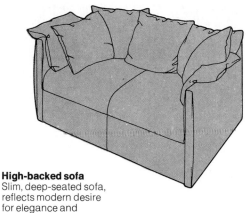

High-backed sofa
Slim, deep-seated sofa, reflects modern desire for elegance and comfort.

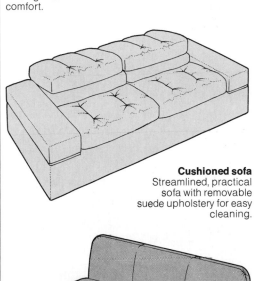

Cushioned sofa
Streamlined, practical sofa with removable suede upholstery for easy cleaning.

Modular sofa
Armless sofa, can also be joined to single chairs or stools.

Chaises Longues

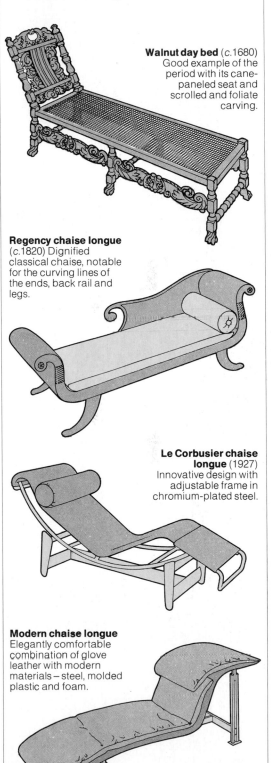

Walnut day bed (c.1680)
Good example of the period with its cane-paneled seat and scrolled and foliate carving.

Regency chaise longue
(c.1820) Dignified classical chaise, notable for the curving lines of the ends, back rail and legs.

Le Corbusier chaise longue (1927)
Innovative design with adjustable frame in chromium-plated steel.

Modern chaise longue
Elegantly comfortable combination of glove leather with modern materials — steel, molded plastic and foam.

TABLES AND DESKS

Until the mid-sixteenth century, when the frame table was introduced, most regularly used domestic tables were only roughly-made trestles. Refinements, such as draw- and flap-top tables, which could be extended or contracted as desired, soon followed. Today, a variety of different occasional pieces for tea, cards, gaming and display are available, as well as writing tables, and desks, ranging from small, elegant secretaires to tall bureau-bookcases.

Tables

Regency rosewood table (*c.*1820) Large, circular table with tripod-shaped pedestal and Boulle decoration, popular throughout the period.

Wood and glass table Self-assembly table with X-framed wooden base and glass top.

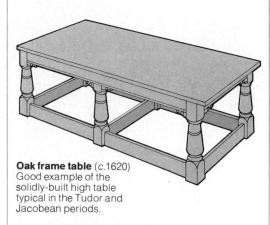

Oak frame table (*c.*1620) Good example of the solidly-built high table typical in the Tudor and Jacobean periods.

Art Nouveau table (*c.*1900) Tea table by Charles Rennie Mackintosh, in white enameled wood with flattened legs and slender top.

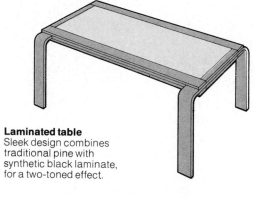

Laminated table Sleek design combines traditional pine with synthetic black laminate, for a two-toned effect.

New England Butterfly table (*c.*1720) Graceful American version of the gate-leg table, derives its name from the hinged top and movable supports.

Saarinen table (1950) Pedestal table with white plastic laminate top and cast aluminum base, the first mass-produced "classic" using synthetic materials.

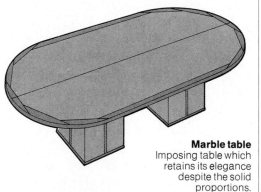

Marble table Imposing table which retains its elegance despite the solid proportions.

Pembroke table (*c.*1790) Elegantly-styled table introduced by Hepplewhite and developed by Sheraton.

Parsons' table Simple and now ubiquitous American design for dining and occasional tables.

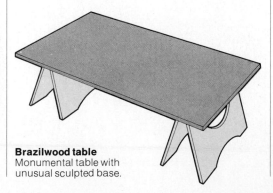

Brazilwood table Monumental table with unusual sculpted base.

Occasional Tables

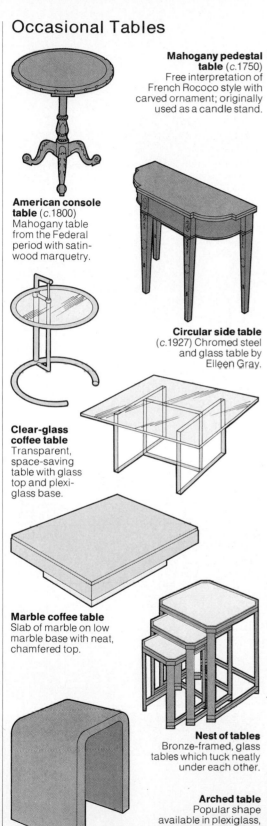

Mahogany pedestal table (*c.*1750)
Free interpretation of French Rococo style with carved ornament; originally used as a candle stand.

American console table (*c.*1800)
Mahogany table from the Federal period with satin-wood marquetry.

Clear-glass coffee table
Transparent, space-saving table with glass top and plexi-glass base.

Circular side table (*c.*1927) Chromed steel and glass table by Eileen Gray.

Marble coffee table
Slab of marble on low marble base with neat, chamfered top.

Nest of tables
Bronze-framed, glass tables which tuck neatly under each other.

Arched table
Popular shape available in plexiglass, travertine, marble and plain wood.

Desks

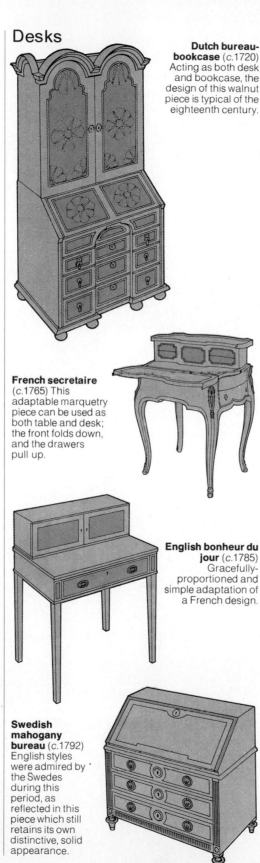

Dutch bureau-bookcase (*c.*1720)
Acting as both desk and bookcase, the design of this walnut piece is typical of the eighteenth century.

French secretaire (*c.*1765) This adaptable marquetry piece can be used as both table and desk; the front folds down, and the drawers pull up.

English bonheur du jour (*c.*1785) Gracefully-proportioned and simple adaptation of a French design.

Swedish mahogany bureau (*c.*1792) English styles were admired by the Swedes during this period, as reflected in this piece which still retains its own distinctive, solid appearance.

Mahogany knee-hole desk (*c.*1860)
Popular variation on the massive, eighteenth century French pedestal or library tables.

English davenport (*c.*1900) Small desk with solid front, fold-down top and drawers at the side, ubiquitous at the turn of the century.

Steel-framed desk
Scandinavian-style, neat, steel-framed desk with laminate top edged in light oak.

Modern knee-hole desk
Large, leather-topped variation on the pedestal desk, with decorative steel banding on one side.

CABINETS

The term cabinet originally applied to a multi-drawed chest on a stand which was designed to hold jewelry and small precious items. Because of its luxurious contents, a cabinet was often elaborately decorated. Among the most spectacular examples were the ebony and tortoiseshell inlays of the Antwerp chests, popular in the seventeenth century, and Boulle's marvellous veneers in the eighteenth. More recently, cabinets have been used to store a great variety of objects, and different shapes and sizes have developed accordingly. Despite the possibilities of built-in storage, modern cabinets continue to be popular.

Corner cabinet (c.1750) *Encoignure*, or hanging cabinet, which fits neatly into corners. This early space-saver was originally used for porcelain or glassware.

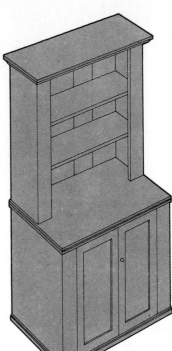

Pine hutch (c.1850) Traditional open-topped hutch, perenially popular for its clean lines and ample storage capacity. Most countries produce their own equivalent of this hutch, and it is to the original craftsmens' credit that their work is accommodated in the style of furnishing of successive generations.

Japanese cabinet (c.1670) Lacquered cabinets in this style became popular in the West as a result of new trade routes to the Orient. The stretcher of the ornately-carved, Baroque-style legs would traditionally support a Chinese vase.

Breakfront cabinet-bookcase (c.1820) Popular piece of "architectural" furniture, with elaborate leaded glass doors and molded mahogany framework.

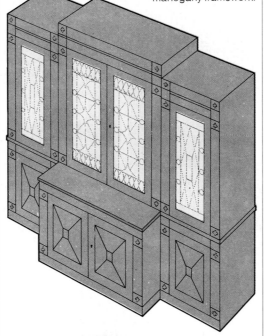

Lacquer and glass cabinet Modern houses and apartments are generally on the small side and storage space is frequently provided by built-in units, not individual pieces of furniture. However, this lacquered cabinet provides ample storage and display space while retaining a light appearance.

Walnut cabinet (c.1710) Tall, narrow piece with double glass doors. Although the cabinet was produced during Queen Anne's reign, its simple, unadorned lines reflect the more sober designs of the William and Mary period.

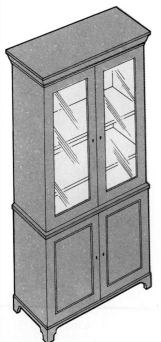

Jelly cabinet (c.1840) Simple, folk piece with bun feet, made in poplar and walnut, originally used for preserves. With the revival of interest in early American history combined with a modern desire for uncluttered furniture this cabinet remains a popular piece to this day.

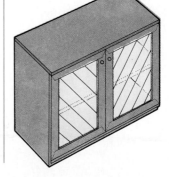

Wood and glass cabinet Polished wood and diagonally-etched glass cabinet; can be left freestanding or wall-hung.

SIDEBOARDS

Early sideboards were also called credenzas, buffets and dressers and although always used for storage, they did not become uniquely connected with dining rooms until the Scottish architect, Robert Adam, adapted them for that purpose in the eighteenth century. Designs then moved away from the massive ornamentation of the Renaissance and Baroque periods, and under Adam's influence, sideboards became light and graceful. It was these pieces which were introduced into American dining rooms during the Federal period (1785–1810). Contemporary sideboards are generally neat and streamlined and frequently form part of a built-in unit.

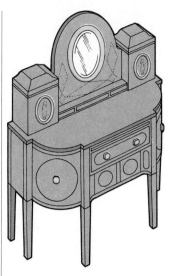

Renaissance sideboard
(*c.*1550) Heavy walnut sideboard with column-like carving, reflects classical influence.

Combined cabinet-sideboard (*c.*1790) American Sheraton-style sideboard with typical body, legs and ornamentation. The elaborate design is notable for the mirror, handsome rectangular boxes for knives and silverware, and inlaid, convex sides. It was probably made in Baltimore, one of the last centers of furniture design in the Federal period.

Italian sideboard
Good-looking, functional sideboard, the top of which is especially useful as a serving table.

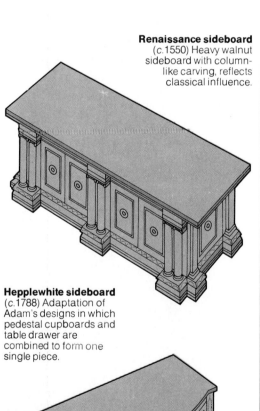

Hepplewhite sideboard
(*c.*1788) Adaptation of Adam's designs in which pedestal cupboards and table drawer are combined to form one single piece.

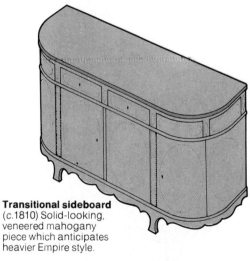

Transitional sideboard
(*c.*1810) Solid-looking, veneered mahogany piece which anticipates heavier Empire style.

French sideboard unit
Adaptable modern steel-legged unit which can be used singly or as a component of built-in storage.

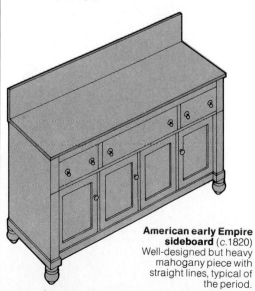

American early Empire sideboard (*c.*1820) Well-designed but heavy mahogany piece with straight lines, typical of the period.

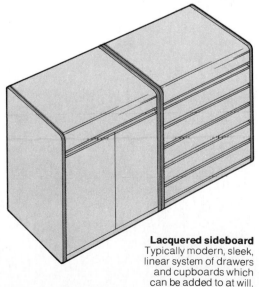

Lacquered sideboard
Typically modern, sleek, linear system of drawers and cupboards which can be added to at will.

CHESTS AND WARDROBES

Chests were the main pieces of furniture for many years. They were used not only for storage, but also as seats, and tables, and when covered with a palliasse, as beds. Originally just crudely carved boxes, they gradually evolved into armoires, closets, hutches and wardrobes, on the one hand, and lowboys, highboys, chests of drawers and dressers on the other. During the sixteenth and seventeenth centuries, chests and *cassone* were the popular decorated pieces, but by the eighteenth century, large items of furniture like highboys and dressers were in general use, especially in America. Heavy carving was replaced by the subtle, elegant carving of the William and Mary and Queen Anne periods, a trend also reflected in the chests of drawers, closets and armoires produced in the seventeenth and eighteenth centuries. Large pieces of furniture such as these are impractical in many modern houses and apartments, and most rooms are now designed with built-in storage systems.

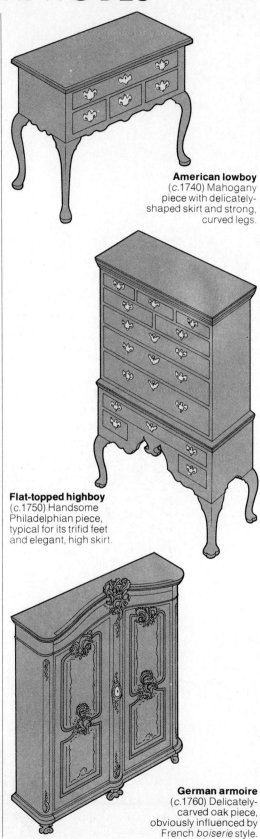

American lowboy
(*c*.1740) Mahogany piece with delicately-shaped skirt and strong, curved legs.

Flat-topped highboy
(*c*.1750) Handsome Philadelphian piece, typical for its trifid feet and elegant, high skirt.

Italian cassone
(*c*.1490) Solidly-made oak chest, with intarsia of various woods.

Chest of drawers
(*c*.1700) Severely-shaped chest with simple brass handles and ball feet.

German armoire
(*c*.1760) Delicately-carved oak piece, obviously influenced by French *boiserie* style.

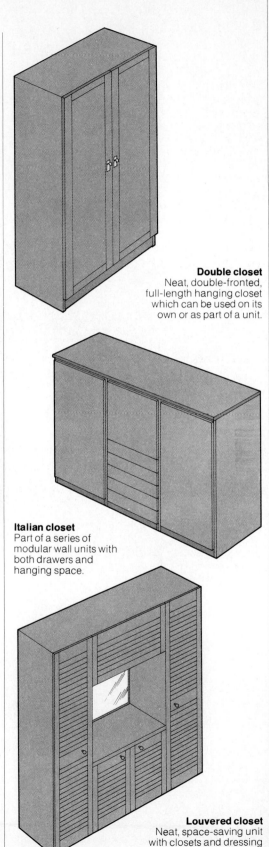

Double closet
Neat, double-fronted, full-length hanging closet which can be used on its own or as part of a unit.

Italian closet
Part of a series of modular wall units with both drawers and hanging space.

Louvered closet
Neat, space-saving unit with closets and dressing table combined.

BEDS

In the sixteenth and seventeenth centuries, beds were people's most valuable possessions, prized not only for the imposing appearance of their frames, but also for their hangings. A more compact, formal style was developed towards the end of the eighteenth century, and by the nineteenth and twentieth centuries, beds were notable for the new materials used, and for the diversity of their designs.

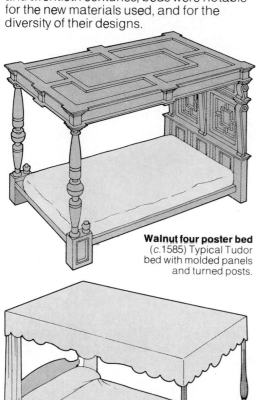

Walnut four poster bed
(c.1585) Typical Tudor bed with molded panels and turned posts.

Federal-style bed
(c.1790) Graceful bed reflects influence of Hepplewhite and Sheraton.

Directoire-style bed
(c.1795) Neoclassical-style bed, using steel for the first time.

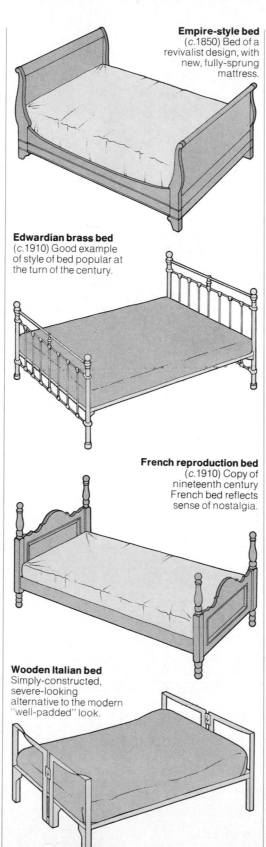

Empire-style bed
(c.1850) Bed of a revivalist design, with new, fully-sprung mattress.

Edwardian brass bed
(c.1910) Good example of style of bed popular at the turn of the century.

French reproduction bed
(c.1910) Copy of nineteenth century French bed reflects sense of nostalgia.

Wooden Italian bed
Simply-constructed, severe-looking alternative to the modern "well-padded" look.

Convertible sofa bed
Space-saving answer for one-room living or other cramped rooms.

Tailored modern bed
Crisp, no-nonsense design characterizes this neat, low-line bed.

Storage bed
Economical use of space with large storage drawer slotted under wooden bed frame.

Pine bunk beds
Good space-saving kit for children's rooms.

STAIRCASES

It is unusual to have to buy a staircase unless a house is being built from scratch or totally remodeled. Demolition yards provide an especially useful source, as do old, condemned houses and it is comforting to know that when bought in this way, staircases will rarely be more expensive than a good-quality stair carpet.

Always consider the physical aspects of the staircase as well as its visual appeal.

For example, it is a great temptation to put a spiral staircase into a small area but do remember that it will occupy an area about six feet (two meters) square. You will also lose valuable storage space.

The appearance of existing staircases can be changed out of all recognition without too much difficulty. Actual parts of the staircase such as the *banisters* (handrails), the *balusters* (parts linking the handrail to

the treads) or the *newelposts* (large pieces at the head, foot and middle of a staircase) can be renewed. Alternatively, they can be decorated by painting, staining, polishing or covering. Handrails can be painted in contrasting colors to the walls as can any moldings or panels. Treads can be fully carpeted (as an alternative to being left bare, or half-carpeted) to make the stairs look much wider.

Staircases
Most staircases run straight from ground to upper levels and the flights of stairs can be broken with landings (the position of which will vary according to the design). Spiral stairs are often used when the space available is small and square in area.

Staircase with landing

Straight stairs with solid banisters

Curved staircase

Wrought-iron staircase

Wooden staircase

Wooden spiral staircase

Open-plan staircase

High-Tech staircase

Metal spiral staircase without banisters

Spiral staircase with round treads

Balusters and newelposts
Balusters link the handrail to each tread of the staircase, while newelposts are the uprights at the ends or corners of the handrail. Both provide a decorative finish to the staircase.

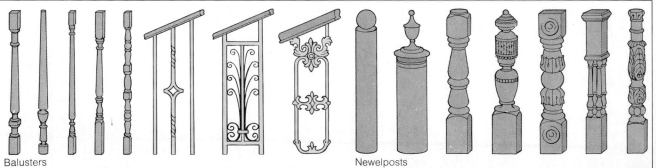

Balusters

Newelposts

DOORS

Doors, both internal and external, make an immediate difference to the feel and quality of a house or apartment. They can be bought both ready- and custom-made out of glass, wood or aluminum; they can be solid or hollow, paneled or louvered, carved, etched or plain. Like staircases, old doors can be found in demolition yards or at antique dealers specializing in architectural and structural pieces of old houses.

Large, traditional-style double doors will immediately enhance an otherwise plain, undistinguished room, as do floor-to-ceiling ones. High-Tech steel or aluminum doors always look functional but also rather cold, whereas plain, flush doors covered with suede, leather or fabric give a much warmer effect. Paneled doors, whether plain or covered, add relief to and soften the effect of a rather austere room.

Door fittings is the usual umbrella title for knobs, handles, knockers, hinges, hooks and locks. They are apt to be expensive but it is worth buying the best you can afford because they will add unexpected character to a door's appearance. Brass fittings look best on old doors whereas iron, unless it is genuinely old or very simple, tends to look bogus. Stripped wooden doors look equally good with china or colored plastic knobs.

Doors
The style and structure of a door will give an immediate feel to the whole decorative scheme of a room. The most common materials are wood and glass but within these categories there is a wide enough variety of shapes and designs to cater for all tastes.

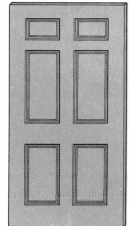 Paneled wooden door
 Sculpted wooden door
 Wooden relief door
 Wooden louvered door
Wood and glass door

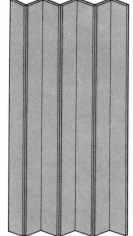 Folding wooden door
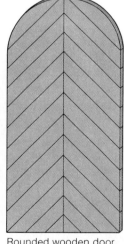 Rounded wooden door
 Wooden swing doors
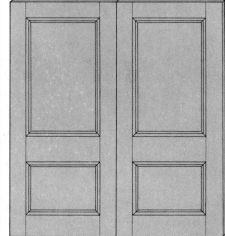 Steel pivot door
Double wooden doors

Door knobs
Knobs, whatever their design, add distinction to otherwise plain doors. Prices vary according to style and material (whether china, glass, bronze or acrylic).

Door handles
Choose the handle according to the door's situation. Plastic handles are suitable for kitchens and children's rooms, while more ornate handles generally look best on living room doors.

FIREPLACES AND STOVES

There can be few things more comforting than the flickering flames and sweet-smelling, smoldering wood of an open fire or stove. Fireplaces are produced in brick, marble, slate, wood, steel and aluminum and provide an immediate focal point to a room. It is wise to keep an original fireplace because it will probably suit the design and proportions of the room better than a modern alternative.

If, however, you decide that the fireplace has to go, there are a number of choices open to you. It is comparatively easy to remove the original one and either install another style of period fireplace, or to neaten up the aperture with a plain wooden or metal surround. The logs can either be burned directly on the brick ground or placed in a basket grate or on firedogs. Or the whole chimney breast can be stripped of plaster and the bare brick either left exposed or painted. There is no reason why the hearth should not be raised a couple of feet or more and the hearth then extended along one or both walls to provide extra seating as well as a long base for storing logs, magazines, books or a television.

Woodburning stoves

However beautiful a fire and however well-controlled the draft, a straight-forward fireplace can never be fully efficient as a heating supplier. Free-standing, woodburning stoves, similar to those so popular in Europe and America in the nineteenth century, are efficient and increasingly popular alternatives to fireplaces. They are both practical and attractive (indeed, they are frequently used simply as sources of decoration in apartments and houses with central heating). Most stoves are made of cast iron (although they are occasionally seen in ceramic and soapstone) and the commonest designs are *box*, *open-door Franklin* and *workshop*. Their decline in popularity, due to the passage of time and innovations in heating systems, has been reversed in recent years, largely because of the high rise in modern fuel prices.

Fireplaces
The efficiency of a working fireplace is of greater importance than its physical appearance, and the draft, which provides air for combustion, should be drawn from the chimney. If the fireplace is on an outside wall, pipes to provide draft can be inserted from behind and beneath the hearth.

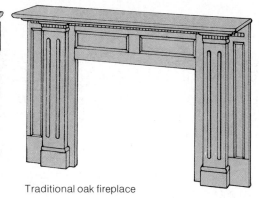
Plain stone fireplace

Sculpted marble fireplace

Traditional oak fireplace

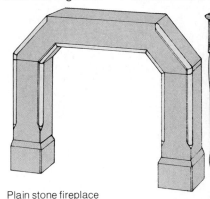
Edwardian tiled fireplace

Georgian marble fireplace

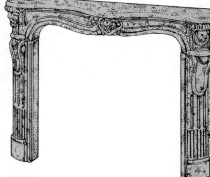
Marble Rococo fireplace

Cast-iron Victorian fireplace

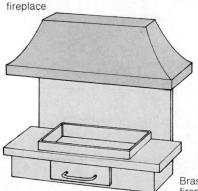
Brass-canopied fireplace

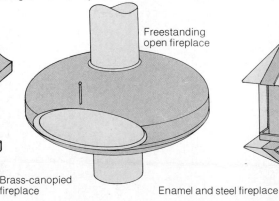
Freestanding open fireplace

Enamel and steel fireplace

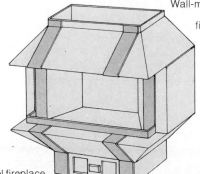
Wall-mounted steel fireplace

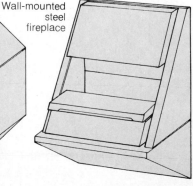

Firebaskets and Firedogs

These provide support for burning logs and are generally made from cast iron, although some of the more decorative firedogs are bronze. In addition to firebaskets and firedogs you will probably need other pieces of equipment, such as a fireguard, scuttle and fire irons.

Woodburning Stoves

Once again, wood-burning stoves are back in fashion and both stores and specialist mail-order houses are useful sources for stove buyers. But it is not only old stoves which are sought after. With increased research into efficiency, new stoves are now being produced which are both airtight and thermostatically controlled for maximum heat radiation.

1–4 Box stoves
5–10 Open-door Franklin stoves
11–15 Workshop stoves

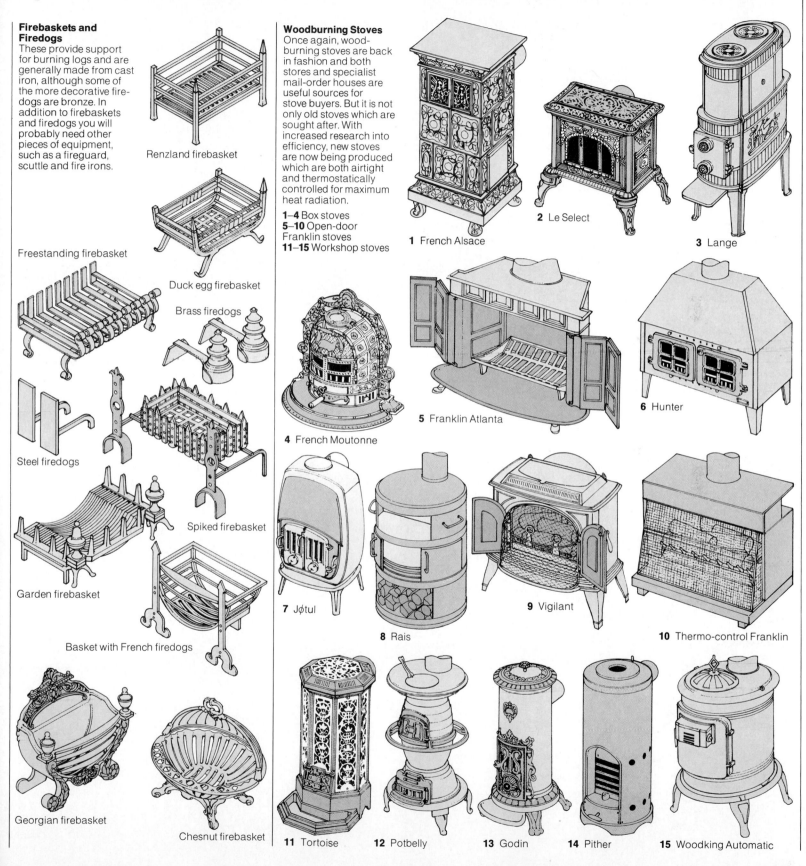

Renzland firebasket

Freestanding firebasket

Duck egg firebasket

Brass firedogs

Steel firedogs

Spiked firebasket

Garden firebasket

Basket with French firedogs

Georgian firebasket

Chesnut firebasket

1 French Alsace

2 Le Select

3 Lange

4 French Moutonne

5 Franklin Atlanta

6 Hunter

7 Jøtul

8 Rais

9 Vigilant

10 Thermo-control Franklin

11 Tortoise

12 Potbelly

13 Godin

14 Pither

15 Woodking Automatic

LIGHT FITTINGS

There are basically four types of domestic lighting: conventional or incandescent lights (including ceiling, wall, table and floor lamps); fluorescent lights; industrial or theatrical lights (including spotlights, floodlights, uplights and downlights); and neon or sculptural lights. There is an enormous range of choice in lighting and it is important to choose the best type for the job. Whenever possible, visit lighting showrooms, even if it is only to get an idea of current trends. Also, try taking note of any pleasing lighting (and how it is produced) whether you see it in houses, restaurants or galleries.

Ceiling-mounted fixtures

These give good overall light, but tend to look "flat" unless used with accent lights, such as table lamps, floor lamps or uplights.

Shatterproof shade with aluminum collar

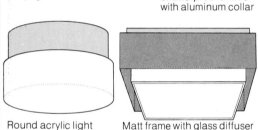

Round acrylic light   Matt frame with glass diffuser

Latticed bronze and acrylic light

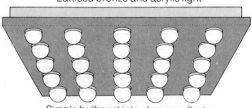

Simple bulbs set into chrome reflector

Polished brass rods with chrome reflector

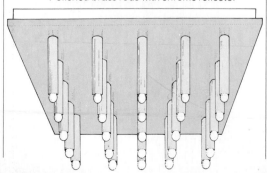

Pendant fixtures

These are the most commonly used ceiling lights. The type of light they give varies according to the shade used. The larger the shade, the more subtle the light cast. To direct the maximum light downwards (as over tables), use opaque, conical shades. Both types of shade can be mounted on rise and fall fixtures.

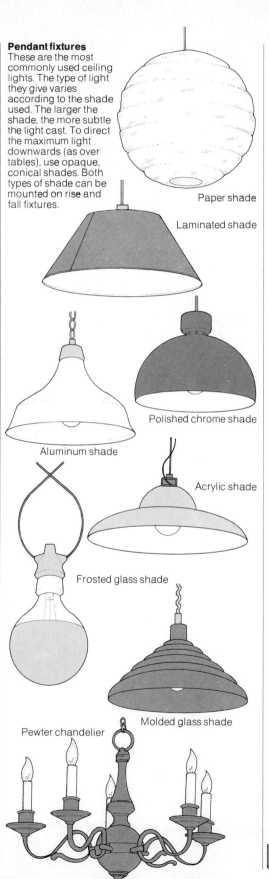

Paper shade

Laminated shade

Polished chrome shade

Aluminum shade

Acrylic shade

Frosted glass shade

Molded glass shade

Pewter chandelier

Wall lamps

These are best used as directional lights, to bounce off the ceiling or walls, or to light an object, picture or surface.

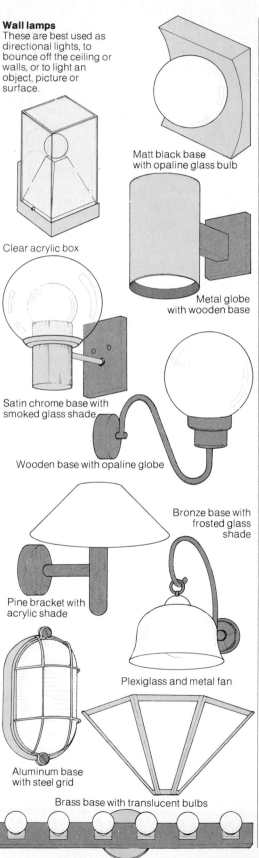

Matt black base with opaline glass bulb

Clear acrylic box

Metal globe with wooden base

Satin chrome base with smoked glass shade

Wooden base with opaline globe

Bronze base with frosted glass shade

Pine bracket with acrylic shade

Plexiglass and metal fan

Aluminum base with steel grid

Brass base with translucent bulbs

Floor lamps

These give general or directional light depending on the shape and the shade. They give a good reading light when set at shoulder height.

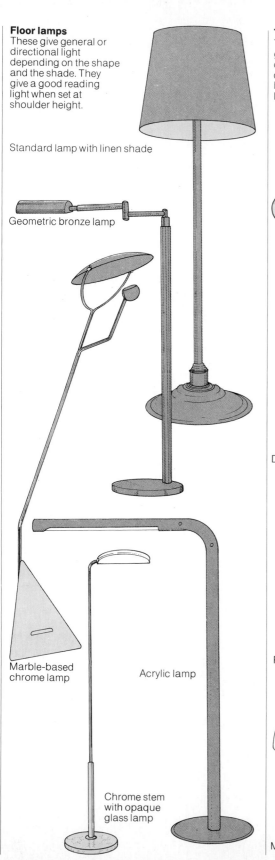

Standard lamp with linen shade

Geometric bronze lamp

Marble-based chrome lamp

Acrylic lamp

Chrome stem with opaque glass lamp

Table lamps

These are designed to give concentrated areas of light. When used for close work, they should be adjustable so that the light fall can be altered.

Coiled lamp

Articulated lamp

High-Tech lamp

Director's desk lamp

Pottery-based lamp

Tiffany lamp

Acrylic lamp

Mushroom lamp

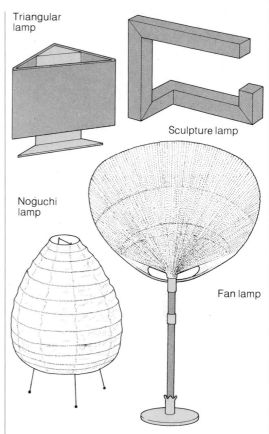

Triangular lamp

Sculpture lamp

Noguchi lamp

Fan lamp

Neon sculptures

Marketed in an infinite number of shapes, neon sculptures make a novel alternative to traditional lamps.

LIGHT FITTINGS

Spotlights

These are used for strong, punchy directional lighting as well as for accent lighting. The simplest variety have a reflector surface and take an ordinary bulb; the most complicated have specialized low-voltage transformers for casting very narrow and precise beams. They can be mounted straight onto the ceiling, set into it or attached to a track. Tracks are a useful way of getting a lot of light from one outlet without extra or expensive electrical work.

General-purpose spotlight

Clip-on spotlight

Square-based spotlight

Parabolic spotlight

Low-illumination spotlight

Spherical spotlight

Sculpted spotlight

Box spotlight

High-illumination spotlight

Downlights and uplights

Downlights are generally used to cast pools of light on the surface below. Some directional varieties can be used for wallwashing. Uplights are ideal for bouncing light through plants and furniture, or off ceilings, and they are particularly useful when it is expensive or difficult to have built-in lighting.

Recessed wallwasher

Downlight

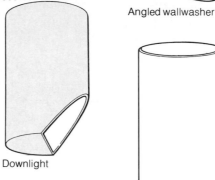
Angled uplight

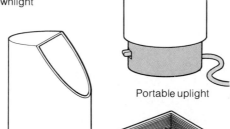
Boxed uplight

Simple wallwasher

Shuttered wallwasher

Angled wallwasher

Portable uplight

Grid uplight

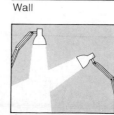
Sandbag uplight

Fluorescents

These are more economical to use than incandescent bulbs, in terms of energy and money, although they give off a much cooler light. They are good for lighting kitchens, bedheads and shelves.

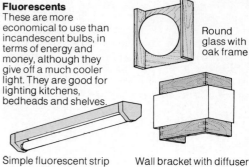
Round glass with oak frame

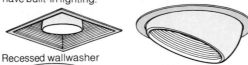

Simple fluorescent strip

Wall bracket with diffuser

Pine box strip

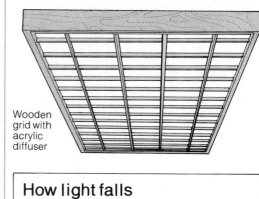

Wooden grid with acrylic diffuser

How light falls

These diagrams of the most popular fittings show the varying ways in which light falls.

Ceiling-mounted

Pendant

Wall

Table and floor

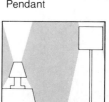
Articulated

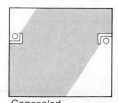
Concealed

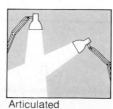

BATHROOM FITTINGS

You can improve the look of a bathroom as much by the choice of fittings as by the choice of fixtures. Fittings are removable and are a cheap way of altering a bathroom's appearance without having to obtain any expensive fixtures. Fittings for a bathroom include soap holders, toilet paper holders, towel rails, drying racks, sink and shower faucets, and they are usually made from china, plastic, steel, aluminum or acrylic. It is worth remembering that manufacturers often produce matching sets of fittings and these frequently complement the colors in their range of bathroom tiles.

Electrical appliances must always be installed with regard to all safety regulations. Hair dryers, sun lamps and extractors should be wired directly into the wall; shaver sockets should be low voltage. All bathroom sockets must be well away from the bathtub or shower, and lights should either have a pull cord or be switched on from outside the bathroom door.

Soap and toothbrush holders
These are usually mounted onto the walls by bathtubs or sinks and are commonly made of ceramic, plastic or chrome.

Toilet paper holders
These are either mounted on the wall (when they are usually ceramic) or they are recessed into the wall behind chrome or plastic plates.

Towel rails
These are an integral part of a bathroom's fittings. They are produced in both rod and ring form and are usually made of chrome, acrylic or plastic. Some models are electrically heated.

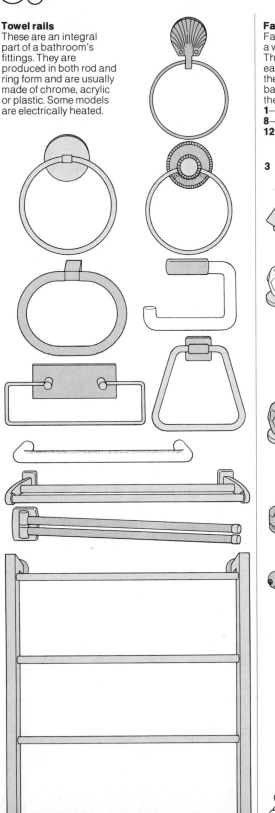

Faucets
Faucets are available in a wide variety of styles. They can be fitted very easily and can change the appearance of a bathroom according to their style and design.
1–7 Angular faucets
8–11 Curved faucets
12–15 Single-unit faucets

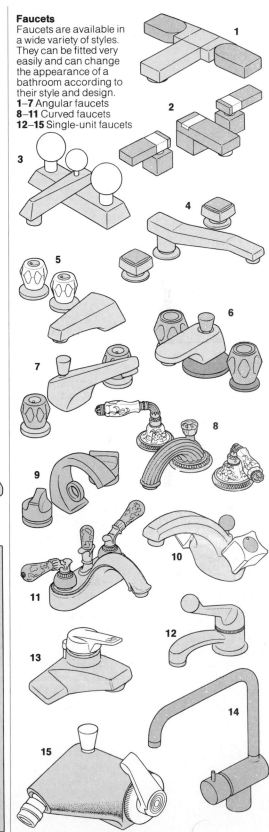

BATHROOM FIXTURES

Bathroom fixtures include bathtubs, washbasins, showers, toilets and bidets. Your choice in these fixtures should be dictated by two things, other than appearance: the size of the fixture in relation to the space available, and its practicality. The standard dimensions for bathtubs are 5ft 6in by 2ft 4in (1700mm by 700mm); depths range from 20 to 24in (508 to 610mm). Alternatives to standard fixtures include short, oval, sunken and corner bathtubs, whirlpool baths and hot tubs. Basins should be large enough for hair or hand washing. The sizes vary enormously, from 14in by 10in to 25in by 18in (350mm by 255mm to 635mm by 460mm). They can be mounted on a wall or a pedestal or fitted into counter tops. Basins can also be plumbed into corners so that they take up the minimum amount of room.

The fixtures should suit the varied needs of the family. Remember that children and elderly people generally need low-sided bathtubs and that side handles help the bather to get out. If the bathtub is to double as a shower, it is advisable to pick a wide, flat-bottomed one.

Showers

These can either be fixed over the tub, set apart in the corner of the room or installed as a ready-made unit.

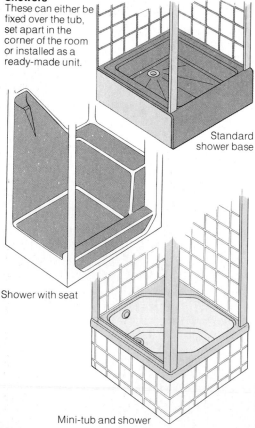

Standard shower base

Shower with seat

Mini-tub and shower

Bathtubs

These range from the traditional porcelain-coated cast iron tubs to the modern, lightweight acrylic-sheeted or synthetic-resined tubs reinforced with fiber-glass. Acrylic tubs are made in subtle colors and are warmer to the touch. The tub sides, which are often removable, can be covered in tiles, wallcoverings or carpet.

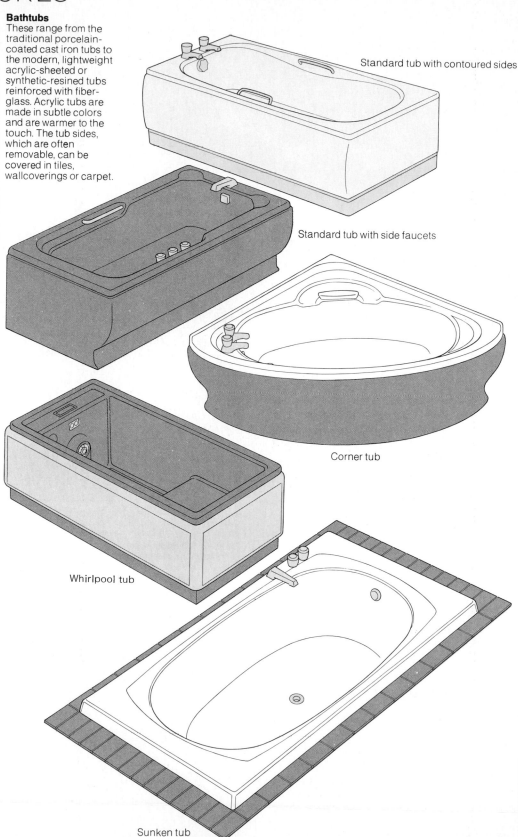

Standard tub with contoured sides

Standard tub with side faucets

Corner tub

Whirlpool tub

Sunken tub

Basins

These are made from vitreous-enameled steel, acrylic, china, or marble. They are made in a wide range of shapes and are most neat and practical when set into vanity units.

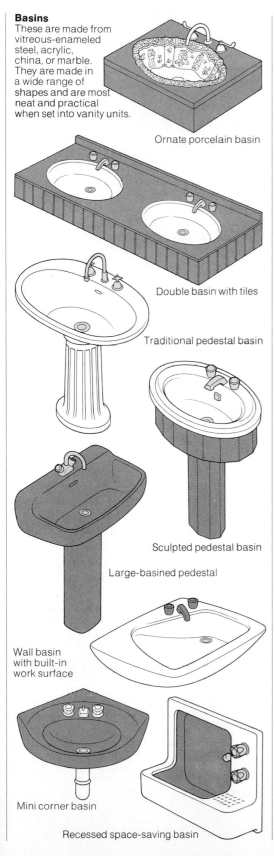

Ornate porcelain basin

Double basin with tiles

Traditional pedestal basin

Sculpted pedestal basin

Large-basined pedestal

Wall basin with built-in work surface

Mini corner basin

Recessed space-saving basin

Toilets

Apart from the range of designs, toilets have different ways of operating. Some have siphonic action, others a flush of water. Some are supplied with seats, for others you may choose your own. The cisterns can be recessed or wall-mounted.

Contoured toilet

Traditional porcelain toilet

Toilet with wall-mounted cistern

Standard toilet with oblong seat

One-piece toilet with waterfall tank cover

One-piece wall-mounted toilet

Bidets

These look best when they match the color and design of the toilet. The simplest types have plain faucets, overflow and plug; the most expensive have a flushing rim, spray mechanism and pop-up waste unit.

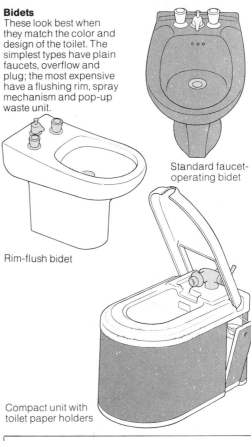

Standard faucet-operating bidet

Rim-flush bidet

Compact unit with toilet paper holders

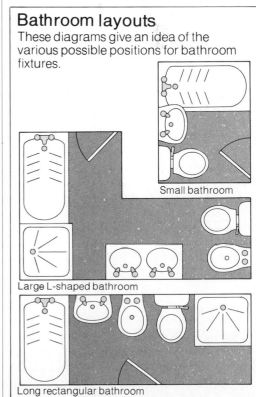

Bathroom layouts

These diagrams give an idea of the various possible positions for bathroom fixtures.

Small bathroom

Large L-shaped bathroom

Long rectangular bathroom

LIVING ROOM STORAGE

Well-planned storage is essential for a neat, efficiently run house or apartment. Good storage is expensive so be prepared to spend about as much on storage as on carpeting, unless you can manage a good deal of clever improvisation. In any room it helps if, at the outset, you are clear in your mind about what you want to store.

The main room for both relaxing and entertaining is the living room, in which you will probably want an assortment of items within easy reach, while maintaining the room's neat, uncluttered appearance. This will include some, if not all, of the following: books, magazines, drinks, glasses, hi-fi equipment including tape deck, records, tapes, television, video, typewriter, files, papers, stationery, board games, sewing machine, movie camera, projector, screen, slides, objets d'art and general memorabilia.

Choosing the right system

Before you decide on a specific storage system there are certain questions about your lifestyle which you should consider: is a move anticipated in the near future? If it is, you may choose moveable rather than fixed storage. Do you want everything stored out of sight or are there certain objects that you want left out on show? Finally, how much can you afford?

The answers to these questions should give some idea of the storage system most suited to you and your family. The next thing to consider is how well will it fit into your room? Bearing in mind the fact that the system used must fit in unobtrusively, take a detached view of the space available, paying special attention to proportion and architectural detail and choose a system which reflects the style of the room.

There are three basic systems for storage: *Freestanding*, moveable furniture, which includes traditional pieces like buffets, chests, cabinets, desks and bookcases, as well as industrial shelving, *built-in* shelves and closets, which are firmly attached to the wall, and finally, standard-sized, *modular* units which are specifically designed to fit flush against the wall or to form a solid dividing unit. All these types are available in solid wood, particle board or chipboard (with a melamine veneer) and, occasionally, metal and can be painted or varnished, veneered or laminated. Keep finishes simple and continue any moldings or baseboards across the top and bottom of new fittings to maintain a regular appearance in the room.

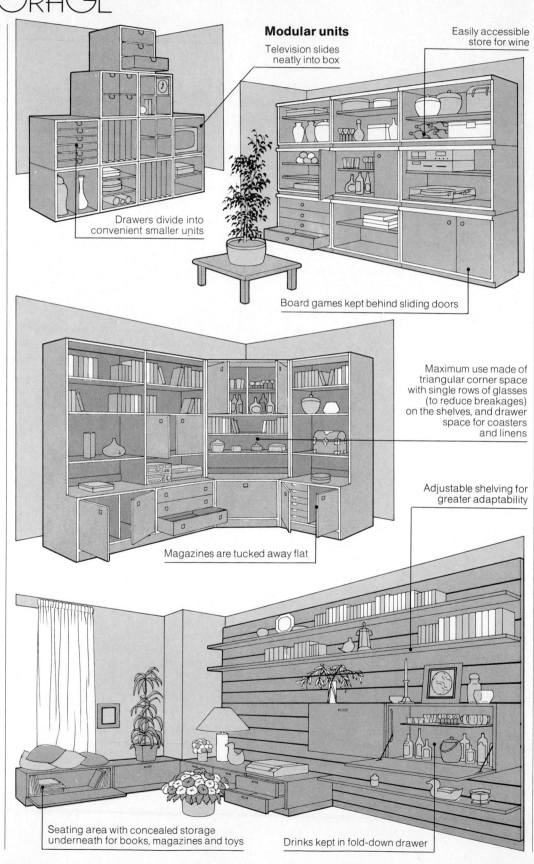

Modular units

Television slides neatly into box

Easily accessible store for wine

Drawers divide into convenient smaller units

Board games kept behind sliding doors

Maximum use made of triangular corner space with single rows of glasses (to reduce breakages) on the shelves, and drawer space for coasters and linens

Magazines are tucked away flat

Adjustable shelving for greater adaptability

Seating area with concealed storage underneath for books, magazines and toys

Drinks kept in fold-down drawer

Freestanding units

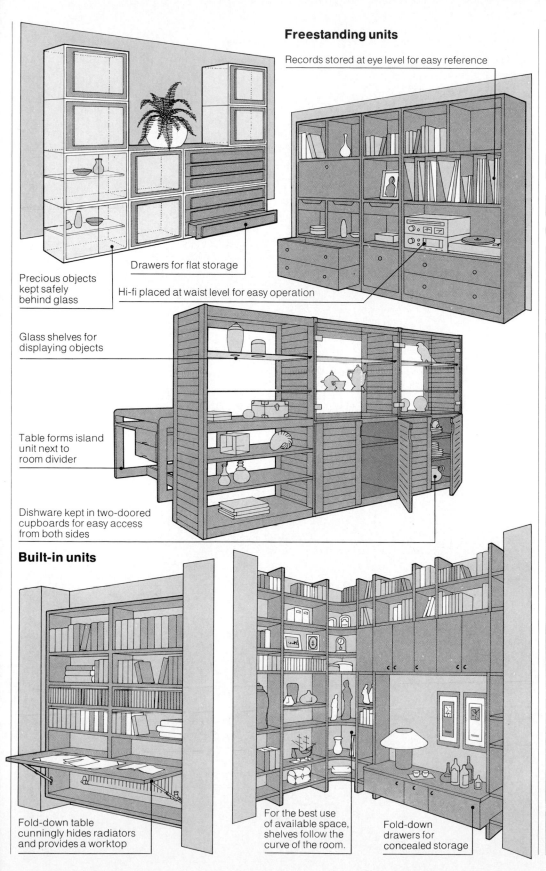

Records stored at eye level for easy reference

Precious objects kept safely behind glass

Drawers for flat storage

Hi-fi placed at waist level for easy operation

Glass shelves for displaying objects

Table forms island unit next to room divider

Dishware kept in two-doored cupboards for easy access from both sides

Built-in units

Fold-down table cunningly hides radiators and provides a worktop

For the best use of available space, shelves follow the curve of the room.

Fold-down drawers for concealed storage

Living room improvisation

As an alternative to these standard choices try improvising storage ideas by using objects in ways that they were not designed for. Laboratory shelving, for example, can be used instead of the conventional types.

Upturned plexiglass table for drinks

Ethnic basket for drinks

Re-cycled tin cans

Printer's type tray

Laboratory shelving

Hospital trolley

KITCHEN STORAGE

You can never have enough kitchen storage. Pots and pans, casseroles, serving dishes, mixing bowls, mixers, juice extractors, coffee grinders, kitchen knives and utensils, cutlery, plates, cups, saucers and mugs, soup bowls, glasses, table linen, herbs and spices, dry and packaged foods, jams, jellies and marmalades, staple foods, bottles of oil, vinegar and wine, fruit and vegetables, baskets, candles, matches, strings and cleaning goods – all must somehow be fitted in.

Kitchen units, which exist in a variety of standardized sizes, are the most usual means of storage. These usually have adjustable shelves and come in a variety of easy-to-clean, durable finishes. The shelves need be no wider than 12 inches (305mm) to accommodate most sizes of dishware in single rows (thus avoiding the need to reach over one row to get to another). Special fittings can be bought to fit into awkward or narrow spaces and they all provide for vegetables, canned foods and household implements.

Storing dishware and pans

Pots, pans and other large or heavy utensils should be stored on low shelves within easy reach of the stove. Pans can also be hung from hooks on the back of any adjacent cupboard doors or from butcher's rails above the cooking or preparation area. Large cooking gadgets like mixers can be set into specially designed, space-saving units.

In clean-air areas dishware can be left displayed on open shelves. In most urban kitchens, however, there is too much dust and dirt for this to be practical and dishware should be stored on covered shelves. A cheap alternative for storing cutlery, table linen and odds and ends is to use deep wicker baskets which could be kept dust-free if slotted under a work surface. Cups, mugs and jugs will look decorative hanging from hooks fixed to wooden shelves. This treatment looks especially effective on traditional hutches. Plates in everyday use can be left in a good-looking plate rack.

Dry goods should be stored in a dark, cool cupboard or a pantry. Salt can be kept in an earthenware jar by the stove; herbs and spices can be kept in glass jars for easy identification. Bottles of oil, vinegar and cooking wine can either be stored in a basket or left in two-tiered wine racks. Vegetables should be stored in cool airy racks (whether free-standing in the kitchen area, or included in the kitchen units themselves).

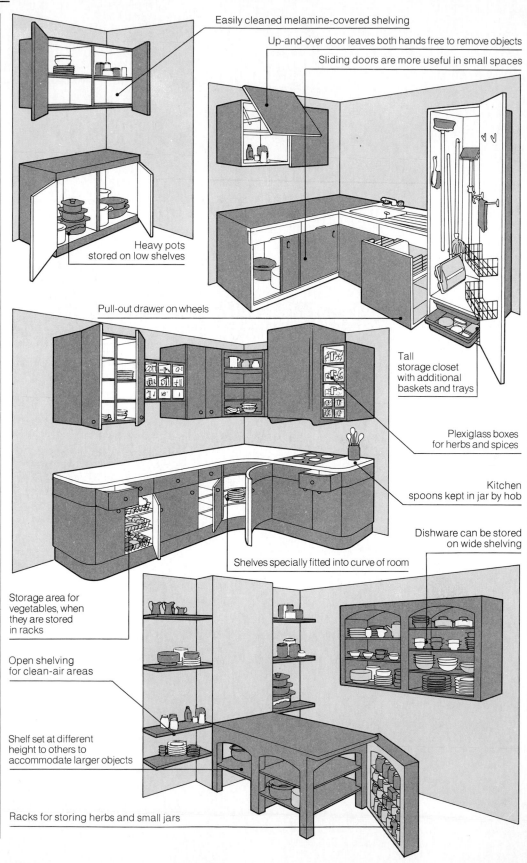

Easily cleaned melamine-covered shelving

Up-and-over door leaves both hands free to remove objects

Sliding doors are more useful in small spaces

Heavy pots stored on low shelves

Pull-out drawer on wheels

Tall storage closet with additional baskets and trays

Plexiglass boxes for herbs and spices

Kitchen spoons kept in jar by hob

Dishware can be stored on wide shelving

Shelves specially fitted into curve of room

Storage area for vegetables, when they are stored in racks

Open shelving for clean-air areas

Shelf set at different height to others to accommodate larger objects

Racks for storing herbs and small jars

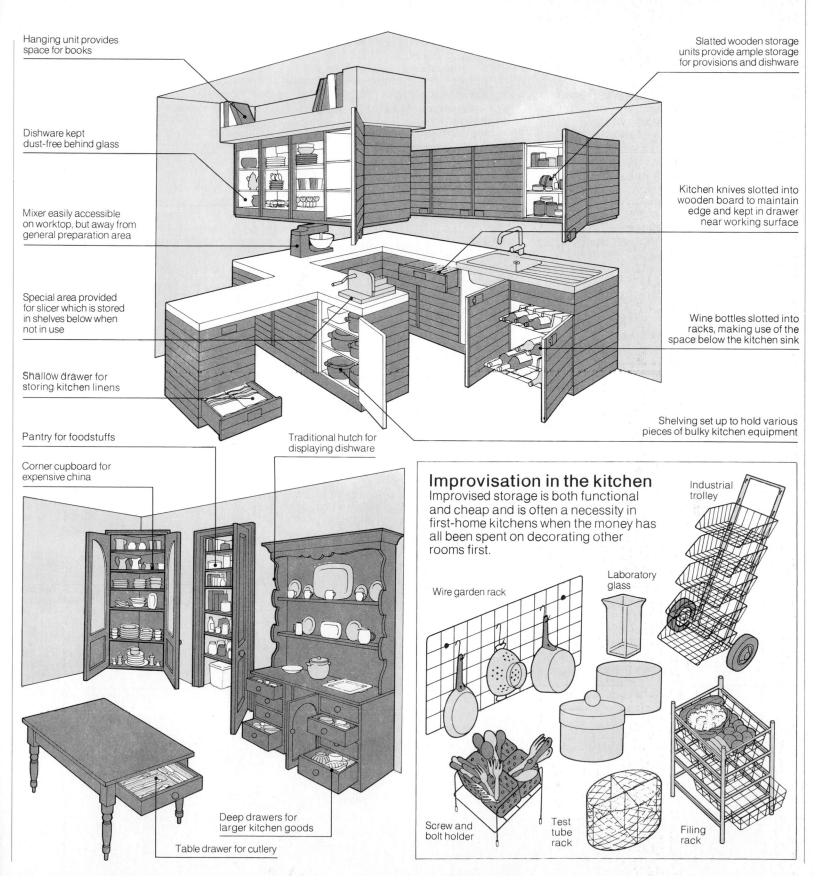

Hanging unit provides space for books

Dishware kept dust-free behind glass

Mixer easily accessible on worktop, but away from general preparation area

Special area provided for slicer which is stored in shelves below when not in use

Shallow drawer for storing kitchen linens

Pantry for foodstuffs

Corner cupboard for expensive china

Traditional hutch for displaying dishware

Deep drawers for larger kitchen goods

Table drawer for cutlery

Slatted wooden storage units provide ample storage for provisions and dishware

Kitchen knives slotted into wooden board to maintain edge and kept in drawer near working surface

Wine bottles slotted into racks, making use of the space below the kitchen sink

Shelving set up to hold various pieces of bulky kitchen equipment

Improvisation in the kitchen

Improvised storage is both functional and cheap and is often a necessity in first-home kitchens when the money has all been spent on decorating other rooms first.

Wire garden rack

Laboratory glass

Industrial trolley

Screw and bolt holder

Test tube rack

Filing rack

BEDROOM STORAGE

Well organized storage space is essential if you want a neat and reasonably spacious bedroom. The more clothing, shoes, accessories and luggage that can be tucked away, the greater the feeling of space you will create, providing the storage system you choose fits unobtrusively into the general scheme. Whether you have built-in closets, free-standing ones, or have improvised with curtains or some other sort of screening, the arrangement inside the storage unit must be practical. To maximize space use shop display rails or even sailing rope for hanging clothes on; stacks of plastic pull-out trays, wire racks, filing cabinets or narrow shelves are good for sweaters, socks, ties or cosmetics.

Young children are invariably untidy and will probably need extra storage units for their toys and books. While it is preferable to give them adult-sized furniture which can still be used when they are grown up, improvised storage should not be forgotten. Children love brightly-colored objects, so try painting a variety of well-sanded wooden boxes to hold shoes, books and toys. You can use space under beds by propping the bed up on cube storage units.

Orange boxes

Filing cabinet

Shop display rail

BATHROOM STORAGE

Bathroom storage, in what is usually the smallest room in the house, is all too often left out of the general budget, with the result that towels, washcloths, tooth brushes, tooth mugs, soaps, powders, essences, toilet waters, shampoos, medicines and cleaning implements are either scattered all over the place, or crammed into one small cabinet and left to overflow onto the bathtub and basin edges. However restricted the space may seem, there is usually room for more open shelving. Bathrooms are periodically damp and steamy and the most practical shelving is therefore melamine-covered or veneered wood. The shelves can be placed up the wall along the length of the bathtub, or at a higher level along the perimeter of the room. By combining shallow shelves with large pigeon holes you will be able to accommodate most items, from small bottles to bath towels. Hanging bags with clear, plastic pockets make good alternatives for storing small objects, and bulkier items like toilet paper can be placed in wire baskets similar to those used in kitchen storage. Instead of always buying new cabinets, shelving or containers, think about adapting small chests and old drug store jars from junk shops.

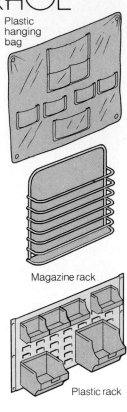

Plastic hanging bag

Magazine rack

Plastic rack

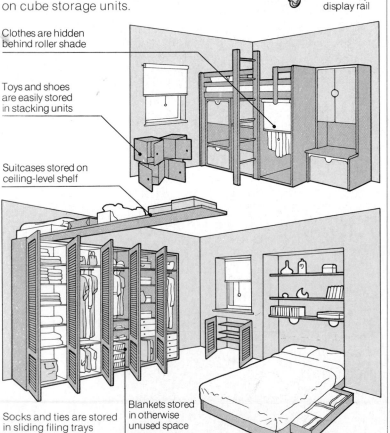

Clothes are hidden behind roller shade

Toys and shoes are easily stored in stacking units

Suitcases stored on ceiling-level shelf

Socks and ties are stored in sliding filing trays

Blankets stored in otherwise unused space

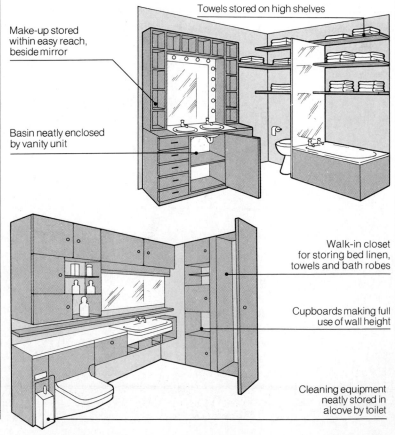

Make-up stored within easy reach, beside mirror

Basin neatly enclosed by vanity unit

Towels stored on high shelves

Walk-in closet for storing bed linen, towels and bath robes

Cupboards making full use of wall height

Cleaning equipment neatly stored in alcove by toilet

AN EYE FOR DETAIL

Once the framework of a room is completed, the decorating done to satisfaction and the furniture chosen, it is time to concentrate on putting together the sort of arrangements and decorative objects that will make a room seem both distinctive and memorable.

An eye for detail can be cultivated – just as color sense can be cultivated – by constant observation and practice. Notice what arrangements and collections seem especially attractive in other people's homes, in public spaces such as hotels and galleries, and in photographs in magazines or books. Look at them in detail and analyze them. Decide which ingredients make a room pleasing to the eye and adapt them to your own environment and pocket.

While there can be no watertight rules for arrangements, no blueprints for success, it is worth bearing in mind the following basic guidelines about proportion, shape and color. Seemingly minor details, they will make the difference between careless and polished living space.

The importance of balance

Symmetry is of prime importance when it comes to arrangments. A solid piece of furniture, such as a large sofa, should be balanced by another such as a desk or work-table; balance the mass of bookshelves on one wall with a large painting or a group of pictures and prints on the wall opposite. Take care never to choose a painting or mirror that is actually larger than the object beneath it, or the effect will be top heavy. Too small a painting or mirror on a large expanse of wall will look similarly unfortunate. Table lamps usually look best if shades are kept to one shape and one color, and if they are, as far as possible, kept at one level. They do not necessarily have to be the same size, but a lamp on a desk or side table, for example, should be shorter or squatter, so that their tops appear to be at the same level as taller floor lamps.

Balance is equally important when it comes to color. The color of a chair at one end of a room can be repeated in a painting or in throw pillows at the other. Colors in the base of a lamp can be picked up in an object or a rug somewhere else; one color from a patterned fabric or wallpaper can be used again in the background matt to a print, or a collection of prints, on the wall.

Choosing and displaying collections

For a truly personal room, the objects must be personal, too. They should always be selected for their intrinsic interest or beauty, or for some sentimental reason. They should never be chosen because of fashion, except, perhaps, for fun, or because other people have similar objects.

There are two quite different schools of thought on the display of possessions and collections; those who believe in owning one or two exquisite or interesting pieces and offering them up in isolation, and those who are inveterate collectors of memorabilia. The trouble with the first group is that the

The combination of massed plants and flowers and similarly patterned fabric for tablecloths and upholstery makes this a perpetually summery room.

few chosen objects really must be beautiful, or made to appear so without being self-conscious. The difficulty with the second is that the accretions of objects must be well-organized or they will certainly degenerate into mere clutter. This involves careful assemblage of shapes, colors and textures, after all, the object is to create a still life, or a series of still lifes, in just the same way as a painter or photographer visualizes and lines up his subject.

Collections on walls

Walls are the most obvious background for any collections. Some people want maximum space for their serious collections, while others use a wall to fill it with objects. Followers of the first school of thought use walls as a blank canvas, and move paintings, prints and constructions around as their collection expands or contracts. Those whose aim is simply to fill up space must try to find a common element, a color, texture or shape which gives cohesion to disparate possessions. This type of collection need look no less charming or interesting than its grander counterpart.

Small objects can be massed alongside books on shelves, on shelves by themselves, on windowsills, ledges and mantelpieces, and on tables. Improvise with collections of quite commonplace objects: old bottles, keys or tins; they often make for more memorable rooms than much rarer items.

Objects as sculpture

Something sculptural, whether figurative or abstract, ancient or modern, will always add distinction to a room. Properly lit and starkly displayed against a bare wall or window or mirror, interesting shapes like a decoy duck, an old clock or an antique stove, can be shown off in a room as though they, too, were pieces of sculpture.

The way daily objects are absorbed into the general ambience also points up an eye for detail; here, what is *not* shown is equally as important as what is. In a well-arranged living or family room, television sets and hi-fi equipment will be tucked away onto shelves, or into cupboards or corners. Radiators will be decorated to blend in with walls or wall-coverings, and pipes are cased or painted in, or they might be boldly treated as decorative shapes in their own right.

A good sense of arrangement also stretches to the many ways beds and windows can be treated; the way different-colored pillows are juxtaposed on a sofa or chair; the different types of elaborate beds, the infinite number of window treatments, ranging from elaborately ruched and tucked shades and romantic drapery to stark windows which serve simply as a frame for a spectacular view. All raise decoration from the competent to the memorable. The vital point to remember in all this is that accessorizing and arrangement must not be too self-conscious. Too rigid or over serious an approach will have a stultifying effect. Remember, too, that a sense of humor in decoration, a lightness of touch, a certain irreverence, particularly when dealing with rather grand objects, is far more beguiling than great perfection.

Opposite page, top:
A wallful of assorted dogs in assorted sizes are the dominant feature in an eclectic living room with its mixture of different, but related patterns in tiling, rug and upholstery. Piled logs mix casually with piled books and a mixture of porcelain, glass and antique tools.

Below:
In a room which is so full of plants it is practically a conservatory, the variegated pattern of the natural foliage is underlined by the leaf-patterned fabric and by the natural textures of the chairs and matting.

This page, top:
Paintings, exotic zebra rug, exotic plants and exotica in general give a hothouse atmosphere to this sitting room, where different periods, objects, shapes and colors are mixed in a thoroughly rarified way.

Below left:
Paintings, prints and objects juxtaposed pleasingly on a brown velvet wall are lit by uplights placed against the baseboards. Both the edges of the wallcovering and the inset bookshelves are defined by lengths of gilt picture-framing. The wall-mounted reading lamps are set at just the right height for reading.

Below right:
Inset bookshelves either side of a fireplace, a collection of shells flanked by cacti and surmounted by an engraving, and a mass of foliage at ground level, all add to the pleasantly crowded composition of this small sitting room.

HANGING ART

Balance and scale are of prime importance when it comes to hanging pictures on walls. Remember that large paintings should not be any bigger than a piece of furniture underneath them, and that small paintings or prints should not be hung in isolation on a large wall. But whatever the size of the piece you are hanging, try to place it at eye level, taking either standing or sitting levels into account. The same applies to landings, where pictures will be seen by people coming up and down stairs. With a large grouping, keep the central pieces at eye level, but do be careful not to hang paintings so close to sofas and chairs that they get knocked by people's heads.

Working out arrangements

Vertical arrangements will, of course, make a room seem higher, just as horizontal ones will make an area seem wider. Play around with different sizes of pictures to find the sort of arrangement that works best on the wall space available and with any other objects or arrangements in the room.

If you are thinking of hanging a large group of different-sized pictures, decide on the overall shape of the arrangement first of all, and mark out the area in an *impermanent* way (very important this). Now lay out all the items on the floor, as you hope to position them on the wall. This should save a lot of unwanted damage to the wall as well as frayed tempers. The same procedure can be followed when mixing objects with paintings, prints, photographs and general memorabilia, marking on the wall where the top and bottom of each object will be. To balance a larger painting or as a substitute for one, a number of very small paintings or prints can be hung together on another wall. A large picture in the middle of a group of smaller ones gives the impression of tailing off, so if one painting or print is much larger than the others, place it at one end of a grouping. The large picture can be balanced at the other end by a plant, flowers or a piece of sculpture – any tall object. A collection of miscellaneous prints without much in common can be given a unity if each one has a matt with the same, distinctive color (bearing in mind the colors of the room) and framed with the same chrome or brass.

The disparate elements of an oddly assorted group will work well together if they share a predominant color: all sepia tints perhaps, or all green and white prints, all black or white, or all photographs. If, of course, the subjects share an affinity, there is no need to worry about shapes, sizes and oddities of frames, because the theme will

Left:
The straight line of Japanese pictures is placed high enough above the sofa to avoid reclining heads, and topped with a miscellany of totally different objects which are held together more by the symmetry of their arrangement than any kind of link. The solidity of the clock is counterbalanced by the slightness of the disparate objects around it.

Some suggested arrangements
Picture and object hanging can be worked within a number of different self-imposed frameworks. Do not forget that vertical arrangements will make a room seem higher; and that horizontal lines will make it seem wider. Larger paintings or objects can be balanced, perhaps, by a pair of smaller prints, or one long object which takes up much the same amount of room as whatever it happens to be counter-balancing can be set beside two smaller ones. The arrangement below effectively balances different sizes.

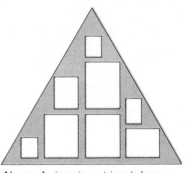

Above: An imaginary triangle frames this pyramid arrangement with the smallest painting placed on top.
Below: A hypothetical circle surrounds this interesting collection.

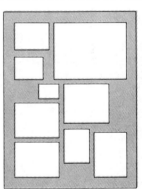

Above: One larger painting at one corner is balanced by two smaller ones diametrically below, with two groups of three filling in the gaps.
Below: A close-knit group of small prints on wide matts.

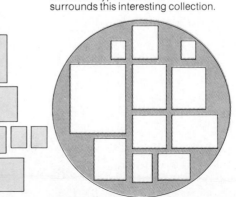

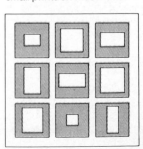

at once have provided the protection of collection status. And once such status has been given, disparate shapes and sizes will serve to make the whole more interesting, rather than being in any way detracting. A useful point to remember, though, is always to leave at least half the width of the smallest item you are hanging between each picture. This gives a balance of its own.

Hanging posters

Posters can be preserved in special holders or framed in plexiglass so that they do not curl at the edges. Balance them by size, subject or color, or use them rather like wallpaper on an all-white wall, filling if not all the space, enough to cover up the large blankness. Blow-ups of photographs come into much the same category, and used in careful sequence can be treated like a mural, or scenic wallpaper. Anything likely to be ephemeral can be stuck up with adhesive which does not mark walls.

Most artwork looks best hung on dark walls, though it adds a particular vivacity to white walls, particularly if colors are clear. If a wall is strongly patterned it is best to mount prints and drawings on very deep matts of toning, or handsomely contrasting colors to the background; the subject is then becalmed in an area of its own rather than being lost in the overall design.

Wall hangings

Wallhangings, which might include rugs, tapestries, woven wool and silk pictures, collages of every description and macramé, old quilts, patchwork, bedspreads of every description, or just a piece of well-designed fabric, can be displayed in one of several ways. Try attaching heavier hangings to a slim curtain rod suspended from hooks, or clipped into strong, thin clamps running the requisite length. Frame cotton and lighter fabrics in plexiglass cut to measure, or plain sheets of glass clipped to board, or stretch them over a thin wood frame in the same way that canvas for a painting is stretched and mounted. If a hanging is coarsely woven and you do not mind about the walls too much, it can just be suspended with long nails, or hung from small hooks latched onto picture wire or nylon thread which is attached in its turn to conventional wall hooks. It is important, of course, to be sure that any strong spotlight or any other light fitting, mounted to show off such hangings, should not be placed near enough to cause a burn. Concentrated light on one area can easily do this. More information about lighting art and possessions is given on page 23.

Top left:
A large Indian portrait on one wall is balanced by a similar-sized mirror on the other, and the space in between filled by smaller prints, miniatures and paintings. Colors in the pictures are repeated in the massed throw cushions heaped on the seating units.

Far left:
The height of the largest picture in this group is counter-balanced by the octagonal clock, initials and bunch of herbs set in among the smaller prints. Darker coloring is also balanced by lighter backgrounds.

Near left:
A fetching collection of portrait miniatures and profiles has been harmoniously and nicely haphazardly hung within a stepped framework. Although frames and shapes are different, the collection has the homogeneity of common subject matter.

Below left:
Yet another example of a harmonious balance of disparate objects, in which even the lamp-shade seems part of the whole.

DISPLAYING COLLECTIONS

All too often, so much money has been spent on the decoration and furnishings in a room that there is very little left for filling the gaps on the walls, let alone for starting a serious collection. Alternatively, money might be available, but ideas are short, and until such time as money becomes more elastic, or the right piece becomes obvious, it is perfectly possible to improvize interesting wall fillers. In any event, whatever the cause of the original blank wall, improvizations are often so successful and so personal, that they are kept on permanently.

Ideas for wall fillers

The fact of the matter is that almost anything, given some imagination, can be made to look unexpectedly good.

Among the less usual ideas, straw hats of every conceivable shape and size, or just different hats from various countries (military headgear for example) look lively and can be hung up in a square or rectangle; so can keys of every size and description; old tools; a series of chains looped and dangling; lids from casseroles; terrines; old paste dishes and toothpaste jars; old postcards or cigarette cards; a large montage of interesting tickets; bi-colored ping-pong balls stuck into painted plywood drilled with holes; a montage of old transfers or autumn leaves; even six or seven different varieties of corn, neatly labelled and mounted on black or brown velvet and simply framed. Trellis is cheap, and a piece of it can be pinned to a wall and used as an easy pinboard for a hotchpotch of cards, clippings, sketches, labels, which can all look quite decorative. Scrap wood is often cheap and a square or rectangle of some sort of boarding can be covered in dark felt or burlap to tone in with a room, and mounted with a collection of belts, or just belt buckles for that matter, which are often highly ornamental. Nineteenth century buttons and cuff-links can be shown off in much the same manner, and arranged in squares, triangles, diamonds and circles, according to taste and the type of collection.

Old kitchen utensils, long since discarded but tucked away for some forgotten reason in the backs of drawers, can be stuck to more board and the whole spray painted with shiny white or black, or any color that suits.

Montages

Other good ideas I have seen include a whole patchwork of pieces of wallpaper stuck together on plywood to form an interesting, abstract design. This montage

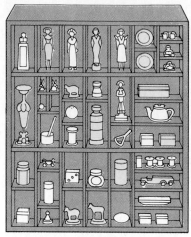

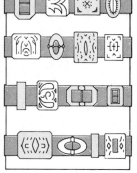

Left: An old printers' type drawer hung on a wall and filled with every kind of collectible miniature. Right: Glass rolling pins, first used during the Napoleonic Wars as salt holders, can look decorative massed together. Below: Shoe and belt buckles mounted on lengths of velvet ribbon.

Left: A series of decorated masks from Bali, China, Japan and Nigeria makes another unusual collection. Right: Decorative hair combs are quite easy to come by; they can be mounted on felt or painted board.

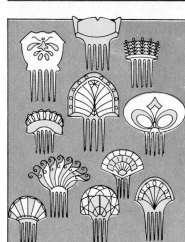

Below: Collector's plates (most of the china manufacturers bring out commemorative plates from time to time) can be hung on wires or propped on shelves.

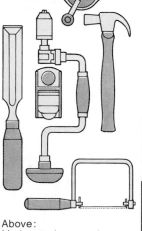

Above: Modern tools can make attractive sculptural shapes when silhouetted against a wall, and can easily be attached to pegboard or cork tiles. Antique tools are equally interesting.

Below: Cards, calendars, invitations, messages and general memorabilia stuck into a length of ordinary garden trellis. This can be attached to a wall from floor to ceiling and added to at will.

326

idea can be repeated with squares of brightly colored felt – available in the sewing sections of most department stores – which can be simply stuck onto some sort of backing to form a brilliant checker board. And of course, anyone with the ability, ideas and will, can make their own collages with a mixture of scraps of fabric, feathers, cards, cut out messages, tin lids, labels, whatever seems appropriate.

Fabric wallhangings

More conventionally, old quilts look splendid attached to walls, as of course, do ethnic rugs, shawls, large antique scarves, and indeed, any piece of graphically designed fabric, stretched and framed like a canvas.

Mirrors

Mirrors can be used in many effective ways. Plain mirror, of course, doubles or trebles space, as well as covering walls, reflecting light and exaggerating images. If a whole wall of mirror is too expensive, a fair substitute can be made with a series of similarly framed mirrors hung side-by-side, one above the other. Huge, nineteenth-century mirrors with elaborate frames are often very much cheaper than one might imagine, and granted that there is space will more than adequately fill a blank wall.

Screens

Screens are another useful filler. Old ones can be bought in junk shops or thrift stores, recovered with calico or burlap and painted with a design. They can be used as a sophisticated pin board; made into a modern version of a scrap screen with fragments of magazine illustrations, bits of cards, and so on; or covered in with patterned fabric to tie in with a room scheme.

Balance and scale

One last point: if you are assembling any sort of collection for mounting on the wall, or putting on a shelf or table for that matter, try to see that all the objects are much the same size. Pieces which are too much out of proportion to the others will stand out. If this is unavoidable, at least try to balance the larger piece with something else of similar size nearby. Objects that are disparate with no real relation to each other should be grouped by colors, textures or at least shapes. And once again, all due attention should be paid to proportion and scale to achieve the best-looking results. More ideas about balance and scale are given at the beginning of this section.

Left:
Ceilings, no less than walls, can be used as areas of decoration, sometimes with as cheap a solution as bunches of herbs and dried flowers marched in tight rows, as in this lobby.

Below:
An overkill of M's in various shapes and sizes are pinned to the wall above a pine chest, itself arranged with stoneware bottles and mugs. Any other initial capital with an interesting shape – X, H, B, K, for example – could easily be used instead.

Many otherwise perfect rooms have an inexplicably stultifying effect which can often, eventually, be traced to too self-conscious an approach to detailing. Decoration, like oneself, should, after all, never be taken too seriously, and one of the nicest things to discover in any room is that its owner, or owners, has a sense of humor.

Humor in decoration

In some areas humor will show in the way objects are arranged. Or themes may be deliberately repeated (see the scheme on page 142 of the Room-by-Room Guide, in which the design on the bathtub was taken as the point of departure and repeated and elaborated on elsewhere in the room). This repetition may involve different themes, or subjects, which can recur in different scales or be taken from different periods. Thus an object illustrated in a painting or photograph on a wall may actually be repeating a real view beyond the window – photographs or montages of skyscrapers hung on walls repeating the urban view outside, for example, are a great favorite, as are bowls of fruit or vases of flowers which imitate the theme of a print or painting on a wall. The painting of a house echoed by objects on a table on page 350 makes this point nicely.

Left:
All sorts and shapes of baskets are hung on this kitchen wall, and look very decorative mixed with the odd wooden mat and fruit-picking hook, with the crowning glory of an elaborately framed piece of nineteenth century embroidery.

Below left:
Yellow walls have been used as an effective backing for a miscellaneous variety of cards, flags, posters, letters and general memorabilia in this small bathroom.

Below right:
Free-form painted shapes, filled in with scratchy designs, act as original frames for sweaters, embroidered jackets. They also act as a pinboard for postcards, memorabilia and anything else that seems amusing or notable. To achieve a reasonable balance however, some are left completely empty and converge onto the ceiling like clouds.

OBJECTS AS SCULPTURE

Recognizing the sculptural quality in an object, of course, is an integral part of good decorating. The capacity to isolate a beautiful shape and show it off for its intrinsic esthetic qualities, however basic or primitive, is what having an eye for detail is all about.

Any sort of sculpture whether African or Oceanic, Indian or Islamic, Oriental or Pre-Columbian, figurative or abstract, heads or torsos, miniature or bulky, bronze, kinetic, neon, stone, marble, wood or two-toned plexiglass, will add at least interest if not distinction to a room.

Displaying objects

Lighting is important to show sculpture at its best advantage (see pages 19 to 24 for information about lighting) and so are the kinds of stands or plinths on which pieces are displayed. Small pieces look good on clear lucite blocks; large pieces should have plinths made to scale whether in natural or painted or lacquered wood, marble, plaster or plexiglass. But then almost anything with a good line looks good displayed on a plinth whether it's a piece of drift wood, a beautiful box, an urn or even a basket of plants or flowers. For a truly personal room, though, the objects must be liked for their own sake.

Left:
Simple, quite ulitarian objects are often un-expectedly decorative as proved by this wood-burning stove, trug of wood, rough frame filled with straw, old grids and pots full of geraniums, set against a background of tongue-and-grooved pine.

Below left:
The solid silhouette of this ancient, West African wood-carving set on a plexiglass plinth against an interesting window, makes a pleasing composition.

Below right:
A decoy duck and an oversize wooden fish set on a primitive chest stand out starkly against the white wall. Set out like this they make as much dramatic impact as pieces of sculpture ten times their price.

ELABORATE BEDS

While some people prefer to minimize the bulk of a bed, others like it to be the most important decorative element in a room. Four-poster beds, for instance, have been popular for centuries, and whatever the fabric treatment, they fill in the wasted space above a bed, making for a feeling of grandeur and privacy. Four-posters look best in largish bedrooms with high ceilings, but quite ordinary-sized beds can be dressed up, less elaborately perhaps, yet to no less effect, with draperies and canopies.

Four-poster beds

Four-poster structures can be made in metal, such as brass or steel, as well as in wood, cane and rattan, or they can be made from deliberately rough planks of wood and even natural boughs.

Modern steel or cane four-posters look best left open and undraped so that they are a mere skeletal framework. More traditional versions can be canopied to match the bed treatment beneath, with the sides left undraped, or partially draped and tied back. Or a four-poster can be given the full traditional treatment and all-round drapes added to coordinate or contrast with the bedcoverings. The side drapes can be made in a luxuriance of light, flimsy fabric such as batiste, cheesecloth or muslin, for example, or they can be neat and tailored in heavier fabric.

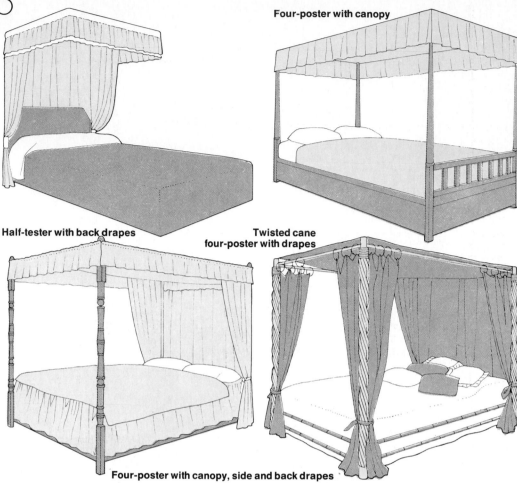

Four-poster with canopy

Half-tester with back drapes

Twisted cane four-poster with drapes

Four-poster with canopy, side and back drapes

Far left:
An elegant four-poster with an elaborately shaped, chintz canopy and matching back drape and dust ruffle.

Left:
A traditional pine bed with the interesting addition of an half-tester, framed in the same wood. Side drapes match the throw-over bed cover.

Fabric "four-posters"

It is perfectly possible and considerably less expensive to achieve the effect of a four-post bed with fabric alone. Small tracks can be fixed to the ceiling at each corner of the bed to support side drapes (as in the bedroom on page 112); or a fabric-covered ply canopy or valance can be attached to the ceiling or suspended from it above the bed; or a canopy can be cantilevered out from the wall behind the bed, with covering and drapes chosen to coordinate with the bedcoverings, valance or dust ruffle. An equally effective alternative to the full four-poster is the half-canopy or tester which consists of the same sort of fabric-covered ply, but about a third of the size, with drapes hanging down beside the pillows, which are then caught with tie-backs and often finished with a back drape.

Canopies

A canopied or "baldechin" effect can also be achieved with a length of fabric the width of the bed. This material is brought up from behind the pillows and shaped over a rod suspended from the ceiling about two feet (61cm) out from the wall. An even longer length can be casually looped over yet another rod at the foot of the bed and from there dropped to the floor. Or simply attach a drape to a semi-circular coronet fixed well above the head of the bed (as on page 117).

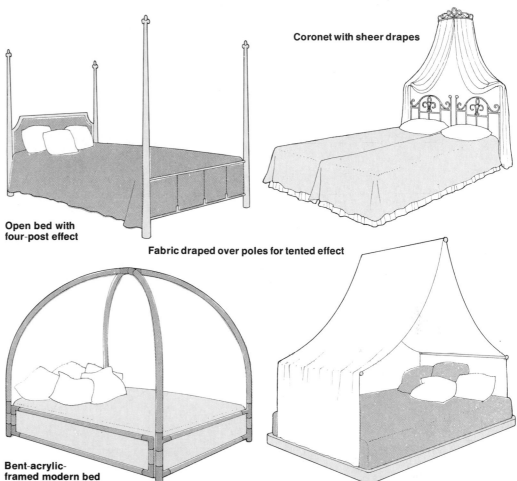

Open bed with four-post effect

Coronet with sheer drapes

Fabric draped over poles for tented effect

Bent-acrylic-framed modern bed

Far left:
An elaborate mirror frame hung between two windows makes a handsome bedhead, picture frame and bedhead shelf, all in one. Horizontally striped pillows add an interesting variation to the vertical pattern of the tuck-in cover and fur throw.

Left:
A nineteenth-century, American bed with sculptural, undraped posts, dressed up here with pristine lace covers and generous pillows.

IDEAS FOR DRAPES

Coinciding with an increased general interest in decorating, there is certainly also a revival of the more elaborate draperies and curtain treatments of the past.

Ideal lengths for drapes

The correct length for a drape is a moot point. Short drapes only really look good in tiny cottage windows or in attic rooms, although café curtains suspended from a slim rod can look neat in kitchens and bathrooms. Short windows in living rooms and bedrooms look better if covered with shades of one description or another (see pages 263 and 334). Full-length drapes should either just touch the floor, or be allowed to fall down onto it, Thirties style. On no account should there be a gap between hem and floor, so always make sure that long drapes have more than generous hems to allow for some shrinkage during washing.

Fabric for drapes

The fabric you choose for the drapes will depend on taste and budget, but whatever material you finally decide on, don't skimp; rather buy plenty of slightly cheaper material than too little of an expensive one. And remember that drapes look much more finished off if they are bound, edged or bordered, or a mixture of all three. Many fabrics have their own borders now which can be cut and sewn on to all four sides of a drape and the lower edge of the valance, if there is one. Above all, drapes must be lined, and preferably interlined as well, with an insulating material to muffle cold and noise and, incidentally, draw dirt away from the drape. There is no comparison between the way properly-lined and interlined drapes will hang, and the bedraggled droop of unlined ones.

Hanging drapes

The most common method of hanging drapes is from a track, and although without a valance, track can look bare, this does mean that the drapes can be pulled open or drawn by a pulley system at the side.

Rods made either of brass, or natural, stained, or painted wood look particularly appropriate in a fairly traditional room, but this often means that the drapes have to be pulled by hand, which results in the edges becoming dirty more quickly. Always make sure the rods are wider than the actual windows so the drapes can be pulled well back. An alternative would be to have them permanently closed at the top and looped gracefully back at the sides with tie-bands during the day.

Left:
A graceful full-length window has been given an equally graceful and deceptively simple treatment by winding an extra long length of fabric over a wooden pole. The fabric, which has been softly pleated, is allowed to fall in generous, train-like folds onto the floor.

Headings for drapes

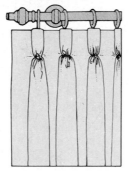

Single "goblet" pleats like this, take less fabric than French heads.

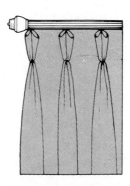

Pinch-pleat headings discipline fabric into neat folds.

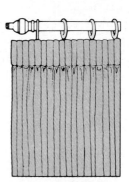

Pencil pleats need three times the width of the window in fabric.

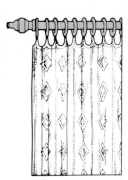

Sheers can be simply hemmed and clipped to rings attached to a rod.

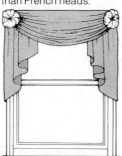

A simplified form of swags and tails softens bare windows.

A simple, gathered pelmet, with longer sides to give a tailed effect.

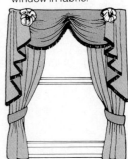

More elaborate swags and tails used over long drapes.

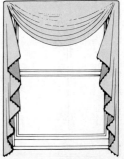

Long swags and tails used to soften neat blinds or shades.

Elegant though it may be, you do have to have plenty of light coming through the windows for this sort of treatment.

Hard and soft valances

If you decide to have a valance you can choose from a soft, fabric one made to match the drapes, or you can have a wooden one which is then covered with interlining and matching or contrasting fabric. Sometimes a cornice or piece of furniture in a room suggests the shape, or perhaps it may be the design of the fabric to be used for the drapes. Hard valances are generally more expensive than soft ones because they have to be shaped.

Headings for drapes

There are a number of different headings (the gathers or pleats at the top of drapes) to choose from, ranging from the very simple to the elaborate. The most popular is the French head. This treatment normally takes two-and-a-half widths of material for each side: the gathers can be in groups of three pleats of two inches (5 cm) of material, anywhere between four and five inches (10 and 12·5 cm) apart. Drapes gathered all the way along in pencil heads make another attractive heading. They usually take more material than French heads, and depending on the height of the window, vary from between four to six inches (10 to 15 cm) deep.

Single pleats take up less fabric, for being less full than French headings, they need only one-and-a-half widths of material. Each pleat is generally some three inches deep (7·5 cm), set about four inches (10 cm) apart.

Double pleats are usually just barely sewn down, about half an inch (1 cm) from the top, so that the drape seems almost to flow from the top of the window. Goblet heads are basically one pleat, but sewn down three (7·5 cm) or four (10 cm) inches vertically, with the base of the pleat sewn down and flattened against the drape, making for a gentler effect than a French heading. Gathered and smocked headings give an effect very similar to smocked dresses. Swags and tails are the most elaborate type of heading, with fabric twisted gracefully around a pole and dropping down the sides of the actual drapes.

Finally, for those who prefer a lighter, airier look, there are sheer fabrics (which, of course, cannot be lined). These include muslins, nets or lace and can be left to hang free or be caught up or back in graceful swags.

Valances

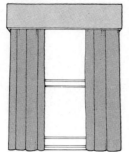
A straight, fabric-covered valance made of wood.

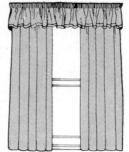
A gathered and lined soft valance with a similar heading to the drapes.

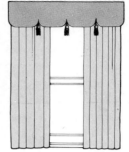
A shaped, stiffened valance made of wood or buckram.

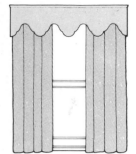
An elaborately-shaped wooden valance inter-lined and fabric-covered.

Tie-backs

Traditional tassled cord tie-backs for holding back heavy drapes.

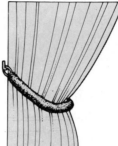
Plumply-padded variety made from the same fabric as the drapes.

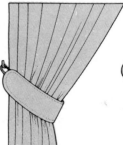
Stiff crescent-shaped buckram-lined tie-back, fixed to a small hook.

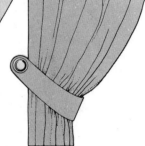
Longer tie-back for fuller drapes with a more elab-orate, medallion fixing.

Far left:
An arched track has the advantage of showing off graceful windows and supporting equally handsome drapes. Tie-backs are set low here, but would look just as well fixed higher up the frames.

Near left:
Elaborately-ruched soft valances provide the only softening to this pair of long windows over-looking a garden, although some sort of shade could just as easily be concealed beneath the deep folds.

Below left:
An entire bedroom lined in cotton drapes gathered onto a series of brass traverse rods and caught back over windows and doors.

Below right:
Festoon blinds like this with their permanent vertical gathers have a particularly feminine air about them. Used in con-junction with sheers, they also act as a valance.

SHADES

When it comes to window treatments, people tend to think mainly of drapes. But there are several practical, equally decorative alternatives.

Roller shades

These are the simplest type of shades. They can be made from almost any thin, closely woven fabric and look neat on their own or teamed with sheers or heavier drapes. Because they are easy to keep clean, roller shades are especially useful in kitchens and bathrooms. They can be bought ready-made, or in kit form, or you can make them yourself, using a favorite fabric. Any tightly woven material, such as cotton or linen, is ideal.

Roman shades

When hanging down, these look very much like roller shades, but when drawn up, they form a series of horizontal, concertina folds. The fabric, which should be lined, is attached to a wooden batten and has rows of eyelets at the back, one above the other, through which the cords are attached. To keep these shades from sagging in the middle, many people fix wooden battens at each eyelet interval, which makes for very even pleats. Roman shades are neat and tailored and look good in modern, uncluttered living or dining rooms. They can be made in most firmly woven fabrics, and look especially effective with a contrasting border, or teamed with matching drapes, tied back.

Pull-up drapes

These work on much the same principle as Roman shades. In spite of the horizontal gathers, pull-up drapes hang flat when the cords are loose. They make for a much softer, more feminine effect than Roman shades and look prettiest when drawn partly up. They are especially effective in light fabrics, with pleated or gathered headings, or scalloped swags.

Festoon or Austrian shades

While pull-up drapes have horizontal gathers, these are ruched in vertical panels; they remain permanently gathered even when hanging down to their full length.

Both festoon blinds and pull-up drapes look good in small rooms, or where full-length drapery would look cramped. Apart from the standard measure, ready-made shades dealt with in the Sample Book, fabric shades can be custom-made to suit individual requirements. For information about making shades yourself, see page 202 of the Sample Book.

Roller shades
A plain fabric shade, **above**, provides good screening against bright sunlight. A close-up of the spring mechanism, **right**. The shade clips neatly into brackets fixed to the edge of the window. To tension the spring, unroll the shade by hand, re-roll, hang and pull down shade; it should now lock.

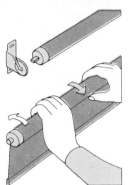

Roman shades
A plain shade edged with a pale border, **above**, looks especially effective in this traditional study. **Right**, a close-up of the back of a Roman shade. Cords threaded through rows of eyelets enable the shade to be pulled up.

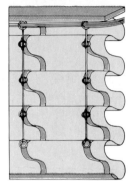

Pull-up shades
This striped shade edged with a fringe looks good against plain walls, **above**. These shades look prettiest drawn halfway up, when let down, they hang flat. **Right**, details showing how the material falls into horizontal gathers.

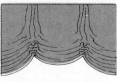

Festoon or Austrian shades
Essentially feminine in character, these shades look particularly good when made in sheer fabric, as above. The details, **right**, show how the material falls in ruched, vertical panels.

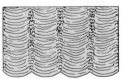

SHUTTERS AND BLINDS

Blinds will protect a room from strong light without making it dark or gloomy.

Matchstick or pinoleum blinds
Made from thin spills of wood sewn together with cotton, these can be pulled up with cords or are sometimes sold with a spring mechanism. Usually available in untreated wood, they are also sometimes painted or stained. Slatted blinds, which have wider strips of wood, can also be used as screens.

Bamboo blinds
These consist of strips of bamboo of varying widths, woven together. They are available in natural wood, which sometimes has an interesting tortoiseshell look.

Venetian blinds
These are made of wood, metal or plastic; the thinner the slats, the smarter their appearance. They give good light control by day and night.

Vertical louver blinds
Made of vertical strips of metal, wood or fabric, these blinds pivot open and shut; they look particularly effective hung right across a window wall.

Venetian blinds
Aluminum blinds look especially good in clean-lined, functional kitchens, as above. The slats are easily cleaned with a damp cloth. The detail, **right**, shows the cords which control the angle of the slats, which in turn affects the amount of light let in through the window.

Vertical louver blinds
The broad slats of this vertical blind have a softening effect on the large expanse of window, **above**. The louvers can be made of wood, canvas or man-made materials. The detail, **right**, shows how the slats pivot open, or they can be fixed shut, or pulled back.

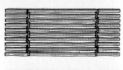

Matchstick or pinoleum blinds
Tortoiseshell blinds make an attractive window covering in the kitchen-dining room, **above**. As shown, **right**, the slats of these blinds come in varying widths; they are usually pulled up in the same way as roller shades.

Shutters

Many older houses still retain their original internal shutters, in which case there is little need for drapes and shades as well.

Both paneled and louvered shutters can be stripped and left bare, or they can be decorated in a variety of ways. Ordinary shutters can be painted all one color, or the folding panels can be picked out in different colors; or they can be treated like an artist's canvas and painted with designs. They can also be stained or stenciled. Louvered shutters can be hung vertically or horizontally. An interesting visual treatment for wide windows is to hang some louvered shutters vertically and some horizontally. Shutters seldom, if ever, need replacing.

Solid shutters can be painted in plain colors or painted or stenciled with interesting designs.

Folding louvered shutters are particularly versatile and can be left half open to let in both air and light.

PROBLEM WINDOWS

Few people are fortunate to have perfect, elegant windows. Many, living in rentals perhaps, or apartments converted from larger buildings, are faced with finding the right treatment for skylights or dormer windows. For others in larger houses or apartments, long French windows pose a problem, and not all windows are perfectly shaped or well-proportioned. Here are some ideas to suit awkward windows.

Windows set in pairs

Treat them as a single unit. Hang drapes from one rod fixed above both windows. If shades are used, make sure they match.

Windows which open inwards or pivot

Where privacy is important, mount sheers or drapes onto the windows themselves. For windows which pivot horizontally, attach a rod to the inner frame and hang café curtains. For vertical pivoting windows, fix drapes or sheers to the frame, as above.

Windows set right up to a corner

Use just one drape, drawn or looped back. Or use a shade instead.

French windows

If both doors open, treat them as a single unit with drapes drawn to the sides. Or use shades set *above* the frames, if possible, so the doors open easily.

Arched windows

Don't try to conceal the arch. Mount drapes on an arched wire or bendable rod and loop them back with ties. Or make a fixed head above the arch, and hang drapes, which should be tied back during the day, or matchstick blinds.

Windows set at angles to each other in a corner

Vertical louver blinds or screens are the only other solution, since shades would snag at the corners where they met.

Dormer windows

These look best with blinds or shades only, or with sheers attached to top and bottom of the frame.

Oddly shaped windows

Use the highest point to carry the horizontal line of the drape rod at the top of a shade or blind.

Skylights

Sheers can be fixed onto the frame, or roller, Venetian or matchstick blinds can be mounted on a special fixture.

Windows set close together can share a pole to make them seem a deliberate pair. Here one is threaded straight through the fabric for a neat heading.

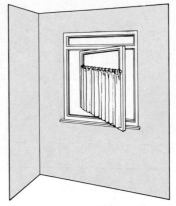

Whether you use a blind, café curtain or drapes on pivot windows, all have to be fixed onto the frame so that they open with the window.

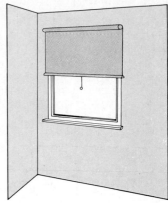

Use a shade or blind if a window is set tight into a corner; drapes would look constricted. Or use glass shelves and objects, stretched across window.

French windows have to be opened easily, so if you want a decorative treatment, drapes should be kept well to the side and suspended from a heading above the frame.

If arched windows need to be covered, drapes should not be allowed to hide the arch. Use a shaped track and have fabric meeting in the centre, tied back.

With windows set at angles and only minimum space in between, tie each drape back so that when drawn they will meet together in the corner where the walls join.

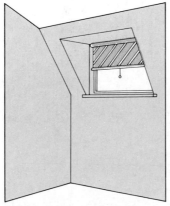

Dormer windows are best with a blind or shade fitted inside the frame, or fit a net or sheer with stretch wire at top and bottom of the frame to keep it looking neat.

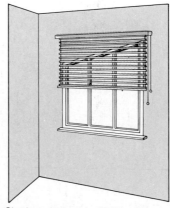

Sloping windows look better if the top can be concealed with an ordinary blind or shade, or with drapes meeting in the middle.

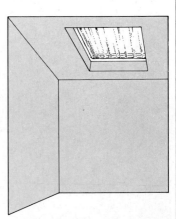

If you want to filter light, or prevent it from entering through a skylight, mount blinds, shades or a sheer straight onto the frame. Attach the sheer with stretch wires.

WINDOW TREATMENTS

Generally speaking, windows are worthy of rather more serious thought than they get, judging by the majority of conventional treatments around. They are often highly decorative in their own right and certainly form a major part of the architecture in a room, quite apart from acting as a base for handsome drapes and shades and as a source of light and air.

Obviously, it would be a mistake to cover completely any particularly beautiful window, one with an arched top, a round window, or a narrow, clerestory shape.

Far left:
A window acting as a frame to encapsulate a dramatic view. A simple roller shade can be pulled down at night.

Left:
Another deeply-recessed window enclosing a pleasant view. The dark red of the frame and repeating colors within the room, delineate the pleasing arch as well as emphasizing the wealth of greenery outside.

Below, left:
In a kitchen too small to lose space, the window is used as a luminous backing for rows of storage shelves.

Below, right:
Awkward dormer windows with their deep embrasure make a good base for plants or objects.

It would be equally criminal to cover up windows which give out onto particularly striking scenery and which are not overlooked. Such windows should be allowed to remain uncovered, effectively framing the view beyond like a picture. Shades or blinds could be fixed to provide a screen of sorts if wished, but they need not detract from the view.

Window frames

Examine your window frames carefully – they are a source of not inconsiderable decorative potential. There is no reason why quite ordinary ones should not be imaginatively treated as long as they will fit in with the rest of the room. Extra trims of wood can always be added to make the frames seem more substantial. Nondescript, short windows, for example, can be made to look like the floor-to-ceiling variety if you use stock lumber cut to the measurements that will fit from the floor to the architrave. Apply the wood with the thin edges butting up to the original frame and the windows will suddenly seem considerably deeper. If you then add long shades that fall to the floor at night, the illusion of beautifully proportioned, long windows will be complete. A more cosmetic solution, which also makes windows seem more substantial, would be to stain the frame to match the floor; or the frames could be painted in vivid colors to make them stand out. If the windows are set in such a way as to leave quite deep side walls, these reveals can be mirrored to great effect. Not only will you get much more reflected light, but all sorts of unexpected glimpses of views will now be visible. Do remember, however, to have the edges of the mirror beaded or bevelled to do away with sharp corners and edges.

Disguising the view outside

Windows with dreary views that are nevertheless needed for the light they give can be hung with plants suspended either from the ceiling or from transverse rods. Or they can be shelved with glass and accoutered with a collection of glasses or old bottles through which the light shines. One of the most effective windows I have seen was in a gloomy basement apartment which was so filled with plants and bird cages and blooms that you might as well have been in Tahiti.

Another unconventional treatment for windows with a less than exciting view is to surround them with bookshelves, which make them look deeply inset. Or ordinary glass can be removed and replaced with panes of tinted glass which exclude the

view, filter light and make the outside world seem almost like an early aquatint. Occasionally, an old stained glass panel can be bought which will fit a window exactly, or new glass can be commissioned; or glass can be painted with designs in special glass paint which does not wash or wear off. Stained glass windows, used to such effect during the 1920s and 1930s in the suburbs of most cities, can themselves be taken up as the basis for a whole scheme.

Very tiny windows with deep sills can often be made to look spectacularly beautiful with the simple addition of a single flower in a small vase, an old jug or glass, or a small plant. It is all a question of the imagination.

Do remember never to think of altering a window physically (as opposed to cosmetically) without first considering the effect on the outside of the building. Windows are just as visible from the outside as they are from indoors, by day as well as by night. On the other hand, thin slits of windows, pierced through a wall of a house, either side of a fireplace, for instance, can add intriguing extra light as well as unexpected slivers of view.

Opposite page, top:
Shelves stretched across
window panes are used
here to show off colored
glasses and other
objects, which look
spectacular against the
rural backing.

Below:
In an unconventional
treatment in a bathroom,
an arched window is
filled with a pane of
frosted and etched glass.
It blocks out an un-
fortunate view, without
detracting from the
interesting shape of
the surround.

This page, right:
Double arched windows
like these are so pretty
that it would be a pity
(and difficult) to drape
them. Instead, they are
left bare to make a gentle
background for the
plants which serve as
natural screening
at night.

Far right:
Glass shelves full of
plants stretched right
across a window provide
a neat greenhouse area
as well as welcome
respite from an un-
attractive view outside.
This is a useful treatment
for kitchen windows
where shelves can be
filled with herbs.

Below:
Necessary but ugly
protective-screening is
disguised here by an
eclectic collection of
objects. The window sill
is painted in *faux* mal-
achite to add variety to
the predominant
lacquered green of
the walls.

DECORATING WITH PLANTS

Indoor plants and trees add a new dimension to a room, giving a liveliness and freshness that is gratifyingly cheap in relation to the pleasure given. The plants you choose will, of course, be governed by the kind of light a room gets and its mean temperature, but there can be few rooms that will not benefit from some sort of greenery, few gaps that would not be filled best of all by foliage, few pieces of furniture that would not look better balanced by a spread of leaves.

Plants as "furniture"

Scale and proportion play a key role when it comes to choosing the right plants for a certain room. Large ones will probably dwarf a tiny space, whereas smaller plants may become lost in more spacious areas. Tall plants and indoor trees, such as palms and weeping figs, make good room-dividers and can be used to separate living from dining areas, for demarcating conversation areas, balancing masses like doors and big cupboards. They are often used to replace drapes or shades at windows. Place them in deep baskets, metal or mirrored containers, in neat wood Versailles boxes or terracotta pots – whatever suits the room best.

Big plants look especially good at night. Light them from below with uplights or small spots, so the light filters up through the leaves and casts patterns on the ceiling. Downlights, too, can be used to throw shafts of light down from the ceiling through the foliage.

Plants in groups

Small plants can be arranged singly or in groups, on shelves, table tops, windowsills and mantelpieces. Shape, color and texture should always be taken into consideration, though, so the plants blend in or contrast well with their background.

In a large room, the same varieties often look best massed together. Sculptural plants like *dracaenas* look especially effective in groups of two or three. Flowering plants give particularly fresh and often unexpected accent colors to a room if chosen carefully to repeat the tones in a pillow, or in a piece of fabric or porcelain.

It is important to research into the sort of plants that will do well in your particular space, and important, too, to take sound advice on the subject. Most plants are surprisingly adaptable, and it is usually possible to tell after a week or so if a plant has settled well into its new environment. Plants which haven't, usually begin to look sick and deteriorate very rapidly.

Opposite page, top:
In an otherwise totally white space, plants are used as the main decorating feature, reaching to the ceiling, masking bare windows, and acting as dividing screens.

Below left:
Plants in baskets, in troughs, and balanced on every ledge give a relaxed feel to this glass-roofed corridor, turning it into a pleasantly verdant extra seating area.

Below right:
In a visual link-up between accessories and furniture, the brilliant rose of the upholstery and the lacquered green of the occasional table are repeated by the roses and the mass of foliage.

This page, top:
Large plants in baskets make appropriate room dividers in a space already filled with foliage. The garden-room feeling is further built up by flowery motifs and the allied textures of cane and matting.

Below left:
Indoor plants with variegated foliage always look good massed against stone walls or a tiled floor.

Below right:
For a comfortably tropical feeling in a bathroom, a miscellaneous collection of plants and bulbs surrounds this sunken jacuzzi tub.

USING KITCHEN WALLS

Of all the rooms in a home, the kitchen is best able to dictate its own arrangements from purely natural ingredients. Pots and pans, casseroles, the whole *batterie de cuisine*; the raw ingredients of food preparation – strings of herbs, onions and garlic, sausages, hams, dried flowers, old jelly and pudding molds, gingerbread, cookie and butter molds, nice old wooden implements and plates, jars, mugs, jugs – all are decorative in their own right and inject character, warmth, idiosyncrasy (and, many would say, extra dust) into a kitchen as nothing else will.

Tiles in the kitchen

Ceramic tiles will probably play a large part on any kitchen wall. They come in a huge range of colors and designs from a good many different countries. Floor tiles are frequently rather larger and tougher than the wall variety, but they can also be used on walls as well. And slick aluminum, cork, quarry and mirror tiles as well as laminates can all be used to give widely different effects. For extensive examples, see pages 236 to 239 and 264 to 271 in the Sample Book. And old designs and odd tiles can generally be found around the place with a bit of diligent searching.

Hanging utensils on walls

Pegboard or cork makes an efficient backing for a collection of kitchen implements like colanders, sieves, graters, whisks, salad shakers, and brightly colored metal, plasticised metal or plain metal grids have a strong, no-nonsense look. Kitchen implements like these, especially if they are much the same size, can also look interesting hung from butchers' hooks or rails to form a frieze around most of the room, or on just one wall. A collection of baskets or pans can be hung from a circular iron saucepan rail, conveniently placed near the stove. And bread baskets, fruit baskets, fly swats, wine racks, old glass or porcelain rolling pins and fruit juicers are all good to look at, too.

Improvising wall fillers

If there is some wall space left over after units, closets and the usual impedimenta of implements have been fitted in, food posters, old shop signs and advertisements can be used to cheer the place up. Oversize pin-boards are also, of course, extremely useful for lists, messages, recipes, cuttings and the ever increasing collections of paper inherent in contemporary day-to-day living. It is even quite acceptable to have nothing whatsoever on beautiful, bare, clean walls.

Left:
White-painted brick walls made a good unifying background for the disparate objects common to most kitchens. Here, a shallow basket and a carpet beater look quite at home beside wall-hung wine racks which in turn act as supports for various bits of equipment.

Below:
Natural tiled walls are equally as good, acting as a richly-colored foil for saucepans, casseroles, pottery and books. The rack above the stove is a very practical, yet good looking space-saver.

Opposite page, top:
Forming a satisfying still life, a splendid gradated collection of unglazed dishes is hung in a semi-circle over wooden shelves of more pots, mugs and casseroles.

Below left:
Neat rows of baskets hanging from the ceiling form an original frieze in this generously-windowed kitchen-dining room.

Below right:
White-painted pegboard makes a carefully arranged assembly of kitchen tools look very pleasing, and the row of pots and pans suspended from the painted beam give a feeling of extra depth to the space. Note the patterned blue and white floor tiles set at random among the terracottas.

USING BATHROOM WALLS

Because they are not usually on general view, and because occupants are a more or less captive audience for whatever time they take in there, bathrooms can be the basis for some of the most personal, idiosyncratic and eclectic of all collections, and it would be a pity not to indulge the opportunities.

The list of possibilities is surprisingly long: memorabilia of all types – maquettes, miniatures, cartoons of whatever age, profiles, plaques, old paste lids, butterflies and moths, pressed flowers and herbs, children's drawings, plates, old soap, toothpaste and tooth powder containers, old or new posters, samplers, needlework pictures, stuffed birds, animals, glass cases of shellwork, woolwork, thimbles and all the other things that the Victorian ladies were so fond of framing, ships in glass bottles, old post-cards. Almost anything as long as it looks good or interesting, can go on a bathroom wall, or shelf, or both.

Bathrooms and powder rooms also provide particularly good backgrounds for decorative spoofs, or the sort of mild teasing (*not* lavatorial humor) which is all part and parcel of humor in design. Humor after all, is quite as pleasing a quality to find in a room as it is in a person, and in bathrooms one can reflect at leisure on a wallful of printer's errors, misquotations, visual puns or what you will. Given the inclination, even very elaborate spoofs or pastiches can be indulged in, like creating a grotto, a Disneyland forest, Roman bath, or just an Edwardian boudoir. It all depends on taste, funds in hand, and, of course, space.

Tile treatments

Tiles, too, can be treated in both conventional and unconventional ways. They can be arranged in stepped, pyramidical or castellated designs, neatened-off with interesting contrasting borders, or manipulated to form a patchwork quilt effect by putting unmatched, but in some way related designs together. Tiles in much the same or harmonious coloring can be grouped together, as can ones with similarly-scaled patterns or motifs. This type of treatment is especially effective with a collection of those old tiles which can often be found in junk yards and thrift stores, as well as antique shops.

A mosaic of fragments of broken tiles embedded in plaster can also look effective as well as being satisfyingly cheap, and do not forget that several coats of polyurethane can make wallpaper or applied fabric just as durable as tile.

Quite interesting effects can be made by sticking odd clippings, pictures, postcards and so on together to form a wall which will look rather like an old scrap screen; this should be covered with polyurethane to prevent damp. Or a dado could be made with a collection of old cigarette cards or post cards, taking them half way up the walls and again protecting them with polyurethane. Used together with a shiny dark color taken from the designs, even the most meager little box of a room can be made to look quite appealing. As with all other decoration, it is all a matter of taste.

Opposite page:
Walls have been titivated in this bathroom with a mixture of mirror, tiles, drawings, paintings and shell-encrusted shelving to hold an array of toilet waters.

This page, right:
Pleasantly colorful walls have been achieved here with variegated stripes of brightly-toned, plain tiles interspersed with a mosaic made up from broken tile fragments.

Far right:
A seabed mural etched on bronze-colored mirror forms a handsome marine background in a mainly brown bathroom.

Below:
An eclectic collection of prints, silhouettes, drawings, etchings and embroidered pictures make this pleasing room a source of perpetual visual interest.

COLLECTIONS ON SHELVES

Objects on narrow shelves or mantelpieces are governed by the same rules concerning balance of color, shape and texture as more general room arrangements, if you want to avoid a jumble.

Grouping objects

Collections of very small objects always look better grouped together rather than scattered throughout a room. Glass or china goblets make useful containers for tiny things and look especially effective if displayed in a window, or on glass shelves or tables, and lit from below by uplight. If they are not a transparent surface, try lighting them from above with a downlight or a spot to give extra brilliance.

Books generally look better grouped by size as well as by subject, and look all the more interesting for being interspersed here and there with objects. Again, the objects can be pulled out by subtle lighting from above, or by pencil-beam spotlights on miniature tracks or nestling among the objects themselves. The actual shelves may be made of wood, glass or plexiglass, but whatever the material, be sure that they fit in with the rest of the room.

Collections kept in glass-fronted cabinets, whatnots or étagères should not be allowed to deteriorate into becoming just a jumble of objects. However different the possessions, try to group them so that they have, say, color in common, or texture, or shape, or choose objects which have some sort of relationship to one another.

Plants, single flowers, dried flowers and twigs can all be used as appropriate to give a touch of extra color to arrangements without distracting from the overall cohesiveness.

Shelves in kitchens and bathrooms can be used to great effect for displaying objects indigenous to the rooms. Storage jars, teapots, plates, spice boxes, all are necessities which look naturally at home on show in the kitchen.

Bathroom accessories

On the whole, bath beauty products are decorative in their own right, so they can be displayed on open shelves. Deep shelves can be used to hold pretty towels for a splash of color; narrow shelves can hold a series of toiletries. Filled with colored water, old measuring jugs or jars can look highly decorative. Small soaps can look interesting masked in large goblets or old drug-store jars.

The main points to remember, as ever, are the rules of balance and scale; these are dealt with in detail on page 321.

This page, left:
In an interesting mixture of colors and textures, ceramic and real fruit are combined with nuts, pewter, pottery and dried flowers and herbs for a horn-of-plenty effect.

Below:
The firm, incisive quality of this composition of primitive painting, prim row of painted tinware, severely square mantel and round table is achieved as much by the clear-cut shapes as by the objects themselves.

Opposite page, top left:
Kitchen storage need never be dull. This miscellany of storage jars, bottles, books and a general *batterie de cuisine* is made to look surprisingly ordered on slick industrial shelving.

Top right:
In a disparate but pleasing collection, books, boxes, pommanders, early figures and models of churches and houses are combined with a smoothly-carved bird and ceramic fruit. The solid shapes of the books are nicely offset by the angular lines of the other objects.

Below left:
A build-up of gleaming treen gives interest to an otherwise undistinguished window. The collection is softened by the dried grasses and everlasting flowers.

Below right:
Even the narrowest recess can be used to show off an interesting collection. These glass shelves are fitted into a slim, yet well-lit alcove to show off a number of Pre-Columbian artefacts.

BED TREATMENTS

Dressing a bed is much like dressing a person: there is a huge gamut of approaches from tailored to romantic and an equally large range of bed linen available to achieve these effects. All the same, there are certain fairly commonsense rulings to follow if the bed is not to assume too great an importance in a space. For more ideas for bed treatments, see pages 108 to 133 of the Room-by-Room Guide.

Fitted bedspreads

If a room is small and single or part of a studio or one-room apartment, it is wise to have the bed covered with a fitted spread neatly tucked in over a straight valance or dust ruffle; ideally, this would be of the same color as the walls, drapes or shades. The addition of a long bolster or squab, or a long one and a short one placed at right angles, if the bed is against a corner, will make the bed look much more like a sofa, especially if small pillows or throw cushions are added as well. Neat, spare, fitted spreads are available which will crisply jacket a bed and base, or they can be custom-made.

In a small double room, the bed will look less substantial if the cover is the same color as the walls or the carpet, and again, a bolster in the same fabric as the spread will neaten up the appearance. Minimal but comfortable bedheads can be made from two tailored pillows or squabs slung on a brass or wooden pole and suspended behind the bed; or a plain rectangular bedhead can be comfortably upholstered in the same material as the bedcover.

There is now an immense range of neat looking, warm comforters, blanket covers and matching dust ruffles and pillow shams available in the stores. There is an equally large range of differently shaped and sized pillows and covers to be massed together in a luxurious way at the head of the bed; the look of deep comfort is well worth the tedium of having to take them all off again to actually get into bed.

Quilted spreads

If, however, a traditional spread or quilt is still preferred, a wide range of ready-made styles is available. Throw-over quilts or spreads have the advantage that they can be made in any choice of fabric and look soft and relaxed resting over a matching or coordinating valance or dust ruffle. On the whole, most custom-made bedspreads (unless very tailored or made from a firm fabric such as suede or corduroy) benefit from being quilted. Quilting resists creases and wrinkles, and it folds easily.

Opposite page, top:
Diagonally-striped fabric, covering the bed-head (squares of cotton-covered foam slung on a pole) and the mattress, make the bed look both tailored and interesting. Throw pillows which match the valance and bed tables tie up the whole treatment.

Below:
In this indoor-outdoor space, pleated fabric on the walls contrasts with the tight-covered, flower-strewn mattress and pillows. The tree trunk bedhead and side tables complete the treatment.

This page, right:
A low divan set in the middle of a midnight blue room is piled with different colors, patterns and textures to make a haphazard, but undoubtedly comfortable lounging cum sleeping space.

Far right:
Old patchwork quilts, pristine white lace, *broderie anglaise*, pink-lined lace drapes, luxuriant daisy plants and a flickering fire combine to make a temptingly sensuous bedroom. Three rows of plump, lace-trimmed pillows make the brass bed seem especially inviting.

Below:
Effective four-poster treatments can be made with fabric. Here, the drapes have been hung from a frame attached directly to the ceiling. They were chosen to match the scalloped bedcover as well as the window drapes. Different-sized pillows are piled luxuriously against a bolster, while the decorative mirror on the end wall adds to the feeling of a room-within-a-room.

TABLESCAPES

For want of a better word, collections laid out on tables are generally known as table-scapes, and bearing in mind this painterly connotation, the aim is to arrange them as carefully and as symmetrically as an artist or photographer would arrange a still-life.

Occasional tables offer the greatest scope for any sort of display, although library tables, chests, and the odd large side table also provide tempting, generous surfaces. Think of them as blank canvases, to be filled in with strokes of color, harmonizing shapes and textures. But beware of being tempted into beautiful arrangements on any table you intend to eat on, unless you are sanguine about clearing it all away each time you need to lay for dinner – and putting it all back afterwards.

Building up arrangements

Most coffee and cocktail table arrangements need to be kept fairly low so that people seated either side can still see each other clearly over the top. As always, try to keep a sense of scale and proportion: large objects will look top-heavy on a small table, whereas a few carefully-chosen small items will just seem lost on a larger surface. Always leave enough dumping space for the general appurtenances of day-to-day living. It should certainly be possible to set down glasses, coffee cups, ashtrays, books and magazines without destroying the effect. Arrangements that would be ruined should be kept to consoles, chests and side tables alongside a wall, or small round skirted tables.

Scale and proportion

Height is as important on a table as it is in a room, especially on a surface of normal height as opposed to low coffee tables. A lamp on a table, of course, will provide height as well as illumination, and can look gently dramatic at night, casting a pool of light down on the objects around it. And a picture above a chest will have much the same proportional effect. If you add a plant, or some flowers, or an arrangement of, perhaps, dried flowers or grasses, you will have a good background for smaller objects. Keep the plant or flowers in direct proportion to the height of the lamp, or the bottom of the picture so that it fills in the space between it, or the lampshade, and the top of the table. This will also give a pleasing softness to the whole.

Building up shapes

To build up an interesting shape, quite apart from the actual content of the arrangement, choose an object (it could be a small piece of sculpture, a jug, or a large glass), which comes about halfway between the bottom of the lampshade and the tabletop. The smallest elements of all could be boxes of every shape, size, purpose and period: bowls, early mugs, stones, glass, minerals, treen, silver, paper-weights, paste pots, card cases and vestas (matchbox cases of the 19th and early 20th century which are now much prized), miniature ceramic fruits, cigarette cases, antique spectacle cases, photographs and miniatures. Similar objects should, if possible, be more or less of a size. If they are not, try grouping objects of similar origin (like, for instance, all *chinoiserie*, or classical antiquities, or pre-Columbian artefacts). If that, too, is impossible, mass together objects with something in common.

Opposite page, far left:
When it comes to interesting arrangements, repetition can be used to make a memorable visual point. Here, the model placed immediately under the house painting, and surrounded by a formal arrangement of boxes is pleasingly harmonious, as is the juxtaposition of subtle, golden tones.

Near left, above:
Cut glass, porcelain and silver against an Art Nouveau panel make a pleasant, *fin de siècle* composition. Though different, these objects have been grouped together because they all share a gentle gleam.

Near left, below:
Tartan and shagreen objects look colorful massed together on the top of a painted chest.

This page, near right:
Chinese porcelain, ivory and malachite objects set on brown velvet against a Coromandel screen make a gentle, cohesive arrangement of different colors, patterns and textures.

Far right:
Lalique glass on a glass-topped table with a suitable array of lilies makes an arresting display. Single pieces would have looked far less effective.

Below:
Similar tones bind together this collection of different objects. The major colors are cleverly repeated in the pattern of the drapes and the table top.

Groups of quite unrelated objects can still manage to look both cohesive and interesting if linked by color, texture pattern or shape.

Another useful way to get things to look good together is either by contrasting textures so that you get the shiny with the matt, abrasive roughness with the silky smooth, the clear with the opaque, or, on the contrary, to collect objects with similar surfaces and sheens, different sorts of glass and silverware, for example. Try to use color too, as deftly as possible, so that as if with the eye of the artist, other colors in the room are picked up in the arrangements, repeating flashes here and there. Vary a principal color with the seasons, and use, say, green or white for summer, and more rusty, earthy in the fall and winter. Or alter the weight of coloring from time to time, so that a fairly inconspicuous color in a room can be repeated again in arrangements and given more importance, thus altering the balance.

Flexibility is the key

Above all, try to be flexible. There is no need to take the whole concept of still-lives literally, keeping the same arrangements frozen for years. Move your possessions around occasionally, get rid of some, import others; and move things around from room to room.

It is interesting how different objects can be made to look when placed against different backgrounds and against different lights. Possessions can be noticed much more in certain arrangements of objects than in others, and it is more a question of experiment than premeditated thought.

However small the actual change in the arrangements, there could still be subtle changes in emphasis so that there is a pleasurable sense of constant renewal and freshness in a room. If, for example, you always keep a vase of flowers or a plant on a table, you could change the flowers or colors or foliage from month to month (or week to week according to budget), and introduce some new object that is the same color or has some relation to the flowers, hanging, for example a small print of a daisy by a jug of the same. Or you could add an overcloth on top of a skirted table to give a new background color to whatever collection is there already. It will make a quite unexpected difference. Ultimately, the important thing to strive for is a good sense of balance in color, texture and scale even if the objects you have bear no resemblance to each other, and have nothing whatsoever in common except the fact that you happen to have liked and bought them.

Left:
A pine dresser or hutch base makes a suitably neutral setting against which to hang a very much more sophisticated painting. Objects of equal weight, chosen as much for their color as size, are balanced either side.

Below:
Each object on this old table has charm in its own right. While there is no tangible link between them, the arrangement beside a generous bowl of flowers and toning ceramics is a particularly pleasing one.

APPENDIX

SAMPLE BOOK CREDITS

For addresses of stores and showrooms where goods – or similar goods – can be obtained, see the Directory of Sources, pages 355 to 359.

211 1, 2, 5, 6, 11 *Dulux*; 3, 7, 9, 12 *Winfield*; 4 *Berger*; 8 *Sandtex*; 10 *International Paint Company*

212 1–7 *Osborne and Little*; 8–14 *J. Pallu and Lake Furnishings Ltd*

213 1, 2, 6, 16–20, 23 *Osborne and Little*; 3, 4 *Cole and Son*; 5 *Habitat*; 7–15 *Hill and Knowles*; 21 *Paper Moon*; 22 *David Ison*; 24 *Brunschwig and Fils at David Ison*

214–215 1, 16 *Laura Ashley*; 2, 11, 24, 25 *Osborne and Little*; 3, 26 *Cole and Son*; 4, 7 *Paper Moon*; 5, 6, 18 *Marimekko at Paper Moon*; 8, 10 *Habitat*; 9, 17, 27 *First Editions at TT Designs*; 28 *Connaisance at TT Designs*; 29 *Magnum Designs at TT Designs*; 30 *Papillion at TT Designs*; 31 *South Bay at TT Designs*; 12, 13, 15, 19, 20, 21, 22 *Groundworks at Homeworks*; 14, 23 *Pallu and Lake Furnishings Ltd*

216–217 1 *Paper Moon*; 2, 6, 8–15, 24 *Laura Ashley*; 3, 7, 26, 27, 30 *David Ison*; 4 *Habitat*; 16 *Duro at Paper Moon*; 17–20, 22 *Osborne and Little*; 21 *Marimekko at Paper Moon*; 23 *Soleiado at Brother Sun*; 25 *Pallu and Lake Furnishings Ltd*; 28, 29 *Schumacher at David Ison*; 5, 7 *Felber at David Ison*

218–219 1, 2, 4–6, 11, 15, 17 *Osborne and Little*; 3 *Cole and Son*; 7, 18, 19 *Charterhouse at TT Designs*; 8, 10, 12, 16 *David Ison*; 9 *First Editions at TT Designs*; 13 *Habitat*; 14 *David and Dash at David Ison*

220–221 1, 17, 19, 22, 23, 25 *Sandersons*; 2, 15, 18 *G. P. and J. Baker*; 3 *Brunschwig and Fils*; 4–11, 21, 29, 30 *Cole and Son*; 12–14, 20, 24 *David Ison*; 27 *Old Stone Mills at David Ison*; 16, 26 *Greef Fabrics at Warner and Sons Ltd*; 28 *Groundworks at Homeworks*

222–223 1 *Zandra Rhodes at CVP Designs*; 2 *Schumacher at David Ison*; 3 *Habitat*; 4–7, 26 *Marimekko at Paper Moon*; 8, 9, 11–14 *Groundworks at Homeworks*; 10 *David Ison*; 15, 23 *Osborne and Little*; 16 *Brunschwig and Fils at J. Pallu and Lake Furnishings Ltd*; 17, 18 *J. Pallu and Lake Furnishings Ltd*; 19 *First Editions at TT Designs*; 20 *John Oliver*; 21, 22, 24, 25 *Paper Moon*; 27–30 *David and Dash at David Ison*

224–225 1 *Sanderson*; 2, 3, 10 *Vescom (UK) Ltd*; 4, 5, 7–9 *Arbutus at K and K Designs Ltd*; 6, 24 *Schumacher at David Ison*; 11, 23 *Kingfisher Vinyls at Nairn Coated Products Ltd*; 12, 14, 15 *Paper Moon*; 13, 16–22, 28–30 *ICI Vymura*; 25, 26 *Soleiado at Brother Sun*; 27 *Habitat*

226 1–3 *Nairn Coated Products Ltd*; 4–15 *Sanderson*

227 1–15 *Crown Decorative Products Ltd*

228–229 1–3, 16, 19, 20–22 *Architectural Textiles*; 4, 5, 15, 27–29 *Vescom (UK) Ltd*; 6, 7 *Home Decorating (Wallpapers) Ltd*; 8–11, 17 *Sidlaw Textiles*; 12 *Habitat*; 13, 14 *Osborne and Little*; 18 *Helen Sheane Wallcoverings Ltd*; 23–26 *Wallco (USA) Ltd*

230–231 1, 7 *B. Brown*; 2–5 *Vescom (UK) Ltd*; 6, 17 *Ebroplan Ltd*; 9–13 *Marvic Products*; 14 *Helen Sheane Wallcoverings*; 15, 16, 18 *Muraspec*; 19–22 *Tekko and Salubra*

232 1–10 *Perstorp Warerite*; 11–15 *Formica Ltd*

233 1–3 *Mirror Wall at Garfield Glass Ltd*; 4–7 *Hoyne International (UK) Inc*; 8–11 *Egecaral Tiles at Abstracta Construction*; 12–15 *Slatex Metallics at Decorette Marketing Services Ltd*

234–235 1–5, 11–21 *Applied Accoustics – Venables Ltd*; 6–10 *C. F. Anderson and Son Ltd*

236–237 1, 3, 8–10, 13, 15–17, 19, 23, 25, 26, 30–32 *The Master Tiler*; 2 *Laura Ashley*; 4, 6, 7, 11, 14, 24, 27–29, 33 *The Tile Mart*; 5 *Domus*; 12, 18, 20, 21 *World's End Tiles*; 22 *Langley London Ltd*

238–239 1–11 *Elon Tiles Ltd*; 12–19 *The Tile Mart*; 20–41, 43, 48, 50–53 *The Master Tiler*; 42, 44–47, 49 *Langley London Ltd*

240 1, 2, 4 *Alison Britton*; 3 *Hoyer and Snowdon/Vision International*; 5, 6 *Lucinda Lambton/Vision International*

241 1, 2, 4, 5, 8, 9, 12, 13, 15 *The Kenyon Collection*; 3, 6, 7, 10, 11, 14 *Angelo Hornak/Vision International*

242 1–13 *Jim Sullivan/Ronseal Stains*; 14 *Jim Sullivan/Lyn Le Grice Stencils*

243 1–6 *Jim Sullivan*

244–245 1–9, 11, 14–18, 35–40 *Conran's*; 10, 22 *Baumann*; 12, 13 *Pierre Frey at Tissunique*; 19 *Luxurious Textiles Ltd*; 20 *Bute Fabrics*; 21 *Leather Goods*; 23–27 *Tissunique*; 28–34 *Margo International*

246 1–6 *Baumann*; 7–14 *Tissunique*; 15, 17 *Pic et Pic at Marvic Textiles*; 16 *Eaglesham*; 18–20, 23 *Margo International*; 21–22 *Jack Lenor Larson at Homeworks*

247 1, 3, 4 *Marvic Textiles*; 2 *Tissunique*; 5, 6 *Dekorativna Ljubljana*; 7–39 *Apogee*

248 1, 6, 12 *Ciel*; 2–4 *Margo International*; 5 *Conran's*; 7 *Eaglesham*; 8 *Valentino at Tissunique*; 9–11, 13 *Lee/Jofa at Hammonds*; 14, 15 *Jack Lenor Larsen at Homeworks*

249 1–12 *Californian Drop Cloths Ltd*

250 1–6; 10–12; 14; 15 *Laura Ashley*; 7–9 *Debenhams*; 13; 16; 17; 22–32 *Sandersons*; 18–21 *Baumann*; 33–38 *Ebroplan*

251 1–5; 9; 10; 13; 14 *Laura Ashley*; 6 *T & J Vestor at Margo International*; 7 *Marimekko at Margo International*; 11; 12; 15; 19 *Ciel*; 16 *Eaglesham*; 8; 17–23 *Conran's*

252 1, 2, 4–6, 9 *Conran's*; 3, 17 *Marimekko at Margo International*; 7, 8, 11, 15 *Ebroplan Ltd*; 10 *Ciel*; 12–14 *Groundworks at Homeworks*; 16 *Canovas at Tissunique*

253 2–4, 9–10 *Conran's*; 1, 5, 6, 14, 15 *Ciel*; 7 *Paper Moon*; 8 *Eaglesham*; 12, 13 *T. and J. Vestor at Margo International*; 11, 16 *Groundworks at Homeworks*

254–255 1–11, 45 *Marimekko*; 12–23, 27, 33, 38, 42–44 *Conran's*; 24–26, 28–32, 34 *Groundworks at Homeworks*; 35–37 *Zandra Rhodes at CVP Designs*; 39 *Wicker Works at Homeworks*; 40, 41 *Heals*

256 1, 5 *Christopher Lawrence at Ciel*; 10 *John Stefanidis at Ciel*; 2, 3, 6–8 *Jack Lenor Larsen at Homeworks*; 4 *J. Pallu and Lake Furnishings Ltd*; 9, 11 *Clarence House at Osborne and Little*

257 1, 5, 7 *Canovas at Tissunique*; 2 *Groundworks at Homeworks*; 3 *Jack Lenor Larsen at Homeworks*; 4 *Clarence House at Osborne and Little*; 6 *Ciel*; 8, 13 *Lee/Jofa at Hammonds*; 9, 10 *J. Pallu and Lake Furnishings Ltd*; 11, 12 *Zumsteg at J. Pallu and Lake Furnishings Ltd*; 14 *Marimekko at Margo International*

258–259 1–3 *G. P. and J. Baker*; 4, 21 *Hammonds*; 5, 6 *Warners*; 7–16, 18 *Liberty's*; 17 *T. and J. Vestor at Margo International*; 19 *Conran's*; 20 *Groundworks*; 22–25 *J. Pallu and Lake Furnishings Ltd*; 26–28 *Ebroplan Ltd*

260–261 1–3, 10–13 *Margo International*; 4–9 *Tamesa Fabrics*; 14–18 *Susanne Garry*

262 1, 2 *Sunstore Blinds*; 3 *General Trading Company Ltd*; 4 *Tidmarsh and Sons*; 5 *Habitat*; 6 *Blind Alley Ltd*

263 1 *Habitat*; 2–4 *Blind Alley Ltd*; 5 *Sunway*; 6 *Louverdrape*

264 1–6, 8 *Wicanders*; 7 *Vigers*; 9–14 *Robinson Cork at Vigers*

265 1, 2 *Penrhyn Slate Quarries*; 3–10, 12, 13 *Fired Earth*; 11, 14 *World's End Tiles*; 15–17 *Elon Tiles*

266–267 1–11 *Domus*; 12–15 *The Tile Mart*; 16–26 *World's End Tiles*; 27–32 *Langley London Ltd*; 33–41 *Elon Tiles*; 42–45 *The Master Tiler*

268–269 1–7 *Fritztile (UK) Ltd*; 8–20 *Reed Harris Ltd*; 21–35 *Konrad Stewart*

270–271 1–19 *Harmony Carpets USA*; 20–21 *GAF*; 22–33 *Amtico*

272–273 1, 3, 4, 8, 9, 11, 13, 17, 18, 24, 25 *Afia Carpets*; 6, 10, 20–23 *Tintawn Ltd*; 2, 5, 7, 14, 16, 26, 27 *Huega UK Ltd*; 28 *Tretford Carpets Ltd*; 12, 15, 19 *Bosanquet Ives Ltd*

274 1–28 *Afia Carpets*

275 1, 5, 8, 9, 29–46 *Afia Carpets*; 2–4, 6, 7 *David Hicks*; 10–13 *Stark Carpet Corporation*

276–277 1, 3, 6, 7, 9, 11, 17–19, 21, 22, 24, 25 *Bosanquet Ives Ltd*; 12, 14, 15 *Afia Carpets*; 2, 4, 5, 8, 10, 13, 16, 20, 23 *Stark Carpet Corporation*

278–279 1–6 *Afia Carpets*; 7–24 *Bosanquet Ives Ltd*

280–281 1, 2 *Byzantium*; 3 *Craftwork*; 4 *General Trading Company*; 5 *Liberty's*; 6–9 *Anonymous*; 10–13 *Inca*

282–283 1, 4, 5 *Christie's*; 2, 3, 7 *David Black*; 6 *C. John*

284–285 1, 5 *Victor Frances*; 2, 6 *Christie's*; 3 *C. John*; 4, 7, 8 *P and O Carpets*

286–287 *David Black Oriental Carpets*

288 *Liberty's*

DIRECTORY OF SOURCES

The following list of sources gives details of where you can obtain samples of materials shown in the Sample Book, or very similar styles. All addresses marked with an asterisk mean that you must either be accompanied by an interior designer or have a letter of introduction, but since many of the commodities shown can either be obtained or ordered from good local stores, it is worth showing a chosen style to the appropriate department head.

In each category we have tried to quote addresses in major geographical locations since space makes it impossible to list every source. However, by telephoning your nearest listed outlet, you should be able to obtain further information about showrooms in your immediate area.

WALLCOVERINGS

Paints

Du Pont De Nemours
1007 Market
Wilmington
Delaware 19801

Janovic/Plaza
1292 1st Ave
New York
NY 10021

Martin-Senour Co
2500 S Senour Ave
Chicago
Illinois 60608

The O'Brien Corp
450 E Grand Ave
South San Francisco
California 94080

Sinclair Paint & Wallcoverings
2500 S Atlantic Blvd
Los Angeles
California 90040

Paint techniques

Angelus Consol Industry
2911 Whittier Blvd
Los Angeles
California 90023

Samuel Cabot
1 Union St
Boston
Massachusetts 02108

Irving Jacobson
3375 Livonia Ave
Los Angeles
California 90034

Murals

Robert Crowder Assoc
8417 Melrose Pl
Los Angeles
California 90069

Crown Wallcovering Corp
979 3rd Ave
New York
NY 10022

Charles R Gracie & Sons Inc
979 3rd Ave
New York
NY 10022

***S M Hexter Co**
2800 E Superior Ave
Cleveland
Ohio 44114

Sinclair Paint & Wallcoverings
2500 S Atlantic Blvd
Los Angeles
California 90040

The Warner Co
108 S Desplaines
Chicago
Illinois 60606

Wallpapers

***Architectural Paneling Inc**
979 3rd Ave
New York
NY 10022

Laura Ashley:

Laura Ashley
714 Madison Ave
New York
NY 10021

Laura Ashley
1827 Union St
San Francisco
California 94123

Laura Ashley
6–26 Watertower Place
835 N Michigan Ave
Chicago
Illinois 60611

Laura Ashley
Lenox Sq
3393 Peachtree Road
Atlanta
Georgia 30326

Brunschwig & Fils Inc:

***Ellouise Abbott Showroom**
PO Box 66172
1911 W Alabama
Houston
Texas 77006

***Brunschwig & Fils Inc**
351 Peachtree Hills
Ave NE
Atlanta
Georgia 30305

***Brunschwig & Fils Inc**
653 Pacific Design
Center
Los Angeles
California 90069

***Designer's Showroom**
500 South Findlay St
Seattle
Washington 98108

Charterhouse Designs Ltd:

***Charterhouse Designs Ltd**
979 3rd Ave
New York
NY 10022

***John Edward Hughes Inc**
100 Oak Lawn Plaza
Dallas
Texas 75207

***Mitchell Mann Inc**
8687 Melrose Ave
Los Angeles
California 90069

Cole & Son:

***Clarence House**
Room 801
111 8th Ave
New York
NY 10011

***Clarence House**
The Merchandise Mart
Space 1254
Chicago
Illinois

***Walter Lee Culp**
Suite 119
1444 Oak Lawn Plaza
Dallas
Texas 75207

***Kneedler-Fauchere**
Space 600
Pacific Design Center
8687 Melrose Ave
Los Angeles
California 90069

***Kneedler-Fauchere**
Suite 238
5701 6th Ave S
Seattle
Washington 98108

Conran's:

Conran's
The Market
The City Corp Center
160 E 54th St
New York
NY 10022

Conran's
3255 Grace St NW
Washington
DC 20007

Conran's
10 Cedar St
New Rochelle
NY 10801

***Ian Crawford Ltd**
140 E 56th St
New York
NY 10022

Donghia Showrooms Inc:

***Donghia Showrooms Inc**
3841 NE 2nd Ave
Miami
Florida 33137

Donghia Showrooms Inc
The Marketplace
2400 Market St
Philadelphia
Pennsylvania 19103

Du Pont De Nemours
1007 Market
Wilmington
Delaware 19898

Fashion Wallcoverings
4005 Carnegie Ave
Cleveland
Ohio 44103

***Laurence Handprints Ltd**
979 3rd Ave
New York
NY 10022

***S M Hexter Co**
2800 E Superior Ave
Cleveland
Ohio 44114

***Lee/Jofa**
New York City
Showroom
Decoration and Design
Building
979 3rd Ave
New York
NY 10022

Karl Mann Assoc
232 E 59th St
New York
NY 10022

Osborne & Little:

***Clarence House**
40 E 57th St
New York
NY 10022

***Clarence House**
Space 170
101 Henry Adams St
San Francisco
California 94103

***Clarence House**
Suite 119
1444 Oak Lawn Plaza
Dallas
Texas 75207

Sandersons:

Southwest
Wallcoverings
4422 W 12th St
Houston
Texas 77055

R E Thibault
315 5th Ave
New York
NY 10016

Thybonny
Wallcoverings
2435 W Belmont Ave
Chicago
Illinois 60657

***Scalamandre**
950 3rd Ave
New York
NY 10022

Sinclair Paint & Wallcoverings
2500 S Atlantic Blvd
Los Angeles
California 90040

Warner & Sons:

***Greeff Fabrics Inc**
150 Midland Ave
Port Chester
NY 10573

The Warner Co
108 S Desplaines
Chicago
Illinois 60606

Textured and fabric wallcoverings

Antel Designs Ltd:

McCormack & Associates
351 Peachtree Hills
Ave NE
Atlanta
Georgia 30305

Auget Designs:

*Perceptive Concepts Inc
979 3rd Ave
New York
NY 10022

Charles Barone Inc
8687 Melrose Ave
Los Angeles
California 90069

Bayberry Handprints Inc
3600 NE 2nd Ave
Miami
Florida 33137

Belgian Linen Assoc
280 Madison Ave
New York
NY 10016

Norton Blumenthal
979 3rd Ave
New York
NY 10022

Kirk-Brummel Assoc
979 3rd Ave
New York
NY 10022

Brunschwig & Fils Inc
979 3rd Ave
New York
NY 10022

Henry Calvin Fabrics
724 Battery
San Francisco
California 94111

Carousel Designs Inc
35 NE 40th St
Miami
Florida 33137

China Seas Inc:

China Seas Inc
979 3rd Ave
New York
NY 10022

China Seas Home/Port
21 E 4th St
New York
NY 10003

Clarence House Imports Ltd
40 E 57th St
New York
NY 10022

Ian Crawford Ltd
140 E 56th St
New York
NY 10022

Crown Wallcovering Corp
979 3rd Ave
New York
NY 10022

David & Dash Inc
2445 N Miami Ave
Florida 33137

Donghia Showrooms Inc
3841 NE 2nd Ave
Miami
Florida

Donghia Showrooms Inc
The Marketplace
2400 Market St
Philadelphia
Pennsylvania 19103

Fashion Wallcoverings
4005 Carnegie Ave
Cleveland
Ohio 44103

First Editions
979 3rd Ave
New York
NY 10022

Philip Graf Wallpapers Inc
979 3rd Ave
New York
NY 10022

Greeff Fabric Inc
155 E 56th St
New York
NY 10022

S M Hexter
979 3rd Ave
New York
NY 10022

Jack Lenor Larsen:

Jack Lenor Larsen
232 E 59th St
New York
NY 10022

Jack Lenor Larsen
6–140 Merchandise Mart
Chicago
Illinois 60654

Laurence Handprints Ltd
979 3rd Ave
New York
NY 10022

Lee/Jofa:

New York City Showroom
Decoration and Design Building
979 3rd Ave
New York
NY 10022

Lee/Jofa
590 Decorative Center
Dallas
Texas 75207

Lee/Jofa
Pacific Design Center
8687 Melrose Ave
Los Angeles
California 90069

Lee/Jofa
6–140 Merchandise Mart
Chicago
Illinois 60654

Karl Mann Assoc
232 E 59th St
New York
NY 10022

Profilewood Paneling System
Ostermann & Scheiwe
PO Box 668
Spanaway
Washington 98387

Prouty Designs Inc
444 N La Salle
Chicago
Illinois 60610

Pryor/Sof-Tex
6001 Telegraph Rd
Los Angeles
California 90040

Reed Wallcoverings
PO Box 105293
Atlanta
Georgia 30348

M L Rose & Sons Inc
4500 E 11th Ave
Hialeah
Florida 33013

F Schumacher & Co
939 3rd Ave
New York
NY 10022

Sinclair Paint & Wallcoverings
2500 S Atlantic Blvd
Los Angeles
California 90040

Tropicraft
568 Howard
San Francisco
California 94105

The Warner Co
108 S Desplaines
Chicago
Illinois 60606

Laminates, vinyls, and paneling

Architectural Paneling
979 3rd Ave
New York
NY 10022

Durawall Inc
979 3rd Ave
New York
NY 10022

Fashion Wallcoverings
4005 Carnegie Ave
Cleveland
Ohio 44103

First Editions
979 3rd Ave
New York
NY 10022

General Tire & Rubber Co
979 3rd Ave
New York
NY 10022

*Groundworks Inc
231 E 58th St
New York
NY 10022

Laurence Handprints Ltd
979 3rd Ave
New York
NY 10022

S M Hexter Co
2800 E Superior Ave
Cleveland
Ohio 44114

Laminating Services
PO Box 32159
Louisville
Kentucky 40232

Palette Prints Inc
2021 N 63rd St
Philadelphia
Pennsylvania 19151

Profilewood Paneling System
Ostermann & Scheiwe
PO Box 668
Spanaway
Washington 98387

Prouty Designs Inc
444 N La Salle
Chicago
Illinois 60610

The Warner Co
108 S Desplaines
Chicago
Illinois 60606

Zumsteg Inc
979 3rd Ave
New York
NY 10022

FABRICS

General upholstery and drapery

Apogee:

Jerry Pair and Associate
351 Peachtree Hills
Ave NE
Atlanta
Georgia 30305

Patterson Flynn and Martin
Space 1226
Merchandise Mart
Chicago
Illinois 60654

J Robert Scott
8727 Melrose Ave
Los Angeles
California 90069

Shears and Window
Galleria Design Center
101 Henry Adams St
San Francisco
California 94103

David Sutherland
1707 Oak Lawn
Dallas
Texas 75207

Laura Ashley:

Laura Ashley
714 Madison Ave
New York
NY 10021

Laura Ashley
1827 Union St
San Francisco
California 94123

G P & J Baker:

*Brunschwig & Fils Inc
410 E 62nd St
New York
NY 10021

*Greeff Fabrics
150 Midland Ave
Port Chester
NY 10573

*S Harris & Co
580 South Douglas St
El Segundo
California 90245

Baumann:

*Baumann
72 Hayter St
Toronto
Ontario M4G 1J8

*Carnegie Fabrics Inc
110 North Center Ave
Rockville Cr
New York
NY 11570

Bayberry Handprints Inc

3600 NE 2nd Ave
Miami
Florida 33137

California Drop Cloths:

*Shears and Window
Galleria Design Center
101 Henry Adams St
San Francisco
California 94103

*David Sutherland Inc
1707 Oak Lawn
Dallas
Texas 75207

*Vice Versa
979 3rd Ave
New York
NY 10022

Manuel Canovas Inc:

*Bill Curran
351 Peachtree Hills
Ave NE
Atlanta
Georgia 30305

*Donghia Showrooms Inc
Space 610
Merchandise Mart
Chicago
Illinois 60654

*Donghia Showrooms Inc
8715 Melrose Ave
Los Angeles
California 90069

*Donghia Showrooms Inc
1700 Stutz Dr
Troy
Michigan 48084

*David Sutherland Inc
1707 Oak Lawn
Dallas
Texas 75207

*China Seas Inc
979 3rd Ave
New York
NY 10022

Clarence House:

*Clarence House
Suite 20
351 Peachtree Hills
Ave NE
Atlanta
Georgia 30305

*Clarence House
Suite 119
1444 Oak Lawn
Dallas
Texas 75207

*Clarence House
40 E 57th St
New York
NY 10022

*Clarence House
Space 170
101 Henry Adams St
San Francisco
California 94103

*Houston Decorative Center
Suite 115
5120 Woodway Dr
Houston
Texas 77127

*Pacific Design Center
Space 600
8687 Melrose Ave
Los Angeles
California 90069

Conran's:

Conran's
The Merchandise
Market
The City Corp Center
160 E 54th St
New York
NY 10022

Conran's
3255 Grace St NW
Washington
DC 20007

Conran's
10 Cedar St
New Rochelle
NY 10801

Robert Crowder Assoc

8417 Melrose Pl
Los Angeles
California 90069

Donghia Textiles:

*Donghia Showrooms
Inc
The Merchandise Mart
Chicago
Illinois 60654

*Kneedler-Fauchere
101 Henry Adams St
San Francisco
California 94103

*David Sutherland Inc
1444 Oak Lawn
Dallas
Texas 75207

*Vice Versa
979 3rd Ave
New York
NY 10022

Eaglesham Prints:

*Decoration and Design
Building
979 3rd Ave
New York
NY 10022

*Design Center
Northwest
Cahill Rubin Showroom
Space 238
5701 6th Ave S
Seattle
Washington 98108

Fabrications
146 E 56th St
New York
NY 10022

*Gerald Hargett Inc
5120 Woodway Dr
Houston
Texas 77506

*John Strauss
Showroom Inc
160 E Erie St
Chicago
Illinois 60611

Gian Fabrics

3431 W Vickery
Fort Worth
Texas 76107

Greeff:

*Greeff
155 E 56th St
New York
NY 10022

*Greeff
351 Peachtree Hills
Ave NE
Atlanta
Georgia 30305

*Greeff
Room 6–125
Merchandise Market
Chicago
Illinois 60654

Groundworks Inc:

*Groundworks Inc
629-A Merchandise
Market
Chicago
Illinois 60654

*Groundworks Inc
231 E 58th St
New York
NY 10028

*Walter Lee Culp Assoc
Suite 115
5120 Woodway Dr
Houston
Texas 77056

*Designer Showroom
500 S Findlay St
Seattle
Washington 98108

*Jerry Pair & Associate
351 Peachtree Hills
Ave NE
Atlanta
Georgia 30305

*Shears & Window
101 Henry Adams St
San Francisco
California 94103

Laurence Handprints Ltd

979 3rd Ave
New York
NY 10022

Jack Lenor Larsen:

*Linn Ledford
100 S Madison St
Denver
Colorado 80209

*Jack Lenor Larsen
590 Decorative Center
Dallas
Texas 75207

*Jack Lenor Larsen
601 Pacific Design
Center
8687 Melrose Ave
Los Angeles
California 90069

*Jack Lenor Larsen
232 E 59th St
New York
NY 10022

*Jack Lenor Larsen
415 Jackson St
San Francisco
California 94111

*Jerry Pair & Associate
351 Peachtree Hills
Ave NE
Atlanta
Georgia 30305

Liberty of London Inc:

Liberty of London
Shop
229 E 60th St
New York
NY 10022

Karl Mann Assoc

232 E 59th St
New York
NY 10022

Marimekko:

Marimekko
7 W 56th St
New York
NY 10019

Crate & Barrel
1510 N Wells
Chicago
Illinois 60610

*Wall Pride
Suite 100
5701 6th Ave S
Seattle
Washington 98108

*Wall Pride
Pacific Design Center
8687 Melrose Ave
Los Angeles
California 90069

*Scalamandre
950 3rd Ave
New York
NY 10022

Stroheim & Romann:

*Design Center
Northwest
Cahill Rubin Showroom
Space 238
5701 6th Ave S
Seattle
Washington 98108

*Stroheim & Romann
155 E 56th St
New York
NY 10022

Warner & Sons:

*Greeff Fabrics Inc
150 Midland Ave
Port Chester
NY 10573

Zuckerman
101 Henry Adams St
San Francisco
California 94103

*Zumsteg Inc
979 3rd Ave
New York
NY 10022

Corduroys, suedes, and velvets

Artmark Fabrics Co Inc
480 Lancaster Pike
Frazer
Pennsylvania 19355

Auget Designs:

*Perceptive Concepts Inc
979 3rd Ave
New York
NY 10022

Basset McNab Co
1032 Arch
Philadelphia
Pennsylvania 19107

*Brunschwig & Fils Inc
979 3rd Ave
New York
NY 10022

Henry Calvin Fabrics
724 Battery
San Francisco
California 94111

Carousel Designs Inc
35 NE 40th St
Miami
Florida 33127

Clarence House
Space 170
101 Henry Adams St
San Francisco
California 94103

*Connaissance Fabrics Inc
979 3rd Ave
New York
NY 10022

*David & Dash Inc
2445 N Miami Ave
Miami
Florida 33137

*Duralee Fabrics Ltd
979 3rd Ave
New York
NY 10022

Gian Fabrics Inc
3431 W Vickery Blvd
Fort Worth
Texas 76107

*Laurence Handprints Ltd
979 3rd Ave
New York
NY 10022

J P Marion Co
1140 Santee
Los Angeles
California 90015

Reed Wallcoverings
PO Box 105293
Atlanta
Georgia 30348

Sinclair Paint & Wallcoverings
2500 S Atlantic Blvd
Los Angeles
California 90040

Sheers

Artmark Fabrics Co Inc
480 Lancaster Pike
Frazer
Pennsylvania 19355

Henry Calvin Fabrics
724 Battery
San Francisco
California 94111

Caro & Upright Inc
2416 E 27th St
Los Angeles
California 90058

Carousel Designs Inc
35 NE 40th St
Miami
Florida 33127

Cavalier Fabrics
4716 Richneil Rd
Richmond
Virginia 23231

*Ian Crawford Ltd
140 E 56th St
New York
NY 10022

*David & Dash Inc
2445 N Miami Ave
Miami
Florida 33137

*Gardisette USA Inc
PO Box 2586
Hwy 24
Anderson
South Carolina 29622

*Greeff Fabrics Inc
155 E 56th St
New York
NY 10022

Paul Kaiser Assoc
PO Box 766
Buena Vista Station
Miami
Florida 33137

Maen Line Fabrics Inc
219 Chestnut
Philadelphia
Pennsylvania 19106

Norman's of Salisbury
PO Box 799
Salisbury
North Carolina 28144

BLINDS AND SHADES

Art Rattan Co of California
1218 Miller Ave
Oakland
California 94601

Auget Designs:

*Perceptive Concepts Inc
979 3rd Ave
New York
NY 10022

Bali Blinds
Loyalsock Ave
Montoursville
Pennsylvania 17754

Breneman Inc
1133 Sycamore St
Cincinnati
Ohio 45210

Al Burkhardt Custom Shade Co
1152 2nd Ave
New York
NY 10021

*Frank's Window Fashions
979 3rd Ave
New York
NY 10022

*Graber Blinds
Modern Window Corp
39–40 30th St
Long Island City
NY 11101

Holland Shade Co
306 E 61st St
New York
NY 10021

*Levelor Blinds
128 Wall St W
Lyndhurst
New Jersey 07071

*Louver Drape Inc
Dept F8
1100 Colorado Ave
Santa Monica
California 90401

Majestic Window Shades
5400 Northwest 101st St
Miami
Florida 33014

Minne Roman Shades
8203 Melrose Ave
Los Angeles
California 90069

Nanik
PO Box 1766
Wausau
Wisconsin 54401

*Ohline Corp
1930 W 139th St
Gardena
California 90249

*Paramount Shade Co
979 3rd Ave
New York
NY 10022

Payne Fabrics
3500 Kettering Blvd
Dayton
Ohio 45439

Shade & Shutter
2400 Market St
Philadelphia
Pennsylvania 19103

Standard Trimmings Corp
1114 1st Ave
New York
NY 10021

FLOORINGS

Ceramics and marbles

American Olean Tile:

*American Olean Tile
Suite 802
964 3rd Ave
New York
NY 10155

*American Olean Tile
2105 Silber Road
Hines Industrial Park
Houston
Texas 77055

American Olean Tile
2029 15th Ave W
Seattle
Washington 98119

Country Floors Inc
300 E 61st St
New York
NY 10021

Designers Tile Gallery
65 S Colorado Blvd
Denver
Colorado 80222

Elon Tile Inc:

*Elon Tile Inc
Architects and
Designers Building
150 E 58th St
New York
NY 10022

*Elon Tile Inc
642 Sawmill River Rd
Ardsley
New York 10502

*Elon Tile of Florida Inc
1320A Stirling Rd
Dania
Florida 33004

*Elon Washington DC
Tile Gallery Inc
810 Potomac Ave SE
Washington
DC 20003

*Elon Tile Inc
2546 Pratt Blvd
Elk Grove
Illinois 60007

Judson Studios
200 South Ave
Los Angeles
California 90001

Latco Products Inc
3371 Glendale Blvd
Los Angeles
California 90039

Saxony Carpets Co Inc
979 3rd Ave
New York
NY 10022

Vinyls, woods, and corks

Armstrong World Industries Inc
PO Box 3001
Lancaster
Pennsylvania 17604

*Eden Manufacturing Corp
979 3rd Ave
New York
NY 10022

Forms & Surfaces Inc
130 NE 40th St
Miami
Florida 33137

*Harmony Carpet Corp
979 3rd Ave
New York
NY 10022

*Kentile Inc
979 3rd Ave
New York
NY 10022

Carl Marias Carpet Co
8793 Beverly St
Los Angeles
California 90048

Natural Vinyl Floor Company Inc
Box 173
Route 2
Killen
Alabama 35645

*SMT Custom Vinyl Tile
979 3rd Ave
New York
NY 10022

Tarkette Inc
140 West 51st St
New York
NY 10022

Carpets

Harmony Carpet Corp:

*Harmony Carpets
12th Floor
979 3rd Ave
New York
NY 10022

*James Goldman & Associates
Design Center
Northwest
Suite 120
5701 6th Ave S
Seattle
Washington 98108

*McCormack & Co Inc
351 Peachtree Hills
Ave NE
Atlanta
Georgia 30305

Schrader Fabrics Inc
705 Oak Lawn Plaza
Dallas
Texas 75202

J Robert Scott
8727 Melrose Ave
Los Angeles
California 90069

*Jack Lenor Larsen Inc
232 E 62nd St
New York
NY 10021

Scalamandre
950 3rd Ave
New York
NY 10022

Stark Carpet Corp:

*Pacific Design Center
8687 Melrose Ave
Los Angeles
California 90069

*Shears & Window
Galleria Design Center
101 Henry Adams St
San Francisco
California 94103

*Stark Carpet Corp
Miami Decorating &
Design Center
3841 NE 2nd Ave
Miami
Florida 33132

*Stark Carpet Corp
111 Oak Lawn Plaza
Dallas
Texas 75207

*Stark Carpet Corp
Space 1270
Merchandise Mart
Chicago
Illinois 60654

*Stark Carpet Corp
420 Boylston St
Boston
Massachusetts 02116

*Waitman Martin
5120 Woodway Dr
170 Decorative Center
Suite 111
Houston
Texas 77056

Saxony Carpets Co Inc:

*Saxony Carpets Co Inc
979 3rd Ave
New York
NY 10022

*Smith-Watson
6 – 127 Merchandise Mart
Chicago
Illinois 60654

*Earnest Treganowan Inc:

*Earnest Treganowan
286 Congress St
Boston
Massachusetts 02210

David Sutherland Inc
1707 Oak Lawn
Dallas
Texas 75207

Ethnic Rugs

Tom Bahti Indian Art Shop
1708 E Speedway
Tucson
Arizona 85719

Elizabeth Eakins
The Collectors Choice
404 E 14th St
New York
NY 10009

*Harmony Carpet Corp
979 3rd Ave
New York
NY 10022

Marvin Kegan Inc
991 Madison Ave
New York
NY 10021

Karl Mann Assoc
232 E 59th St
New York
NY 10022

Oriental Rug Exchange
349 N La Cienega Blvd
Los Angeles
California 90048

*Patterson Flynn & Martin Inc
950 3rd Ave
New York
NY 10022

*Saxony Carpet Co Inc
979 3rd Ave
New York
NY 10022

*Stark Carpet Corp
979 3rd Ave
New York
NY 10022

Earnest Treganowan Inc:

*Earnest Treganowan
Inc
306 E 61st St
New York
NY 10021

*Earnest Treganowan
Inc
286 Congress St
Boston
Massachusetts 02210

Oriental rugs and carpets

*Connaissance Fabrics Inc
979 3rd Ave
New York
NY 10022

Couristan:

*Design Center
Northwest
Cahill Rubin Showroom
Space 238
5701 6th Ave S
Seattle
Washington 98108

Dildarian Inc
595 Madison Ave
New York
NY 10022

G A Gertmenian & Sons
1130 W 2nd St
Los Angeles
California 90012

*S M Hexter Co
2800 E Superior Ave
Cleveland
Ohio 44114

Karl Mann Assoc
232 E 59th St
New York
NY 10022

*Pande Cameron
200 Lexington Ave
New York
NY 10016

*Earnest Treganowan Inc
306 E 61st St
New York
NY 10021

GLOSSARY

A

Accent Colors: contrast colors used to spice up room schemes.

Apron: the shaped piece of a chair or table below the seat rail or table top: in a window, the molding below the sill.

Architrave: a molded or decorated band framing a panel or an opening such as a door or window.

Armoire: a tall, heavy, storage cabinet with two doors.

Aubusson: the name applied to the decorative, flat-patterned weaves of rugs, carpets and fabrics made at Aubusson, France.

B

Balance: arrangement of objects around an imaginary central point to achieve a pleasing result. Balance can either be symmetrical (where objects on one side of the "point" are mirrored by those on the other) or asymmetrical (in which case they are not).

Banquette: a long, upholstered seat, frequently built-in along one side of a wall.

Baroque: a corruption of Spanish word *barrueco*, an irregularly-shaped pearl. Baroque denotes the florid lines of furnishings and architecture of the last half of the seventeenth century.

Batik: an Indonesian technique of hand-printing textiles; the coating of the areas not to be dyed with wax produces a delicate, mottled effect.

Bentwood: a technique in which the wood is steam-heated and then bent into shape.

Bergère: a French name, originally used to describe an upholstered chair. Bergère chairs frequently have caned backs and sides, with long seats.

Bevel: a process whereby surface edges are cut to a slant eg, on glass, wood or worktops.

Bibelot: a small decorative object or trinket.

Bolster: a long pillow or cushion which forms an integral part of a chair, sofa or bed.

Bombé: a term for case furniture (q.v.) which has an outward curve or bulge towards the base.

Breakfront: a large cabinet or bookcase whose center section protrudes beyond the sections at each side; the top half is frequently made of glass.

Brocade: a heavy textile with a raised design resembling embroidery.

Bureau: a chest of drawers, often with a mirror at the top; an English desk or writing table with drawers.

Bureau-bookcase: a flap-top desk with bookshelves on top, and glass, wood or mirrored doors.

Butler's tray: a large wooden serving tray with hinged flaps; the sides are usually about $3\frac{1}{2}$ inches (9cm) deep.

C

Cabriole: the style of leg on furniture where the top curves out, the center curves in and the foot curves out. It became popular at the end of the seventeenth century.

Campaign furniture: pieces of furniture, like chests and desks, with metal corners and handles typical of those used on military campaigns.

Cane: slender, flexible, woody stems, split into narrow strands and woven into chair backs, seats, and occasional furniture.

Case furniture: a collective term for cabinets, escritoires, and bureau-bookcases.

Celadon: a pale green color.

Chiffonier: a piece of furniture which has open shelves for books, and a drawer or cabinet.

Chinoiserie: the collective term for Chinese or Chinese-style pieces.

Chintz: a cotton printed in several colors on a light or white background.

Claw-and-ball foot: the foot of a piece of furniture in the shape of a bird clutching a ball. Much used in the eighteenth century.

Cloissoné: a style of enamel decoration in which colored areas are separated by thin metal bands or *cloisons*.

Cloqué: an embossed material.

Commode: the French name for a low cabinet with drawers or shelves, usually set against a wall. May frequently have a semi-circular or serpentine front.

Console table: a small rectangular table, longer than it is wide, usually set against the wall.

Cornice: a decorative, horizontal band of plaster, metal or wood used to surmount a wall or to conceal drapery fixtures.

Cosmetic decoration: purely decorative as opposed to structural alteration, which improves appearance.

Credenza: a sideboard or buffet.

D

Dado: the lower part of a wall where separated by a rail known as the dado rail.

Dhurrie (also durry; dhurry): an Indian cotton carpet.

Dormer: a vertical window set into a sloping roof.

E

Eclectic: to choose from various sources; not following any one system, but selecting from and using the best components of several styles.

Empire style: the style developed during the French Empire (1804–15), which was a revival of the classical ideas of decoration.

Etagère: a set of open shelves supported by columns or corner posts.

F

Faience: a glazed and decorated form of earthenware.

Faux bamboo: simulated bamboo.

Faux malachite: simulated malachite.

Fretwork: form of decoration where the wood is cut into a fine, trellis-like pattern.

G

Gateleg table: a table with drop leaves. The legs are attached to a hinged frame which swings out to support the leaves.

Gesso: a mixture of plaster of paris or whiting, used for making bas reliefs, or as a base for gilding.

Ghiordes: the symmetrical knot used by the Turks and Caucasians for their rugs, as opposed to the non-symmetrical Senneh or Persian knot used by Persian weavers.

Gul: an octagonal motif frequently found in Turkoman rugs and carpets.

H

Half-tester: a small canopy or tester (q.v.) over a bed, covering only the pillow end.
Highboy: the American term for a tallboy. A high chest with seven or more drawers, three or four on the top part and three or four on the bottom; sometimes mounted on legs.
High-Tech: Contemporary style adapting industrial components for domestic use.
Hutch (or dresser): the word generally used to describe a large storage cupboard which has a two-doored unit below and open shelves above.

I

Inlay: a method of decorating the surface of furniture whereby cuts or grooves in the wood are filled with differently-colored wood, mother-of-pearl, ceramic or metal.
Intarsia: a decorative wood inlay, which is usually pictorial.

J

Jacobean: in furniture, the term used to describe pieces either made during the reign of James I of England (1603–25), or those styles designed to imitate them.
Japanned: a black lacquered finish, used to decorate furniture in the Japanese manner.

L

Lacquer: a durable varnish which is applied in layers and then polished to a mirror-like shine.
Lambrequin: a stiff, three-sided case which is fixed along the top of draperies to conceal their attachment to the wall. It can also be used above a bed.
Laminate: a very strong, multi-layered material.
Love seat (or settee): a small, two-seater sofa or chaise.

M

Malachite: a green-colored mineral used for ornamental objects.
Marquetry: inlaid work, usually of wood, metal, ivory or tortoiseshell.
Matt finish: a completely flat paint finish, with no shine or luster.
Moiré: the wavy design on silk, or other fabrics, which gives a watered appearance.
Monochromatic scheme: design using one basic color as its theme, in a variety of shades and textures.

O

Ormolu: ornament used on furniture made of imitation gold.
Ottoman: a long, low upholstered seat with no back; alternatively, a circular seat divided into four, with a central back.

P

Parquet: a form of wooden flooring where the grain of one square of wood runs at right angles to that in the adjacent square.
Parsons table: a square or rectangular table with wide, straight legs.
Pedestal table: any table supported by a single, central post.

R

Reveal (embrazure): the sides of a window between the frame and the outer surface of the wall.
Rococo: an ornate, curving style developed in the early eighteenth century in France from Chinese forms. Characteristic motifs are rocks and shells.

S

Secretary (escritoire, secretaire): a piece of furniture fitted with a hinged writing surface which can be pulled down for use.
Splat: the major, central support in a dining chair back.
Stretcher: a crosspiece joining table or chair legs.
Stucco: smooth plaster decoration for interior walls.
Swag and tail: elaborate valance-like treatment for drapes. The fabric is caught up near each end so that the middle part, or swag, falls in a graceful curve, and the ends hang in tails.

T

Tester: a wood or fabric canopy, covering the whole bed area.
Travertine: a form of pale limestone, often used on floors.
Treen: small articles made entirely of wood, especially eating and drinking vessels.
Trompe l'oeil: anything which deceives the eye.

V

Valance: a drapery heading, usually made of fabric, which hides drapery hardware. The English term for a dust ruffle on a bed.
Vanity units: storage units which usually enclose the basin.
Veneer: the thin layer of wood laminated on top of another.

W

Wicker (wicker-work): slender, pliant twigs, plaited or woven to make chairs or baskets.
Windsor chair: a general name for wooden chairs of stick construction.
Wing chair: an upholstered chair with high back and projecting sides.

BIBLIOGRAPHY

The Apartment Book
New York: Harmony Books, 1979

Allen, Phyllis S.
The Beginnings of Interior Environment
Utah: Brigham Young University Press, 1975

Conran, Terence.
The Bed and Bath Book
New York: Crown, 1978

Conran, Terence.
The House Book
New York: Crown, 1974

Conran, Terence.
The Kitchen Book
New York: Crown, 1977

Felcher, Cecilia.
The Complete Book of Rug Making
New York: Hawthorne Books, 1975

Gilliatt, Mary.
Bathrooms
New York: Viking Press, 1971

Gilliatt, Mary.
Decorating. A Realistic Guide
New York: Pantheon, 1977

Gilliatt, Mary.
English Style
New York: Viking Press, 1967

Gilliatt, Mary & Baker, Douglas.
Lighting your Home. A Practical Guide
New York: Pantheon, 1979

Gilliatt, Mary.
Kitchens and Dining Rooms
New York: Viking Press, 1970

Guild, Robin.
The Finishing Touch
New York: Van Nostrand Reinhold, 1979

Harrington, Geri.
The Wood-Burning Stove Book
New York: Macmillan Publishing Co Inc, 1977

Hughes, Therle.
The Country Life Collectors Pocket Book of Furniture
New York: Hawthorne Books, 1968

Jackson, Albert & Day, David.
Good Housekeeping Do-It-Yourself Book
New York: Good Housekeeping Books, 1977

Hatje, G & Kaspar, P.
Decorating Ideas for Modern Living
New York: Abrams, 1975

Ketchum, William C.
The Catalog of American Antiques
New York: Rutledge Books, 1977

Lenor Larsen, Jack and Weeks, Jeanne.
Fabrics for Interiors
New York: Van Nostrand Reinhold, 1975

Magnani, Franco.
Interiors for Today
New York: Whitney Library of Design, 1975

Malino, Emily.
Super Living Rooms
New York: Random House, 1976

Plumb, Barbara.
Young Designs in Color
New York: Viking Press, 1972

Skurka, Norma.
The New York Times Book of Interior Design and Decoration
New York: Quadrangle, 1976

INDEX

PICTURE CREDITS

Own = Owner; Des = Designer; b = bottom; c = center; l = left; r = right; t = top

2 *Michael Nicholson/Elizabeth Whiting and Associates*; 6 Des *Chester Jones*; *Michael Nicholson/Elizabeth Whiting and Associates*; 7 *Steve Oliver*; 10t Own/Des *Filippa Naess*; *Michael Dunne*; 10b Own/Des *Pauline Vogelpoel*; *Michael Dunne*; 11t Own *Shirley W. Wray*; *Michael Dunne*; 11bl *Brigitte Baert/Vision International*; 11br Own *Ida Bjorn Hansen*; Des *Filippa Naess*; *Michael Dunne*; 12 Des *Peter Wilson*; *Norman McGrath/Vision International*; 13tl Own/Des *La Comtesse Roussy de Sales*; *Michael Dunne*; 13tr Des *Mary Gilliatt*; *Michael Dunne*; 13bl Own *Mrs David Hidary*; *Michael Dunne*; 13br Own/Des *William Waldron*; *Michael Nicholson/Elizabeth Whiting and Associates*; 14t Des *Richard Holley (CVP)*; *Gerry Mudford/Elizabeth Whiting and Associates*; 14b *Tom Yee*; 15t Own *Louis Muller*; Des *Louis Muller and William Murphy*; 15bl *Michael Nicholson/Elizabeth Whiting and Associates*; 15br Des *Alan Buchsbaum/Design Coalition*; 16t Own/Des *William Barnes*; *Michael Dunne*; 16bl *Tom Yee*; 16br Own *Mrs Fran Moscowitz*; Des *Louis Muller and William Murphy*; 17t *Alain Dovifat/Brigitte Baert/Vision International*; 17b *Tom Yee*; 18t,bl *Alain Dovifat/Brigitte Baert/Vision International*; 18br *Tom Yee*; 19 Own/Des *Borus and Borus*; *Michael Dunne*; 20l Own/Des *Jeffrey Stubbs and Glen McVey*; *Michael Dunne*; 20r Own/Des *Robert Mihalik*; *Michael Dunne*; 21t Own *Susanne Zevon*, Des *Sam Neustadt*; *Michael Dunne*; 21bl Des *Adrian Gale*; *Tim Street-Porter/Elizabeth Whiting and Associates*; 21br *Tim Street-Porter/Elizabeth Whiting and Associates*; 22t *Brigitte Baert/Vision International*; 22bl Des *Stan Peskett*; *Tim Street-Porter/Elizabeth Whiting and Associates*; 22br Own/Des *Borus and Borus*; *Michael Dunne*; 22t *Brigitte Baert/Vision International*; 23t *Michel Nahmias*; 23br Own/Des *Mary Gilliatt*; *Michael Dunne*; 23bl Own *Martin Corke*; *Michael Dunne*; 24t Own *Mrs Kagan*, Des *Barbara Littman*; *Michael Dunne*; 24b Own/Des *Mark Hampton*; *Michael Dunne*; 25t Own/Des *Mr and Mrs Frank Avray-Wilson*; *Michael Dunne*; 25b *Tom Yee*; 26t Own/Des *Anthony Hail*; *Michael Nicholson/Elizabeth Whiting and Associates*; 26b *Tim Street-Porter/Elizabeth Whiting and Associates*; 27t *Jerry Tubby/Elizabeth Whiting and Associates*; 27bl *Bill McLaughlin*; 27br *Brigitte Baert/Vision International*; 28t *Neil Lorrimer/Elizabeth Whiting and Associates*; 28b Own/Des *Filippa Naess*; *Michael Dunne*; 28tl *Neil Lorrimer/Elizabeth Whiting and Associates*; 28tr Des *Ed Pearlman*; *Michael Dunne*; 29b Des *Leila Corbett*; *Michael Nicholson/Elizabeth Whiting and Associates*; 30t Des *Tricia Guild*; *David Cripps/Elizabeth Whiting and Associates*; 30b *Tom Yee*; 31t *Alain Dovifat/Brigitte Baert/Vision International*; 31b Own/Des *Filippa Naess*; *Michael Dunne*; 32t *Michael Boys/Susan Griggs*; 32b *Michel Nahmias*; 34 *Alain Dovifat/Brigitte Baert/Vision International*; 35t Own/Des *Mrs Patricia Rawlinson*; *Michael Dunne*; 35bl *Chris Mead*; 35br *Michael Nicholson/Elizabeth Whiting and Associates*; 37 Own/Des *Mary Gilliatt*; *Michael Dunne*; 39 Own *Shirley W. Wray*; *Michael Dunne*; 41 *Michael Dunne*; 43 Own/Des *Mary Gilliatt*; *Michael Dunne*; 45 *Michael Dunne*; 46 *Chris Mead*; 47tl Own/Des *Filippa Naess*; *Michael Dunne*; 47tr Own/Des *Robert Mihalik*; 47b *Femina/Camera Press*; 49 Own/Des *Mary Gilliatt*; *Michael Dunne*; 51 *Clive Helm/Elizabeth Whiting and Associates*; 53 Own/Des *Sue and David Leigh*; *Michael Dunne*; 55 *Brigitte Baert/Vision International*; 57 *Tom Yee*;

59 *Elizabeth Whiting and Associates*; 61 *Tom Yee*; 63 Own *Mr and Mrs Michael Koplik*, Des *Earl Burns Combs*; *Michael Dunne*; 65 Own/Des *Mrs Helen Preston*; *Michael Dunne*; 66 Own/Des *William Rousseau and Michael Kennedy*; *Michael Dunne*; 67 Own *Ida Bjorn Hansen*, Des *Filippa Naess*; *Michael Dunne*; 69 Own/Des *Luis Villa*; *Michael Dunne*; 71 Own/Des *Patricia Sayad*; *Michael Dunne*; 72 Own/Des *Filippa Naess*; *Michael Dunne*; 73t Own *Jackie Breslow*, Des *Earl Burns Combs*; *Michael Dunne*; 73bl Des *Howard Phillips*; *Michael Nicholson/Elizabeth Whiting and Associates*; 73b *Michael Nicholson/Elizabeth Whiting and Associates*; 75 *Chris Mead*; 77 *Tom Yee*; 79 Own/Des *Mary Gilliatt*; *Michael Dunne*; 81 *Ezra Stoller/Esto Photographic*; 83 Own *Susie Martin*; *Michael Dunne*; 85tl Own/Des *Joan Sinclair*; 85tr *Tom Yee*; 85bl Own *Mrs Marshall Cogan*; 85br *Chris Mead*; 87 *Tom Yee*; 89 Own/Des *Mary Gilliatt*; *Michael Dunne*; 91 *Zühause/Camera Press*; 93 *Tom Yee*; 94 *Spike Powell/Elizabeth Whiting and Associates*; 95 *ICI Paints*; 97 Des *Nicholas Hills*; *Clive Helm/Elizabeth Whiting and Associates*; 99 Own/Des *Alan Buchsbaum/Design Coalition*; *Norman McGrath/Vision International*; 101 Own *Shirley W. Wray*; *Michael Dunne*; 103 Own *Mrs Block*, Des *Barbara Littman*; *Michael Dunne*; 105 Own/Des *Hilary Green*; *Michael Dunne*; 107 Own/Des *Mark Hudson*; *Michael Dunne*; 108bl Own *Shirley W. Wray*; *Michael Dunne*; 108br Own/Des *Mary Gilliatt*; 109t *ICI Paints*; 109b Own *Mrs Kagan*, Des *Barbara Littman*; *Michael Dunne*; 111 Own/Des *Barbara Littman*; *Michael Dunne*; 113 Own/Des *Sue and David Leigh*; *Michael Dunne*; 115 Own *Mr and Mrs Michael Koplik*, Des *Earl Burns Combs with Leigh Hammond*; *Michael Dunne*; 117 Own/Des *Mary Gilliatt*; *Michael Dunne*; 119 *Syndication International*; 121 Own *Mrs Rose*; *Michael Dunne*; 123 Own *Mrs Susan Block*, Des *Barbara Littman*; *Michael Dunne*; 125 Des *Magenta Yglesias/Designare Ltd Interiors*; *Michael Dunne*; 127 *Zühause/Camera Press*; 128 Own *Teddy Millington-Drake*, Des *John Stefanidis*; *Michael Boys/Susan Griggs*; 129 Own/Des *Hilary Green*; *Michael Dunne*; 131 Own/Des *Sophia Gilliatt*; *Michael Dunne*; 133 Own/Des *Andrew Usiskin*; *Michael Dunne*; 135t *ICI Paints*; 135bl *Tom Yee*; 135br Own/Des *Larry Durham*; *Michael Dunne*; 137 Own/Des *Helene Fesenmaier*; *Michael Dunne*; 139 *Femina/Camera Press*; 141 Own/Des *Joan Sinclair*; *Michael Dunne*; 143 Own/Des *Sue and David Leigh*; *Michael Dunne*; 144 *Michael Dunne*; 145 Own/Des *Filippa Naess*; *Michael Dunne*; 147 *Zühause/Camera Press*; 149 *Alain Dovifat/Brigitte Baert/Vision International*; 151 *Tom Yee*; 153 *Femina/Camera Press*; 154 *Alain Buchsbaum/Design Coalition*; 155tl Own/Des *Madame La Comtesse Roussy de Sales*; 155tr *Michael Nicholson/Elizabeth Whiting and Associates*; 155b Own/Des *Mr and Mrs Robert Chapman*; *Michael Dunne*; 157 Own/Des *Mary Gilliatt*; *Michael Dunne*; 159 Own/Des *Mary Gilliatt*; *Michael Dunne*; 160 Own *Mrs Dushey*, Des *Borus and Borus*; *Michael Dunne*; 161tr *Shirley W. Wray*; *Michael Dunne*; 161b *Alain Dovifat/Brigitte Baert/Vision International*; 163 Own/Des *Mary Gilliatt*; *Michael Dunne*; 165 Own/Des *Andrew Usiskin*; *Michael Dunne*; 167 Own/Des *Filippa Naess*; *Michael Dunne*; 169 *Alain Dovifat/Brigitte Baert/Vision International*; 170 Own *Mrs Cogan*, Des *Borus and Borus*; *Michael Dunne*; 171t *Esto Photographics Inc*; 171b Des *Peter Wilson*; *Norman McGrath/Vision International*; 173 Own *Larry Durham*, *Michael Dunne*; 175 *Michael Dunne*;

Appendix/Credits and Acknowledgments

176 *Robert Belton*; 177l *Michael Boys/Susan Griggs*; 177tr Des *Mario Buarto*; *Michael Dunne*; 177br Own *Mr Rosenthal*, Des *Horace Gifford*; *Michael Dunne*; 179 Own *Mr and Mrs William H. Johnstone*, Des *Tom Moore*; *Michael Dunne*; 181 Own *Ray Bain*; *Michael Dunne*; 183 Des *Frank R. Angel*; *Michael Dunne*; 184–5 Own/Des *Mary Gilliatt*; 200 *Michael Dunne*; 201 *Michael Dunne*; 203 *Michael Dunne*; 211–88 (except 240–1, 282–7) *Michael Dunne*; 282–7 *Alison Britton*; 240tr *Hoyer and Snowdon/Vision International*; 240cl *Alison Britton*; 240bl *Alison Britton*; 240bc *Lucinda Lambton/Vision International*; 240br *Lucinda Lambton/Vision International*; 241 *All Kenyon Collection*, except numbers 3, 6, 7, 10, 11, 14 *Angelo Hornak/Vision International*; 282t *Christie's, London*; 282bl,br *David Black*; 283t *Christie's, London*; 283bl *Christie's, London*; 283bc *C. John*; 283br *David Black*; 284t *Victor Frances*; 284bl *Christie's, London*; 284bc *C. John*; 284br *P. and O. Carpets*; 285tl *Victor Frances*; 285tr *Christie's, London*; 285bl,br *P. and O. Carpets*; 286–287 *David Black*; 290–295 *Victoria and Albert Museum, London*; 321 *Chris Mead*; 322t *Chris Mead*; 322 Des *Val Arnold*; *Michael Nicholson/ Elizabeth Whiting and Associates*; 323br Own/Des *Helene Tomasi*; *Julian Nieman/Elizabeth Whiting and Associates*; 323t *Tim Street-Porter/Elizabeth Whiting Associates*; 323bl Own/Des *Diana Phipps*; *Michael Dunne*; 324 Own/Des *Tony and Gay Firth*; *Michael Nicholson/Elizabeth Whiting and Associates*; 325t *Michael Nicholson/Elizabeth Whiting and Associates*; 325cl *Elizabeth Whiting and Associates*; 325cr *Chris Mead*; 325b *Elizabeth Whiting and Associates*; 327t *Elizabeth Whiting and Associates*; 327b *Michael Boys/Susan Griggs*; 328t Own/Des *Virginia and Bobby Chapman*; *Michael Dunne*; 328bl *Spike Powell/Elizabeth Whiting and Associates*; 328br Des *Jim O'Connor*; *Michael Dunne*; 329t *Michael Dunne*; 329b *Chris Mead*; 330bl Des *Roy A. Klein*; *Michael Dunne*; 330br Own/Des *Anthony Paul*; *Michael Nicholson/Elizabeth Whiting and Associates*; 331bl Des *Don Clay*; *Peter M. Fine*; 331br *Michael Nicholson/Elizabeth Whiting and Associates*; 332 Des *D. L. Freeman Interiors*; *Michael Dunne*; 333tl,tr *Michael Dunne*; 333bl *Chris Mead*; 333br Own/Des *Louise Pleydell-Bouverie*; *Michael Dunne*; 334tl Own *Carl Burden*, Des *Mark Hampton*; *Michael Dunne*; 334tr Des *John Guest*; *Tim Street-Porter/Elizabeth Whiting and Associates*; 334bl Own/Des *Paul Anstee*; *Michael Dunne*; 334br Own/Des *Jack and Elizabeth Lambert*; *Michael Dunne*; 335 Own *Marina de Brant*, Des *Louis Muller and William Murphy*; *Michael Dunne*; 335tl *Tim Street-Porter/Elizabeth Whiting and Associates*; 335tr *Tim Street-Porter/Elizabeth Whiting and Associates*; 335 c *Alain Dovifat/Brigitte Baert/ Vision International*; 335bl *Spike Powell/Elizabeth Whiting and Associates*; 335br *Clive Helm/Elizabeth Whiting and Associates*; 337tl *Tim Street-Porter/ Elizabeth Whiting and Associates*; 337tr *David Cripps/ Elizabeth Whiting and Associates*; 337bl *Elizabeth Whiting and Associates*; 337br *Clive Helm/Elizabeth Whiting and Associates*; 338t *Chris Mead*; 338b Des *Phillip Castle*; *Tim Street-Porter/Elizabeth Whiting and Associates*; 338tl *Michael Dunne*; 339tr *Tim Street-Porter/Elizabeth Whiting and Associates*; 339b Own/ Des *Filippa Naess*; *Michael Dunne*; 340t Own/Des *Jack Ceglic*; *Michael Dunne*; 340bl Own/Des *Anthony Paul*; *Michael Nicholson/Elizabeth Whiting and Associates*; 340br Own/Des *Filippa Naess*; *Michael Dunne*; 341t Des *Dorit Egli*; *Michael Nicholson/ Elizabeth Whiting and Associates*; 341bl Own/Des *Signora Ponti*; *Michael Dunne*; 341br Own/Des *Alan Buchsbaum/Design Coalition*; 342t Own/Des *Elizabeth Dickson*; *Michael Nicholson/Elizabeth Whiting and Associates*; 342b Des *E. Hannah and P. Rosenquet*; *Michael Dunne*; 343t,bl *Chris Mead*;

343br *Peter M. Fine*; 344 Own/Des *Paul Anstee*; *Michael Dunne*; 345tl *Michael Dunne*; 345tr Des *Max Clendinning*; *Tim Street-Porter/Elizabeth Whiting and Associates*; 345b Own/Des *Mrs Chapman*; *Michael Dunne*; 346 *Chris Mead*; 347tl Own/Des *Alan Buchsbaum/Design Coalition*; *Michael Dunne*; 347tr *Chris Mead*; 347bl *Michael Boys/Susan Griggs*; 347br Own *Mrs C. Diker*, Des *Mark Hampton*; *Michael Dunne*; 348t Des *Granville Dixon Designs*; *Michael Crockett/Elizabeth Whiting and Associates*; 348b Des *Barbara Brickman Associates*; *Michael Dunne*; 349tl Own *Mrs Marlow Stone*; *Michael Dunne*; 349tr Own/Des *Filippa Naess*; *Michael Dunne*; 349b *Brigitte Baert/Vision International*; 350l Own/Des *Mrs Chapman*; *Michael Dunne*; 350t *Steve Colby/ Elizabeth Whiting and Associates*; 350 Own/Des *Paul Anstee*; *Michael Dunne*; 351tl *William Rousseau and Michael Kennedy*; *Michael Dunne*; 351tr Own/Des *Christopher Vane-Percy*; *Michael Dunne*; 351b *Christine Hanscomb*; 352t Own/Des *Filippa Naess*; 352b *Chris Mead*

Acknowledgments

It is certainly no exaggeration to say that I could in no way have achieved this book without the support, hard work, constructive criticism, generosity and creativity of the small team who worked all along with me: my special thanks then to Yvonne McFarlane, Ron Pickless, Fiona MacIntyre, Derek Coombes, Amy Carroll and Peter Kindersley who also made the time spent on the project one of the happiest, funniest and most memorable periods of my working life.

I would also like to thank Barbara Plumb for her equal generosity, encouragement, insights and patience, as well as Betsy Amster, Ursula Bender, Jill Danzig, André Schiffrin and Robin Stevens at Pantheon, who always make my contact with them such a pleasure; my assistant, Susie Hanmer for her constancy and invaluable aid; my splendidly efficient and sympathetic agent, Felicity Bryan, and, as usual, my long-suffering and understanding family who put up with so much.

Clearly, no book of this size could have been undertaken without the cooperation and help of all the people who so kindly let their homes be photographed or gave me ideas. Nor could it have been achieved without the excellence of the artists and photographers, and especially the peripatetic attitude, sheer hard work and keen eye of Michael Dunne, who took the majority of the pictures.

Mary Gilliatt

Dorling Kindersley would like to give special thanks to Ian O'Leary for the daunting task of photographing the Sample Book; to John Bishop, and to the artists at Hayward and Martin for setting the style and producing most of the illustrations; to Richard Lewis, particularly for the Design Kit illustrations; to Ian Carr, Ron Williamson and Tony Wallace at Contact Graphics for setting the text; and to Michael Burman for reproducing the illustrations.

Thanks also to Sarie Forster, Steve Oliver, Jemima Dunne, Sue Meads, Julia Harris, Judy Robinson and Sue Rawkins.

Illustrators and Studio Services
John Bishop
Hayward and Martin Ltd
Richard Lewis
Les Smith
Jim Robins
Gary Marsh
Intermedia Design Assoc

Photographic Services
Negs
W Photoprint
Quicksilver
Gilchrist Studios

Typesetting
Contact Graphics
Focus

Lithographic Reproduction
F. E. Burman